Rhea County, Tennessee

LAND ENTRY BOOK

(Surveyors Book No. 1)

1824–1889

AND

1902–1929

જેન્ડ

Transcribed by
Bettye J. Broyles

Rhea County Historical and
Genealogical Society

Heritage Books
2024

HERITAGE BOOKS
AN IMPRINT OF HERITAGE BOOKS, INC.

Books, CDs, and more—Worldwide

For our listing of thousands of titles see our website
at
www.HeritageBooks.com

A Facsimile Reprint
Published 2024 by
HERITAGE BOOKS, INC.
Publishing Division
5810 Ruatan Street
Berwyn Heights, MD 20740

Printed 1992
Rhea County Historical and Genealogical Society

International Standard Book Number
Paperbound: 978-0-7884-8895-5

FOREWORD

The Land Entry Book (Surveyor's Book No. 1) was transcribed exactly as written because the original book has become so fragile and worn that it should not be used until some method of preservation has been accomplished. Pages 45, 46, 49 through 70, 217, and 218 are already missing from the book. The edge and bottom line on many pages are so frayed that they cannot be read, and a few pages contain brown spots that obliterate the text. A xerox copy of the book is in the files of the Historical Society and the book is included on Microfilm Roll No. 130 (Register's Office) at the Tennessee State Library and Archives.

This book has been in use for over 100 years, although the first entries were made 168 years ago (in 1824). The first 209 pages of the book contain entries made prior to 1860, and eleven entries were made from 1871 through 1873. By this time, the condition of the book evidently had reached a similar condition since it was re-copied by the Register, Young Colville. At the January 1874 Term of the County Court (Minutes, page 213), the following statement was made:

"It appearing from the mutilated condition of the registers book in the Office of Register of Rhea County that it is necessary that said book be transcribed in a good book or books suitable for said records, commencing at Book A and continuing to Books B,C, & D, inclusive, & furnish and index said transcribed work & furnish suitable index . . . books E,F,G,H, & I, and Young Colville appeared in open Court and agreed to furnish books and indexes . . ." for the sum of $140.00.

In April, 1874, Young Colville was allowed $21.00 for the blank books and John M. Willis was appointed to assist him in collating the books to be transcribed. The project was completed by July and Colville was allowed $119.00, the balance due him for transcribing the first five books and indexing five others. At the January, 1875, Term, Willis was allowed $19.50 for 13 days work. Although there is no mention of the Entry Takers Book being transcribed, a note on page 196 (page 115 of typed copy) indicates that Colville transcribed the book in 1880.

The beautiful handwriting of Young Colville was easy to read, but the last 53 pages of the book contained several entries that were almost impossible to read. Most of the later entries (1902-1929) were processioning records, and many pages were covered with plats that required reduction to fit the typed copy.

All of the plats included with the various entries were xeroxed and added to the typed copy. A one-inch scale was added to the few plats that were reduced.

The index to the original book has been included as an Appendix (begins on page 169). It contains an alphabetical listing of the enterers, the page number (original book), entry number, and number of acres. Because there were many other names included in the book, a complete index was also prepared (begins on page 162). Streams and other landmarks also are included in this index.

This book is important to researchers because it supplements the Deed Books. Many of the entries were never registered and do not appear in the Deed Books, and the addition of the individual plats assist in the location of the various tracts of land.

Bettye J. Broyles

ENTRY TAKERS OF RHEA COUNTY

Robert Locke	1824-1836 (resigned)
James Berry	1836-1837 (resigned)
James A. Darwin	1837-1840 (resigned)
William H. Shelton	1840-1843
Henry Griffett	1843-1846
John W. Chambers	1846- ?

SURVEYORS OF RHEA COUNTY

James Wilson	1820-1828
David Shelton	1828-1832
Crispien E. Shelton	1832-1836
Jesse Thompson	1836-1837 (died in office)
Alfred Collins	1837-1840
William H. Bell	1840-1848
Franklin Locke	1848-1852
Jesse P. Thompson	1859-1871
R.F. McDonald	1871
Jesse P. Thompson	1871-1880
E.F. Waterhouse	1882-1888
G.C. McKenzie	1888-1889
Jim Gillespie	1889-1890
J.L. Daniel	1904-1903
J.W. Truex	1917-1929

DEPUTY SURVEYORS

John Purris	1826
Franklin Locke	1827-1828
Jesse Thompson	1831-1836
Richard Waterhouse	1836-1841
John Locke	1837
Jesse P. Thompson	1848
James W. Clift	1849
R.F. McDonald	1857
J.L. Daniel	1889

NOTE— The above lists are incomplete.

State of Tennessee, Rhea County
October 15th 1824. Surveyed for John Hammel by virtue
of preference entry No. 1 dated the 15th 1824, Sixty
acres of land on the West fork of Piney River adjoining
his One Hundred acre tract on Wallens Ridge of Cumberland Mountain in Said County. BEGINNING on two Post
oaks on South side of Said creek corner to his One Hundred acre tract; then North Sixty nine West one hundred
and forty two poles crossing the creek to an oak; then
North twenty one East fifty three and one eighth poles
crossing a branch and the trace turnpike road; then
South Sixty nine East one hundred and forty two poles
crossing the creek below the bridge to said road to a Postoak on his own line;
then to the beginning containing Sixty acres agreeable to Survey. J. Wilson
John Hammel and James Wilson, Chain Carriers

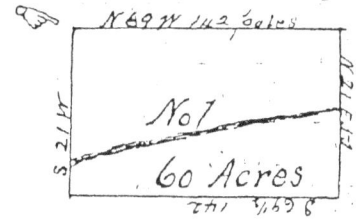

J. BISHOP

State of Tennessee, Rhea County
October 19th 1824. By virtue of an Entry of Preference,
certified by the Entry Taker of Said County No. 2, dated
the 3rd July 1824 made by Joseph Bishop, I have Surveyed
for Said Bishop fifty acres of land in the Said County on
Wallens Ridge on both sides of the Kiuka turnpike road
near the fork of the road. BEGINNING on a Postoak corner
to a five acre tract granted to Jeremiah Qualls; then
South crossing Said road eighty poles to a Postoak; then
East crossing the road one hundred poles to a Blackoak, then North eighty poles
to a hickory; then to the beginning. J. Wilson
David Ragsdale and William Gothard, Chain Carriers

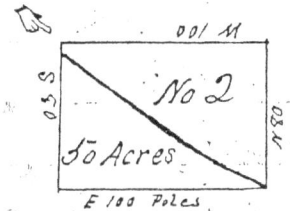

Note— The transfers were made on the certificate previous to Surveying and the
certificate Sent on to the Register and not received, was Sent back and new one
made out on which the transfers alluded to were [remainder of sentence missing]

D. RAGSDALE

State of Tennessee, Rhea County
August 14th 1824. Surveyed for David Ragsdale fifty
acres of land agreeable to a certificate of entry made
by him dated the 14th of July 1824, No. 3, on the waters of Richland Creek in Said County on Wallens Ridge
of Cumberland Mountain. BEGINNING on a Hickory on
Keedy Road about half a mile from the fork on the South
Side of the road; then South Seventy West one hundred
and twenty eight poles to a Postoak on the North Side
of the road; then North twenty West Sixty Six poles to
a Gum Saplin near a Spring, then North Seventy East including the Spring and
crossing a bend of the creek one hundred and twenty eight poles, then to the
beginning. J. Wilson S.R.C.
C. Brown and William Gothard, Chain Carriers

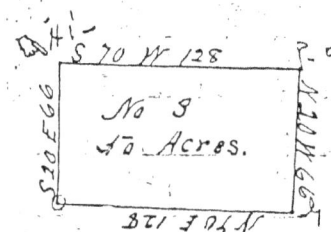

D. RAGSDALE

State of Tennessee, Rhea County
August 14th 1824. Surveyed for David Ragsdale fifty
acres of land on Wallens Ridge Rhea County on the waters of Richland Creek on both sides of the Kiuka
Turnpike road including the improvement on which
Josiah Cranmore now lives certificate of Entry No. 4
and dated the 14th of July 1824. BEGINNING on a White
oak on the South Side of the road then West crossing
a branch one hundred and eighty nine poles to a Post
oak; then North Seventy eight poles to an oak; then
East one hundred and eighty nine poles crossing the road to a postoak; then South
crossing the road to the beginning.   J. Wilson S.R.C.
C. Brown and William Gothard, Chain Carriers

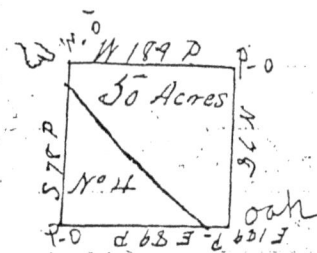

(blank)   (pages 3 and 4)

R.G. WATERHOUSE   50 acres   (page 5)

November 12th 1824. Surveyed for Richard G. Waterhouse fifty acres of land in
Said County on Wallens Ridge on the waters of Whites Creek entry No. 8 dated 12th
September 1824 on the South Side of Said creek below the South fork and lick
branch on both Sides of a path leading from Tennessee Valley to Knoxes and Red-
wines. BEGINNING on a hickory and Whiteoak marked "D" on the South Side of a
Small branch; then South Seventy East one hundred and twenty Six poles crossing
Said branch Several times to a Maple and Black Gum mark "X"; then South twenty
West crossing the path Sixty three poles to a Chestnut marked "A"; then North
Seventy West one hundred and twenty Six poles; then a direct line to the beginning.
Blackstone Waterhouse and Cyrus Waterhouse, Chain Carriers

R.G. WATERHOUSE   51 acres

Nov 6th 1824. Surveyed for Richard G. Waterhouse Fifty one acres agreeable
to his entry No. 9 certificate dated 16th of September 1824, a general entry
lying on Wallens Ridge in Said County between the South fork of Whites Creek and
the middle fork of Said creek below Whyley Redwines. BEGINNING at four Whiteoaks and two Blackoaks marked "W"; thence South ten West Ninety and one half
poles to two Chestnuts marked "E"; then South eighty East ninety and one half
poles to a Stake on the South fork of Whites Creek; then North ten East ninety
and one half poles; thence direct line to the beginning being an equilateral
parallelogram.
Richard Waterhouse and Blackstone Waterhouse, Chain Carriers

R.G. WATERHOUSE   52 acres   (page 6)

Nov 7th 1824. Surveyed for Richard G. Waterhouse Fifty Two acres of land on the
Mountain in Said County on the middle fork of Whites Creek below David Knoxes.
BEGINNING on two Whiteoaks marked "H" on the South Side of the Spring branch;
thence North Sixty Five West one hundred and twenty nine poles crossing a path
to four blackoak Saplins; then South twenty five West crossing the middle fork
Sixty four and a half poles; then South Sixty five East one hundred and twenty
nine poles; then a direct line to the beginning.
Richard Waterhouse and Blackstone Waterhouse, Chain Carriers

R.G. WATERHOUSE   160 acres   & 53 acres

Nov 13th 1824. Surveyed for Richard G. Waterhouse one hundred and Sixty acres
of land on Wallens Ridge on Cumberland Mountain in Said County agreeably to two
certificates of entry No. 11 dated 13th of September 1824 and No. 18 dated November
11th 1824 of fifty three acres each making a right angle equilateral Tetragon on both sides of Devils Fork of Piney above the Big Falls. BEGINNING on four
blackgums marked "R.C.E." on the South Side of the path leading to Swaggarthys
and Grassy Coves, and on the South Side of both forks of Said Creek, running
thence North fifty two East crossing Said path and the West branch five times
one hundred and thirty poles to a Chestnutoak and Whiteoak marked "G"; then
South thirty eight East crossing the Devils fork one hundred and thirty poles to
a whiteoak marked "B"; then South fifty two West one hundred and thirty poles to
a Blackoak and chestnut marked "I"; then crossing the path and Said Creek above
the fork to the beginning.
Blackstone Waterhouse and Cyrus Waterhouse, Chain Carriers

R.G. WATERHOUSE   62½ acres   No. 12   (page 7)

November 4th 1824. Certificate of Entry No. 12 dated 16th of September 1824.
Surveyed for Richard G. Waterhouse Sixty two and a half acres of land on the
Mountain on the waters of Piney and Clear Creek in Said County lying on both
sides of Girtmans trace or turnpike road including a cave Spring nearly opposite
Oliver Pikes. BEGINNING on a postoak marked "H" and redoak and postoak Saplins
on the South Side of Said road; running thence South Sixty five East one hundred
poles to a chestnut and small hickory; then North twenty five [East] one hundred
poles to a hickory, then North Sixty five West crossing the Waggon road one hundred poles; then to the beginning.
Oliver Pike and Cyrus Waterhouse, Chain Carriers

ROB'T FERGUSON   80 acres   No. 13

November 4th 1824. Agreeably to a certificate of Entry No. 13 dated 16th of
September 1824, I have Surveyed for Robert Ferguson Eighty acres of land of the
face of the mountain on the waters of Piney in Said County. BEGINNING on a
hickory corner to Samuel Ferguson at the foot of the mountain; then North Sixty
West forty Six poles to a chestnutoak under the clift of the mountain about ten
poles North of a Calybeate Spring; then South thirty West down the clift two
hundred and Seventy eight poles; then South Sixty East fifty poles to the foot
of the mountain, then along the foot of the Mountain with Samuel Fergusons line
to the beginning.
James Ferguson and Cyrus Waterhouse, Chain Carriers

R.G. WATERHOUSE   65 acres
Sept 4th 1824. Surveyed for Richard G. Waterhouse Sixty five acres of land on
the Mountain on the waters of Clear Creek on the North fork of Said creek in
Said County, including Calibeate and one other Spring in an oblong on both sides
of Girtmans trace going up the mountain. BEGINNING   (page 8)
on two Spanishoaks one marked "C" and two small hickorys on the west side of
Said North fork; thence North twenty East up said fork one hundred and forty four
poles to or near the lower line of James Smiths five acre entry; then South
twenty East with Said line crossing the Waggon road Seventy two poles; then South
twenty West crossing Said road one hundred and forty four poles; then a direct
line to the beginning.
Oliver Pike and Cyrus Waterhouse, Chain Carriers

4

R.G. WATERHOUSE [sic]   50 acres

19th October 1824. Surveyed for Joel Loury fifty acres of land on the Mountain
on the Second fork of Richland Creek about one half mile above ford of the
Kiuka turnpike road in Said County. BEGINNING on a postoak about one hundred
and fifty yards South of an improvement made by said Loury, thence South Seventy
three West ninety Six poles crossing Richland Creek to a chestnut; then North
Seventeen East crossing Said creek above a Spring eighty four poles to a hickory;
then North Seventy three East ninety Six poles to a postoak; then to the beginning.
Nehemiah Vernum and Andrew Vernum, Chain Carriers

R.G. WATERHOUSE   84 acres   No. 17

November 11th 1824. Surveyed for Richard Waterhouse eighty four acres of land
in rectangle equilateral tetragon, certificate of entry dated 11th of November
1824 No. 17 lying on the mountain on both Sides of Sandy fork of Whites Creek
including a cane brake at the fork of Said creek in Said County. BEGINNING on
a Small Whiteoak marked "R" on the South Side of Said Creek; thence North 65 East
crossing one fork of the creek at four poles and the other fork at ten, in all
one hundred and Sixteen poles to a blackoak marked "D.B."; then South twenty five
East one hundred and sixteen poles to a blackoak; then South sixty five West one
hundred and sixteen poles; then a direct line to the beginning.
Blackstone Waterhouse and Cyrus Waterhouse, Chain Carriers

B. WATERHOUSE   55 acres   (page 9)

December 31st 1824. No. 20 Certificate dated 30th Nov. 1824, Surveyed for Blackstone Waterhouse fifty five acres of land on the mountain on the waters of Piney,
on the Western branch of Said Creek including Bonines improvement in Said County.
BEGINNING on a large blackoak marked "A"; thence North fifteen West one hundred
and thirty three poles to a blackoak; then North Seventy five East Sixty Six
poles (crossing a path at thirty four) to two Small hickorys; then South fifteen
East one hundred and thirty three poles to a Stake near a postoak marked "B";
then to the beginning.
Joseph Garrison and Cyrus Waterhouse, Chain Carriers

DAY & MADAN

Scale: 50 poles to an inch

State of Tennessee, Rhea County
Febry 28th 1825. Surveyed for John Day and
John Madan fifty acres of land in Said
County Entry No. 21, and dated the 10th of
Febry 1821 [sic], lying on both sides of
Richland Creek where it comes out of the
mountain. BEGINNING on a Beach (Jesse Witts
corner) a hickory and dogwood on the South
Side of the Creek; from thence North Sixty
Seven East Sixty three poles crossing Said
Creek at twelve poles near to a blackoak
and hickory; then North twenty three West
one hundred and twenty Six poles; then South Sixty Seven West Sixty three poles
crossing the creek; then to the beginning.
Washington Morgan and Robert Parke, Chain Carriers

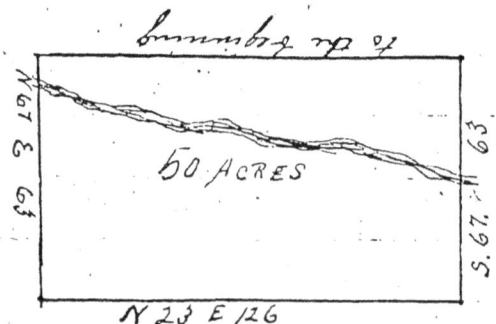

CY. WATERHOUSE   (page 10)

State of Tennessee, Rhea County   Scale: 50 poles to an inch
Friday July 29th 1825
By virtue of Entry No. 24 made in the
Entry Takers Office of Said County by
Cyrus Waterhouse for eighty acres 12th
July 1825 I have Surveyed for Said
Cyrus Waterhouse the enteror eighty
acres of land in an oblong on or near
Said County line and South Side of
Sandy Creek a tributary of Whites
Creek on the Mountain and on both
sides of Gordons turnpike road includ-
ing a Spring, a Mill Shoal and part of
an improvement made by Willis McClen-
don. BEGINNING on a Whiteoak marked
"C.W." on the bank of Said Sandy Creek; then South fifty West through McClendons
old field eighty poles to a blackoak, Whiteoak and hickory; then North forty West
crossing a path and County line one hundred and Sixty poles to two hickorys; then
North fifty East crossing a path and Said Gordons turnpike road eighty poles to a
blackoak and hickory near Said Sandy Creek; then down Said Creek to the beginning.
J. Wilson S.R.C.   Wiley Redwine and David Knox, Chain Carriers

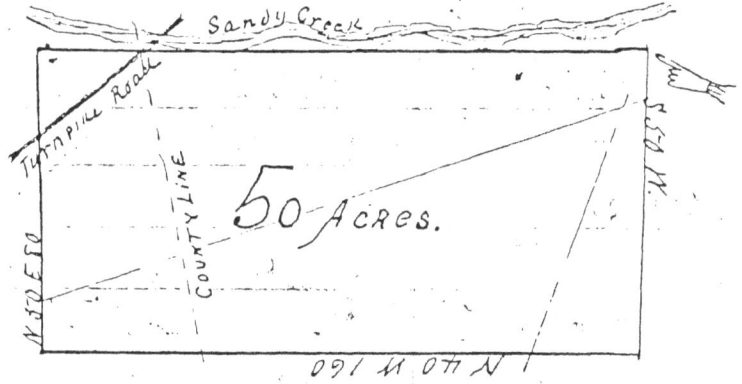

MYRA WATERHOUSE

State of Tennessee, Rhea
County, 30th of July 1825
Cyrus Waterhouse and
Richard Waterhouse, Chain
Carriers. By virtue of
Entry No. 23 made in the
(page 11)
Entry Takers office of
Said County by Myra Wa-
terhouse for one hundred
and forty two and half
acres 2nd of June 1825, I
have Surveyed for Said
Myra Waterhouse the ente-
rer 142½ acres of land in
Said County on the moun-
tain including the Chinque-
pine plains on the South
Side of the Waggon road
and West Side of Piney
River above the bridge.
BEGINNING on a whiteoak and maple marked "M" on the South of a drain; thence
South Seventy East twenty poles to two Small postoaks on the line of Richard Walkers Survey; thence with his line South twenty West crossing a branch at thirty
eight poles in all Sixty poles to a blackoak, postoak & hickory his corner;
thence South Seventy East touching the branch at twenty eight poles crossing a
drain at Sixty Six, leaving the branch at Seventy in all one hundred and fifteen
poles to two Whiteoaks marked "Y" on the top of a low ridge; then South twenty
West one hundred and Sixty poles to three postoaks marked "R" on the West bank

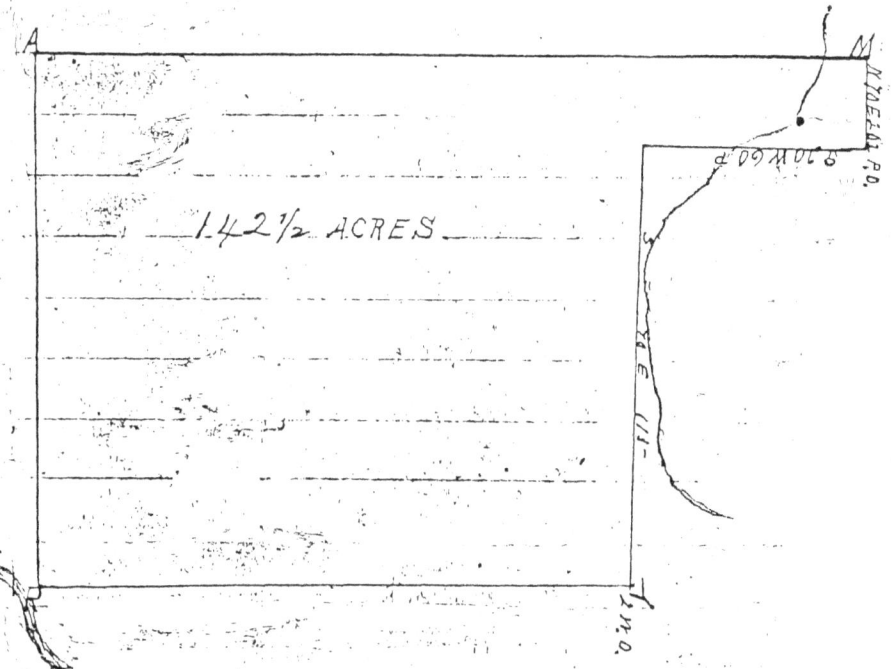

of Piney River, then North Seventy West one hundred and thirty five poles to a
blackoak marked "A"; then N 20 East crossing the branch two hundred and twenty
poles to the beginning forming an irregular right angled hexagon as shown in
the above plot of fifty poles to an inch.   J. Wilson S.R.C.
Cyrus Waterhouse and Richard Waterhouse, Chain Carriers

JOHN GARRISON   (page 12)

State of Tennessee
    Rhea County
Surveyed for John Gar-
rison one hundred and
twenty five acres (No.
32 dated the 23rd of
January 1826 at one
cent per acre) of land
in a rectangular ob-
long parallellagram in
Rhea County [on] the
Mountain on both sides
of the Bumblebee Fork
or branch of Piney Ri-
ver. BEGINNING at
three whiteoaks N 72 West thirteen poles from the old Indian Rock House; thence
North crossing Said fork at 10, 48 and 68 poles in all two Hundred poles to a
postoak and blackoak marked "G"; then West crossing Said fork at 43,54 & 60 poles,
in all one hundred poles to two Small Whiteoaks; then South crossing Selfs trace
at 150 poles, in all two hundred poles; then East crossing Said trace one hundred
poles to the beginning, the 26th day of Jany 1826.   J. Wilson S.R.C.
Joseph Garrison and Richard Waterhouse, Chain Carriers

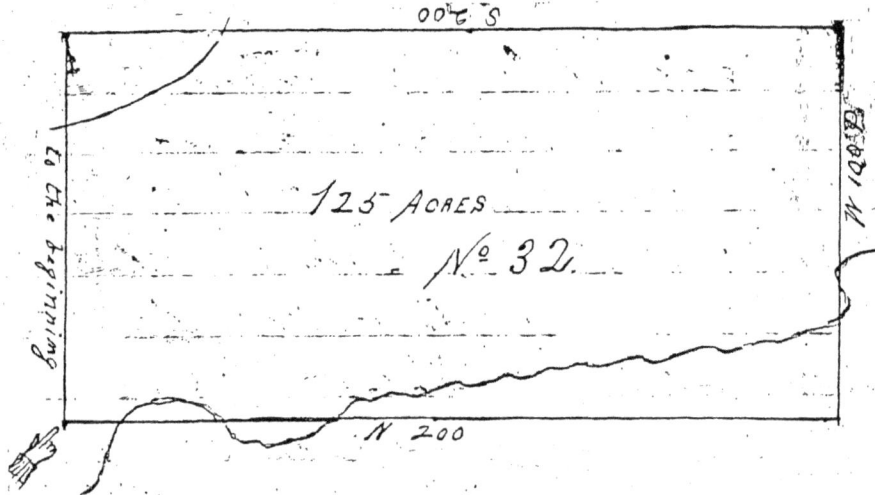

ROBT FERGUSON   (page 13)

State of Tennessee, Rhea County
15th of Febry 1826. Surveyed for Robert Fergason three hundred acres of land
Entry 31 dated 23rd of Jany 1826 on the mountain on the Bumblebee fork of Piney
River including a place known by the name of the old Indian Rock House.
BEGINNING on a blackoak on the South Side of Said fork; then North crossing
Selfs trace and Said fork one hundred and forty four poles to a blackoak and
whiteoak; then West Sixty poles to John Garrisons corner near the Rock House,
then with Garrisons line Same course in all one hundred and sixty poles to Gar-
risons 4th; then North with Garrisons line two hundred poles to a Whiteoak
Garrisons 3rd corner; then West one hundred and two poles to a blackoak; then
South two hundred and forty four poles to a blackoak, then East to the beginning.
                                                  J. Wilson S.R.C.

George Ransom and Ben Irwin, C.C.

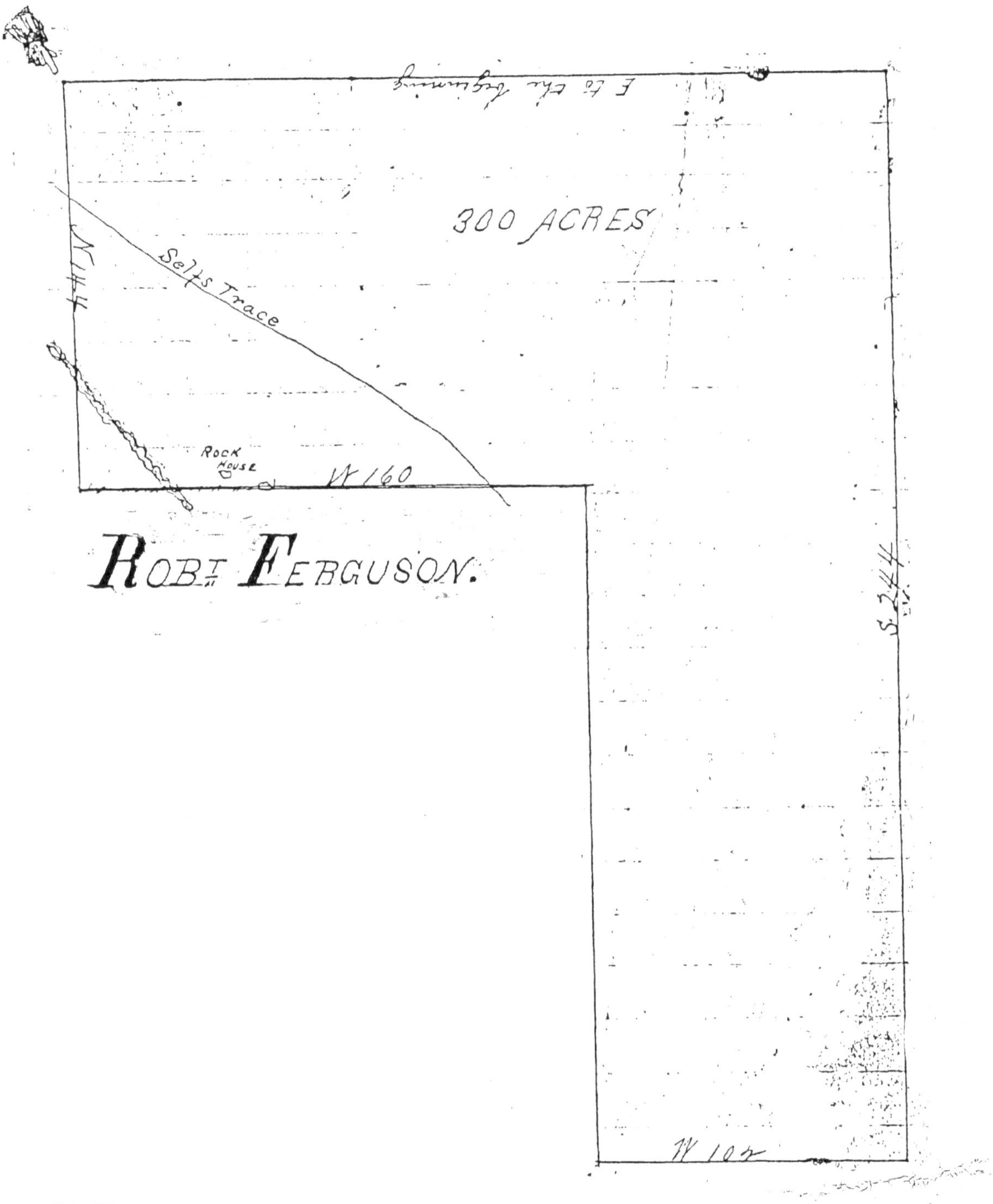

300 ACRES

Selts Trace

ROCK HOUSE W 160

ROBᵀ FERGUSON.

T.M. KIMMEN (page 14)

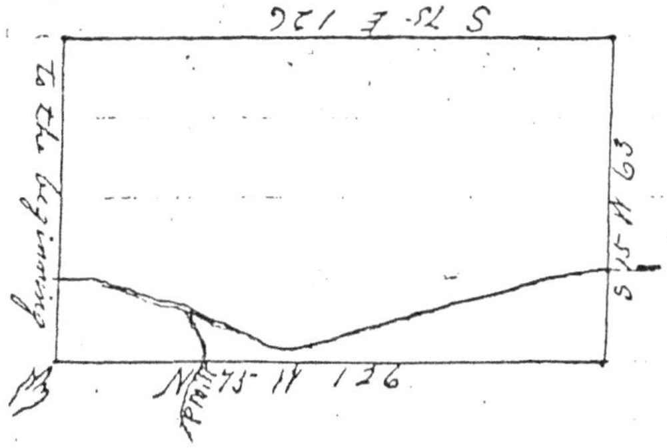

State of Tennessee 29th July 1825
Surveyed for Thomas M. Kimmen fifty acres of
land, Entry No. 22 dated the 22nd of Febry
1825 including the place where Wyley Redwine
now lives in Said County on the mountain on
both sides of the West fork of Whites Creek.
BEGINNING at a large rock marked "A" on the
side of the hill about fifty yards below Redwines house; then North Seventy West crossing
a path, the Powder Mill branch and touching
the main creek one hundred and twenty Six
poles to a large B.O. on the North Side of Said Creek; then South fifteen West

crossing a path and the creek to a Stake and pointers on the hillside; then South
Seventy five East one hundred and twenty Six poles crossing a branch and path;
then to the beginning.   J. Wilson
Richard Waterhouse and Wyley Redwine, Chain Carriers

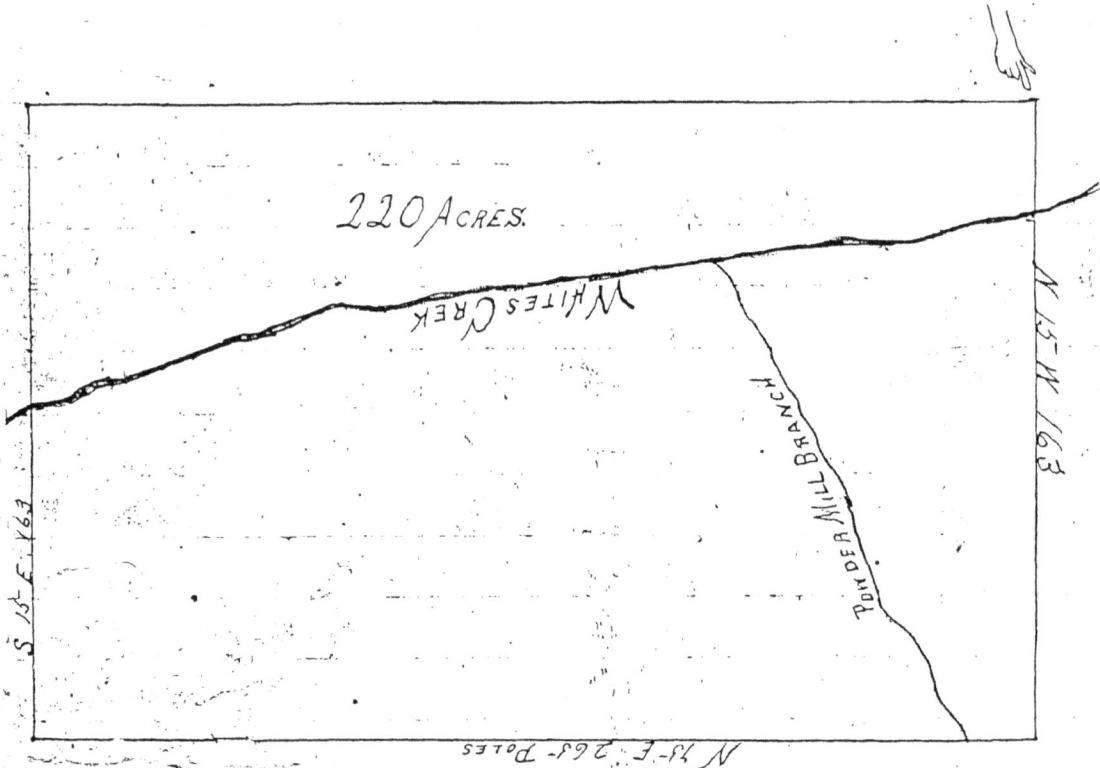

220 Acres.

J. HOWERTON

State of Tennessee, Rhea County 14th of April 1826
Surveyed for Jeremiah Howerton two hundred and twenty acres of land entered agreeably to the late law, at one cent per acre, dated the 27th of March 1826, No. 41
lying on both sides of the West fork of Whites Creek including an entry made by
                                                            (page 15)
Thomas M. Kimmen No. 22. BEGINNING on a large Whiteoak marked J and Small Maple;
then North fifteen West crossing the creek and path one hundred and sixty three
poles to two Postoaks on the top of the ridge; then North Seventy five East crossing the Powder Mill branch at 36 poles and Knox trace to Grassy Cove at 236 in
all two hundred and Sixty two poles to a Whiteoak on the bluff of the Middle Fork
Creek; then South fifteen East one hundred and Sixty three poles crossing Whites
Creek; then to the beginning.   J. Wilson S.R.C.
David Knox and Daniel Knox, Chain Carriers

J. DENTON

State of Tennessee, Rhea County April 10th 1826
Surveyed for Jonathan Denton one hundred acres of land on the mountain entered
agreeably to act of assembly at one cent per acre the 20th of March 1826, No. 39
on the waters of Piney River near the turnpike road. BEGINNING on a Whiteoak
Anthony Smiths corner on Browns line in the edge of a pond; then East Sixty poles
to a whiteoak about four poles the South Side of Said road; then South one hundred and three poles to a postoak; then West crossing the old road, Smiths Spring
branch and a fork of Piney two hundred and Seventy one poles; then North crossing

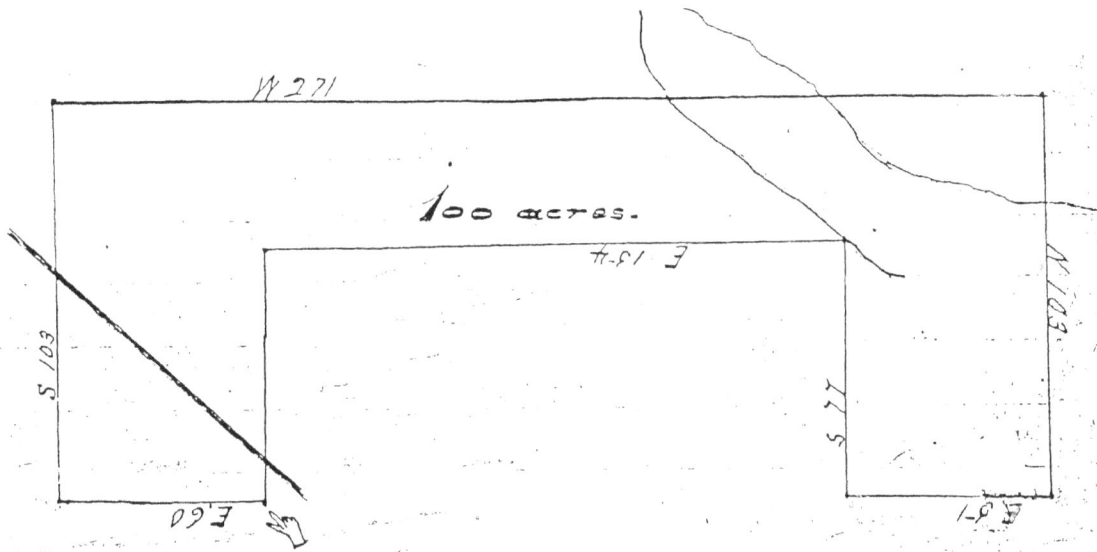

a branch of Piney one hundred and three poles; then East fifty Seven poles to
Smiths corner; then with Smiths line South Seventy Seven and half poles to Smiths
corner; then on with Smiths line East one hundred and fifty four poles; then to
the beginning.   J. Wilson S.R.C.
Anthony G. Smith and G. Hoodenpyle, Chain Carriers

E. WATERHOUSE   (page 16)

State of Tennessee, Rhea County
By virtue of an Entry No. 27 dated the 23rd day of Jany 1826 made in the Entry
Takers [office] of Said County by Euclid Waterhouse a minor for five hundred and
twenty acres of land in Said Rhea County on the mountain at one cent per acre.
I have Surveyed for the Said Euclid Waterhouse in a rectangular, irregular hec-
tagon five hundred and twenty acres of land on the East Side of Richland Creek
in a fork of Said Creek Supposed to be the first large fork on the mountain
East of Said creek. BEGINNING at a postoak bent Laurel and witch hazel in a
branch which is a tributary of the East branch of Said fork third corner of
Darius Waterhouses 640 acre tract of Entry No. 26; then East down Said branch
crossing the Same at 20 & 30 poles another branch at 80 poles 5 poles above its
junction with the former crossing a path at 110 poles in all two hundred to a
large Blackoak marked "J" in the fork of a branch beginning to Blackstone Waterhouses 585 acre tract of Entry No. 28 then South twenty Six poles to the conflu-
ence of Said branch and down the Same crossing it Several times to 68 poles
crossing Said path at 112 poles, a branch at 146, the East branch of Said fork
at 148, 166, 194 & 208   (page 17)
poles in all four hundred poles to a postoak and blackoak; then West crossing
Said East branch at 18 poles in all two hundred and forty poles to a Chestnut,
blackoak and blackgum; then North crossing a drain at 40 poles in all eighty poles
to a blackgum on the closing line of the Said Darius Waterhouses 640 acre tract;
then with the Same East forty poles to a postoak, blackoak and two chestnuts corner to Said tract; then with another line thereof North crossing a branch 153
poles in all three hundred and twenty poles to the beginning. Surveyed the 13th
of April 1826.   J. Wilson   S.R.C.
Richard Waterhouse and Cyrus Waterhouse, Chain Carriers

D. WATERHOUSE

State of Tennessee, Rhea County
By virtue of an Entry No. 26 dated the 3rd day of January 1826 made in the Entry
Takers office of Rhea County made by Darius Waterhouse a minor for six hundred and
forty acres of land at one cent per acre, I have Surveyed for the Said Darius Waterhouse in a rectangular equilateral tetragon Six hundred and forty acres of land
in Said County on the mountain and East Side of main Richland creek in a fork of
Said creek Supposed to be the first main fork on the mountain on Said East Side.
BEGINNING at a blackoak and hickory marked "B" on the top of a ridge about 80
poles East of Said Creek; then North crossing a drain at 108 poles in all three
hundred and twenty poles to a Whiteoak marked 2 and large rock on the [bank?] of
a drain; then East touching a branch one of the tributaries of the East branch of
Said fork 280 poles crossing the Same at 298 & 309 poles in all three
(page 18)
hundred and twenty poles to a postoak bush, laurel and Witch hazel in the branch;
then South crossing a branch at 167 in all three hundred and twenty poles to a
postoak, blackoak and two chestnuts; then West crossing a drain in all three
hundred and twenty poles to the beginning. Surveyed 13th of April 1826.
J. Wilson S.R.C.   Richard Waterhouse and Cyrus Waterhouse, Chain Carriers

B. WATERHOUSE

State of Tennessee, Rhea County
By virtue of an Entry No. 28 dated the 3rd of Jany 1826, made in the Entry Takers
office of Said County by Blackstone Waterhouse for five hundred eighty five acres
of land at one cent per acre. I have Surveyed for the Said Blackstone Waterhouse
in an irregular Septagon 585 acres of land in Said County on the mountain inclu=
ding the headwaters of Richland Creek and Piney River. BEGINNING at a large blackoak marked "J" in the fork of a branch corner to Euclid Waterhouses 520 acre tract
of Entry No. 27 on Richland Creek, then East eighty poles to a large blackoak;
then North passing an old path and branch or drain 120 poles to a redoak and two
hickory bushes; then West 2 ? poles to a postoak corner to his 55 acre tract of
Grant No. 10601; then with two lines of the Same South 75 West 66 poles to a
Blackoak marked "A" and North 15 West 133 poles to a Small blackoak; then West
crossing a branch of Piney River 335 poles; then South 230 poles to the line of
Darius Waterhouses 640 acre Survey of Entry No. 26 on Richland Creek; thence with
a line   (page 19)
of the Same and the first line of Euclid Waterhouses Said Survey East 380 poles
to the beginning. Surveyed 13th of April 1826.   J. Wilson S.R.C.
Richard Waterhouse and Cyrus Waterhouse, Chain Carriers

R.G. WATERHOUSE

State of Tennessee, Rhea County
By virtue of an Entry made by Richard G. Waterhouse in the Entry Takers Office of
Said County of Rhea No. 43 dated the 11th of April 1826 including his two former
entries No. 7 and 16. I have Surveyed for the Said Richard G. Waterhouse Six
hundred and forty acres of land in Said County on the mountain including Glazes
hickory flat on the big fork of Whites Creek. BEGINNING at a Spruce pine on the
bank of the middle fork of Whites Creek; then North 30 West one hundred and thirty
five poles to three blackoaks marked "C" at a path corner to his Said entry No. 7
and 16; then with a line of the former North Sixty West crossing Said middle fork
one hundred and fifteen poles to a chestnut and blackoak marked "B"; then North
30 East crossing Said middle fork below the mouth of David Knoxes Spring branch

pasing above the head of a Spring two hundred and thirty poles to four blackoaks and a postoak marked "A"; then South 60 East crossing Said Spring branch at 185 poles and passing over two large high rocks near Said branch in all five hundred poles to Whites Creek; then up the Creek to the beginning. Surveyed the 25th of July 1826.   J. Wilson S.R.C.
Richard Waterhouse and David Knox, Chain Carriers

J. LONG   (page 20)

State of Tennessee, Rhea County
Surveyed for Joel Long two hundred acres of land on the Side of Wallins Ridge on Whites Creek. BEGINNING on two Maples on the West bank of Said Creek near an old Mill Dam; then South fifty West thirty three poles to a whiteoak under the cliff of the mountain; then South twenty nine West along the cliff of the mountain two hundred and Sixty poles to a blackoak; then South Sixty East Sixty four poles to a blackgum on or near Roddys line; then East crossing a path at 20 in all 21 poles to Roddys corner; thence with Roddys line South Sixty two East thirty five poles; then North twenty Nine East two hundred and Seventy one poles to Whites Creek; then up Said Creek to the beginning. Entered the 7th of January 1826 No. 29, and Surveyed the 20th of Febry 1826.   J. Wilson S.R.C.
David Nelson and Hardeman Cruize, Chain Carriers

C. WATERHOUSE

State of Tennessee, Rhea County
Surveyed for Cyrus Waterhouse One hundred and Seventy acres of land agreeably to an Entry No. 42 dated the 11th of April 1826 at one cent per acre lying on Wallins Ridge on the South Side of Whites Creek in Said County. BEGINNING on a poplar and blackgum nearly opposite the big fork near the Bluff of Said Creek near and below the first branch above the Lick Branch; then South crossing a fork of Lick Branch at one hundred and fifty eight poles in all one hundred and sixty poles to a Chestnutoak and hickory on the bluff; then West one hundred and Seventy poles; then North one hundred and Sixty poles then East crossing a branch to the beginning. The 25th of July 1826.   J. Wilson S.R.C.
David Knox and Richard Waterhouse, Chain Carriers

E. BEAN   (page 21)

State of Tennessee, Rhea County
Surveyed for Edmond Bean fifty acres of land on Wallins Ridge in Said County Entry No. 19 dated the 22nd of Nov 1824 on a branch of Sale Creek near the cliff of the mountain including a bank of Stone coal. BEGINNING on a Small Sassafras and hickory Standing on the bluff about two poles from the coal bank, thence up the bluff South eighty eight West one hundred and twenty six poles to a hickory; then North two East Sixty three poles to a Stake, two hickory, postoak and blackoak; then North eighty eight East one hundred and twenty poles crossing the branch to a Stake; then down the cliff Sixty three poles to the beginning. The 29th of Febry 1825.   J. Wilson S.R.C.
John Witt and Washington Morgan, Chain Carriers

JOHN DAY

State of Tennessee, Rhea County
Surveyed for John Day Six hundred acres of land Entry No. 34, dated the 28th of Jany 1826, lying on Wallins Ridge, waters of Richland Creek. BEGINNING on a

12

Chestnutoak tree marked "J.D." on the South
Side of the Kiuka turnpike road where it
crosses the ridge of the lone mountain,
running North thirty five West along the
road crossing it twice two hundred and
thirty poles to a chestnut, chestnutoak
and pine on the South Side near Said road;
then North fifty five East crossing the
road at a cliff and descends the great
cliff of Richland at 296 poles in all 417
four hundred Seventeen and a half poles,
then South thirty five East two hundred
and thirty poles; then South fifty five West four hundred Seventeen and a half
poles to the beginning. Surveyed 17th July 1826.   J. Wilson S.R.C.

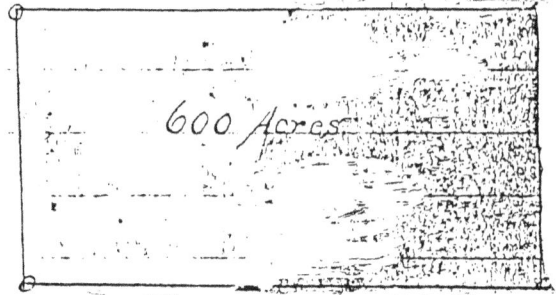

S.B. DYER   (page 22)

State of Tennessee, Rhea County
Surveyed for Spills B. Dyer and John Miller three hundred and Sixty acres of land
Entry No. 36 dated the 30th of January 1826 lying on the Waters of Stinging fork
of Piney River on Wallins Ridge. BEGINNING on a white pine marked "D" on the top
of the North cliff of Stinging fork, running North twenty East crossing a branch
at 200, another at two hundred and forty poles to a whiteoak on the bank thereof;
then up the Same North Seventy West crossing at 14 & 20 poles in all two hundred
and forty poles; then South twenty West two hundred and forty poles to the beginning. Surveyed 25th of July 1826.   J. Wilson S.R.C.
Andrew Wassum and James Wilson, Chain Carriers

GEO. RANSON

State of Tennessee, Rhea County
Surveyed for George Ransom four hundred acres of land on Wallins Ridge on both
sides of Beaty turnpike road on the waters of Piney River all round the 29 acre
tract of land on which he now lives, Entry No. 35. BEGINNING on a Whiteoak tree
on the South Side of Said road corner to Said 25 acre tract of land; then running
South twenty West two hundred and twenty four poles to a Blackoak; then North
Seventy West crossing the turnpike road one hundred and eighty five poles to a
postoak Saplin; then North twenty East four hundred and nine poles; thence Seventy
East one hundred and Eighty five poles to a maple, Sourwood and dogwood on the
bank of a branch; then a direct line to the beginning crossing a branch at 25 poles
and crossing Said turnpike road. Surveyed 15th of Feby 1826. J. Wilson S.R.C.
Robert Ferguson and _____?_ J _?_ , Chain Carriers

J. WASSUM   (page 23)

State of Tennessee, Rhea County
Surveyed for Jacob Wassum 200 acres of land Entry No. 40 dated the 27th of May
1826 on Wallins Ridge, waters of Bumblebee fork of Piney River. BEGINNING at a
Whiteoak marked "W" and a hickory on Robert Fergusons line on the North Side of
Said fork, running East crossing Bumblebee at 160 in all two hundred poles to a
whiteoak marked "J" and a hickory; then South one hundred and Sixty poles to a
hickory crossing Selfs trace at 105 poles, then West two hundred poles to Fergusons line, then with Fergusons line to the beginning. Surveyed the 25th of July
1826.   J. Wilson S.R.C.
Jacob Wassum Junr and Andrew Wassum, Chain Carriers

D. RAGSDALE

State of Tennessee, Rhea County
Surveyed for David Ragsdale One Hundred Acres of land on Wallins Ridge on the waters of Richland Creek, Entry No. 37 dated 25th of Feby 1826. BEGINNING on a blackoak on the South Side of the Kiuka turnpike road; then North five East crossing Said road at one in all one hundred and eighty poles to a whiteoak; then South eighty five East eighty nine poles to two postoaks, pine and blackoak, then South five West one hundred eighty poles to a chestnut and two blackoaks on the East Side of Said road; then a direct line crossing the road to the beginning, the 18th of July 1826.   J. Wilson S.R.C.
John Ellis and Saml Loury, Chain Carriers

JOHN JETT & CO.   (page 24)

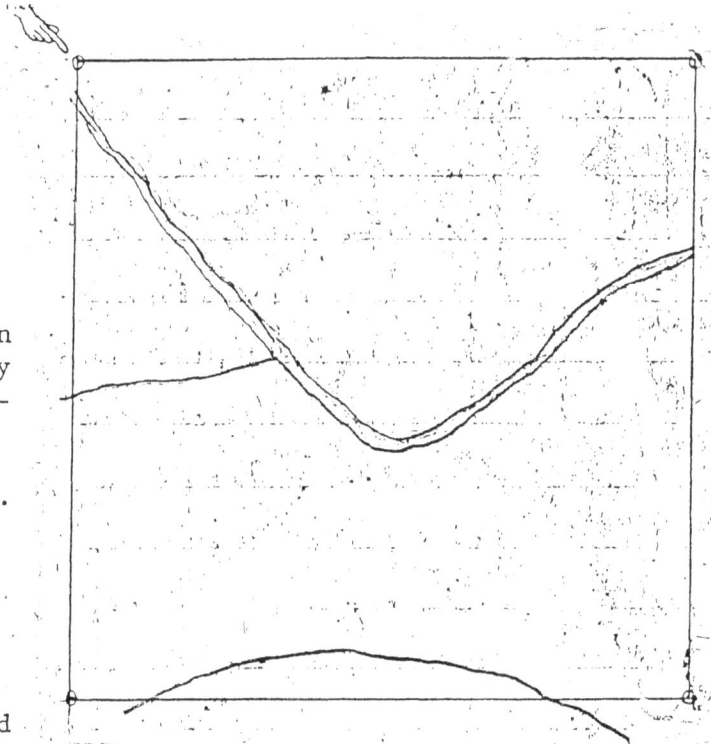

State of Tennessee, Rhea County
October 9th 1826
By virtue of an Entry No. 49 dated the 16th of September 1826 at one cent per acre. Surveyed for John Jett, Jesse Lincoln, Joseph Thomas, John H. Derens & Thomas B. Eastland Six hundred and forty acres of land in Said County of Rhea on Wallins Ridge on a fork of Piney River known by the name of Duskins fork of Piney River which fork leads down from opposite a gap known by Lowes Gap and North of an improvement at the Said Gap called and known by John Ramsey. BEGINNING on a Maple marked "J.T." and two whiteoaks one marked "J.D." the other "J.J." and Standing South of and close to a large rock marked "H" on the South Side and nearly South of the Rock house which is in the cliff above and at the aforesaid trees and large rock on the North Side of Said Duskins fork running then South crossing Duskins or Stinging fork at 20 a branch at 202 in all three hundred and twenty poles to a Stake three chestnuts and two Spanishoaks and one postoak; then East crossing at 56 and 218 in all three hundred and twenty poles to a Blackoak and hickory; then North crossing Said Duskins or Stinging Fork of Piney River at 220 in all three hundred and twenty poles; then to the beginning.   J. Wilson S.R.C.
Robert Ferguson and Edward Robins, Chain Carriers

NAIL & FARMER   (page 25)

State of Tennessee, Rhea County
October 10th 1826. Surveyed for Thomas Nail and Aquilla Farmer three hundred acres of land as general enterers No. 48 dated 1st of Sept 1826 lying on Wallins Ridge of Cumberland mountain. BEGINNING on a Stake about forty poles from and on the South Side of Duskins or Stinging fork of Piney River; thence South forty five East three hundred poles going down the cliff at 100 and runing it again at 200 poles to a Whiteoak blackoak and chestnut; then North forty five East passing

14

the cliff and a branch at 100 then along
the bluff in all one hundred and Sixty
poles to a hickory in the edge of the
bottom; thence North forty five West
crossing the Said creek at 5 in all three
hundred poles; then crossing the creek
to the beginning. A Silver or lead mine
at the (blank) thereof (blank).
                    J. Wilson S.R.C.
George S. Jones
Shamel Parham
        Chain Carriers

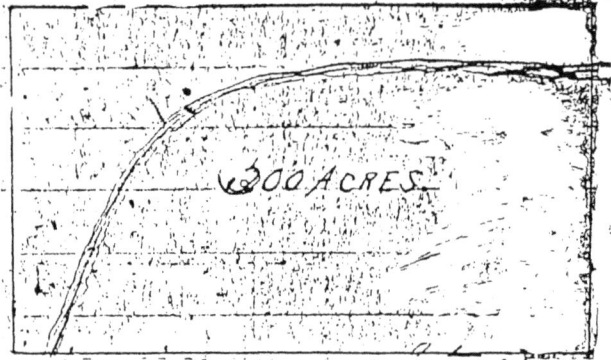

JOHN ELLIS

Scale 100 to an inch

State of Tennessee, Rhea County
Surveyed for John Ellis one hundred acres of land on
Wallens Ridge on the waters of Richland Creek entry No.
44 dated the 3rd of May 1826.   BEGINNING on a Stake
and blackoak on Joel Lowrys line running North fifteen
West one hundred and forty poles to three postoaks and
a blackoak; then South Seventy five West one hundred
and thirteen poles to a blackoak and postoak; then
South fifteen East crossing Halfway of Richland Creek
at 128 in all one hundred and forty; then a direct
line to the beginning crossing the Creek. Surveyed 13th of July 1826.
                                        J. Wilson S.R.C.

David Ragsdale and Samuel Lowry, Chain Carriers

R. RICHARDS   (page 26)

State of Tennessee, Rhea County
In pursuance of an Entry made by Richard
Richards of No. 25, dated Nov 15th 1825
for fifty acres of land at twelve and a
half cents per acre, and by virtue of a
deputation to me given by J. Wilson, Surveyor for Rhea County, I have Surveyed
[for] the Said Richard Richards fifty
acres of land in Said County on the West
Side of Bunks Creek which is the line
between Roane & Rhea County. BEGINNING
in the center of Said Creek on a rock at
the head of what is called the Falling
Water, running with a tremendous and Sub-
lime Cliff N 61 W thirty one poles to a
hickory, then West ninety four poles to
two Chestnutoaks, North Sixty five poles to a Stake; East one hundred and twenty
poles to the creek; thence down the creek to the beginning. Surveyed December
19th 1826.   John Purris, Dep Surveyor for Rhea County
Harvey Crews and Henry Flackner, S.C.C.

Scale 50 poles to an inch

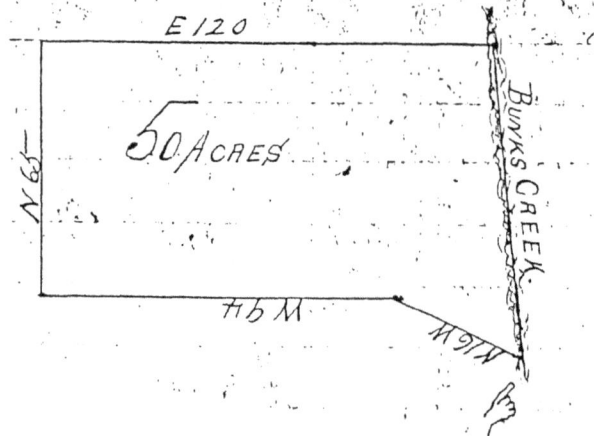

R. COOPER

State of Tennessee, Rhea County
In pursuance of an Entry made by Robert
Cooper of No. 61 dated 21st March 1827
for 100 acres of land at one cent per
acre, and in virtue of a deputation to
me given by Jas Wilson, Surveyor for
Rhea County, I have Surveyed for the
Said Robert Cooper one hundred acres
of land in Sd County on the waters of
Whites   (page 27)
Creek. BEGINNING on a poplar and dogwood on the North Side of a branch
called Camp branch near a drain;
thence South Sixty one degrees East
crossing Said branch eighty four poles
to a dogwood and blackgum on top of a
cliff; thence South ten degrees East
forty six poles to a blackoak and
poplar on the line of Mathew Englishs
24 acre survey; then along Sd line
South Seven degrees West Eight poles
to Gordon road, Same course pursued
in all forty eight poles to a hickory
Sapling on a line of John Purrisses
nine acre Survey; thence with Said
line North Seventy five West forty
six poles to Purris's corner, Same
course continued in all one hundred
and ninety poles to a dogwood and
hickory; thence North thirty degrees
East one hundred and twenty Six poles crossing Gordons road at ninety two poles
to a blackgum and pine near the top of a ridge; thence South Sixty one degrees
East fifty poles to the beginning. Surveyed 16th Nov. 1827 by Franklin Locke,
Deputy Surveyor for Rhea County.
M. English and Wm Garner, S.C.C.

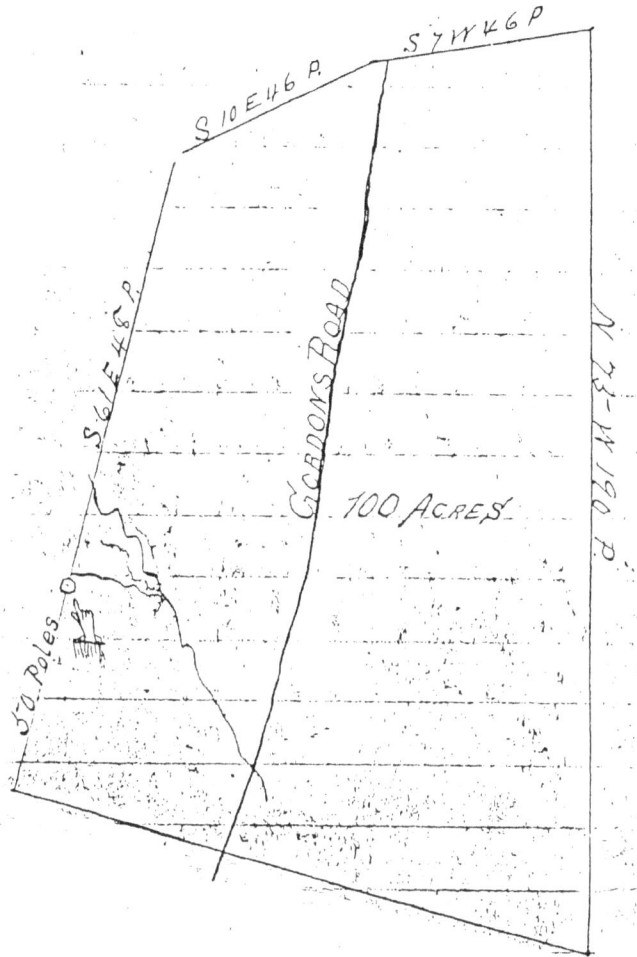

J. & T. PAUL

State of Tennessee, Rhea County
In pursuance of an entry made by James Paul and
Thomas G. Paul of No. 60 dated the 21st March 1827
for one hundred acres of land at one cent per acre
and by virtue of a deputation to me given by James
Wilson, Surveyor in and for Said County, I have
Surveyed for the Sd James & Thomas G. [Paul] one
hundred acres of land lying and being in Sd
County on the West fork of the Devils fork of
Piney Creek or river on the road leading from
Walton Ferry to the Grassy Cove on the mountain.
BEGINNING on a blackgum Southwest Side of Said
Creek about three poles from the Same, thence North
twenty degrees East crossing Sd creek at twenty
eight poles and a branch at _?_   (page 28)

Scale 80 equal parts to
the inch

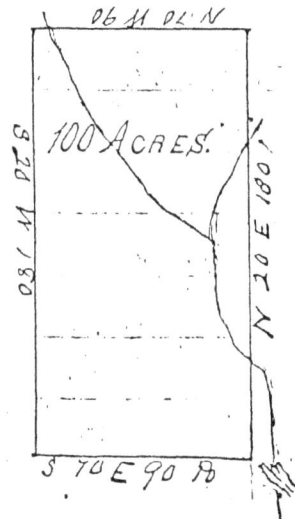

continued in all one hundred and eighty to a chestnut and blackgum on the top of a rise, thence North twenty degrees West ninety poles to a Stake; thence South twenty degrees West one hundred and eighty poles to a Stake; thence South Seventy degrees East ninety poles to the beginning. Surveyed 22nd January 1829.

                          Franklin Locke, D.S.R.C.

Ralph Locke and John Locke, S.C.C.

W.G. ENGLISH

State of Tennessee, Rhea County
In pursuance of an entry made by William G. English of No. 65 dated 10th day of May 1827, for 200 acres of land at one cent per acre and in virtue of a deposition to me given by James Wilson, Surveyor for Rhea County, I have Surveyed for the Sd William G. English 200 acres of land in Sd County. BEGINNING on a Small ash and hickory near the falls of a Small branch on the South Side of Whites Creek on the top of a cliff opposite to the mouth of Piney thence East two hundred and fifty four poles to a Stake; thence South one hundred and twenty Seven poles to a Stake; thence West two hundred and fifty four poles to a Stake; thence North one hundred and twenty Seven poles to the beginning. Surveyed 16 Novr 1827.

Scale 80 equal parts to the inch

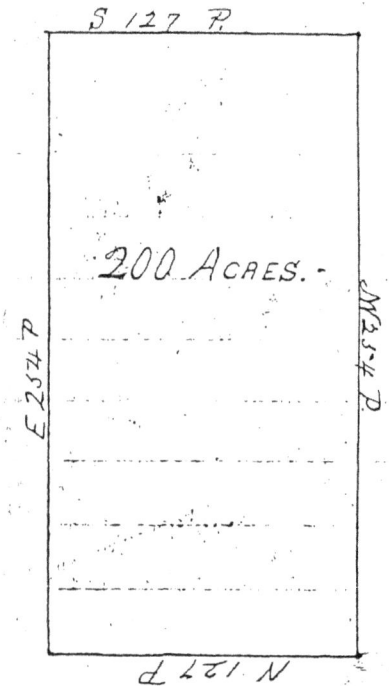

S 127 P.
E 234 P
W 234 P
N 127 P
200 Acres.

                          Franklin Locke
              Deputy Surveyor Rhea County
Matthew English and William Garner, S.C.C.

G.G. ENGLISH

S 16 W 44.7
25 Acres

Scale 40 equal parts to an inch

State of Tennessee, Rhea County
In pursuance of an entry made by George G. English of No. 66 dated the 10th day of May 1827 for 25 acres of land at one cent per acre and [by] virtue of a deputation to me given by James

(page 29)

Wilson Surveyor of Rhea County, I have Surveyed for the Said George G. English 25 acres of land in Said County. BEGINNING near the bank of Whites Creek at the upper end of a place known by the name of "cane brake" opposite the mouth of Piney on the South Side of Whites Creek on a Spruce pine; thence down the creek as it meanders South Seventy four degrees East 89.4 poles to a Stake; thence South Sixteen degrees West 44.7 poles to a Stake; thence North Seventy four degrees West 89.4 poles to a Stake; thence North Sixteen degrees East 44.7 poles to the beginning. Surveyed 16th Novr 1827.

              Franklin Locke, Deputy Surveyor for R.C.
William Garner and Matthew English, S.C.C.

MATTHEW ENGLISH

State of Tennessee, Rhea County
In pursuance of an entry made by Matthew English of No. 67 the 10th day of May 1827 for 200 acres of land at one cent per acre, and in virtue of a deputation to me given by James Wilson Surveyor of Rhea County, I have Surveyed for the Said

Matthew English two hundred acres of land lying and being in the County of Rhea on Wallins Ridge of Cumberland Mountain. BEGINNING on two maples on a bank of a branch of Bear Creek a tributary Stream of Whites Creek near and Northwest of a tar kiln, thence South thirty four degrees West crossing Gordon road at fifty eight poles in all two hundred and fifty four poles to a Stake on Hinses Camp Branch; thence South fifty Six degrees East one hundred and twenty Seven poles to three Chestnuts; thence North thirty four degrees East one hundred and twenty Seven poles to Gordons Road containing in all two hundred and fifty four poles to a Stake; thence North fifty Six West one hundred and twenty Seven poles to the beginning. Surveyed 17 Nov 1827. Thos Rose and John Locke, S.C.C.

Scale 80 equal parts to the inch

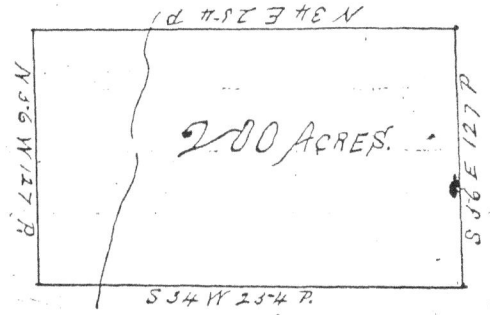

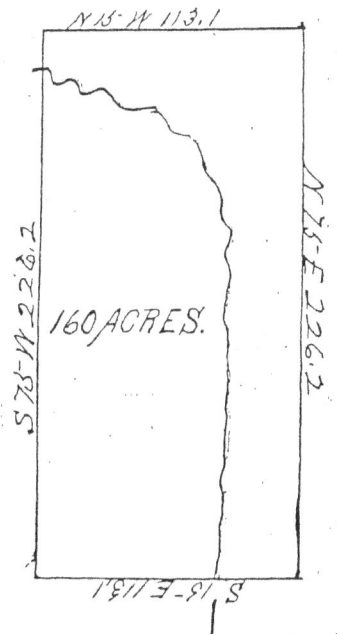

200 ACRES.

Franklin Locke   D.S.R.C.

MARY WHEELER   (page 30)

State of Tennessee, Rhea County
Pursuant to an entry made by Mary Wheeler of No. 89 dated the 1st day of February in the year 1823 for one hundred and Sixty acres of land at one cent per acre, and in virtue of a deputation to me given by James Wilson Surveyor for Rhea County I have Surveyed for the Said Mary Wheeler one hundred and sixty acres of land lying and being in Said County on the waters of Piney in the mountain. BEGINNING on a Whiteoak on a point of ridge in the fork of the Creek near John Hammets line and corner to her other tract of land; thence South fifteen degrees East crossing one fork of Piney at forty poles in all one hundred and thirteen & one tenth poles to three blackoaks; thence South Seventy five West two hundred and twenty Six and two tenths poles to a chestnut, two Postoaks and blackoak, thence North fifteen degrees West one hundred and thirteen and one tenth poles to a Stake & blackoak pointers; thence North Seventy five degrees East two hundred and Seventy Six and two tenth poles to the beginning. Surveyed 16th February 1828. Franklin Locke
                                    Deputy Surveyor R.C.
Andrew Smith and Thomas H. Wheeler, S.C.C.

Scale 80 equal parts to the inch

160 ACRES.

MARY WHEELER   (page 31)

State of Tennessee, Rhea County
Pursuant to an entry made by Mary Wheeler of No. 55, dated the 7th day of February in the year 1827 for two hundred acres of land at one cent per acre, and in virtue of a deputation to me given by James Wilson Surveyor in and for Said Rhea County, I have Surveyed for the Said Mary Wheeler two hundred acres of land lying and being in Rhea County on the waters of Piney. BEGINNING on a whiteoak in the fork of Said Creek corner to her other Survey; thence with line thereof South Seventy five degrees West one hundred and twenty four poles to a blackoak near Myra Waterhouses line; thence North fifteen degrees West eighty four poles to the chincapin fork of Piney Creek continued in all one hundred and sixty five poles to three postoaks and blackoak; thence North Seventy five degrees East crossing

Beaty road at eighty poles in all one hundred and
ninety four poles to two postoaks and hickory;
thence South fifteen degrees East crossing Said
Chincapin fork and Beatys turnpike road to the
beginning. Surveyed 16th Feb 1828.
                    Franklin Locke, D.S.R.C.
Andrew Smith and Thos H. Wheeler, S.C.C.

W.H. CHAPMAN   (page 32)

State of Tennessee, Rhea County
In pursuance of an entry made by Wylis H. Chapman
of No. 62 dated
the 23rd day of
March 1827 for
four hundred
acres of land at
one cent per
acre and by vir-
tue of a deputa-
tion to me given
by James Wilson
Surveyor in and
for Said Rhea County, I have Surveyed for the
Said Wylles H. Chapman four hundred acres of
land in Said County on the waters of Sandy
Creek a tributary Steam of Whites Creek.
BEGINNING on three maples on a cliff on the
East Side of Sandy Creek; thence South fifty
degrees West twenty five poles to the line of
Cyrus Waterhouses eighty acre entry; then with
the line of the Same North forty West Sixty
poles to a Blackoak & hickory corner to Said
entry then with Said line South fifty degrees
West eighty poles to two hickorys; then with
said line South forty East one hundred and
Sixty poles to a blackoak, Whiteoak & hickory;
thence leaving Said Waterhouses line South
fifty degrees West one hundred & three & one

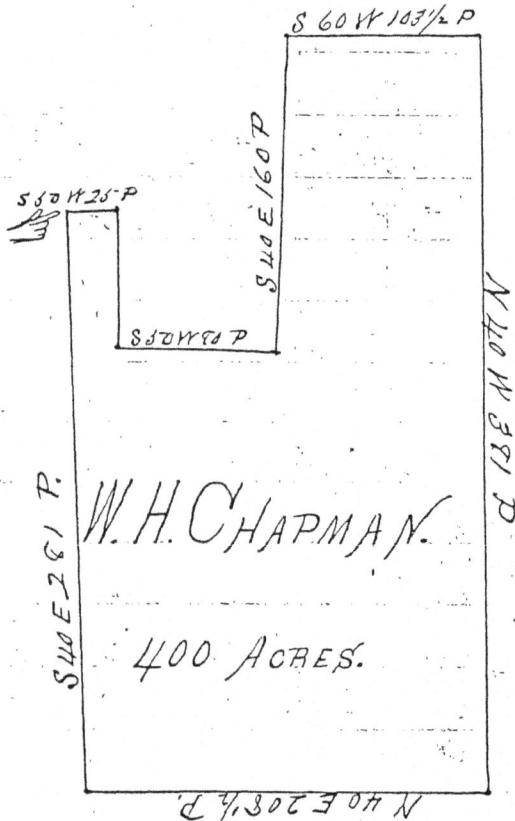

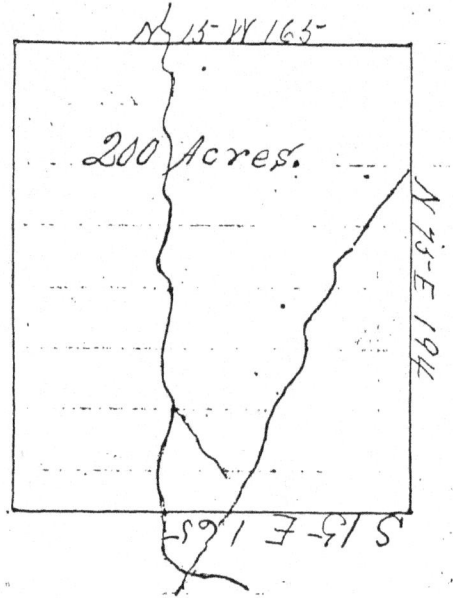

80 equal parts to the inch

Scale 100 poles to the inch

half poles to a blackoak and two whiteoaks;
thence South forty degrees West three hundred
& eighty one poles to a Sourwood & Chestnut; thence North fifty degrees East crossing Gordons road at thirty nine poles in all two hundred & eighty & one half
poles to a Stake; thence South forty degrees East two hundred and eighty one poles
to the beginning. Surveyed the 25 Novr 1827.   Franklin Locke Deputy Surveyor
Henry Henry and Thomas Rose, S.C.C.

ROBT. COOPER   (page 33)

State of Tennessee, Rhea County
In pursuance of an entry made by Robert Cooper of No. 79 dated the 6th October
1827 for fifty acres of land at one cent per acre, and in virtue of deputation to
me given by James Wilson Surveyor for Rhea County, I have Surveyed for the Said
Robert Cooper fifty acres of land in Said County on the waters of Whites Creek on
both Sides of Gordon Road. BEGINNING on the North Side of Said road on a hickory

and pine on a line of said Coopers one hundred acre Survey; thence North thirty degrees East fifteen poles to a blackgum and pine cor- ner to Said one hundred acre Survey; thence North Seventy Seven West Sixty four poles to a blackoak and Whiteoak on the top of a cliff; then South thirty degrees West crossing Gor- dons road at eighteen poles in all one hundred & twenty Six & five tenth poles to a Stake; thence South Seventy Seven East Sixty four poles to the Southwest corner of his Said one hundred acre Survey; thence with the line of Said Survey North thirty degrees East one hundred and five tenth poles to the beginning. Surveyed 17th Nov 1827. Franklin Locke, Deputy Surveyor Matthew English and John Locke, S.C.C.

Scale 40 equal parts to an inch

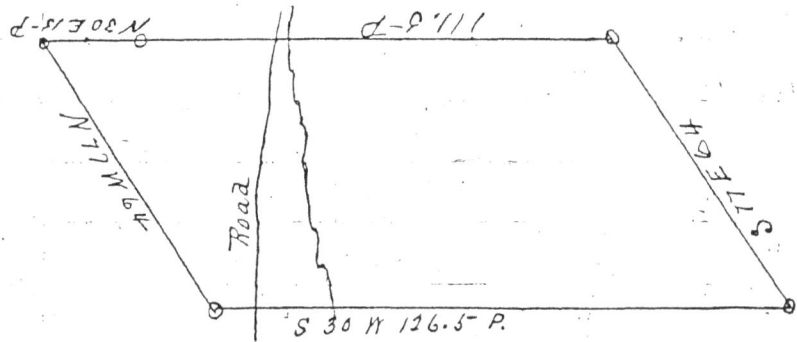

C.D. GIPSON [sic]   (page 34)

State of Tennessee, Rhea County
In pursuance of an entry made by Calvin D. Gibson [sic] of No. 87, dated the 1st day of January 1828 for one hundred acres of land at 1 One cent per acre and in virtue of a depu- tation to me given by James Wilson Surveyor in and for Rhea County, I have Surveyed for the Said Calvin D. Gibson one hundred acres of land in Said County on the mountain. BEGINNING on a dogwood & two Whiteoaks Stand- ing at the edge of a Swamp on the west Side of Sandy Creek a tributary Stream of Whites Creek; thence North Sixty degrees West one hundred and eighty poles to a blackoak; thence South thirty degrees West ninety poles to a chestnut and three pine trees Standing in the laurel on the North fork of Said Creek; thence South Sixty degrees East one hundred & fifty four poles to Sandy Creek continued in all one hundred and eighty poles to a Stake; thence North thirty East ninety poles to the beginning. Surveyed 24 Feb 1828. Franklin Locke, Deputy Surveyor R.C. Pleasant R. Gibson and Allen Looper, S.C.C.

80 equal parts to the inch

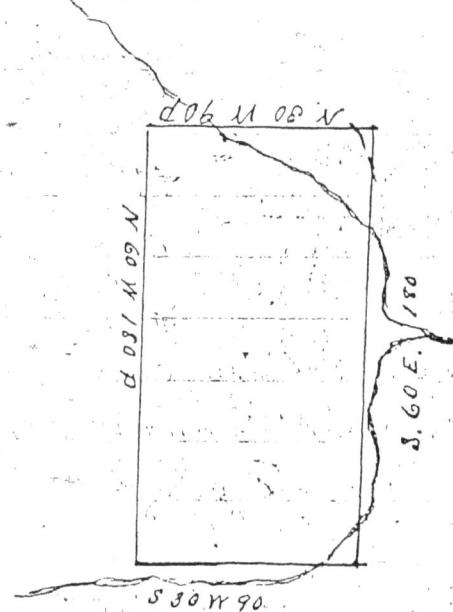

B.G. GIPSON   (page 35)

State of Tennessee, Rhea County
In pursuance of an entry made by John Richards and transfered in the Entry Takers office to Benjamin C. Gibson of No. 51 dated 12 of December in the year 1826 for one hundred acres of land at one cent per acre and in virtue of a deputation to me given by James Wilson Surveyor in and for Rhea County, I have Surveyed for Benjamin C. Gibson one hundred acres of land lying and being in Said County on

Wallins Ridge. BEGINNING on a Small hickory on the divide between Sandy and Basan Creeks tributary Streams of Whites Creek; thence South Sixty degrees East one hundred and eighty poles to a dogwood; thence South thirty degrees West crossing Gordons road at Sixty poles continued in all ninety poles to two Small blackoaks; thence North Sixty West one hundred and twenty poles to Gordons road continued in all one hundred and eighty poles to a Stake and pointers; thence South thirty West to the beginning. Surveyed 23rd January 1828.
Franklin Locke, Deputy Surveyor for Rhea County
Ralph B. Locke and John Locke, S.C.C.

Scale: 80 equal parts to the inch

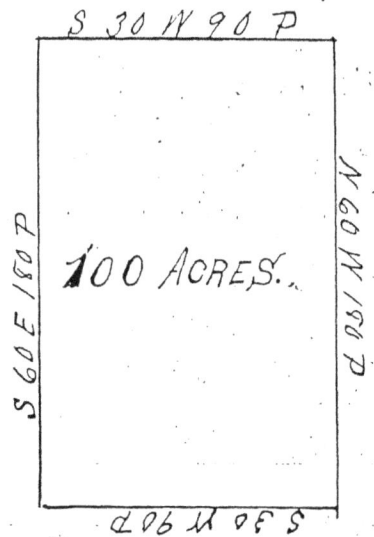

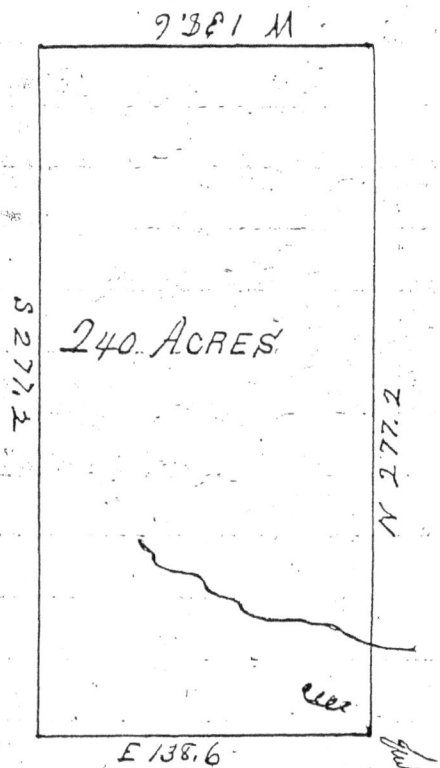

B.C. GIPSON

(page 36)

State of Tennessee, Rhea County
In pursuance of an entry made by Benjamin C. Gibson of No. 53 dated the 2 day of February in the year 1827 for two hundred and forty acres of land at one cent per acre and in virtue of a deputation to me given by James Wilson Surveyor in and for Rhea County, I have Surveyed for Benjamin C. Gibson two hundred and fifty acres of land in Said County lying and being on Wallins Ridge on the Waters of Whites Creek. BEGINNING on a Chestnut about one hundred yards East of the Speewood Spring on the North side of Gordons Road; thence due North crossing the Spring branch at eight poles, Basan Creek at fifty eight poles passing a Small Chestnut and Pine on the cliff of Burks Creek at two hundred and fifty poles continued in all two hundred and Seventy Seven and two tenth poles to a Stake; thence West one hundred and thirty eight and Six tenths poles to a Stake; thence South two hundred and Seventy Seven and two tenth poles to a Stake; thence East to the beginning. Surveyed 23 January 1828. Franklin Locke, Deputy Surveyor Rhea Cty John Locke and Ralph Locke, S.C.C.

80 equal parts to the inch

ALLEN LOOPER

(page 37)

State of Tennessee, Rhea County
In pursuance of an entry made by Allen Looper of No. 54 dated the 2 day of February in year 1827 for one hundred and fifty acres of land at one cent per acre, and in virtue of a deputation to me given by James Wilson Surveyor in and for Rhea County, I have Surveyed for the Said Allen Looper one hundred and fifty acres of land in Said County on the mountain. BEGINNING on a Chestnut tree & Whiteoak Saplin on the North Side of the South fork of Bason Creek a tributary Stream of

Whites Creek near Benjamin C. Gibsons Survey; thence
North Seventy nine degrees East crossing a branch at
one hundred and Seventy two poles continued in all
two hundred and nineteen poles to a Stake and dogwood on the Side of a ridge; thence South eleven
East crossing the South fork of Bason Creek at
Sixty poles continued in all one hundred and nine
and five tenth poles to a Stake, thence South Seventy nine degrees West two hundred and nineteen poles
to a Stake; thence North eleven degrees West one
hundred and nine and five tenth poles to the beginning. Surveyed 24 January 1828.
Franklin Locke, Deputy Surveyor R.C.
Ralph Locke and Pleasant R. Gibson, S.C.C.

60 equal parts to an inch

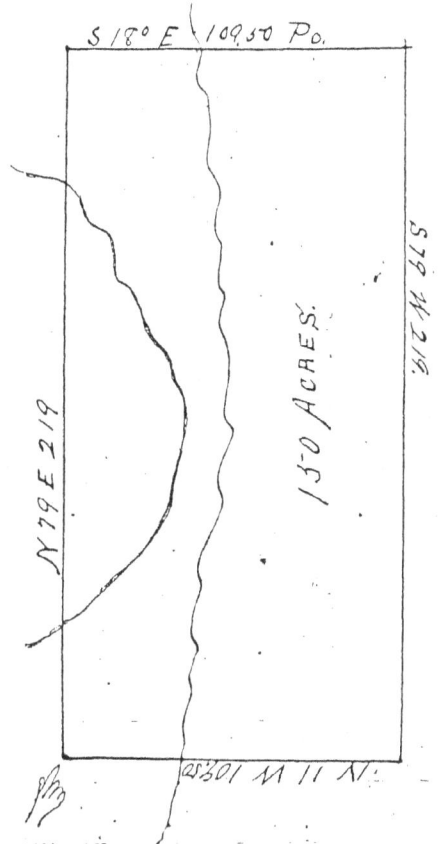

JAMES LEA   (page 38)

State of Tennessee, Rhea County
In pursuance of an entry made by James Lea of No.
50 dated 13 November 1826 for two hundred acres of
land at one cent per acre, I have this day Surveyed for the Said James Lea two hundred acres of
land in Said County on Waldens Ridge of Cumberland
BEGINNING on a Spruce pine on the North side of
Gilbreaths branch a tributary Stream of Sale Creek
on the 3rd line of E. Beans entry of 50 acres;
thence with Said line South 87 [written under this
number was 71½] West 92 [written under this number
72] poles to Beans corner; thence
S 26 W 140 poles to a blackoak;
thence West crossing a Small
branch three times Sixty poles
to a Spanishoak; thence North
twenty three West 23 poles to
a postoak on Said 50 acre Survey, then South 23 poles to
the corner of Said Survey on
two hickorys; thence North 80
poles to a Spanish oak; thence
W 100 poles to the corner of
Said Survey on a blackoak;
thence N 22 E one hundred and
sixty four poles to a blackoak;
thence South 62 East two hundred & Sixty four poles to the
beginning. Surveyed April 15th
1827. James Wilson
     Surveyor for Rhea County
Washington Morgan
John Jarrell   S.C.C.

Scale: 80 equal parts to the inch

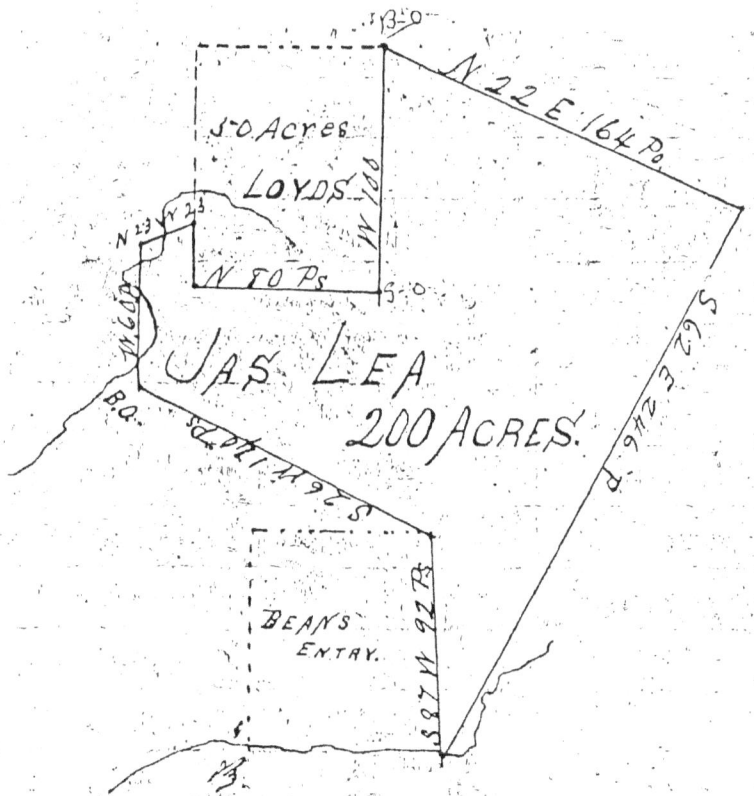

JOHN WITT (page 39)

State of Tennessee, Rhea County
In pursuance of an entry made by
John Witt of No. 94 dated Nov 26
1827 for three hundred acres of
land at one cent per acre, I have
this day Surveyed for the Said
John Witt three hundred and
twenty acres of land in Said
County on Waldens Ridge of Cumberland Mountain. BEGINNING on
a Spruce or white[oak] near the
mouth of a branch of Richland
Creek between what is called the
two laurel forks of Sd Creek;
thence N 10 W one hundred and Sixty
poles to a Stake on top of a ridge;

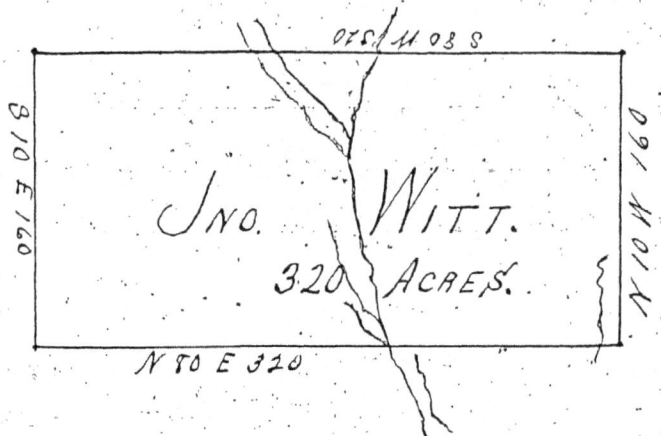

Scale: 80 parts to the inch

thence South eighty degrees West 320 Poles crossing the main laurel fork of Richland Creek to a Whiteoak on a ridge; thence South ten degrees East to a blackoak;
thence a Streight line to the beginning. Surveyed 4th June 1828.
                David Shelton, Surveyor for Rhea County Pro-tem
Wesley Maness and Willson Hudgens, S.C.C.

D. SHELTON

State of Tennessee, Rhea County
In pursuance of an entry made by David Shelton of
No. 76 dated 17th Sept 1827 for one hundred acres
of land at one cent per acre, I have this day
Surveyed for the Sd David Shelton one hundred
acres of land in Sd County on Waldens Ridge of
Cumberland Mountain. BEGINNING on a hickory on
the Southwest Side of the Kiuka turnpike road;
thence North twenty five degrees West crossing
Richland   (page 40)
Creek and Said road one hundred and Seventy eight
poles to a postoak; thence North forty five degrees East near ninety poles to a Stake, a postoak and blackoak pointers; thence South twenty
five degrees East one hundred and Seventy eight
poles crossing Sd Creek to a postoak & blackoak;
thence a strait line to the beginning. Surveyed
June 4th 1828.   David Shelton
    Surveyor for Rhea County pro tem
Wesley Maness and Wilson Hudgins, S.C.C.

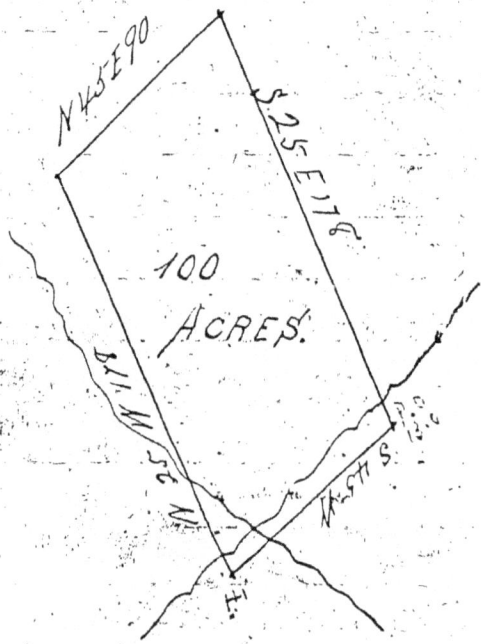

Scale: 80 parts to the inch

T. CLARK

State of Tennessee, Rhea County
In pursuance of an entry made by Thomas Clarke of No. 88 dated January 2nd 1828
for four hundred acres of land at one cent per acre, I have this day Surveyed
for the said Thomas Clarke four hundred acres of land in Rhea County on Walding
Ridge. BEGINNING on a Spruce pine on the North Side of Gilbreaths branch a
tributary Stream of Sale Creek corner of James Lea's 200 acre entry of No. 50;

Scale 100 poles to the inch

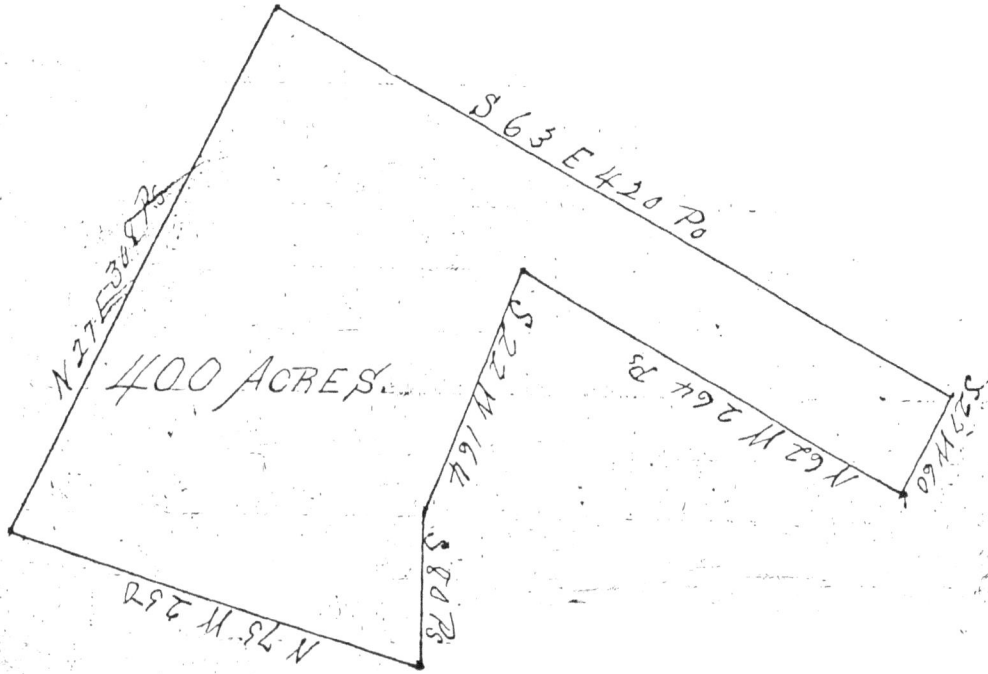

thence with his line crossing Sd branch N 62 W 264 poles to a Blackoak; thence South 22 W 164 poles to a Spanishoak corner of James Lea's 200 acre Survey and James Loids 50 acre entry; thence with Loids line South 80 poles to a hickory; thence North 75 West 250 poles to a Whiteoak and Blackgum; thence North 27 E 308 poles to a Small hickory and blackoak; thence S 63 E 420 poles to a Stake whiteoak blackoak pointers; thence S 27 W 60 poles to the beginning. Surveyed September 8th 1828. David Shelton, Surveyor for R.C. pro tem William Romain and David Ragsdale, S.C.C.

W. MORGAN   (page 41)

State of Tennessee, Rhea County
In pursuance of an entry made by Washington Morgan of No. 75 dated September 15th 1827 for one hundred acres of land at one cent per acre. In pursuance of Sd entry I have Surveyed for the Said W. Morgan one hundred acres of land in Sd County on Walding Ridge on Richland Creek. BEGINNING on the North side of Sd Creek on what is called "Buzzard Point" on a blackoak; thence South ten degrees East crossing the Creek at about twenty poles and the other fork at about one hundred poles in all one hundred and Sixty poles to a Chestnutoak and two hickorys pointers; thence South eighty degrees East ninety two poles to the Bluff in all one hundred poles to a Stake; thence North 10 West 160 poles to a Stake; thence to the beginning so as to include two falls in Said creek near the fork. Surveyed 15th Sept 1828.

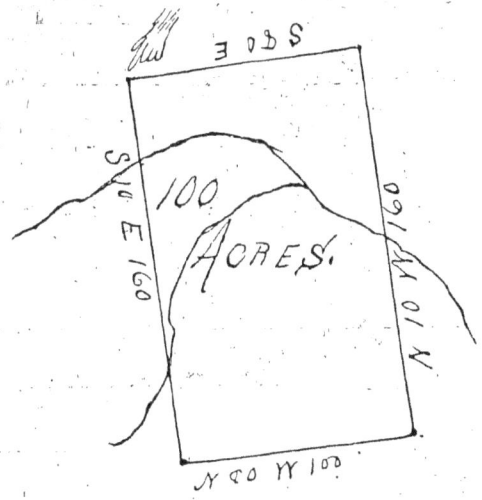

Scale: 80 poles to the inch

David Shelton, S.R.C. pro tem

David Ragsdale and William Runnion, S.C.C.

WILLIAM RUNNION

State of Tennessee, Rhea County
In pursuance of an entry made by William Runnion
of No. 70 dated Sept 3rd 1827, I have this day
Surveyed for the Said Runnion fifty acres of
(page 42)
land in Said County on Waldens Ridge on Richland
Creek. BEGINNING on a crooked postoak joining
another fifty acre entry of his; thence South
eighty poles to three postoak bushes; thence
West eighty poles to hickory and postoak; thence
North one hundred poles to a Stake; thence [to]
the beginning, So as to include Said fifty acres
on both Sides of the Kiuka Trace. Surveyed Sept 9th 1828. David Shelton S.R.C.

Scale: 80 poles to the inch

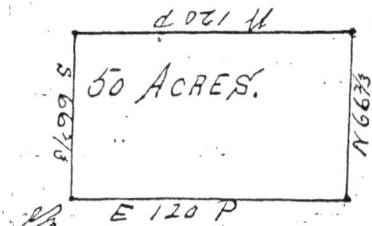

WILLIAM RUNNION

State of Tennessee, Rhea County
In pursuance of an entry made by Wm Runnion of No.
83 dated the 14 November 1827 of fifty acres at
one cent per acre, I have this day Surveyed for
the Sd Wm Runnion fifty acres of land in Sd County
on Waldens Ridge on Richland Creek. BEGINNING on
a crooked postoak corner to Bishops fifty acre
entry and to his other fifty acre entry of No. 70;
thence East one hundred and twenty poles to a postoak bush; thence North 66 2/3 poles to a whiteoak;
thence West one hundred and twenty poles to a
Stake two postoaks and hickory pointer; thence to the beginning. Surveyed September the 9th 1828. David Shelton S.R.C. pro tem
David Ragsdale and Isaac Richard, S.C.C.

Scale: 80 equal parts to the inch

ISAAC RICHARDS
(page 43)

State of Tennessee, Rhea County
In pursuance of an entry made by Isaac Richard
[sic] of No. 81, dated 16th Oct 1827 for one
hundred acres of land at one cent per acre, I
have this day Surveyed for the Sd Isaac Richard one hundred acres of land in Sd County on
Waldens Ridge on both sides of the Kiuka trace
BEGINNING on a blackoak on Ragsdales line on a
Small branch of Richland Creek, thence North
thirty Six poles to Ragsdales corner a blackoak; thence East with Sd line ninety Six poles
to a Small postoak; thence North one hundred
poles to a blackoak; thence West Sixty poles
to Dixons 50 acre Survey; thence South with
Said line twenty eight poles to a blackoak;
thence with Sd line crossing Sd trace eighty
eighty [sic] poles to a postoak on Said line;
thence South one hundred and thirty Six poles
to a postoak; thence to the beginning So as
to include a hundred acres. Surveyed Sept 9th

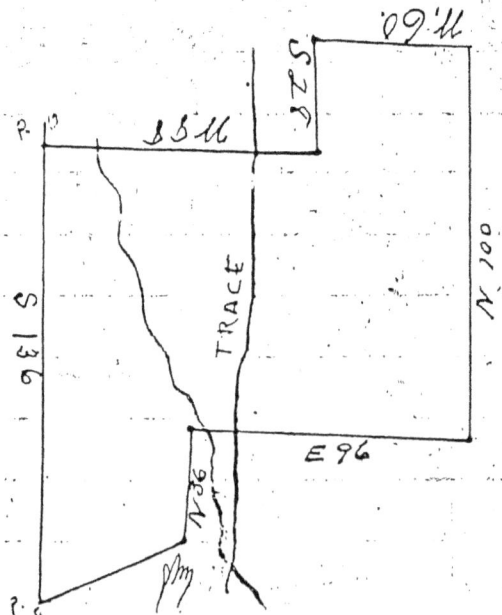

Scale: 50 poles to the inch

1828.   David Shelton S.R.C. pro tem
David Ragsdale and Wm Runnion, S.C.C.

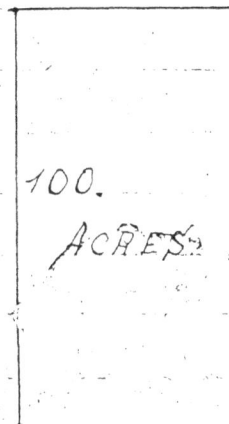

S. ROMINE

State of Tennessee, Rhea County
In pursuance of an entry made by Samuel Romine of No. 82
dated 23rd October 1827 for one hundred acres of land at
one cent per acre, I have this day Surveyed for the Said
Romine one hundred acres of land in Sd County on Waldens
Ridge on Richland Creek. BEGINNING on a postoak on the
Kiuka turnpike (page torn)   (page 44)
North one hundred and Sixty poles to a whiteoak on Isaac
Richards 100 acre entry; thence East one hundred poles to
a blackoak; thence South crossing Said Creek one hundred
and Sixty poles to a hickory; thence to the beginning So
as to include Sd hundred acres. Survey Sept 9th 1828.
                    David Shelton   Pro tem
David Ragsdale
Isaac Richards   S.C.C.

100. ACRES

Scale: 80 poles to the inch

PLEAS. CREECY [sic]

State of Tennessee,
    Rhea County
In pursuance of an entry
made by Pleasant Crecy
[sic] of No. 90 dated the
2nd Feb 1828 for three
hundred and twenty acres
of land at one cent per
acre, I have this [day]
Surveyed for the Sd
Pleasant Crecy three
hundred and twenty acres
of land in Sd County on
Waldens Ridge on the wa-
ters of Piney. BEGINNING
on a blackoak; thence South
crossing a branch of Piney

E 320 P
N 160 P   *PLEAS. CREECY.*   *S 160 P*

Scale: 80 poles to the inch

one hundred and Sixty poles to a chestnut oak; thence West three hundred and
twenty poles to a whiteoak on the top of the ridge; thence North one hundred and
Sixty poles to a Stake; thence East to the beginning So as to include an improvement & (blank) that Isaac Garm--- (page torn) made. Surveyed March 17th
1829.   D. Shelton S.R.C.
David (blank) and Joseph Levrett [Chain Carriers]

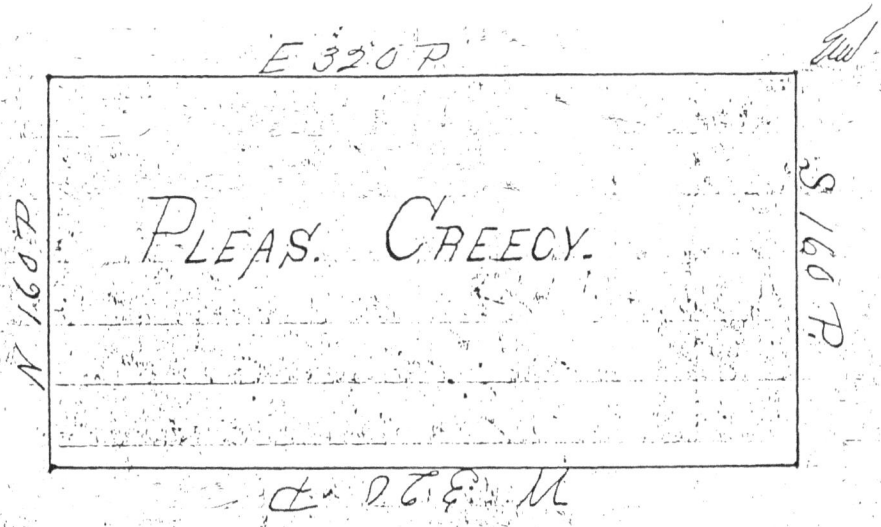

                              =NOTE=

PAGES 45 THROUGH 70 ARE MISSING FROM THIS RECORD BOOK. TWO PAGES (NUMBERS 47

AND 48) WERE INSERTED IN THE BOOK. THE MISSING PAGES WERE NOT MICROFILMED BY

THE TENNESSEE STATE LIBRARY AND ARCHIVES, BUT THE REMAINDER OF THE BOOK CAN BE

FOUND ON ROLL NO. 130 (REGISTER'S OFFICE).

O. PAINE   (page 47)

State of Tennessee, Rhea County
Pursuant to an entry made in the
Entry Takers office in and for Sd
County of No. 104 dated the 21 day
of February 1829, I have Surveyed
for the Said Orville Paine four
hundred and eighty acres of land on
Waldens Ridge of Cumberland Mountain on the waters of Piney Creek
or river. BEGINNING on five hickory
Saplings about two poles East of the
Creek and nearly opposite the mouth
of a fork running from Bonines
Cabbing, thence South eighty three
degrees East two hundred and forty
poles crossing two wet weather
drains to two Chestnut and three
blackoaks near the top of a ridge;
thence North Seven degrees East
three hundred and twenty poles [to]
a Stake; thence North eighty three
degrees West two hundred and forty
poles crossing the Creek to three
post oaks and two hickorys about
twenty poles South of Browns Cowpen
fork; then South Seven degrees West
along line of Sd Paines 640 acre
Survey to the beginning. Survey
Feb 24th 1829. David Shelton, S.R.C.

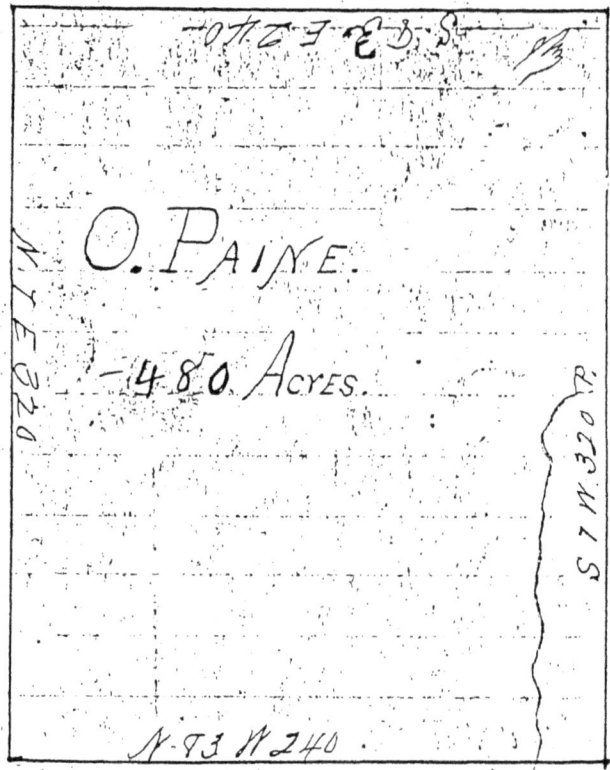

80 to the inch

Wm A. Crawford and Robert Crawford S.C.C.

O. PAINE   (page 48)

State of Tennessee, Rhea County
Pursuant to an entry made in the
Entry Takers office of Said
County of No. 105 dated 21st of
February 1829, I have Surveyed
for Orville Paine Six Hundred
and forty acres of land on Waldens Ridge of Cumberland Mountain in Rhea County on the waters of Richland Creek. BEGIN-
NING on a Spanishoak and hickory
whiteoak and two blackoaks,
Standing immediately on the top
of Ridge on a point above where
a branch breaks down the mountain about one fourth of a mile
above what is called Stewarts
trace; thence North forty five
degrees East along the top of
Said Ridge three hundred and
twenty poles to a Stake; thence

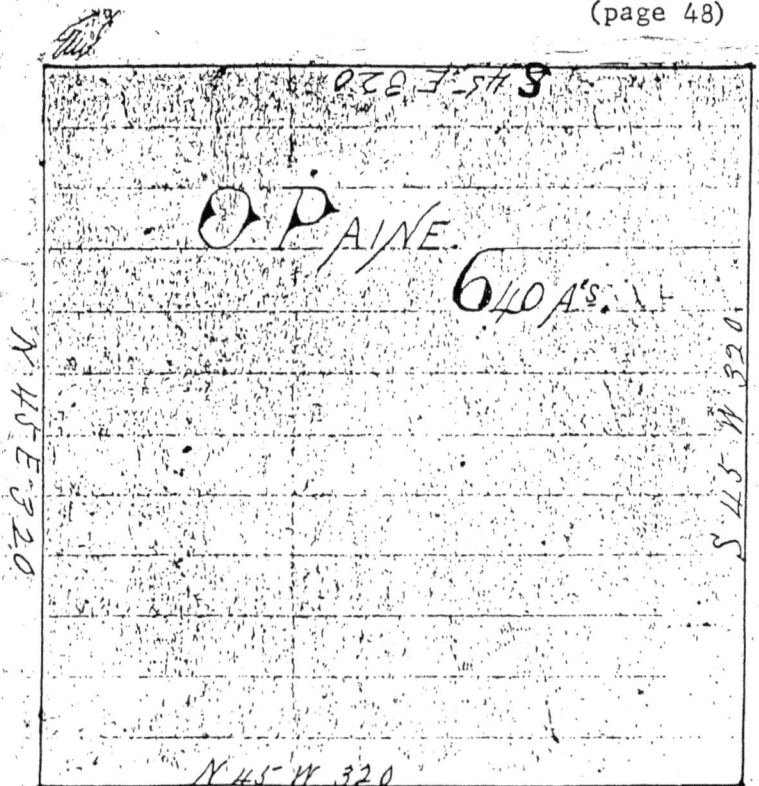

North forty five degrees West three hundred and twenty poles to a Stake; then
South forty five degrees West three hundred and twenty poles to a Stake; then
South forty five degrees East three hundred and twenty poles to the beginning.
Surveyed 24th Feb 1829.   David Shelton, S.R.C., by John Locke
Wm A. Crawford and Robert Crawfotd, S.C.C.

UNKNOWN (top one-fourth of page missing)   (page 71)

. . . from the . . . a whiteoak near a . . . Gordons turnpike road running . . .
degrees West forty poles to a Stake near a house, then South fifty degrees West
twenty twenty [sic] poles to a Stake; then South fifty East forty poles to a
Stake; then to the beginning entered on part of a certificate of No. 500 issued
by Edward Scott to Adam Huntsman for 100 acres, entered November the 15 day 1819.
Survey the 7th March 1831.   Jesse Thompson, Deputy Surveyor
Miles Loving and James Brown, S.C.C.

JESSE DAY

State of Tennessee, Rhea County
In pursuance of an entry made by Jesse Day of No.
116 dated April the 6th 1830 for one hundred acres
of land, I have Surveyed for the Said Day one hundred acres of land in Said County. BEGINNING on
a postoak at foot of Waldens Ridge; then North
Seventy degrees West fourty poles to James Stewarts
line; thence North fifty five degrees West with
Said line eighty Six poles to a Chestnut & Chestnut
oak on Said line; thence North thirty five degrees
East one hundred Seventy Seven poles to a Stake;
then South . . . (continued on top of page 72
which is missing)

30 equal parts to the inch

100 ACRES

EDMUND HOWERTON   (page 72)

State of Tennessee, Rhea County   NOTE: most of plat
. . . ance of an entry . . . Edmund Howerton . . .   was missing
of No. 179 dated the 10 day of February one thousand
eight hundred & thirty two for forty acres of land, I have this day Surveyed for
the Said Edmond Howerton forty acres of land in Said County. BEGINNING on a
blackoak lower corner of William Fowlers entry & on James Darwins mountain line
on the waters of Little Richland Creek; thence South twenty five degrees west
with Said line eighty three poles to Said Darwins corner a Stump and two blackoak
pointers; then North Sixty five degrees West Seventy eight poles to a Stake;
then North twenty five degrees East eighty three poles to Said Fowlers line to a
Stake, then South Sixty five degrees East with Said line to the beginning.
Surveyed February the 15th 1832.   David Shelton, Surveyor for Rhea County
Micajah Howerton and Henderson Compton, S.C.C.

WILLIAM McBRIDE

State of Tennessee, Rhea County
In pursuance of an entry made by Wm McBride of No. 121 dated May the 13th 1830,
I have this day Surveyed for the Said McBride one hundred acres of land in Said
County   (page 73)
in Cranmore Cove in [sic] Waldens Ridge of Cumberland mountain. BEGINNING on

two whiteoaks & gum corner to Lewis Morgans
entry in the upper end of said Cove; then
North fifteen degrees West one hundred poles
to a pine & blackoak pointers; thence West
one hundred and Sixty poles to a Chestnutoak;
then South fifteen degrees East one hundred
poles to a lane(?), a pine, postoak, blackoak & blackjack; thence East one hundred and
Sixty poles to the beginning.
Surveyed March 7th 1832 .

    David Shelton, Surveyor Rhea County
David McBride
James Lea   C.C.

80 parts to the inch

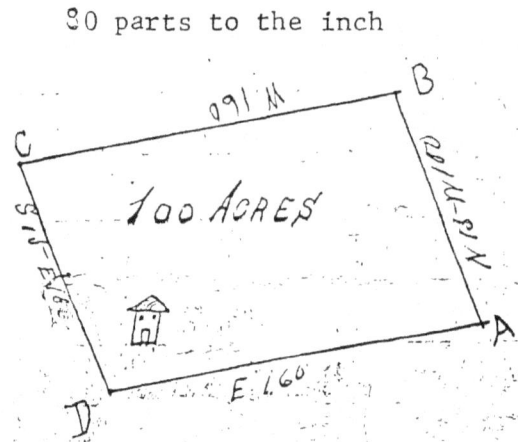

A. TRIPLETT

State of Tennessee, Rhea County
In pursuance of an entry made by Abner Triplett in the
Entry Takers office of No. 146, dated February 24th
1831 for one hundred acres of land, I have this day
Surveyed for the [said] Abner Triplett one hundred
acres of land in Said County on the waters of little
Richland Creek. BEGINNING on a Stake on Howertons
line near a blackoak pointer; then South twenty five
degrees West eight poles to a postoak corner to Jas.
Darwin the Same course continued with his line one
hundred and fifty two poles to Darwins corner a
blackoak Stump; then North Sixty five degrees West
one hundred poles to a Stake, then North twenty five
degrees East one hundred & Sixty poles to a Stake;
then South Sixty five degrees East one hundred poles
to the beginning. Surveyed Feb. 29, 1832
    David Shelton, Surveyor for Rhea County
Micajah and Jackson Howerton, C.C.

80 parts to the inch

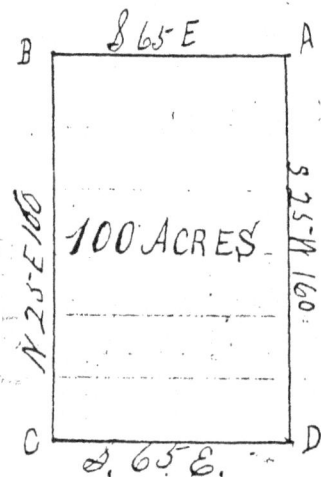

JESSE SAMPLEY

(page 74)

State of Tennessee, Rhea County
In Pursuance of an entry made in the Entry Takers office of Said County of No.
178, dated the January 21st 1832 for Six hundred acres of land, I have this day
for Jesse Samply Surveyed Six hundred acres of land in Said County in Cranmores
Cove on Sale Creek. BEGINNING on a Stake on the West Side of the Lone Mountain
near a blackgum, Chestnut, Chestnutoak pointers, thence North Seventy degrees
West eighty two poles to a blackoak on the top of a ridge; then South fifty five
degrees West forty Six poles to a whiteoak on the bank of Sale Creek; then S in
general with the mianders of Said creek one hundred and thirty eight poles to
the line of Gilbreath; then North Eighty degrees West with Said line forty three
poles to an Ash Same course in all two hundred and fifteen poles to Chestnut
near a good Spring on the foot of the mountain; then North thirty degrees East
along the foot of the mountain four hundred and twenty Six poles to three Chestnuts; then South   (page 75)
eighty degrees East crossing Said Creek three hundred & thirty four poles to a
Stake on the West Side of the Lone mountain; then to the beginning, So as to include a Spring above the dwelling house. Surveyed March 5th 1832
      David Shelton S.R.C
Isaac & David Sampley, C.C.

80 parts to the inch

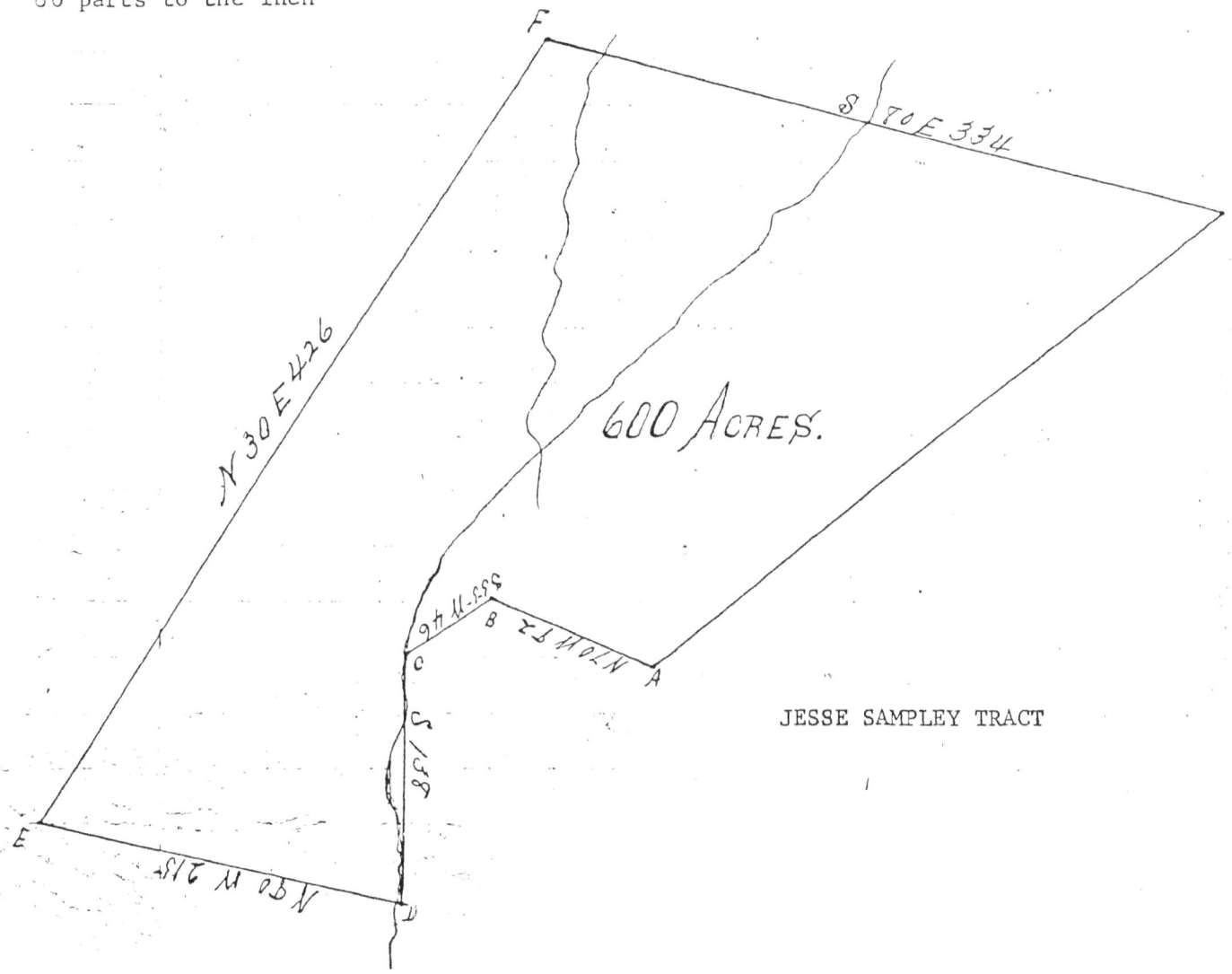

600 ACRES.

N 30 E 426

S 70 E 334

N 80 W 215

JESSE SAMPLEY TRACT

DAVID McBRIDE   (page 75)

State of Tennessee, Rhea County
In pursuance of an entry made by David
McBride for one hundred and forty acres
of land in Said County of No. 120 dated
May 13th 1830, I have this day Surveyed
one hundred and forty acres of land in
Said County in Cranmores Cove of Waldens
Ridge of Cumberland Mountain on the wa-
ters of Sale Creek for Lewis Inlow
assignee of David McBride. BEGINNING on
an ash tree Gilbreaths corner; then
North Seventy nine degrees West ninety
Six poles to two whiteoaks, Gilbreaths
corner; then North Seventeen degrees
East with Romines line one hundred &
thirty four poles to a maple corner to
Said Romine on the bank of Said Creek
near a Spring; then crossing Said Creek

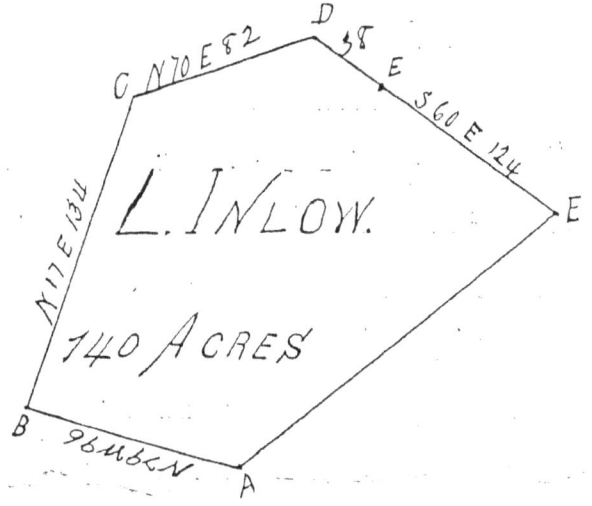

L. INLOW.

140 ACRES

N 70 E 82

S 60 E 124

N 17 E 134

N 79 W 96

80 equal parts to the inch

North Seven degrees East with T. Romines line eighty two poles to a Blackoak corner to Jas. Picket; then with Said Pickets line South Sixty degrees East thirty eight poles to a blackoak, Same course continued one hundred & twenty four poles to a Stake on the North Side of the Lone Mountain, then a direct line to the beginning. Surveyed March 7th 1832. David Shelton S.R.C. Jas Carter and Wm McBride, S.C.C.

B. BREEDING   (page 76)

State of Tennessee, Rhea County
In pursuance of an entry made by Byram Breeding of
No. 108 dated November 2nd 1829 for one hundred acres
of land & by virtue of a deputation to me given by
David Shelton, Surveyor for said County, I have Surveyed for the Said Byram Breeding one hundred acres
of land on Waldens Ridge of Cumberland Mountain on
the waters of Whites Creek on a branch known by Pres-
tons Camp Branch. BEGINNING on a whiteoak & running
North eighty five degrees West one hundred and Sixty
poles to a Small blackjack tree; then North five degrees East one hundred poles to a blackoak; then
South eighty five degrees East one hundred & Sixty

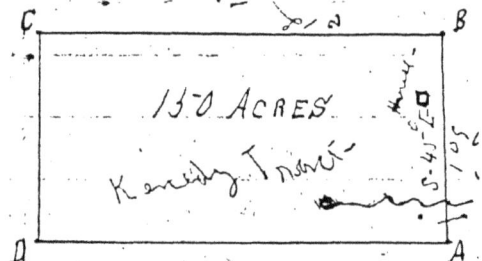

100 equal parts to inch

poles to a Chestnut, blackgum and hickory; then to the beginning. Surveyed the 2nd day of September 1831. Jesse Thompson, Deputy Surveyor for Rhea County Bart L. Stevens and Major Holloway, S.C.C.

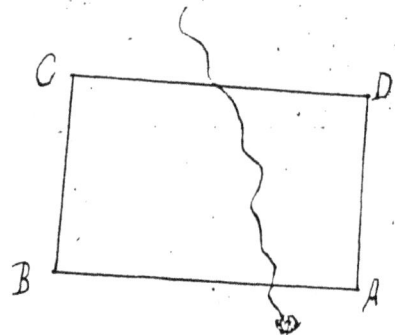

WHEELER & PARSONS

State of Tennessee, Rhea County
In pursuance of an entry made by Thomas H. Wheeler
& Jas. Parsons of No. 109 dated the 7th day of November 1829 & by virtue of a deputation to me given by David Shelton Surveyor for Rhea County, I
have Surveyed for Said Wheeler & Parsons one hundred & fifty acres of land on Waldens Ridge of
Cumberland Mountain on the Moccason Fork of Piney
River. BEGINNING on a whiteoak, running South
forty five degrees West one hundred & nine poles

150 ACRES
Kennedy Tract

100 equal parts to inch

to a Spanishoak; then South Sixty five degrees East two hundred and eighteen poles
                                                                    (page 77)
to a whiteoak; then North forty five degrees East one hundred and nine poles to a
Stake; then to the beginning. Surveyed the 27th day of September 1831.
                    Jesse Thompson, Deputy Surveyor for Rhea County
William Postain & Saml. Igou, S.C.C.

ROBERT BENSON

State of Tennessee, Rhea County
Pursuant to an entry made by Robert Benson of No. 156 for 100
acres dated 18 day of June 1831 & by virtue of a deputation
to me given by Chrispian E. Shelton, Surveyor for Rhea County
I have Surveyed for Said Robert Benson 100 acres of land in
Said County lying & being on the waters of Richland Creek on

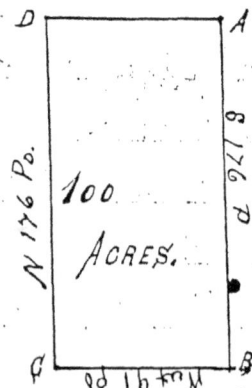

100 ACRES

100 equal parts in inch

South Side of Kiuca trace. BEGINNING on a Spanish oak Stump Said to be Lewis Morgans corner running due South 176 poles to a Small black Jack tree; then due West 91 poles to a blackjack near a path; then due North 176 poles to a Stake; then to the beginning. Surveyed the 20th day of December 1832.

> Jesse Thompson, Deputy Surveyor for Rhea County

Archabald Smallwood and Hezekiel Borden, C.B.

W.G. ENGLISH

(page 78)

State of Tennessee, Rhea County
Pursuant to an entry made by
William G. English of No. 169
dated November the 5th day 1831
of 600 acres of land & by virtue of a deputation to me given
by David Shelton Surveyor of
Rhea County, I have Surveyed
for the Said English Six Hundred
acres in Said County lying &
being on Waldens Ridge on the
South side of Whites Creek.
BEGINNING on a pine tree on a
bluff of Said Creek running
South 45 degrees West 230 poles
to a Whiteoak & blackoak; then
South 45 degrees East 343 poles
to a blackoak & dogwood; then
North 45 East 230 poles to a
Stake; then to the beginning.
Surveyed the 20th day of January 1832

> Jesse Thompson,
> Deputy Surveyor

William Smith & Laban Stewart, S.C.B.

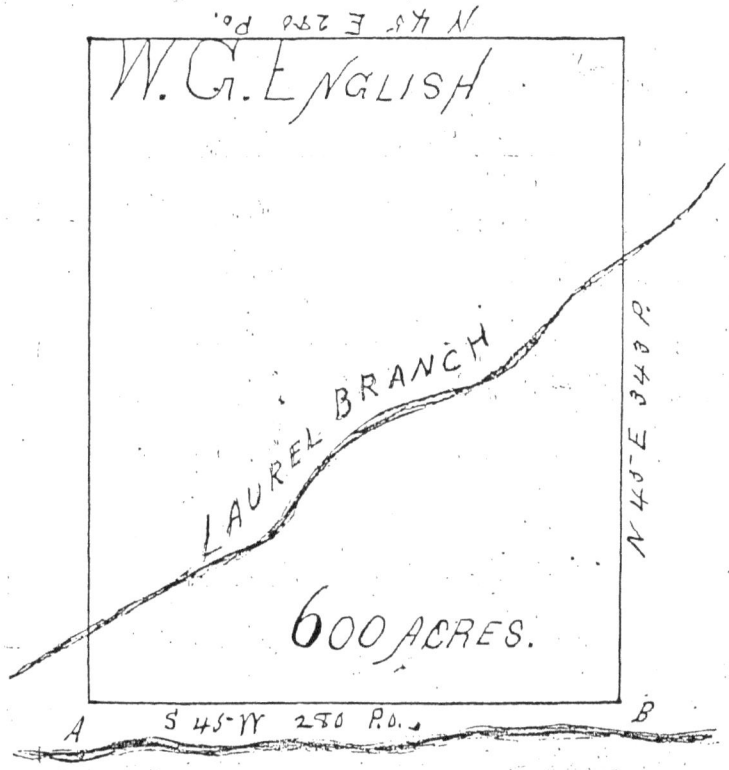

100 equal parts to the inch

W.T. GILLENWATERS

State of Tennessee, Rhea County
Pursuant to an entry made by William T.
Gillenwaters of No. 172 dated the 7th day
of November 1831 for 300 acres of land on
Waldens Ridge & by virtue of a Deputation
to me given by David Shelton Surveyor of
Rhea County, I have Surveyed for Said
Gillenwaters 300 acres of land lying &
being in Said County on the waters of
Whites Creek on two branches called the
Big & Little Laurels. BEGINNING on a
postoak, hickory & Small whiteoak on

(page 79)

the North side of the Little Laurel,
running due North 78 poles to a maple;
then North 45 degrees West 57 poles to
two blackoak bushes David Roddys corner

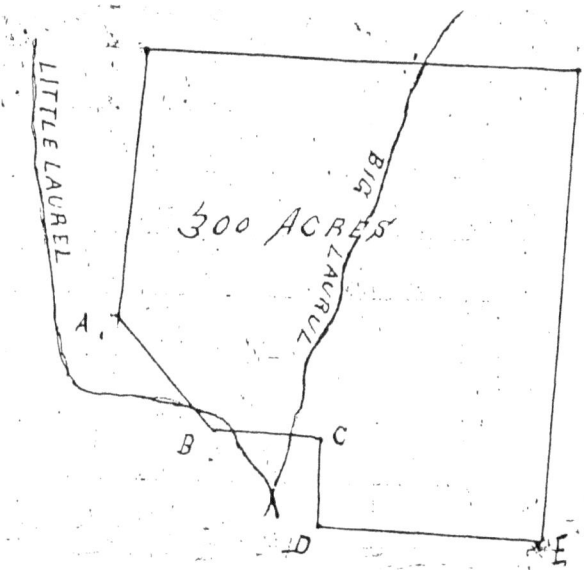

100 equal parts to the inch

then North 45 degrees East 46 poles to William G. Englishs corner of 600 acre
Survey on a Small blackoak & two Whiteoaks; then North 45 degrees West along
Said Englishs line 116 poles to two postoaks on the Side of a Ridge; then South
45 degrees West 239 poles to a Stake; then South 45 degrees East 230 poles to a
Stake, then to the beginning. Surveyed the 13th day of September 1832
                    Jesse Thompson, Deputy Surveyor for Rhea County
Bramillian Holloway and Major Holloway, C.B.

POLLY McBRIDE

State of Tennessee, Rhea County
Pursuant to a entry made by Polly McBride of No. 125 for 100
acres dated 2nd June 1830, I have Surveyed for Sd Polly McBride
100 acres of land in Sd County lying in the Side of Waldens
Ridge & waters of Sale Creek in Cranmores Cove. BEGINNING on a
Whiteoak near a branch running North 50 degrees West 96 poles
to a redoak on a clift or bluff on the Side of Waldens Ridge;
then South 40 West along the clift 22 poles to a little blackoak, then South 35 W 34 poles to a redoak on Said bluff, then
South 15 W 110 poles to a hickory; then South 60 East 100 poles
to a Small hickory on a ridge; thence a Streight line to the beginning. Surveyed
7 March 1832.   C.E. Shelton, Surveyor for Rhea County
Lewis Inlow and Jean Goff, C.B.

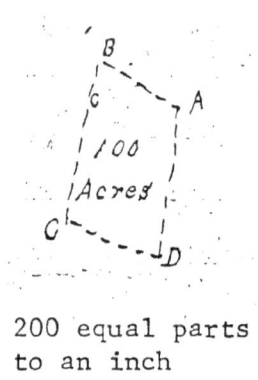

200 equal parts
to an inch

M. STONER   (page 80)

State of Tennessee, Rhea County
Pursuant to an entry made by Michael Stoner of
No. 123 May the 14th 1830 for 300 acres and by
virtue of a deputation to me given by Chrispian
E. Shelton Surveyor of Rhea County, I have Sur-
veyed for Said Harrison Pharris as assignee of
Said Stoner 300 acres of land in Cranmores Cove
on both Sides of a Creek. BEGINNING on Lewis
Morgans corner; then down the foot of the Cove
Mountain & with meanders thereof running from
said Morgans corner to a large whiteoak South
55 West 46 poles to a Whiteoak; then S 30 de-
grees W 217 poles to a large blackoak; then
North 45 W passing Picketts corner on a ridge
148 poles to a Whiteoak at the foot of Waldens
Ridge; then North 23 E 226 poles to a Stake on
Lewis Morgans 100 acre Survey; then with Said
line to the beginning. Surveyed the 19 day of
December 1832.   Jesse Thompson
          Deputy Surveyor for Rhea County
Joseph Stiner and William W. Pharris, C.B.

100 equal parts to the inch

W.B. SMITH

State of Tennessee, Rhea County
Pursuant to an entry made by William B. Smith
of No. 190 for 400 acres of land dated the 20th day of August 1832 and transferred
assignment to Harrison Pharris, and by virtue of a deputation to me given by
Crispien E. Shelton Surveyor of Rhea County, I have Surveyed for Sd Pharris 400

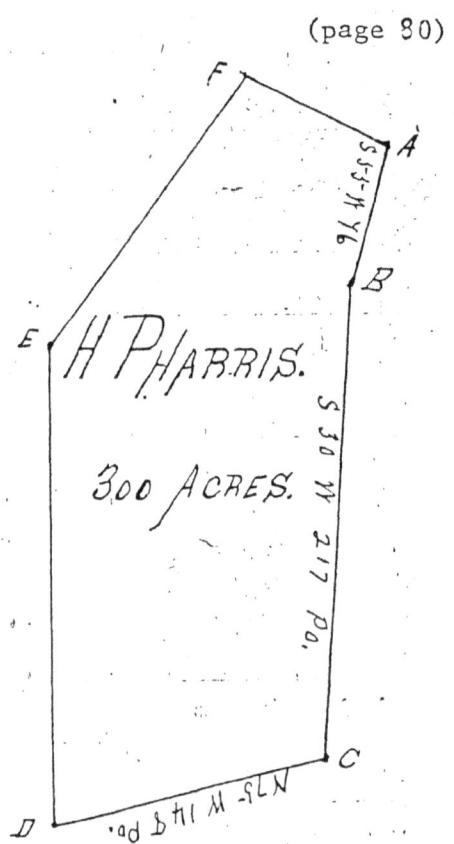

acres of land on Bushy Creek a fork of Sale Creek,
BEGINNING on a Small hickory

(page 81)

tree marked thus (Smith) running North 65 degrees
West 180 poles to a Postoak, whiteoak & hickory; then
North 25 East 398 poles to two whiteoak trees; then
South 53 degrees East 180 poles to a Stake; then
South 25 degrees West 360 poles to the beginning.
Surveyed the 17th day of December 1832.
Jesse Thompson, Deputy Surveyor for Rhea County
William W. Pharis and George Shuster, C.B.

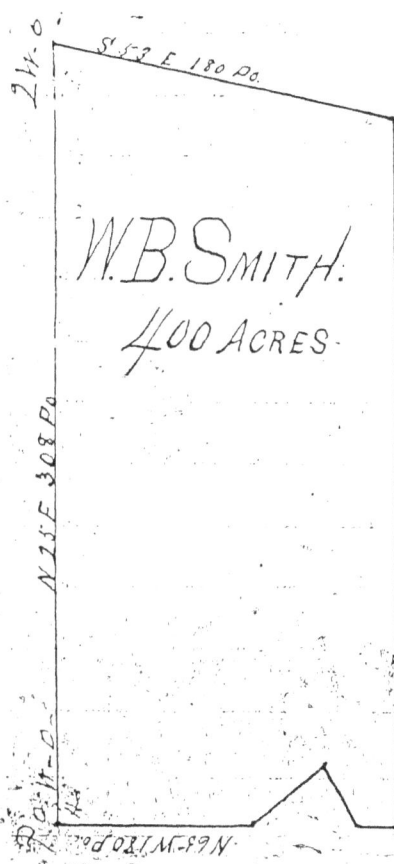

W.B.SMITH. 400 ACRES.

100 equal parts to the inch

A. LOWRY

State of Tennessee, Rhea County
Pursuant to an entry made by Adam Lowry of No. 181
for 100 acres dated March 24th 1832, I have Sur-
veyed for Said Adam Lowry 100 acres of land in Sd
County lying on Waldens Ridge near Ragsdales turn-
pike road.   BEGINNING on a blackoak; thence North
63 West 136 poles to a Postoak;
then North 27 East 125 poles to
a postoak; then South 63 East
136 poles to a Stake, then a
Straight line to the beginning.
Surveyed 20th March 1833.
C.E. Shelton, Surveyor for
Rhea County
Mathew Rawlston
Jacob Lowry   C.B.

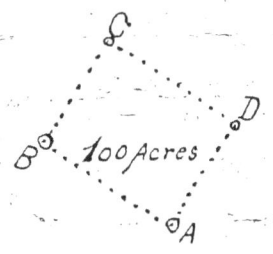

100 Acres

200 equal parts to the inch

E. RAWLSTON [sic]

State of Tennessee, Rhea County
Pursuant to an entry made by Elizabeth Raulston [sic] of
No. 149 for 100 acres of land dated 7th March 1331, I
have Surveyed for Said Elizabeth Raulston 100 acres of
land in Said County lying on the top of Waldens Ridge &
waters of Richland Creek.   BEGINNING on a blackoak;
thence South 75 degrees East 174 poles to a double
hickory; then South 15 W 8? poles to a redoak on a
bluff; then North 75 W 17? poles to a Stake; thence a
Straight line to the beginning.   Surveyed 19th March 1833.
      C.E. Shelton, Surveyor of Rhea County
Thos Dean and Absolom Vernon,   C.B.

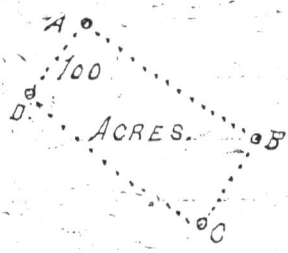

100 ACRES.

200 equal parts to the inch

J. RAWLSTON [sic]

(page 82)

State of Tennessee, Rhea County
Pursuant to a entry made by James Raulston [sic] of No. 182 &
dated March 24th 1832 for 100 acres, I have this day Surveyed
for Absolom Vernon assignee of Said James Raulston 100 acres
of land on Waldens Ridge & waters of Richland Creek.
BEGINNING on a postoak on a little ridge; then North 15 East

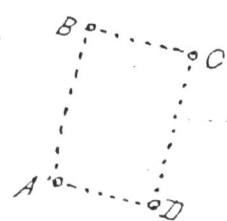

200 equal parts
to the inch

174 poles to a hickory & blackoak; then South 75 E 88 poles to a postoak; then South 15 E 174 poles to a whiteoak, blackoak & postoak; then a Straight line to the beginning. Surveyed 19th March 1833. C.E. Shelton, Surveyor for R.County Thos. Dean and Matthew Raulston, C.B.

J.W. THOMPSON

State of Tennessee, Rhea County
Pursuant to an entry made by James W. Thompson & Elijah Reynolds of No. 173 dated the 7th day of November 1831 for 100 acres, & by virtue of a deputation to me given by David Shelton, Surveyor of Sd County, I have Surveyed for Sd Thompson & Reynolds 100 acres of land in Rhea County on the mountain on Johnsons fork of Piney. BEGINNING on a blackoak running due North 132 poles to a Birch & Spanishoak then due West 121½ poles to a whiteoak & chestnut, then due South 132 poles to a chestnut; then to the beginning. Surveyed March the 24th day 1832. Jesse Thompson, Deputy Surveyor for Rhea County Henry Owens and Alexander Owens, C.C.B.

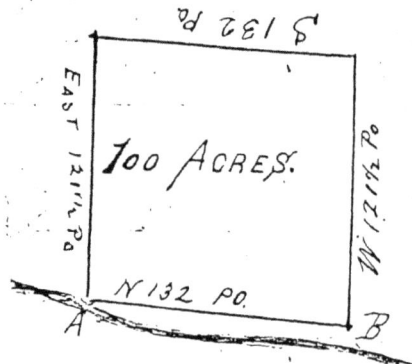

100 equal parts to the inch

D. RODDY   (page 33)

State of Tennessee, Rhea County
Pursuant to a entry made by David Roddy of No. 140 dated the 5th day of November 1831 for 150 acres of land on a branch of the Laurel Fork of Whites Creek running Northwardly, & by virtue of a deputation to me given by David Shelton, Surveyor of Rhea County, I have Surveyed for Sd Roddy 150 acres of land lying & being in Sd County. BEGINNING on a poplar running North 45 degrees West 62 poles to a blackoak & Chestnut on Wm G. Englishs line of 600 acre Survey running & bounded by Said line South 45 West 250 poles to 2 Small black & two hickory trees; then South 45 degrees East 132 poles to a Stake; then to the beginning. Surveyed 20th January 1832. Jesse Thompson, Deputy Surveyor Laban Stuart and William English, C.B.

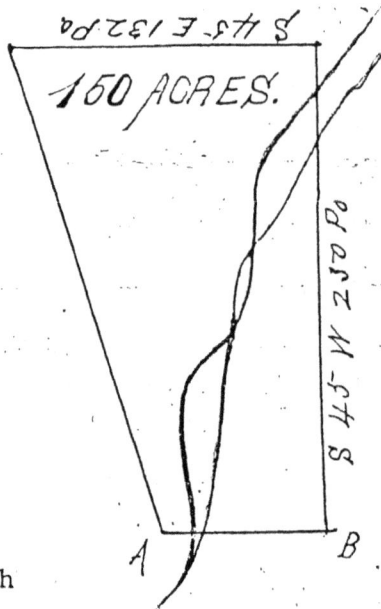

100 equal parts to the inch

SAML LOWRY

State of Tennessee, Rhea County
Pursuant to a entry made by Samuel Lowry of No. 144 dated February 21st 1831 for 100 acres of land, I have this day Surveyed for James Grigsby assignee of Sd Samuel Lowry 100 acres on Waldens Ridge in Sd County on the waters of Richland Creek. BEGINNING on a Small double hickory running North 5 East 140 poles to a postoak; then South 85 D.E 11 poles to a Stake; then South 5 D. W 140 poles to a Stake, then a Straight line to the beginning. Surveyed 22nd April 1833. C.E. Shelton, Surveyor for R.C. Jacob Lowry & Matthew Rawlston, C.B.

100 equal parts to inch

JNO HENDERSON (page 84)

State of Tennessee, Rhea County
Pursuant to a entry made by Adam L. Ellis of No. 145 dated Feb.
21st 1831 for 200 acres, I have Surveyed for John Henderson
assignee of Sd Ellis 200 acres of land in Sd County on Waldens
Ridge on the waters of Richland Creek & on whats called Paines
Trace. BEGINNING on a postoak running South 18 d. E 239 poles
to a Spanishoak; then North 72 E 134 poles to a Stake; then
North 18 D.W. 239 Poles to a Stake, then a Straight line to the
beginning. Surveyed 22nd April 1832.   C.E. Shelton
                              Surveyor for Rhea County
Green Berry McDaniel and William Henderson, C.B.

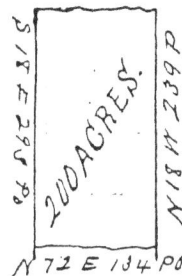

200 equal parts
to the inch

THOS. RIDDLE

State of Tennessee
Pursuant to an entry made by Thomas Riddle of No. 214 &
dated 20th (blank) 1833 for 200 acres of land, I have this
day Surveyed for Thomas Riddle 200 acres on Waldens Ridge
on a branch of Sale Creek called the Roundhouse branch.
BEGINNING on a Whiteoak near a branch running South 10 degrees East 200 poles to a maple and Whiteoak in a Swamp;
then North 80 East 160 poles to a Small blackoak on the
top of a hill; then North 10 West 200 poles to a Stake;
then a Straight line to the beginning. Surveyed 22nd May
1833.   C.E. Shelton, Surveyor for Rhea County
William Clemens and Jesse Crane, C.B.

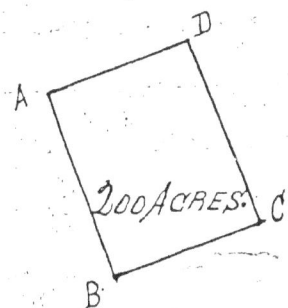

200 equal parts to the
inch

J. BUNDREN (page 85)

State of Tennessee, Rhea County
In pursuance of an entry made by James Bundren of
No. 155 dated June the 18th day 1831 for 300 acres
& by virtue of a deputation to me given by David
Shelton, Surveyor of Rhea County, I have Surveyed
for the Said James Bundren 300 acres of land lying
& being in Sd County on the North side of Whites
Creek. BEGINNING on a Whiteoak, running S 88 degrees East 196 poles to a Sowerwood & maple tree;
then South 244½ poles up or crossing Whites Creek
to a Stake; then North 88 degrees West 196 poles
to a Stake; then North 244½ poles to the beginning.
Surveyed 22nd March 1832.
          Jesse Thompson, Deputy Surveyor for R.C.
George C. Bundren and Benjamin Lawless
          Sworn C. [Chain] Bearers

     100 equal parts to the inch

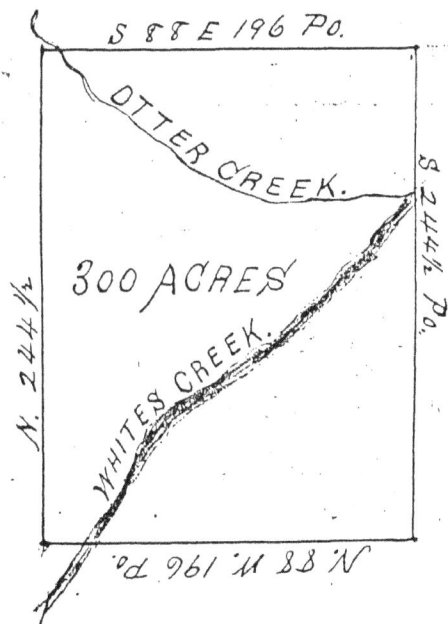

PAUL & CREWS

State of Tennessee, Rhea County
In pursuance of an Entry made by Marten E. Paul & Nancy Crews of No. 167 dated
the 29th day of October 1831 for 500 acres & by virtue of a deputation to me

given by Crispien E. Shelton, Surveyor of
Rhea County, I have Surveyed for Sd Martin
E. Paul & Nancy Crews 500 acres of land on
Waldens Ridge Mountain. BEGINNING on a
Whiteoak, running South 45 degrees West
274 poles to a whiteoak & chestnut, then
North 45 West 292 poles to a Stake; then
(page 86)
North 45 East 274 poles to a Stake; then
South 45 East 292 poles to the beginning.
Surveyed 2 day of September 1833.
Jesse Thompson, Deputy Surveyor for Rhea
        County
Jesse Craig &
Simeon Craig   Sworn C.C.

JESSE THOMPSON

State of Tennessee, Rhea County
Pursuant to an entry made by Jesse Thompson of No. 176 dated November the 26th
day 1831 for 100 acres of land on Waldens
Ridge, & by virtue of a deputation to me
given by Crispian E. Shelton, Surveyor for Rhea County
I have Surveyed for Jesse Thompson 100 acres of land
on Waldens Ridge, lying & being in Sd County on a
branch of Piney, & to include a Camp called Fines
Camp. BEGINNING on the East Side of Sd branch on a
poplar & hickory marked thus "T.E.", and running
West 104 poles to a Black & hickory; then due South
155 poles to a Stake; then East 104 poles to a
Stake; then North to the beginning. Surveyed the
30th day of August 1833
        Jesse Thompson, Deputy Surveyor for Rhea County
William R. Warman & Thomas Dunahoo,
        Sworn Chain Carryers [sic]

100 equal parts to the inch

J. THOMPSON

State of Tennessee, Rhea County
In pursuance of an entry made by Jesse Thompson of
No. 177 dated the 26 day of Nov. 1831 & filed the 2nd
day of Decr 1831 for 150 acres of land on Waldens
Ridge, and by virtue of a deputation to me given by
Chrispian E. Shelton, Surveyor for Rhea County, I
have Surveyed for Jesse Thompson 150 acres of land
lying & being in Said County   (page 87)
on a branch of Piney. BEGINNING on a blackoak and
two Whiteoak trees running from the North East corner of his entry for 50 acres North 75 degrees East
135 poles to a blackoak; then South 38 W 270 poles to
three Small Chestnuts; then North 52 D.W. 125 poles
to a Stake; then to the beginning. Surveyed the 23rd

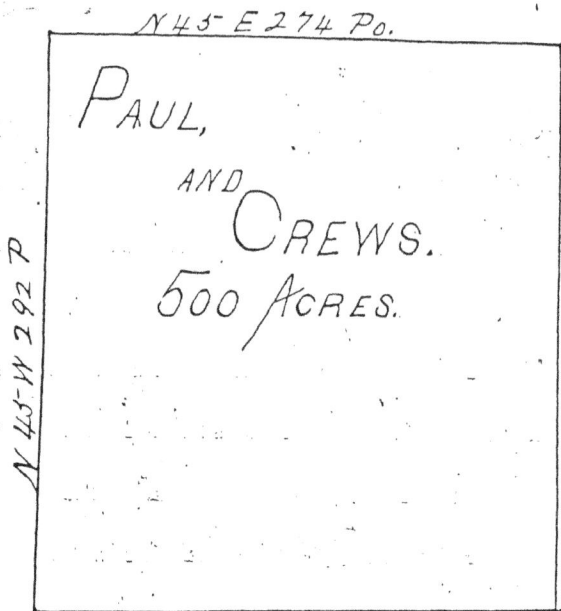

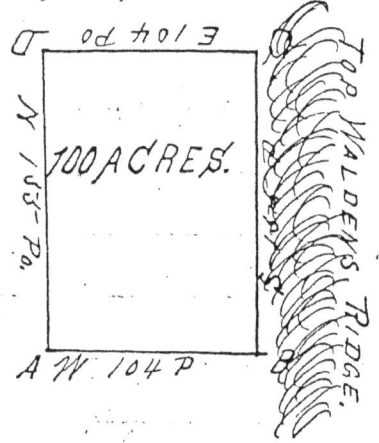

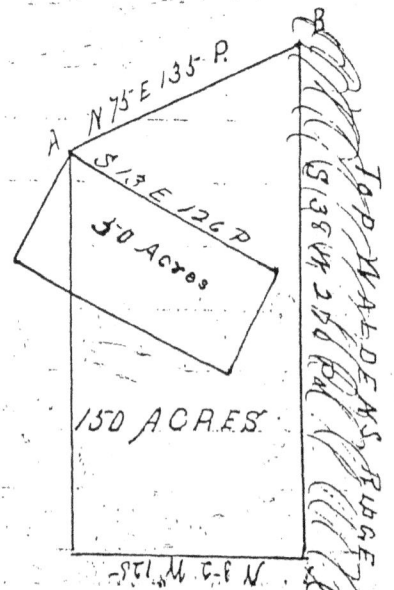

100 equal parts to the inch

day of September 1833.   Jesse Thompson, Deputy Surveyor for Rhea County
Jesse Craig and Simeon Craig, Sworn C.C.

THOS. MAJORS   (page 87)

State of Tennessee, Rhea County
In pursuance of an entry made by Thomas Majors which is re-
gularly assigned to Jesse Thompson of No. 110 dated the 13th
November 1829 and filed in the Same day for 50 acres in Said
Rhea County, and by virtue of a deputation to me given by
Chrispian E. Shelton, Surveyor for Rhea County, I have Surveyed for the Sd Jesse Thompson 50 acres of land lying and
being in the Sd County on Piney Creek or river to include
an improvement made by Isaac Smith in the whiteoak flat.
BEGINNING on a whiteoak marked thus "T.E." running 42 D.
West along a large clift of rocks 40 poles to a Small Ash &
hickory then North 20 D.W. Sixty four poles to a chestnut &
whiteoak; then South 80 D.W. 120 poles to a Stake; then So
10 D. East 40 poles to a Stake then to the beginning.
Surveyed the 30th day of August 1833.
            Jesse Thompson, Deputy Surveyor for Rhea County
William R. Worman and Thomas Dunahoo, Sworn Chain Carriers

100 equal parts to
the inch

WM. MONDAY   (page 88)

State of Tennessee, Rhea County
Pursuant to a entry made by William Munday [sic]
of No. 163 dated the 12 day of October 1831 for
200 acres of [land] on Waldens Ridge of Cumberland Mountain, & by virtue of a deputation to me
given by David Shelton Surveyor for Rhea County,
I have Surveyed for William Monday 200 acres
lying in Said Rhea County on the waters of Whites
Creek. BEGINNING on a Pine tree on a ridge running S 30 D West 200 poles to two hickory trees;
then North 60 West 160 poles to a Stake; then
North 30 E 200 poles to a Stake, then to the beginning. Surveyed the 23rd day March 1832.
            Jesse Thompson, Deputy Surveyor for R.C.
Arthur Monday and Cornelius Harris, Sworn C.C.

100 equal parts to the inch

JAS. HAYS

State of Tennessee, Rhea County
In pursuance of an entry made by James Hayes [sic] of No. 135 dated the 24 September 1830 for 300 acres and by virtue of a deputation to me given by David Shelton
Surveyor for Rhea County, I have Surveyed for the Said Hays [sic] 300 acres of
land lying in the Sd County on Sandy a fork of Whites Creek. BEGINNING Waterhouses corner above the bridge on Sandy on a whiteoak tree running South 45 degrees West 176½   (page 89)
poles with Waterhouses line to a blackoak; then with Chapmans line North 40 D.W.
178 poles to a whiteoak, then South 50 D.W. 146 poles to a Stake; then South 40
D.E. 252 poles to a Stake; then North 45 East 320 poles to a Stake; then to the
beginning. Surveyed 8th day of March 1831.

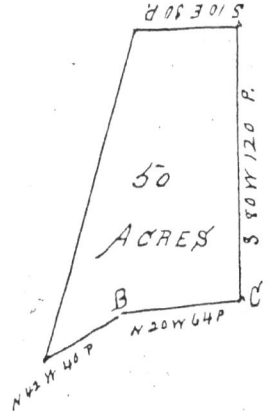

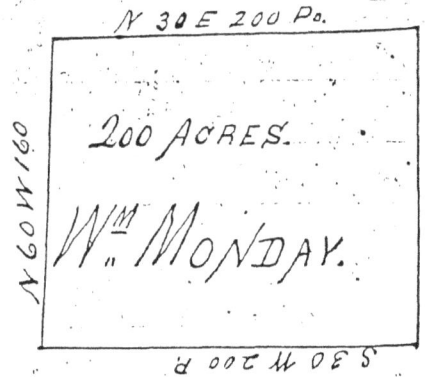

Jesse Thompson, Surveyor
for Rhea County
Arthur Monday
Benjamin M. Barnwell
    [Chain Carriers]

G. QUALLS

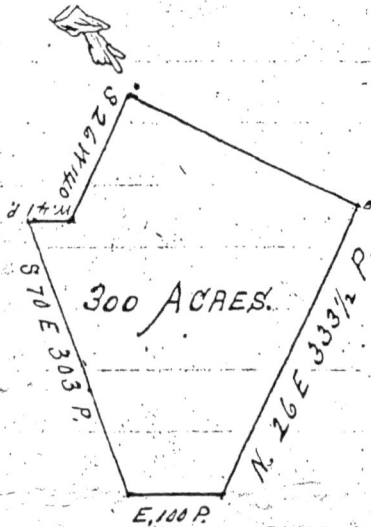

300 ACRES.

200 equal parts to the inch
(QUALLS TRACT)

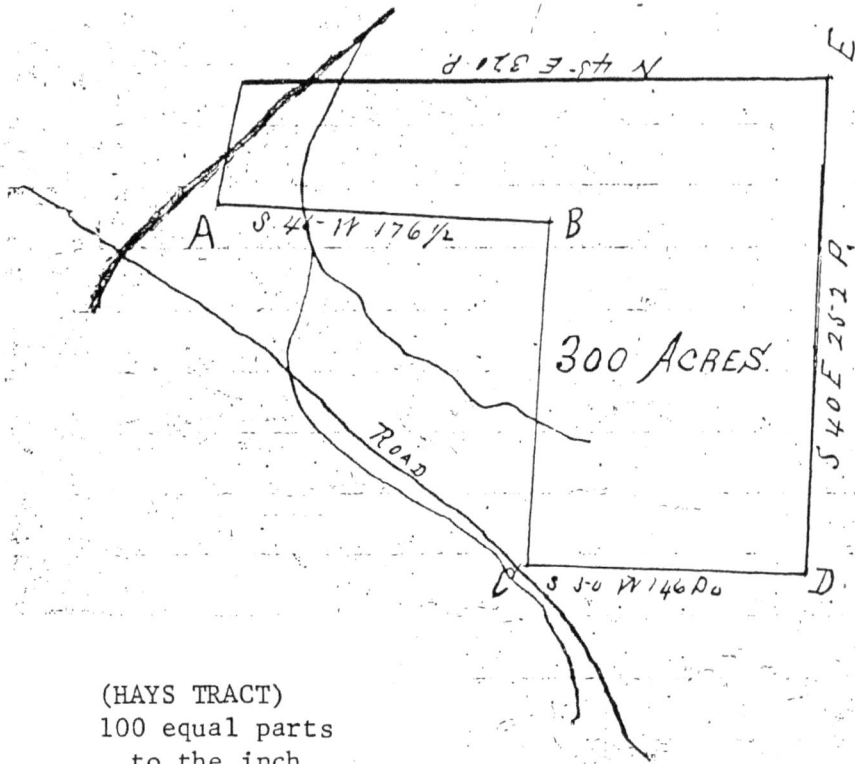

A   S. 41-1W 176½   B

300 ACRES.

C   S. 3-0 W 146 Po   D

N 45-E 321 P.

S 40 E 252 P.

(HAYS TRACT)
100 equal parts
to the inch

State of Tennessee, Rhea County
In pursuance of an entry made by Gatewood Qualls
of No. 199 dated Oct 6th 1832 for 300 acres of
land, I have this day Surveyed 300 acres for
George Shuster assignee of Said G. Qualls lying
on Waldens Ridge waters of Sale Creek. BEGINNING on a whiteoak running South 26
W 140 p. to a corner blackoak; then W 41 P. to where David Sheltons line intersects to a Stake on Leas old line; then with Sheltons old line to a corner
Spanishoak 133 ps; thence the Same course 20 p. in all 304 to a Stake; then East
100 p. to a Stake; then North 26° E. 333 p. to a Stake; then a Straight line to
the beginning. August 25th 1834. C.E. Shelton, Surveyor of R. Cty
Robert Qualls and John Witt, C.B.

B.L. STEPHENS

State of Tennessee, Rhea County
In pursuance of an entry made by Burt L. Stephens
for 75 acres of No. 160 dated the 26th day of
August 1831, filed 13th day of September 1831 in
Rhea County on Waldens Ridge on the waters
                        (page 90)
of Whites Creek. BEGINNING on a chestnut tree
on R. Greens line running North 43 degrees East
100 poles passing Waterhouses corner near a
branch of fifty acre Survey to a Stake on Burt L. Stephens 200 acre Survey; then
due North 20 poles to a Stake on the bluff of Whites Creek; then North 47 degrees
West 220 poles to a Stake beginning along the bluff of Whites Creek to a Stake;
then to the beginning. Surveyed the 13th day of September 1832.
        Jesse Thompson, Deputy Surveyor R. Cty
Robert Green and Major Holloway, S.C.C.

N 47 W 220 P.

75 ACRES

N 43 E 100 P.   N 20 P.

100 equal parts to the inch

A. FULTON   (page 90)

State of Tennessee, Rhea County
In pursuance of an entry made by David W. Brown
& transferred by assignment to Arthur Fulton of
No. 77, dated the 20th September 1827, and filed
the 29th September 1827 for 100 acres of land
on the mountain on Waldens Ridge. BEGINNING on
a whiteoak near Howertons trace; running S. 30
deg. West 100 poles to a Blackoak; then North 55
degrees West 160 poles to a whiteoak and Spanishoak; then North 30 degrees East 100 poles to a
Chestnut corner of a 55 acre Survey; then along
Said line 160 poles to the beginning lying on both Sides of the trace leading to
Sequatchie Valley from Tennessee Valley. Surveyed the 30th day of September 1831
        Jesse Thompson, Deputy Surveyor R. County
John F. Paul & Joshua Taylor, Sworn Chain bearers

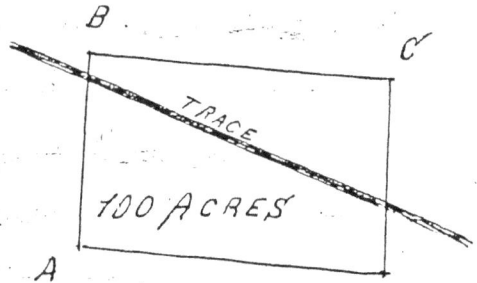

100 equal parts to one inch

A. FULTON   (page 91)

State of Tennessee, Rhea County
In pursuance of an entry made by David W.
Brown & transferred by assignment to
Arthur Fulton of No. 112 dated 13th day
of Nover 1829 and filed the Same day for
55 acres of land on Waldens Ridge of Cumberland Mountain, a deputation by virtue
to me given by Chrispian E. Shelton, Surveyor for Said County, I have Surveyed
for Peter Helton one of assignees of Sd
certificate the Sd 55 acres of land.
BEGINNING on a Blackoak & Postoak N 55 W 134 ps. to a blackoak; then S 20 W 66 ps.
to a chestnut tree; then S 55 E 134 ps to a blackgum; then to the beginning.
Surveyed 30th Sept 1831.   Jesse Thompson, Deputy Surveyor R. Cty
Joshua Taylor & John F. Paul, C.C.

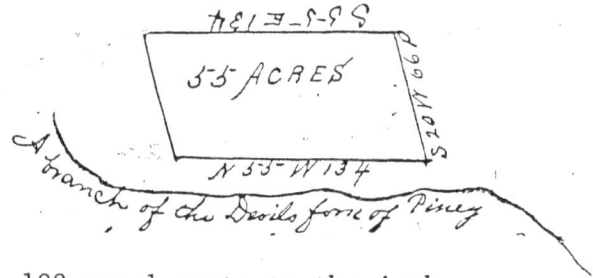

100 equal parts to the inch

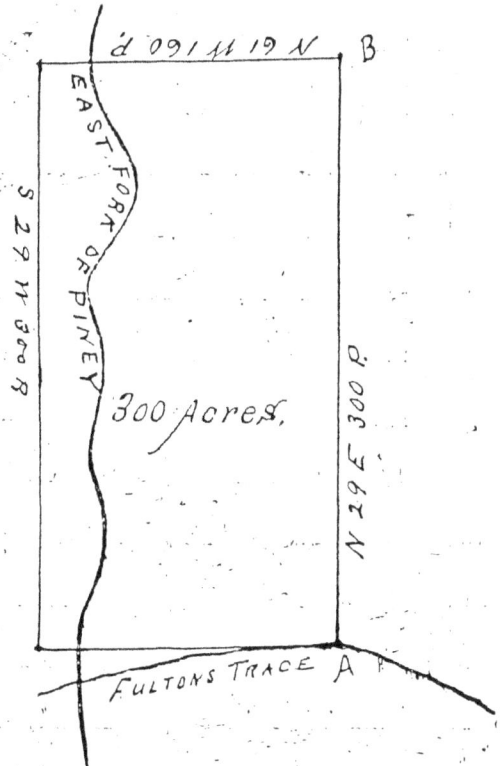

FULTON AND DANIEL

State of Tennessee, Rhea County
In pursuance of an entry made by Arthur Fulton
& Joseph Daniel of 300 acres of No. 168 dated
4 day of Nov. & filed the 5 day of Same Month
in 1831 & by virtue of a deputation to me given
by Chrispian E. Shelton Surveyor for Sd County,
I have Surveyed for the Sd Fulton & Daniel 300
acres of land on Waldens Ridge of Cumberland
Mountain on the East fork of Piney River.
BEGINNING on a Chestnut on the South Side of
Fultons trace running N 29 E 300 ps to 2
chestnut trees; then N 61 W 160 ps to a black
oak; then S 29 W 300 ps to a large chestnut &
hickory, then S 61 E 160 ps to the beginning.
Surveyed 30th day of Sept 1833.
        Jesse Thompson, Deputy Surveyor R. Cty
William R. Worman & Moses Paul, S.C.C.

        100 equal parts to the inch

SILAS IVY   (page 92)

State of Tennessee, Rhea County
In pursuance of an entry made by Silas Ivy of No. 151
and dated 30th March 1831 filed the Same day for 100
acres of land on Waldens Ridge on both sides of George
Gordons Road.   BEGINNING on a Chestnutoak tree on the
South west Side of Gordons road, running North 45 E
46 ps to a blackoak; then N 85 E 112 ps to Allen Lupers
line; then due South 114 ps to a Stake; then due West
140 ps to a Stake; then due East 75 ps to the beginning
Surveyed the 14th day Sept 1832.
        Jesse Thompson, Deputy Surveyor Rhea Cty
Clabourn Bundren & Richd Bundren, S.C.C.

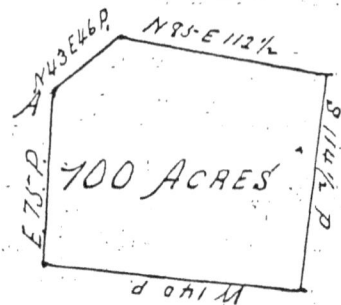

100 equal parts to the inch

R. GREEN

State of Tennessee, Rhea County
In pursuance of an entry made by Rob. Green of
No. 139 and dated & filed the 15th day of Novr.
1830 for 50 acres on Waldens Ridge on Whites
Creek adjoining Said Greens 200 acre Survey by
virtue of a deputation to me given by Chrispian
E. Shelton Surveyor for Sd Rhea County, I have
Surveyed for Sd Green 50 acres of land.
BEGINNING on a chestnut tree on the South Side

100 equal parts to the inch

of Whites Creek running North 10 W 64 ps. to crossing Whites Creek at 200 ps from
the beginning to a Stake; then North 80 E 127 ps to a Stake; then S 10 E 64 to a
Stake; then to the beginning. Surveyed the 27th day of Sept 1833.
        Jesse Thompson, Deputy Surveyor R. County
Burt L. Stephens & John Harvey, S.C.C.

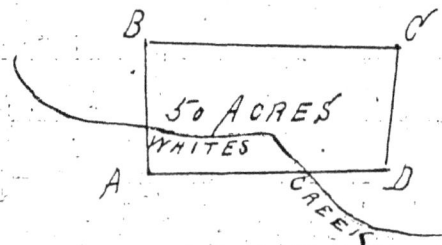

R. GREEN   (page 93)

State of Tennessee, Rhea County
In pursuance of an entry made by Robert
Green for 200 acres of land on Waldens
Ridge of No. 56 filed the 20th day of
February 1827, and by virtue of a depu-
tation to me given by Chrispian E.
Shelton Surveyor for Said County, I
have this day Surveyed for the Said
Green the Said 200 acres. BEGINNING
on a large blackoak running North 45
East 254 ps to a Stake on the bluff of
a North fork of Whites Creek, then
South 45 E 127 poles to a Stake; then
South 45 West 254 poles to a Stake;
then to the beginning. Surveyed the
27th day of September 1833.
        Jesse Thompson, Deputy Surveyor
              R. County
Burt L. Stephens
John Harvey   Sworn C.C.

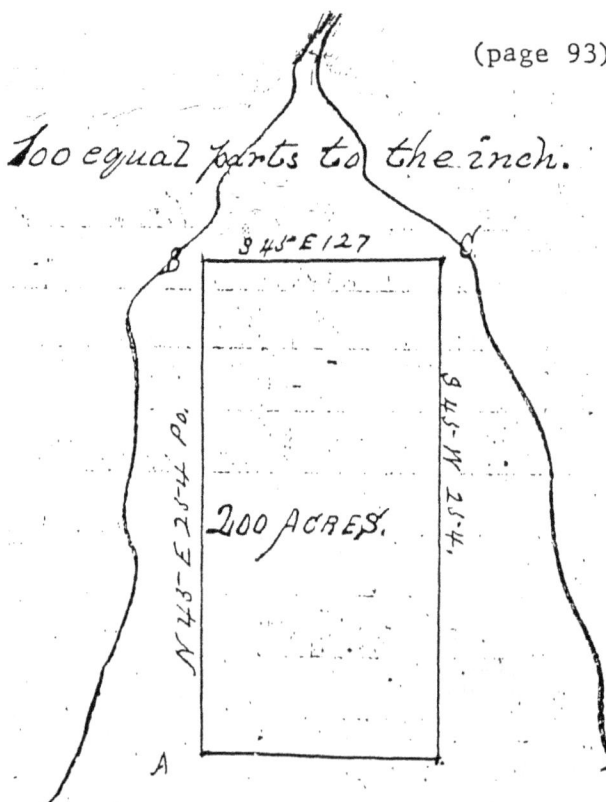

        100 equal parts to the inch

A. FULTON

State of Tennessee, Rhea County
In pursuance of an entry made by
Arthur Fulton of No. 136 filed
May the 7 day 1832 for 300 acres
of land on Waldens Ridge of Cumberland Mountain on a branch
known by the Devils fork of Piney
River by virtue of a deputation
to me given by Chrispian E. Shelton Surveyor of Sd County, I have
Surveyed for the Said Fulton 300
acres. BEGINNING on three blackoak trees on the East Side of the
Devils fork of Piney River West
58 ps to a whiteoak; then No 55 W
30 ps to a gum tree; then N 20 E
66 ps to a blackoak & postoak the
beginning corner of the _?_ th
entry of David W. Brown; then N
55 W   (page 94)
134 poles to a blackoak; then N
50 E 180 poles to a Sowerwood;
then S 40 E 290 p to a Stake;
then S 50 W 150 ps to a Stake;
then a Straight line to the beginning. Surveyed 1st Oct 1833
        Jesse Thompson, Deputy Surveyor R. County
Josep Danld [sic] and Wm R. Warman, S.C.C.

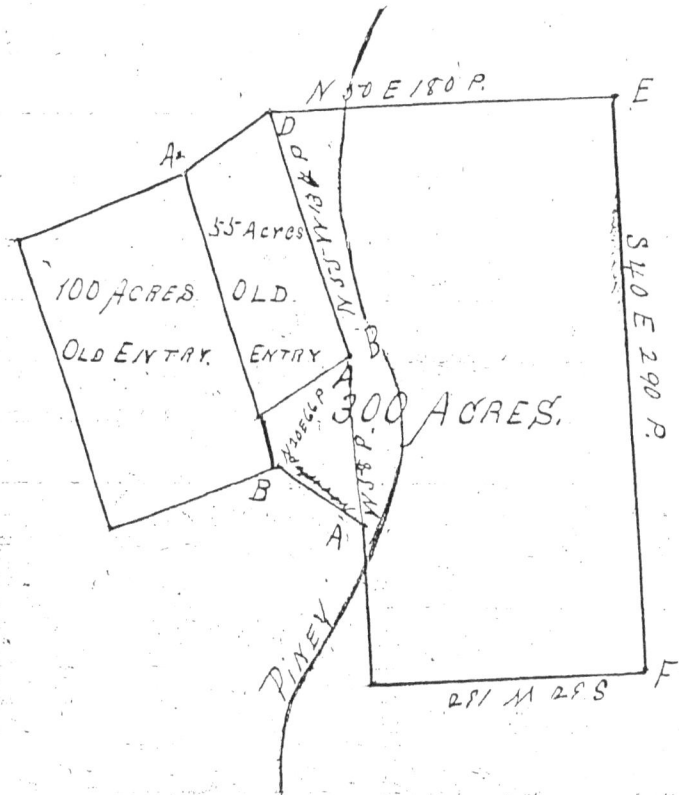

100 equal parts to the inch

T.B. RICE

State of Tennessee, Rhea County
In pursuance of an entry made by George Gillespie and Jesse Thompson of No. 115
& dated the 4th day of February 1830 and transferred by assignment to Theoderick
B. Rice for value received 2000 acres of land on Waldens Ridge of Cumberland
Mountain on the waters of Piney River. BEGINNING on a blackoak tree corner of
Said Rices 500 acre Survey at the Shutin on piney river and by virtue

(page 95)
of a deputation to me given by Chrispian E. Shelton Surveyor for Rhea County, I
have Surveyed for the Said Rice 2000 acres. BEGINNING on a blackoak and Pine
running North 45 E 30 ps to a Spanishoak on the top of the mountain; then North
40 E 320 poles to a hickory & blackoak; then North 50 West 548 ps to a whiteoak;
then South 45 West 640 poles to a Stake, then to the beginning. Surveyed the 30th
of Sept 1833.   Jesse Thompson, Dept Surveyor R. Cty
Asa Glascock and Abraham G. Wright, Sworn C.C.   (Plat on following page)

D. RAGSDALE

State of Tennessee, Rhea County
In pursuance and by virtue of entry No. 279 for 800 acres, I have this 20 day of
October 1836 Surveyed for David Ragsdale eight hundred acres of land in Rhea
County on the mountain on the waters of Sale Creek & Richland Creek. BEGINNING
on a hickory near a blackoak marked "R" then South thirty West two hundred and

42

100 equal parts to the inch.

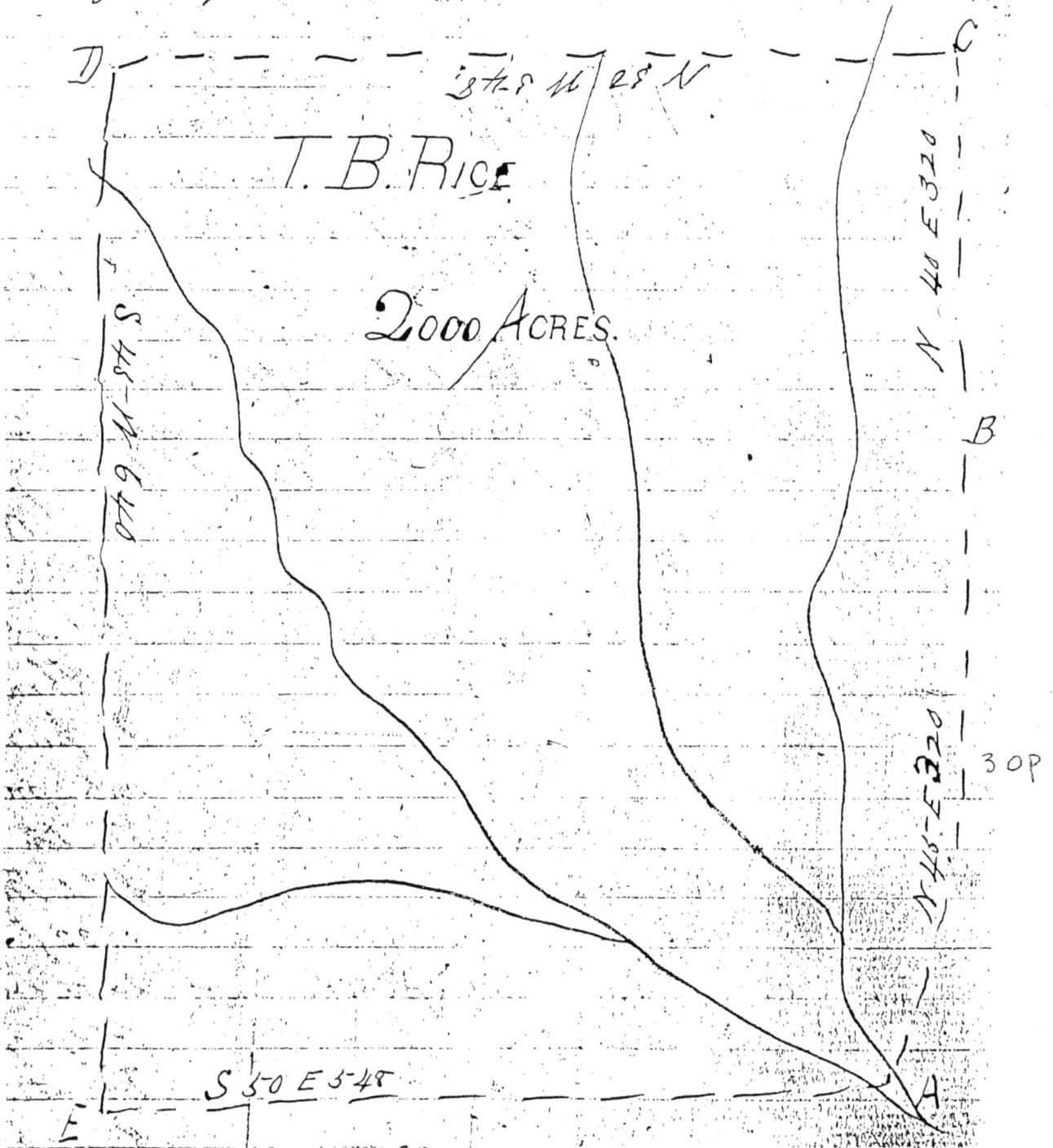

T. B. Rice

2000 Acres.

N 20 W 8-48.

N 40 E 320

B

3 0 P

N 48 E 320

S 48 W 640

D

S 50 E 5-48

E

A

C

43

Scale 100 poles to an inch.

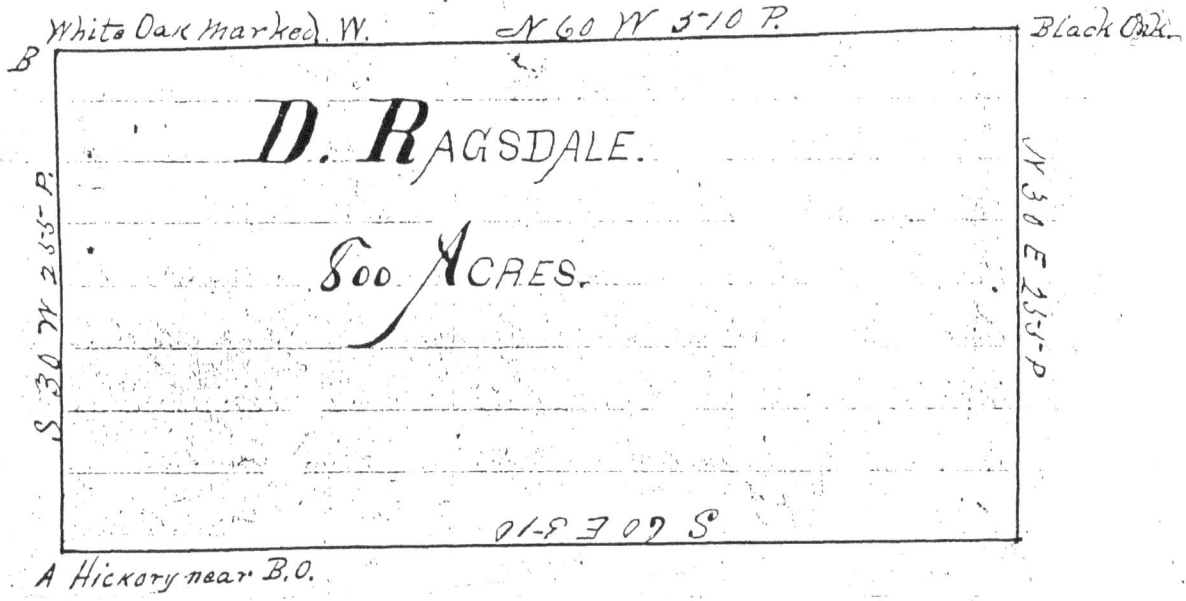

White Oak marked W.   N 60 W 5-10 P.   Black Oak

D. RAGSDALE.

800 ACRES.

A Hickory near B.O.

fifty five poles crossing an old road Several [times] to a whiteoak marked "W", then N 60 W crossing a branch of Richland Creek in all five hundred and ten poles to a large forked blackoak near a postoak, then N 30° E crossing a road and creek two hundred & fifty five poles to a Stake; then a direct line being South Sixty East five hundred and ten poles to the beginning. Surveyed by

(page 96)

me on the 20th October 1836. Richard Waterhouse, Deputy Surveyor
John Smallwood and Franklin Ragsdale, S.C.C.   David Ragsdale, Marker

RANSOM AND WHITEHEAD

State of Tennessee, Rhea County
In pursuance of an entry made by John Ransom and Benjamin Whitehead of No. 100 dated the 8th day of December 1828 for 200 acres of land on Waldens Ridge. BEGINNING on a blackoak running North 10 degrees East 160 poles crossing Waterhouses path to a blackjack tree, then due West 200 poles to a Stake; then South 10 degrees West 160 poles to a Stake; then due East 200 poles to the beginning, and by virtue of a deputation to me given by David Shelton Surveyor for Said County, I have Surveyed for Nusom Cooper having the entry transferred by assignment to him from the original enterers the Said 200 acres on the waters of Piney and to include an improvement made by John Ransom. Surveyed the 13th day of August 1830.

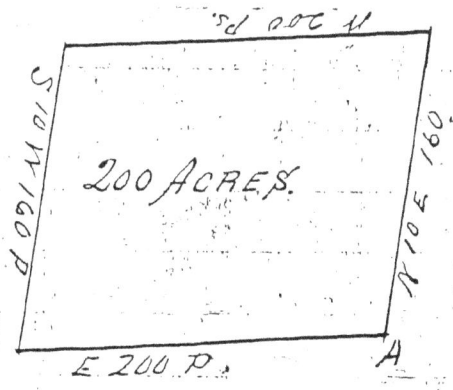

200 ACRES.

100 equal parts to the inch

        Jesse Thompson, Deputy Surveyor for Rhea County
James W. Thompson and John Ferguson, C.B.

J. GARRISON

State of Tennessee,
        Rhea County
Pursuant to
                (page 97)
an entry made by Joseph
Garrison of No. 33 and
dated the 23rd day of
January 1826 for 640
acres of land on Wal-
dens Ridge on both
sides of the Bumble-
bee fork of Piney.
BEGINNING at two
Small whiteoaks the
Northwest corner of
John Garrisons 125
acres running due East
320 poles to a white-
oak marked "A"; then
due North 320 poles
to a maple and white-
oak; then due West
320 poles to a Stake;
then South 320 poles to the beginning, and by virtue of a deputation to me given
by Crispian E. Shelton Surveyor for Rhea County, I have Surveyed as above the Said
640 acres on the waters of Piney River. Surveyed the 3rd day of January 1835.
            Jesse Thompson, D. Surveyor for Rhea Cty
Elijah Snodgrass and Benj Erwin, Chain Bearers

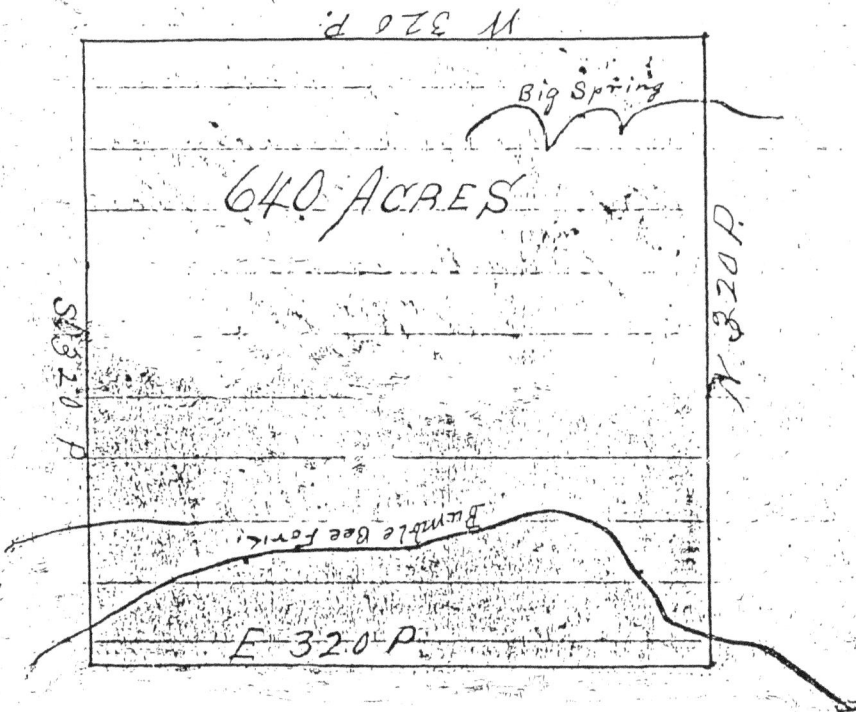

R. FERGUSON ET ALS

200 parts to an inch

State of Tennessee, Rhea County
Pursuant to an entry made by Robert Ferguson, Samuel B.
Ferguson, Thomas Ferguson & Levi W. Ferguson of No. 232
for 1000 acres of land date the 5th day of August 1834
in Sd County on Waldens Ridge a Spur of Cumberland
Mountain, and on the waters of Piney on a Small branch
passing James Fergusons entry of No. 99. BEGINNING on
a White pine near the bluff of Piney River running
South 45 degrees East 283 poles crossing a branch at
123 poles to a Stake on the line of the 19,000 acre
Survey at the foot of the mountain North 40 degrees
East 600 poles to a Stake; then North 45 degrees West
283 poles to a Stake; then a direct line to the beginning and by virtue of a deputation to me given by
Chrispian E. Shelton Surveyor for Said County, I have
Surveyed as above the Said 1000 acres of land as called
for in Said Entry to include the Chestnut pond & Mullins Cabin Situated in the bend of Piney River. Surveyed the ? th day of September   (page 98)
1834.   Jesse Thompson, D. Surveyor for R. County
Jacob L. Wassum & Andrew Wassum, C.B.

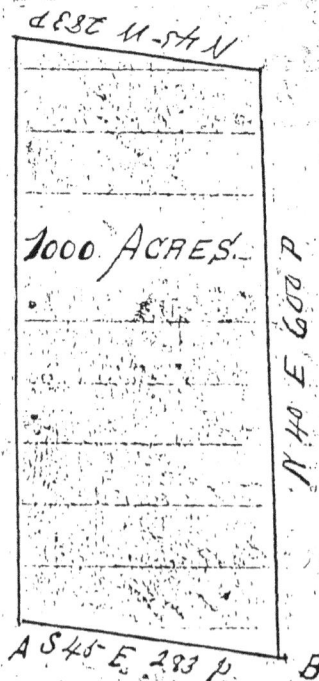

Y.B. MONDAY   (page 98)

State of Tennessee, Rhea County
In pursuance of an entry made by Young B.
Monday of No. 213, dated the 4th day of
March and filed the 8th day of May 1833
for 100 acres of land on Waldens Ridge of
Cumberland Mountain and by virtue of a
deputation to me given by Chrispian E.
Shelton Surveyor for Said County, I have
Surveyed for the Said Young B. Monday 100
acres. BEGINNING on a Small chestnut and
Sowerwood trees, running due North 80
poles to a blackgum near Calvin D. Gipsons
line; then S 45 degrees West 240 poles to
a Stake; then South 45 degrees East 70
poles to a Stake; then North 62 degrees
East 110 poles to a corner of Waterhouses
84 acre grant then North 25 degrees West
116 poles along Said line to a whiteoak
the beginning corner of the 84 acre
grant, then North 65 East with Said
Grant 36 poles to the beginning lying on
Whites Creek on both Sides and to include the mouth of Sandy. Surveyed the
18th day of October 1833.

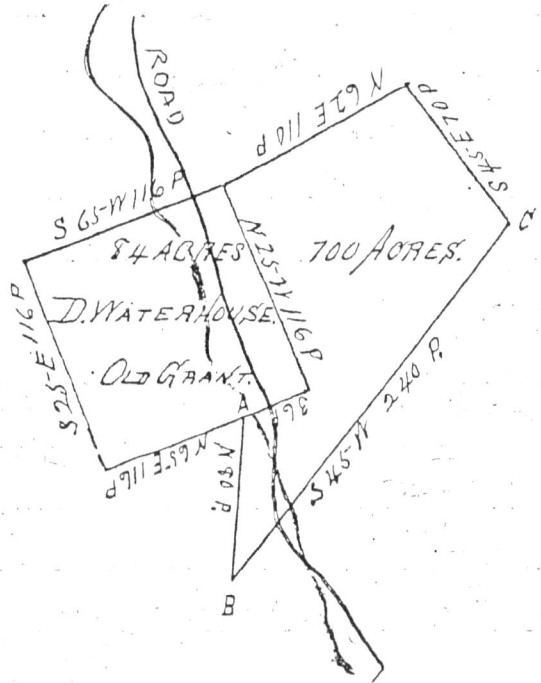

100 equal parts to the inch

        Jesse Thompson, Deputy Surveyor for Rhea County
Absolem L. Thompson & Alexander Smith, Chain Bearers

A.D. PAUL   (page 99)

State of Tennessee, Rhea County
Pursuant to an entry made by Archibald D. Paul of No. 209
dated the 18th of February 1833 for 150 acres of land on
Waldens Ridge on the South fork of Whites Creek to include a Laurel Branch. BEGINNING on a Gum tree running
South 15 degrees East 219 poles to a Stake with two hickorys and a chestnut marked pointers; then South 75 degrees West 110 poles to a Stake with a blackgum and
Whiteoak marked pointers; then N 15 degrees West 219
poles to a chestnut and blackoak; then North 75 degrees
East 110 poles to the beginning, and by virtue of a deputation to me given by Chrispian E. Shelton Surveyor for
Said County, I have Surveyed for the Said Paul as above
150 acres. Surveyed the 19th day of May 1834.

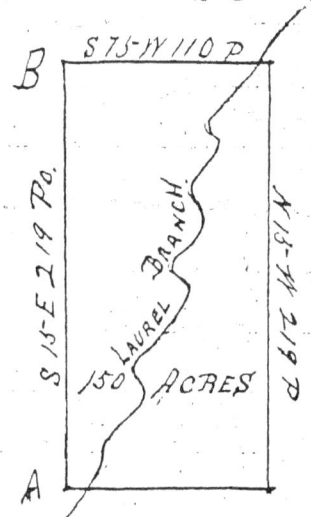

        Jesse Thompson, Deputy Surveyor for Rhea County
Martin E. Paul & Hardy Crews, C.B.   Scale 100 parts to one inch

B. HOLLOWAY

State of Tennessee, Rhea County
In pursuance of an entry made by Bermillion Holloway of No. 166 dated 18th
day of October 1831 for 300 acres. BEGINNING on a Chestnut near Thompsons
trace running South 60 East 160 poles to a Chestnut; then North 30 East 300
poles to a postoak & blackjack; then North 60 West 160 poles to a blackjack

and hickory then to the beginning, and by virtue of a deputation to me given by David Shelton Surveyor for Rhea County

(page 100)

I have Surveyed for the Sd Holloway 300 acres
of land as above lying & being in Sd County
on the waters of Whites Creek. Surveyed 13th
Sept 1832.
Jesse Thompson, Deputy Surveyor for Rhea County
Major Holloway & Wm T. Gillenwaters, C.B.

T. MAJORS

State of Tennessee, Rhea County
In pursuance of an entry made by Thomas Majors
for 50 acres on Waldens Ridge on the waters of
Piney River No. 111 dated the 13th Novr 1829
and transferred by different assignments to Wm
R. Warman, and by virtue of a deputation to me
given by C.E. Shelton Surveyor for Sd County,
I have Surveyed for Sd Warman 50 acres of land.
BEGINNING on a chestnut with 6 blackgum poin-
ters, running South 45 D. W. 63 poles to a
chestnut tree; then No. 45 W. 126 ps to a
Chestnutoak & a blackgum; then No. 45 E 63
poles to a Stake; then to the beginning.
Surveyed 3rd March 1833.
Jesse Thompson, Deputy Surveyor for Rhea County
John Garrison & Absolem Rutherford, C.B.

100 equal parts to the inch

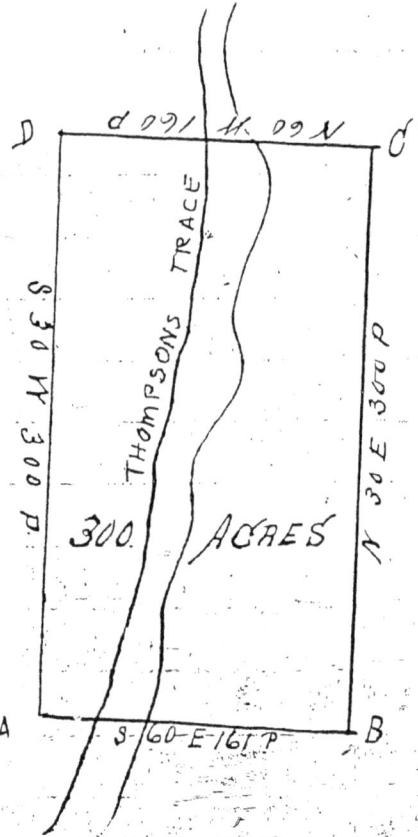

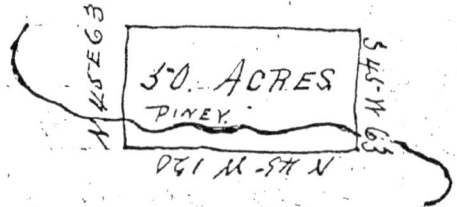

100 equal parts to the inch

100 equal parts to the inch

R. GREEN

State of Tennessee, Rhea County
In pursuance of an entry made by Thompson
Danill for 300 acres of land on Waldens
Ridge on the waters of Whites Creek on a
branch called the Lick branch of No. 191
and dated the 23 day of August

(page 101)

1832, and Thompson by assignment to Robert
Green and by virtue of a deputation to me
given by Chrispian E. Shelton Surveyor for
Sd County, I have Surveyed for the Sd Green
agreeably to Sd entry 300 acres of land.
BEGINNING on a Whiteoak Wm M. Stevens beginning corner of his 500 acre entry, running with Sd line So 30 W 200 ps to a
Whiteoak; then No 85 W 167 ps to a blackoak near Wm B. Gordons corner; then No 36
E 45 ps to a whiteoak near a road; then

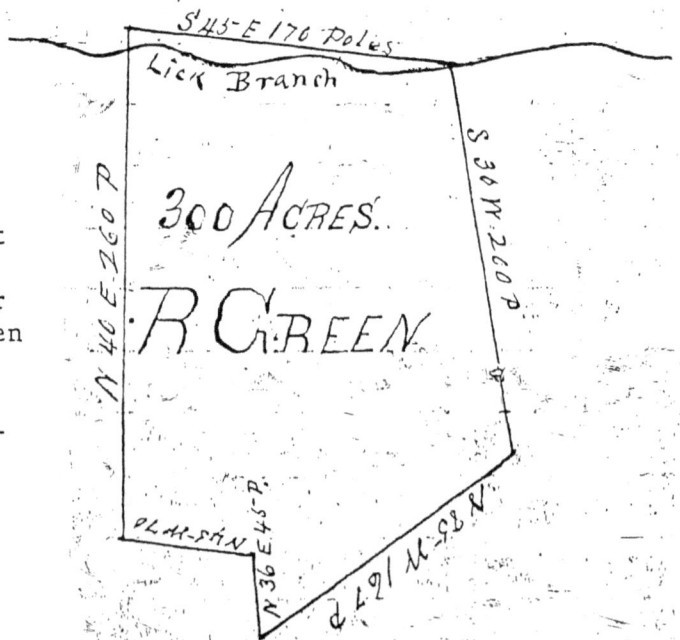

No 45 W 70 ps to a Stake on Gordons line; then No 40 E 260 ps crossing the Lick
Branch to a Stake; then to the beginning. Surveyed 28th Sept 1833.
        Jesse Thompson, Deputy Surveyor of Rhea County
Wm B. Gordon & John Harvey, C.B.

W.H. SEAY   (page 101)

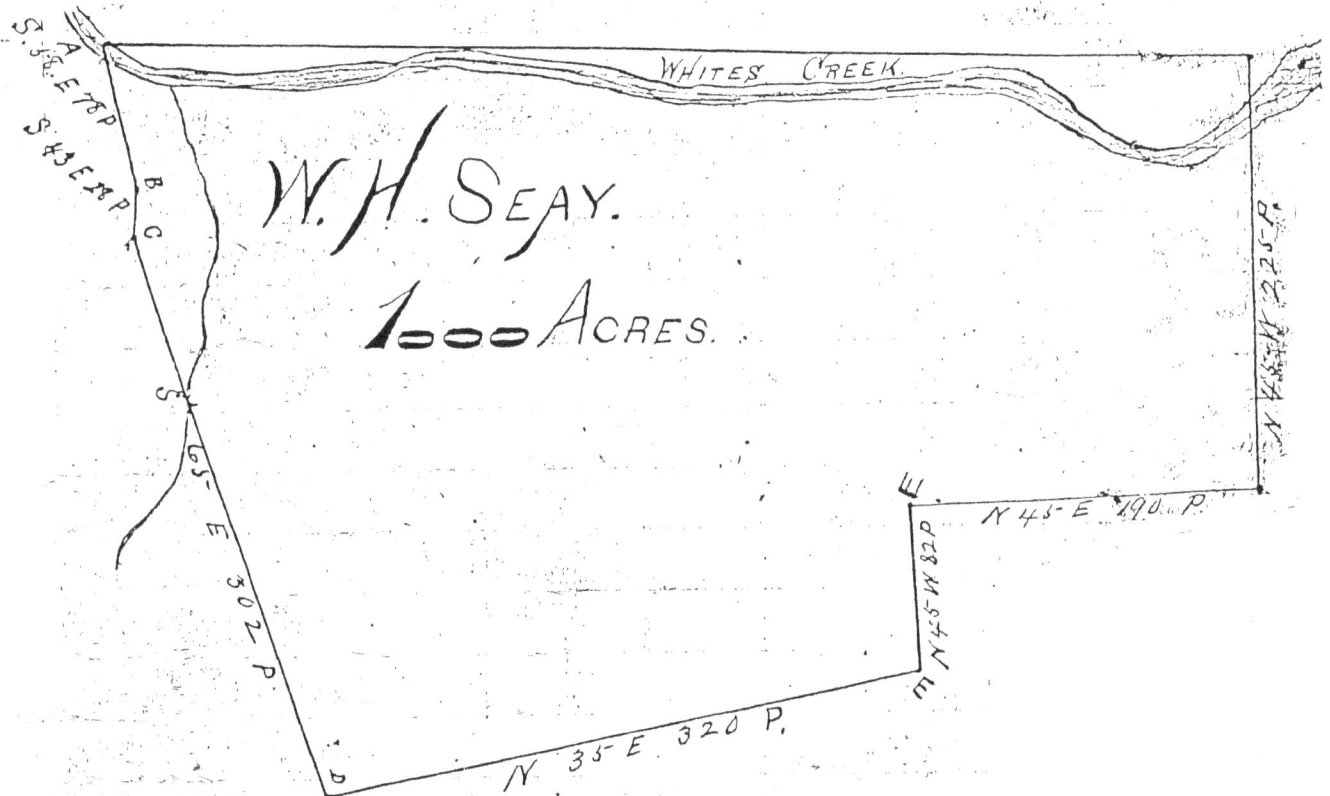

W.H. Seay.
1000 Acres.

100 poles to the inch

State of Tennessee, Rhea County
In pursuance of an entry made by Wm H. Seay of No. 187 and filed   June 30th
day 1832 for 1000 acres of land on Waldens Ridge of Cumberland Mountain on the
South East Side of Whites Creek and by virtue of a deputation to me given by
Chrispian E. Shelton Surveyor for Rhea County, I have Surveyed for the Sd Seay
1000 acres.   (page 102)
BEGINNING on the Northwest Side of a branch on a whiteoak and hickory, running
South 58 degrees East 78 poles to a Maple; then So 43 degrees East 28 poles to a
Chestnut oak to Major Holloways corner; then South 65 degrees East passing Major
Holloways corner to a hickory 302 poles to a postoak, then North 35 degrees East
320 poles to two blackoaks, then North 35 degrees West 82 poles to a Stake on
William T. Gillenwaters line, then North 45 East 190 poles along Sd line to Wm G.
English line of 600 acre Survey; then along Sd line North 45 West 225 poles to
the Bluff of Whites Creek, then a Straight line to the beginning. Surveyed the
2nd day of October 1833. Jesse Thompson, Deputy Surveyor
Major Holloway & Bermillion Holloway, C.B.

A. WASSUM   (page 102)

State of Tennessee, Rhea County
In pursuance of an entry made by Andrew Wassum for 150 acres
of No. 221 dated the 4th day of October 1833 for 150 acres
on the Side of Waldens Ridge.   BEGINNING on a blackoak tree
running North eighty degrees East one hundred and ten poles
to a Stake on the line of a Grant granted to Stockly Donelson for 1000 acres No. 616; then with Said line North ten
degrees East two hundred and twenty poles to a Stake; then
South eighty degrees West one hundred and ten poles to a
Stake; then to the beginning and by virtue of a deputation
to me given by Crispian E. Shelton Surveyor for Said County,
I have Surveyed for the Said Andrew Wassum the Said 150
acres of land in Said County on the waters of Town Creek a
branch of Piney River Situated as above. Surveyed the 4th
day of September 1834.   Jesse Thompson, Deputy Surveyor
Jacob Wassum & Levi W. Ferguson, Sworn C.C.

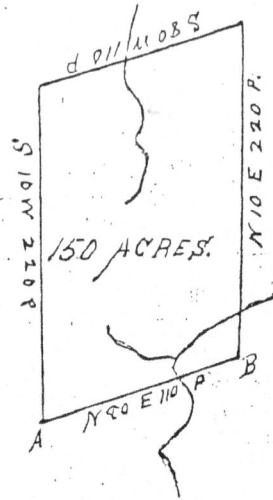

Scale 100 equal parts
to the inch

J. WASSUM   (page 103)

State of Tennessee, Rhea County
In pursuance of an entry made by Jacob Wassum of No. 78
dated the 1 day of October 1827 for 100 acres of land.
BEGINNING near a bluff of Piney River on a poplar marked
thus "A.W." and a double maple running North Sixty eight
degrees East one hundred and Sixty poles to three blackoaks trees; thence North twenty two degrees West one
hundred poles to a Stake; then South Sixty eight degrees
West one hundred and Sixty poles to a Stake, then to the
beginning and [by] virtue of a deputation to me given by
Crispian E. Shelton Surveyor for Rhea County, I have Surveyed for the Said Jacob Wassum the Said 100 acres to include a bear pen and a large pond near the top of the
mountain Situated as above in the Said County. Surveyed
this 30th day of August 1834.

        Jesse Thompson, Deputy Surveyor for Rhea County
Jacob L. Wassum & Hiram Evans, S.C.B.

                Scale: 100 parts to the inch

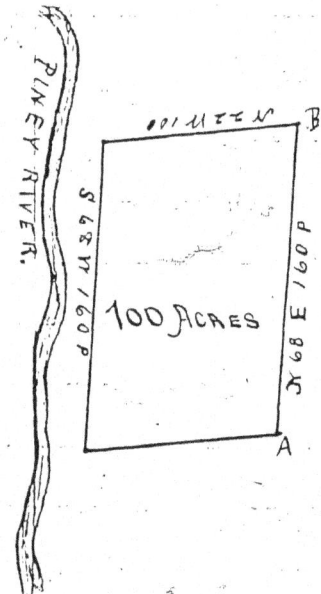

J. BROWN

State of Tennessee, Rhea County
In pursuance of a entry made by James Brown of No. 150 dated 9th day of March
1830 for 200 acres. BEGINNING on a Chestnut tree running South eighty degrees
West Seventy one poles with the line of a 75 acres Surveyed and granted to Thomas Rose to a Whiteoak & Maple, then South ten degrees West down the South
Side of Sandy Creek with the line of James Hays to a White pine tree one hundred
poles; then South forty degrees East Two hundred poles to a Stake; then North 12
                                                                  (page 104)
degrees East two hundred and ninety poles to a Stake; then South eighty degrees
West one hundred and ten poles to the beginning, and Virtue of a deputation to me
given by Crispian E. Shelton Surveyor for Rhea County, I have Surveyed the Said
two hundred acres of land on the East side of Sandy Creek a fork of Whites Creek

Said entry made by James Brown and transferred by assignment to Sd Benjamin Hembree. Surveyed the 9th day of November 1835.

Jesse Thompson, Deputy Surveyor for Rhea County

James Hays Senr & James H. Hays Junr, Sworn C.C.

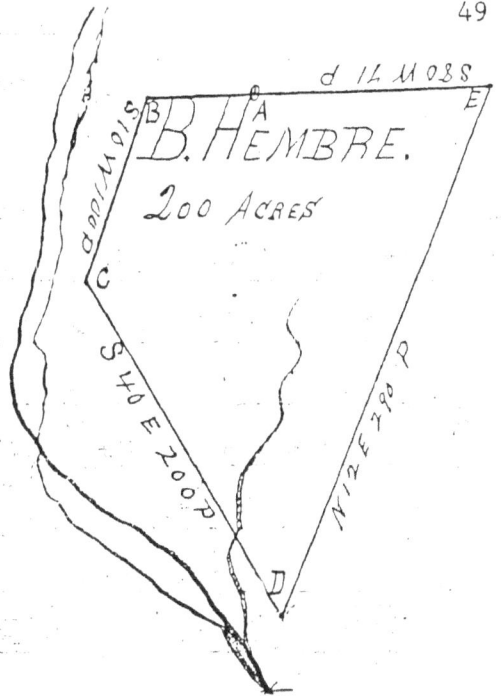

D. KNOX

State of Tennessee, Rhea County
In pursuance of an entry made by David Knox for 100 acres of No. 211 & dated the 16th day of May 1833 for 100 acres of land on Waldens Ridge on the Big fork of Whites Creek. BEGINNING on the South Side of what is called the Allaway Creek on a Chestnut tree; running North Seventy five degrees West one hundred and eighty poles to a blackgum tree; then South fifteen degrees East Ninety poles to a Stake; then South Seventy five degrees East one hundred and eighty poles to a Stake; then N fifteen degrees West 90 poles to the beginning; and by virtue of a deputation to me given by Crispian E. Shelton Surveyor for Said County, I have Surveyed for the Said David Knox the Said land as above Situated in Said County. Surveyed the 23rd day of November 1833.   Jesse Thompson,
Deputy Surveyor for Rhea County

Thompson Daniel & John Harvey, S.C.C.

Scale 100 parts to the inch

100 equal parts to the inch

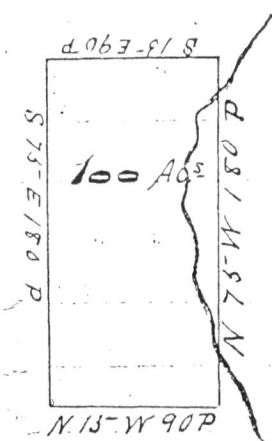

ARTHUR FULTON   (page 105)

State of Tennessee, Rhea County
Pursuant to an entry made by Henry Owens of No. 174 dated the 6th day of Nov 1831 for 150 acres and transferred by assignment to Arthur Fulton, and I have Surveyed for the Said Fulton the Said 150 acres of land. BEGINNING on a chestnut tree below and near Said Fulton trace, running North 25 degrees West 219 poles to a Chestnut and postoak, then South Sixty five degrees West 110 poles to a forked Dogwood near a branch; then South 25 degrees East 47 poles to Waterhouses line; then S 55 degrees East with Said Waterhouses old line 146 poles to a whiteoak his corner; then South 25 degrees East 30 poles to two blackgums, and a Sowerwood; then North 65 degrees East 60 poles to a Stake; then to the beginning, Said land lying and being in Said County of Rhea on Waldens Ridge on a East fork of Piney River on both sides of what is called a trace leading from Fultons to what is called Swaggertys Cove. Surveyed the 24 day of

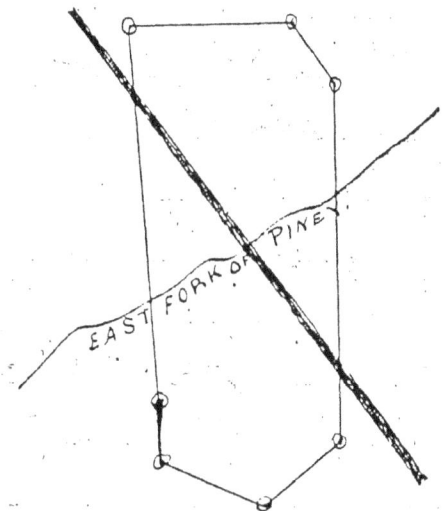

Scale 100 to the inch

March, and re-Surveyed in part the 5th day of October 1835.
        Jesse Thompson, Deputy Surveyor for Rhea County
Elijah Runnels & Alexander Owens, Sworn C.C.

A. OWENS

State of Tennessee, Rhea County
In pursuance of an entry made by Alexander Owens
and transferred by assignment to John Dunlap of
No. 222 dated the 5th day of October 1833 for 200
acres of land on the waters of Piney. BEGINNING
on two blackgum trees running North ten degrees
West 220 poles to a whiteoak; then South 80 degrees West(?) (bottom of page torn)
                                    (page 106)
South ten degrees East 220 poles to a Stake near
a blased maple; then a direct line to the beginning; and by virtue of a deputation to me given
by Crispin E. Shelton Surveyor for Rhea County,
I have Surveyed the Said 200 acres of land agreeable to the calls of Said Entry lying and being
in Said County on both Sides of Fultons trace.
Surveyed the 10th day of January 1835.
        Jesse Thompson, Deputy Surveyor for Rhea County
Elijah Runnels & Henry Owens, Sworn C.C.

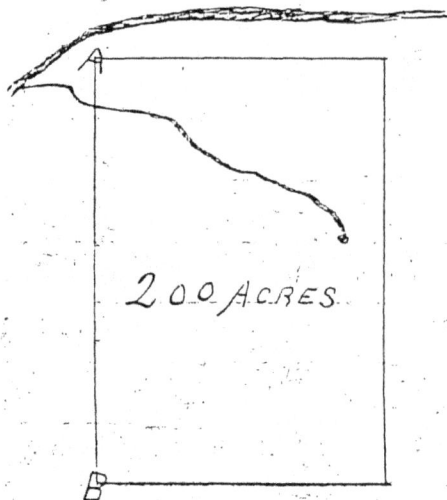

2 0 0 ACRES

Scale 100 parts to one inch

F.H. FULTON   (page 106)

State of Tennessee, Rhea County
In pursuance of an entry made by Flemming H. Fulton of No.
194 for 200 acres of land on Waldens Ridge and on the waters
of Piney River and dated the 17th day of September 1832.
BEGINNING on a chestnut tree near Fultons trace running
South 30 degrees West Ninety poles to Wm M. Stevens corner;
then North Sixty degrees West thirty poles to a Stake on
Said Stevens line; then South thirty degrees West 196 poles
along with James A. Darwin line to a Stake, then South
Sixty degrees East 122 poles to a Stake on Arthur Fultons
and Joseph Daniel line of 300 acre entry; then North twenty
Nine degrees East 288 poles to a Chestnut tree; then North
Sixty degrees West ninety two poles to the beginning, and
by virtue of a deputation to me given by Crispin E. Shelton
Surveyor for Said County, I have Surveyed the Said 200 acres
of land agreeable to the calls of the Said entry lying and
being in Said County on both Sides of the trace that leads
from Fultons Gap. Surveyed the 10th day of October 1833.
        Jesse Thompson, Deputy Surveyor R.C.
Absolem L. Thompson & William M. Stevens, S.C.B.

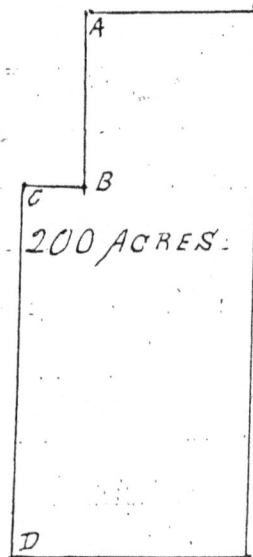

200 ACRES

100 parts to the
inch

JO. GARRISON   (page 107)

State of Tennessee, Rhea County
Pursuant to an entry made by Joseph Garrison of No. 33 and dated the 23rd day of
January 1826 for 640 acres of land on Waldens Ridge on both sides of the Bumble-
bee fork of Piney. BEGINNING at two Small whiteoaks the Northwest corner of John

Garrisons 125 acres, running due
East 320 poles to a whiteoak marked
"A", then due North 320 poles to a
maple and whiteoak; then due West
320 poles to a Stake; then South
320 poles to the beginning, and by
virtue of a deputation to me given
by Crispin E. Shelton Surveyor for
Rhea, I have Surveyed as above the
Said 640 acres on the waters of
Piney River. Surveyed the 3rd day
of January 1835.
Jesse Thompson, A Deputy Surveyor
        for Rhea County
Elijah Snodgrass
Benjamin Erwin
        Sworn Chain Bearers

Jo. GARRISON.
640 ACRES
Bumble Fork of Piney

100 parts to one inch

JAS. GIPSON

State of Tennessee, Rhea County
In pursuance of an entry made by James Gipson for
100 acres of land on Waldens ridge on both sides
of Gordons Road of No. 217 for 100 acres of land
dated the 13 day of August 1833. BEGINNING on a
chestnut tree near Roses line of a 75 acre Survey
running North fifty four degrees East one hundred
and forty poles to a poplar and chestnut; then
North 27 degrees West one hundred and fifteen
poles to a dogwood and hickory; then South fifty
four degrees West one hundred and forty poles
(last line on page missing)

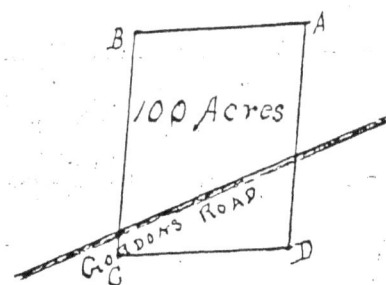

100 Acres
GORDONS ROAD

100 parts to the inch
(page 108)

deputation to me given by Crispin E. Shelton Surveyor for Rhea County, I have
Surveyed the Said 100 acres in Said County on Waldens Ridge agreeable to the
calls of Said Entry. Surveyed the 21st day of July 1834.
        Jesse Thompson, Deputy Surveyor for Rhea County
James Hayse & William Gipson, Sworn C. Bearers

100 parts to the
inch

C. BUNDREN

State of Tennessee, Rhea County
In pursuance of an entry made by Claibourn Bundren of No. 185
for fifty acres of land on Waldens Ridge on Fall Creek a branch
of Whites Creek joining Said Bundrens 150 acre entry and dated
the 25th day of March 1832. BEGINNING on the corner of Said
150 acre entry and dated the 25th day of March 1932, beginning
on a dogwood and double Whiteoak running South forty degrees
West Seventy Six poles to two Chestnuts; then South Sixty degrees East one hundred and Six poles to a Stake; then North
forty degrees East Seventy Six poles to a Stake; then a direct

50 ACRES
N 40 E 76 P
S 60 E 106
S 40 W 76 P

line to the beginning, and by virtue of a deputation to me given by David Shelton
Surveyor for Rhea County, I have Surveyed for the Said Bundren the Said fifty
acres of land on Waldens Ridge agreeable to the calls of Said entry.   Surveyed
the 15th day of September 1832.   Jesse Thompson, Deputy Surveyor for Rhea
Richard Bundren & Gilbert Luper, S.C.B.   County

C. BUNDREN

State of Tennessee, Rhea County
In pursuance of an entry made by Claibourn Bundren of No.
154 dated the 18 day of June 1831 for 150 acres of land
on Waldens Ridge on Bason Creek a fork of Whites Creek.
BEGINNING   (last line on page missing)

(page 109)

of Said Bason Creek on a large White pine, running South
forty degrees East one hundred and ten poles to a maple
near a large rock; then South forty degrees West 219
poles to a dogwood and double whiteoak, then North 40
degrees West 110 poles to a Stake, then to the beginning,
and by virtue of a deputation to me given by David Shelton Surveyor for Rhea County, I have Surveyed the Said
150 acres of land agreeable to the calles of Said entry
lying and being in Said County. Surveyed the 22nd day
of March 1832.   Jesse Thompson, Deputy Surveyor R.C.
George C. Bundren & Benjamin Lawless, S.C.B.

W.T. GILLENWATERS

State of Tennessee, Rhea County
Pursuant to an entry made by Wm T. Gillenwaters and
James Roddy of No. 243 and dated the 13th day of
January 1835 for 150 acres of land on a big ridge
and the Side of Waldens Ridge on the waters of
Whites Creek. BEGINNING on a Whiteoak on William
T. Gillenwaters old line, running North Sixty degrees West 36 poles to a chestnut & poplar, Gillenwaters old corner, then North 81 degrees West two
hundred and Six poles to a Stake; then South 9 degrees West one hundred poles to a Stake; then South
Sixty three degrees East one hundred and thirty
five poles to David M. Roddys line and with his
line to the beginning, and by virtue of a deputation to me given by Crispin E. Shelton Surveyor
for Rhea County, I have Surveyed as above the Said
150 acres on the waters of Whites Creek to include   100 parts to one inch
the ridge called for in Said entry. Surveyed the
9th day of October 1835.   Jesse Thompson, Deputy Surveyor for Rhea County
Abraham G. Wright & David M. Roddy, C.B.

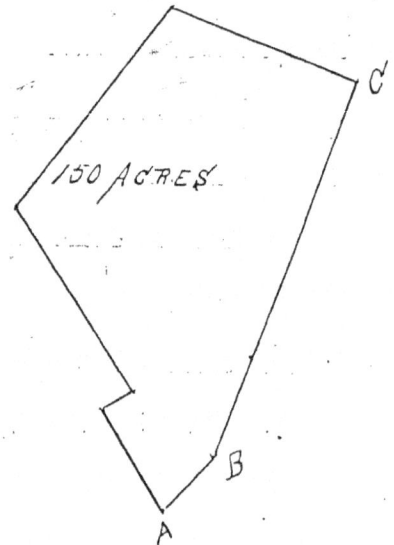

W.T. GILLENWATERS   (page 110)

State of Tennessee, Rhea County
In pursuance of an entry made by William T. Gillenwaters of No. 207 dated the 5th
day of February 1833 for 250 acres of land on the Side of Waldens Ridge on both

sides of what is called Gillenwaters trace.
BEGINNING on a chestnut tree near a Spring
running South 81 degrees East 106 poles to a
blackoak and chestnutoak; then N 30 degrees
West 162 poles to a whiteoak corner on Robert
Walkers line; then North 60 degrees West 30
poles to a whiteoak Walkers corner; then
North 27 degrees West 147 poles to a maple on
a branch; then North 60 degrees West 110
poles to a Stake; then South 34 degrees West
335 poles to a Stake; then South 60 degrees
East 30 poles to the beginning, and by virtue of a deputation to me given by Crispin
E. Shelton, Surveyor for Rhea County, I
have Surveyed for the Said William T. Gillenwaters the Said 250 acres of land as above on
the waters of Camp Creek a branch of Whites
Creek on both sides of what is called Gillenwaters trace. Surveyed the 9th day of October
1835.   Jesse Thompson, Deputy Surveyor
Abraham G. Wright & David M. Roddy, S.C.B.

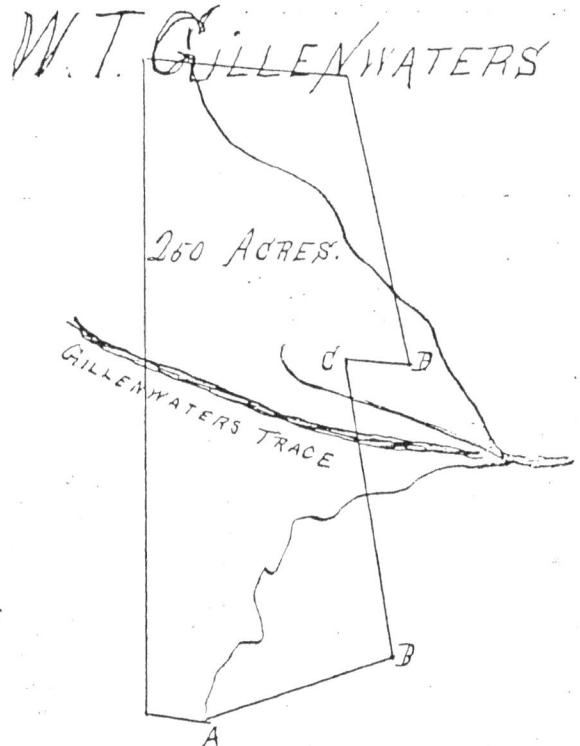

W.T. GILLENWATERS

250 ACRES.

GILLENWATERS TRACE

100 parts to one inch

J. BRUMBLE

State of Tennessee, Rhea County
Pursuant to an entry made by Jesse Brumble of
No. 241 dated the 9th day of December 1834 for
100 acres of land on Waldens Ridge on the North
Side of Gordons Road on the East Side of Bear
Creek. BEGINNING on a chestnut tree on Allen
Lupers line   (page 111)
running due East one hundred and Sixty poles
to a Chestnutoak & Whiteoak; then due North
one hundred poles to a chestnut and hickory;
then due West one hundred and Sixty poles to a

BEARS CREEK.

100 ACRES.

A S 160 P B

BEAR CREEK

100 parts to one inch

large Chestnut; then due South one hundred poles to the beginning and by virtue
of a deputation to me given by Crispin E. Shelton Surveyor for Rhea County, I
have Surveyed the above entry of 100 acres agreeable to the calls of Said entry.
Surveyed the 10th day of November 1835. Jesse Thompson, Deputy Surveyor R.C.
Gilbert Luper & Allen Luper, C.B.

GILLESPIE AND SMITH

State of Tennessee, Rhea County
Pursuant to an entry made by George Smith and John Coldwell jointly, and the Said
John Coldwell having transferred his interest in Said entry to Said George Gillespie Said entry No. 193 dated the 10th day of September 1832 for 1200 acres of
land. BEGINNING on a pine on the South Side of Whites Creek running North Sixty
five degrees West twenty poles to Whites Creek in all four hundred poles to a
blackgum Chestnut & Sowerwood; then North twenty five degrees East four hundred
and ninety poles to a pine and blackoak, then South Sixty five degrees East four
hundred poles to a Chestnut, whiteoak and hickory; then South twenty five degrees
West four hundred & ninety poles to the beginning, and by virtue of a deputation

to me given by Crispin E. Shelton Surveyor for Rhea County, I have Surveyed for the Said George Smith and George Gillespie the Said 1200 acres of land on Waldens Ridge and on both Sides of Whites Creek lying and being in Said County.   Surveyed the 31 day of

October 1834.

Jesse Thompson,
Deputy Surveyor
R.C.
Alexander Smith
& Eli Brewer
S.C.B.

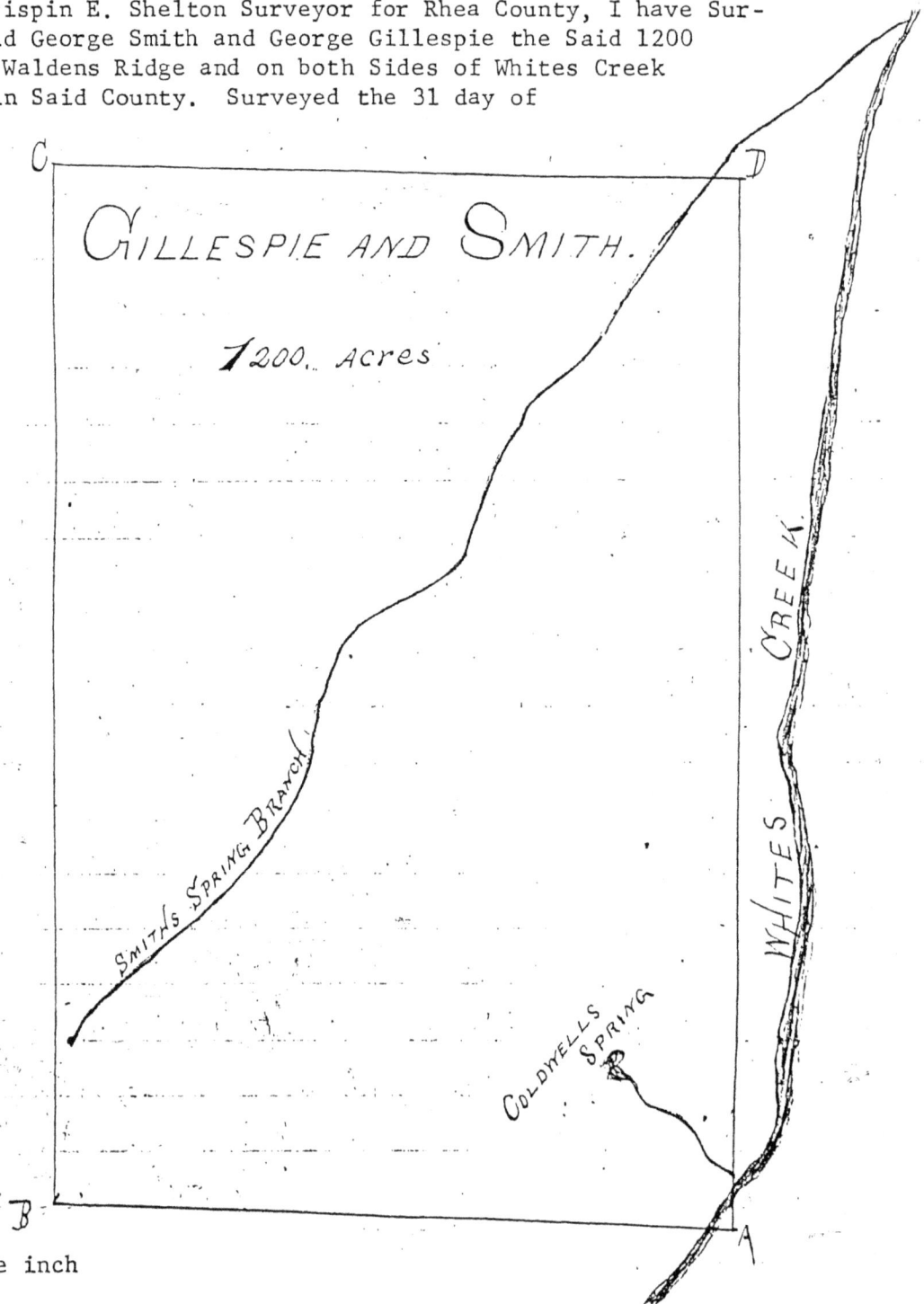

GILLESPIE AND SMITH.

1200. Acres

100 parts to the inch

D.M. RODDY   (page 112)

State of Tennessee, Rhea County
Pursuant to an entry made by David M. Roddye of No. 245 dated January the 13th day 1835 for 100 acres of land on a Spur of Waldens Ridge. BEGINNING on a dogwood tree near a Spring running North 60 degrees West forty poles to a whiteoak and dogwood; then South 45 degrees West 60 poles to a Stake on Said Spur; then North 45 degrees West 15 poles to a Stake; then South 45 degrees West 160 poles to a Stake; then South 45 degrees East 15 poles to a Whiteoak marked as a corner and continuing So 45 degrees East along a marked line 74 po to a Stake on Peter

(page 113)

Majors old line; then North 50 degrees East with Said old
line twenty four poles to a Small hickory; then South fifty
five degrees East ten poles to a blackoak corner of an old
grant for six hundred acres; then a direct line to the beginning, and by virtue of a deputation to me given by Crispien E. Shelton Surveyor for Said County, I have Surveyed
for the Said Roddye one hundred acres on Said Spur of Waldens Ridge on the waters of Camp Creek a branch of Whites
Creek. Surveyed the 17th day of April 1835.

Jesse Thompson, Deputy Surveyor for Rhea County
W.T. Gillenwaters and Jesse Majors, Sworn C.C.

100 parts to one inch

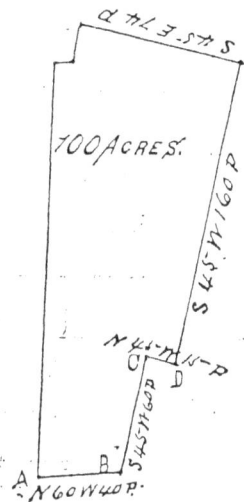

W. REDWINE

State of Tennessee, Rhea County
Pursuant to an entry made by Wilie Redwine of No.
238 dated the 1st day of November 1834 for 100
acres of land on Waldens Ridge a Spur of Cumberland
Mountain on the waters of Whites Creek.
BEGINNING on a chestnut on James Bundrens line of a
300 acre Survey running North twenty poles to a
hickory and chestnut; then West forty poles to
George Smith line of a 1200 acre Survey; then South
twenty five degrees West with Said line one hundred
and forty two poles to a chestnut and blackoak;
then South Sixty five degrees East one hundred and
forty poles to a chestnut; then North thirty five
degrees East thirty poles to a Stake; then West
Seventy five poles to a Stake; then South Sixty
poles to James Bundren line, and with Said line due
East Seventy five poles; then due South one hundred
and thirty poles to the beginning. Surveyed the
13th day of September 1836.

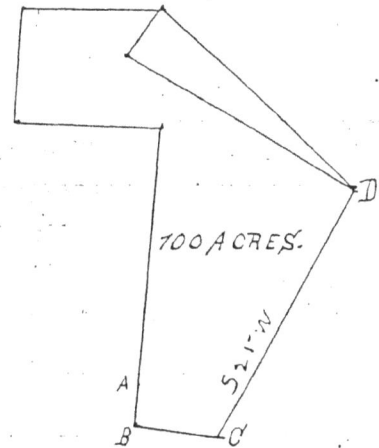

Jesse Thompson, Surveyor for Rhea County
David Knox and Elijah Brewer, Sworn Chain bearers

100 parts to one inch

JAS. RHEA

(page 114)

State of Tennessee, Rhea County
In pursuance of an entry made by James Rhea of No. 240 dated the 11th day of
September 1834 for 5000 acres of land in Said County on the North Side of Tennessee River and on both Sides of Piney River. BEGINNING at a Stake four hundred
and forty poles below the mouth of Piney River; then running South down the meanders of Tennessee River 285 poles to a Stake whiteoak tree near a bluff of rocks
the first bluff of rocks below the mouth of Piney river; then North 80 degrees
West 943 poles crossing the road at 520 poles to a blackjack and postoak on the
top or extreme hight of a ridge; thence up the ridge North 40 East 80 poles to a
blackjack tree; then North 49 East 82 poles to a blackjack tree; then North 20
East 40 poles to a chestnut and hickory; then due N 132 poles to two Postoaks;
then North 22 East 73 poles to a hickory; then North 15 degrees East 93 poles to
a postoak; then North 39° East 77 poles to a blackoak; then North 60° East 24
poles to a blackjack tree; then South 48° East 47 poles to a postoak and black-

100 equal parts to the inch

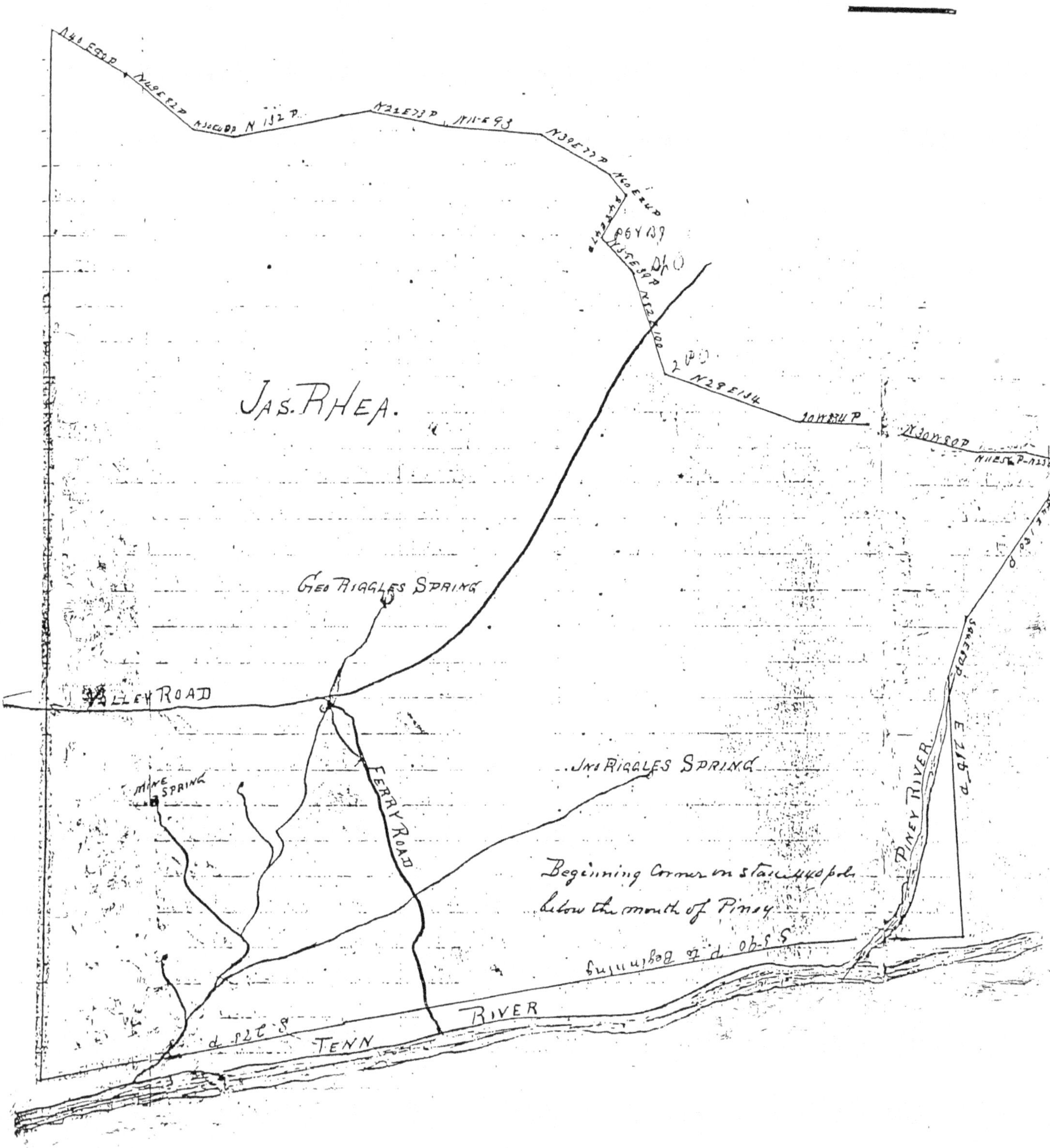

JAS. RHEA.

GEO RIGGLES SPRING

VALLEY ROAD

FERRY ROAD

MINE SPRING

JNO RIGGLES SPRING

Beginning Corner on state 440 pol.
below the mouth of Piney

PINEY RIVER

TENN RIVER

NOTE— The above plat was reduced to fit page; one inch scale added in upper right corner.

jack; then North 58° East 39 poles to Spanishoak; then North 82° East 100 poles to two postoaks; then North 28° East 134 poles to a hickory; then North 20° West 34 poles to a blackjack; then North 30° West 80 poles to a postoak; then North 11° East 56 poles to a postoak; then North 23° East 40 poles to two oaks and hickory where a due East line from the ford of Piney Strikes the top of the ridge; then South 54° E 215 ps to a hickory and cedar Stake on the South bank of Piney river; then So 44° E 50 ps to a Stake; then due East 215 ps to Tennessee River; then down the meanders of the river crossing Piney at one hundred poles in all 590 poles to the beginning. Surveyed the 19th day of November 1834.

      Jesse Thompson, Deputy Surveyor for Rhea County
George W. Riggle & Jacob Riggle, S.C.C.

  NOTE above plat— 3540 Acres being all the lands in the bounds of entry No. 240 entered by James Rhea for 5000 acres, but limited to Special calls of other deeds or grants and I find a deficiency of 1460 acres. Jesse Thompson D.C.

JOHN DOUGLAS [JAMES RODDYE]   (page 116)

State of Tennessee, Rhea County
Pursuant to an entry made by John Doughlas for one hundred acres of land on Waldens Ridge on little Laurel a branch of Whites Creek & transferred to James Roddys by assignment, I have this day Surveyed for the Said Roddye the Said one hundred acres to include a house & improvement made by Said Douglas. BEGINNING on a chestnut oak and hickory & Stake runing South thirty degrees West one hundred and Seventy two poles to a Sowerwood and hickory; then North Sixty degrees West ninety three poles to a Spanishoak; then North thirty degrees East one hundred and Seventy two poles to a Stake; then South Sixty degrees East Ninety three poles to the beginning. Said entry 197 dated the 25 day of Sept 1832. Surveyed the 21 day of September 1836.

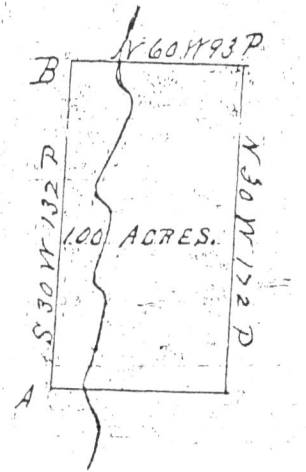

100 parts to one inch

      Jesse Thompson, Surveyor R. County
Jesse Roddye Senior and Dawson Harris, S.C. Bearers

J.H. STEWART

State of Tennessee, Rhea County
Pursuant to an entry made by James H. Stewart of No. 188 dated the 17th day of July 1832 for 100 acres of land on Waldens Ridge of Cumberland Mountain on the West side of the Laurel Fork of Richland Creek. BEGINNING on a Spruce pine tree on the West Side of Said Creek running North 57° West 40 poles to a whiteoak; then South 33° West 180 poles to a black oak; then South 57 E 90 poles to a blackgum; then North 33° E 180 poles to a Stake; then North 57° West 50 poles to the beginning. Surveyed the 4th day of August 1836.   Jesse Thompson, S. R. County
James C. Nelson & Monroe Cunningham, S.C.C.

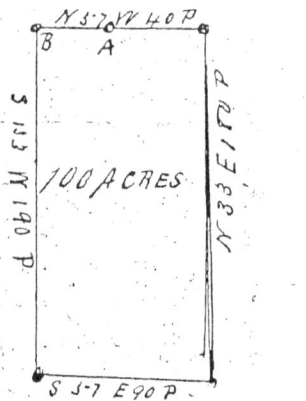

100 parts to one inch

J. STEWART   (page 117)

State of Tennessee, Rhea County
Pursuant to an entry made by James Stewart of No. 264 dated the 10th day of May 1836 for 200 acres of land on Waldens Ridge on the waters of Little Richland

100 parts to the inch

Creek. BEGINNING on a hickory and pine runing North 30° East 292 to a blackoak on Stuarts 1000 acre line; then North 60 West 145 poles along Said line; then South 30 West 145 poles to Lewis Morgans line; then with Said line to the beginning. Surveyed the 3rd day of August 1836. Jesse Thompson, S.R. County Jacob Byerly and James C. Nelson, C.C.

S.B. DYER

State of Tennessee, Rhea County In pursuance of an entry made by Spill Bee Dyer of No. 247, and dated the 5th day of May 1835 for 150 acres of land on the Side of Waldens Ridge to include an improvement made by Nusam Cooper and Massy Duncan, and Said Dyer Still House. BEGINNING on a double chestnut and chestnutoak and runing due North two hundred and twenty poles to a postoak

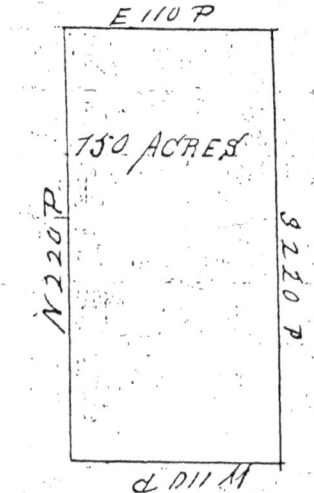

100 parts to the inch

then due East One hundred and ten poles to a blackoak and Maple and Chestnutoak; then South two hundred and twenty poles to a Stake; then West one hundred and ten poles to the beginning and by virtue of a deputation to me given by Crispin E. Shelton Surveyor for Rhea County, I have Surveyed for the Said Dyer the Said 150 acres of land Situated as above lying in Said County on Waters of Piney River. Surveyed the 6th day of May 1836.

Jesse Thompson, Deputy Surveyor for Rhea County
Eli Ferguson and George W. Black, S.C.C.

JAS. STEWART   (page 118)

State of Tennessee, Rhea County
Pursuant to an entry made by James Stewart of No. 273 dated the 28th of July 1836 for 1500 acres of land on the West Side of Big Richland Creek. BEGINNING on a Cucumber tree a corner of a tract of land belonging to Lewis and Washington Morgan runing North 65 E 24 poles to 2 Whiteoaks on the West Side of Richland Creek then due N 140 poles to a long White pine; then N 45 W 800 poles to a Stake; then South 45° W 450 poles to a Stake, then South 45° E 800 poles to a Stake; then South 85 E 280 poles to Lewis Morgans corner, then with his line to the beginning Cucumber tree. Surveyed the 3rd day of August 1836.

Jesse Thompson, Surveyor for Rhea County
James C. Nelson and Jacob Byerly, S.C.C.

(NOTE— The plat on the following page has been reduced to fit the page and a one inch scale added in the upper left corner. The original scale was 100 parts to the inch. A notation in the center of the plat shows that the tract contained "2300 Acres in the whole bounds. 890 Acres older grants.")

100 parts to the inch.

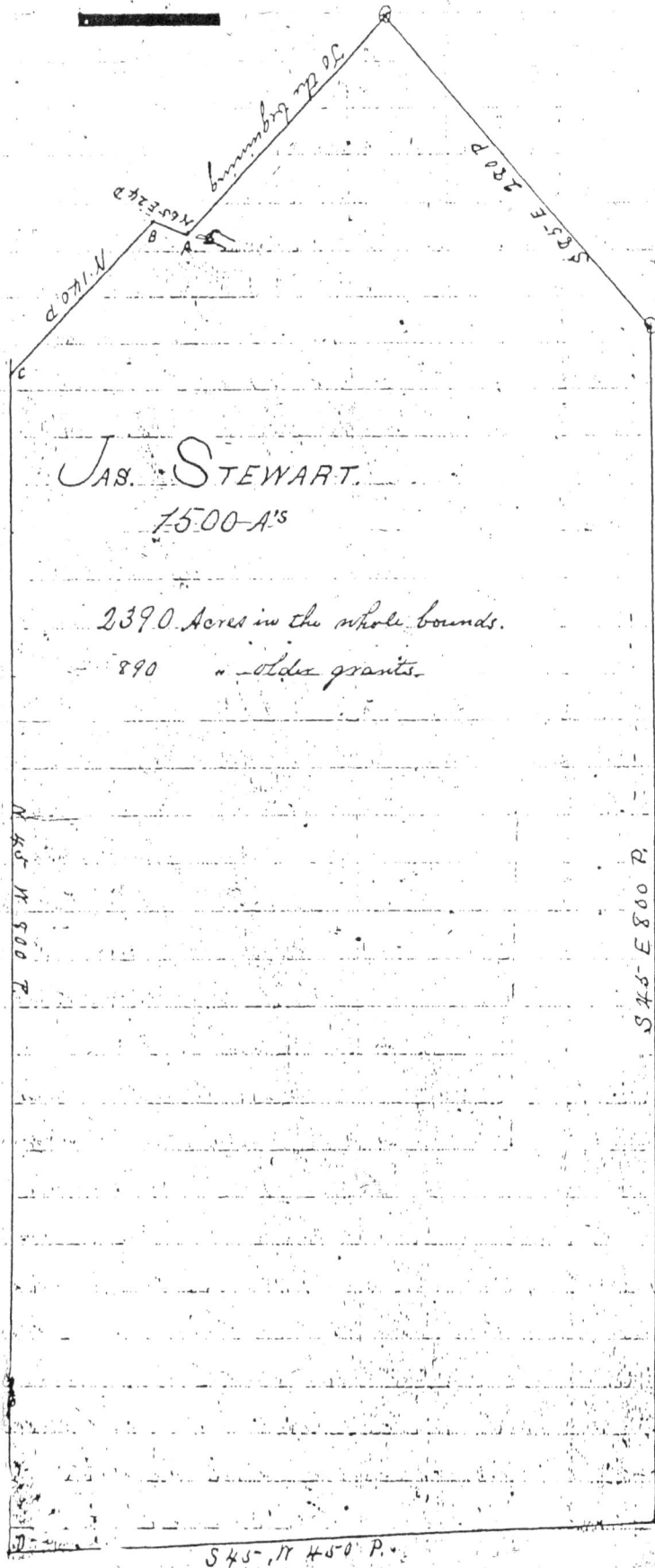

JAS. STEWART.
1500-A's

2390 Acres in the whole bounds.
890 " older grants.

N65-E 24 P
N 160 P
S 45-E 260 P
S 45-E 800 P.
N 45 W 800 P
S 45-W 450 P.

S.B. DYER   (page 119)

State of Tennessee, Rhea County
In pursuance of an entry made by Spills
B. Dyer and John Miller of No. 36 dated
the 30th day of January 1826 for three
hundred and Sixty acres of land in the
fork of Piney River on Waldens Ridge.
BEGINNING on the bluff of Piney on a
white pine marked thus "D" running
North twenty degrees East two hundred
and forty poles to a poplar on a branch
marked thus "D"; then North Seventy degrees West two hundred and forty poles
to a Stake; then South twenty degrees
West two hundred and forty poles to a
Stake; thence South Seventy degrees
East two hundred and forty poles to the
beginning, and by virtue of a deputation
to me given by Crispien E. Shelton Surveyor for Sd County, I have Surveyed for
the Said Miller and Dyer the Said 360

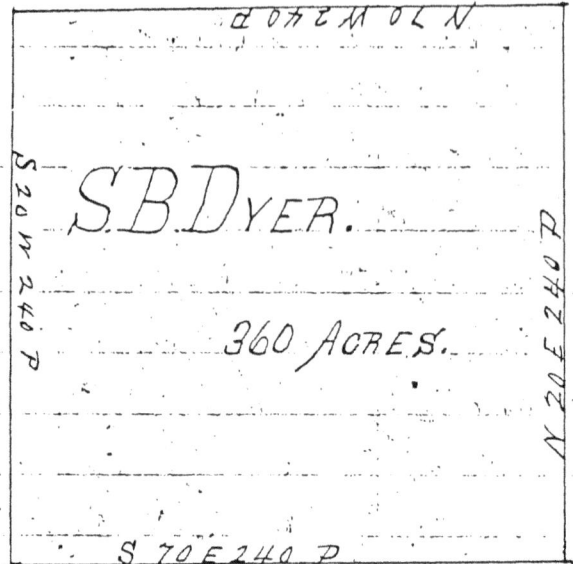

Scale 100 parts to the inch

acres of land as above Situated in Said County in the fork of Piney. Surveyed
the 3rd day of October 1833.   Jesse Thompson, Deputy Surveyor R. County
Benjamin Erwin and Andrew Wassum, S.C.C.

ALLEN LUPER

State of Tennessee, Rhea County
In pursuance of an entry made by Allen Luper of No. 246 and
dated the 27 day of January 1835 for 100 acres of land on Waldens Ridge on the waters of Whites Creek on the South Side of
Bear Creek. BEGINNING on a blackoak on Benjamin C. Gipsons
line of 240 acre entry running 42 poles to a Chestnut Gipsons
corner, then due West four poles to a dead Whiteoak, (corner
of page torn)   (page 120)

100 Acres.

Scale 100
parts to
the inch

then due South with Silas Ivys line crossing Gordons road at
140 poles in all 150 poles to a large hickory tree on a hill;
then due East 40 poles to a Whiteoak and blackgum; then due
North 34 poles to a Whiteoak [marked through] 96 poles to a
chestnut Isham Coxes corner; then due East 20 poles to a poplar; then due North 34 poles to a Whiteoak; then North 72°
West 30 poles to a Stake in a field North 11 deg West to a
Stake 14 poles due East of beginning corner. Surveyed the 12th day of November
1835.   Jesse Thompson, Deputy Surveyor for Rhea County
Isham Cox & Silas Ivy, S.C.C.

JAS. HILTON

State of Tennessee, Rhea County
In pursuance of an entry made by James Hilton in Said County for 200 acres of
land on Waldens Ridge of Cumberland Mountain on Brush Creek a fork of Sale Creek
of No. 192 and dated the 29th day of August 1832. BEGINNING on two postoaks
corner of David Ragsdales 100 acre Survey, running South fifteen degrees East
one hundred and Sixty poles to two postoaks, then North Seventy five degrees East

two hundred poles to a double blackoak on a path; then North fifteen degrees West one hundred and Sixty poles to a Stake; then to the beginning. Surveyed the 18th day of February 1837.

      Jesse Thompson, County Surveyor
David Ragsdale and Charles Pickett [sic]
      Sworn Chain Carriers
James Hilton, Marker

DAVID RAGSDALE (page 121)

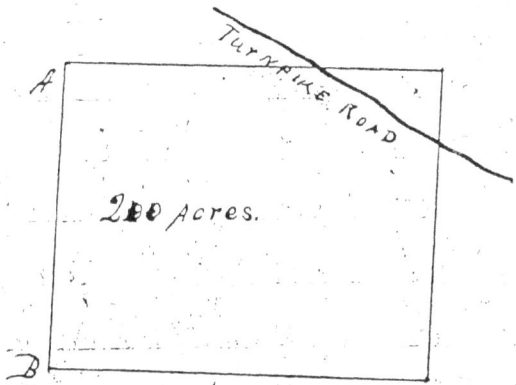

Scale 100 parts in one inch

State of Tennessee, Rhea County
In pursuance of an entry made by David Ragsdale of No. 47 and dated the 7th day of August 1826 for 100 acres of land on Waldens Ridge. BEGINNING on a blackoak Standing on the waters of Richland on the North Side Thedys trace, and on the East Side of an improvement made by David Dane, running North fifteen degrees West one hundred poles to two postoaks on the West side of a branch, thence South Seventy five degrees West one hundred and Sixty poles to a Stake; then South fifteen degrees East one hundred poles to a Stake; thence to the beginning. Surveyed the 8th day of February 1837

      Jesse Thompson, County Surveyor
James Hilton and Charles Pukett [sic], Sworn C.C.
David Ragsdale, Marker

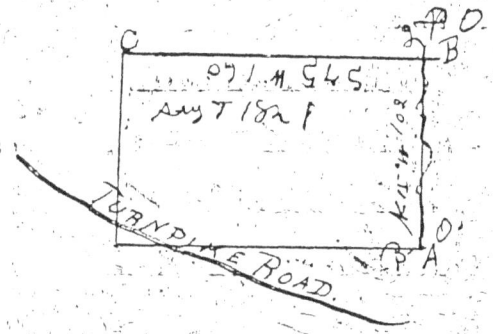

Scale 100 parts to the inch

JNO. HILTON

State of Tennessee, Rhea County
In pursuance of an entry made by John Hilton for 300 acres of land on Waldens Ridge of Cumberland Mountain on the waters of Richland Creek of No. 157 and dated the 4th day of August 1831. BEGINNING on a blackoak on the East line of an entry made by David Ragsdale Known by the name of the Dane place, running North twenty degrees West two hundred and Sixty two poles to two hickory trees; then South Seventy degrees East one hundred and eighty and a half poles to a blackoak and two hickory trees; then South Seventy degrees West with the line (page 122) of Job Romines older entry one hundred and Seven poles to a blackoak Romines corner; then South twenty degrees East two hundred and forty poles to a Stake, then South Seventy degrees West one hundred poles to a Stake; then North twenty degrees West Sixty Six poles to a Stake;

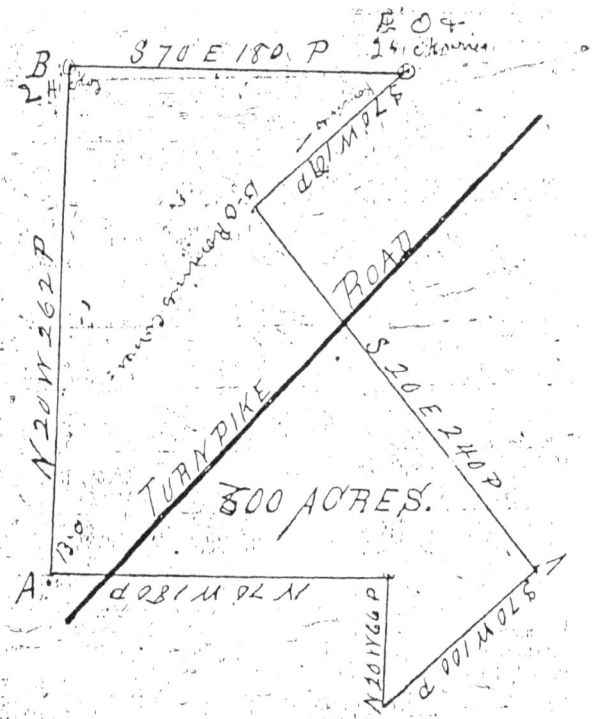

Scale 100 parts to the inch

then to the beginning. Surveyed the 8th day of February 1837.
         Jesse Thompson, Surveyor of Rhea County
David Ragsdale and Chas Pukett, S.C.C.   James Hilton, Marker

W.M. WILSON   (page 122)

State of Tennessee, Rhea County
In pursuance to an entry made by William
M. Wilson for 200 acres of land on Waldens
Ridge of Cumberland Mountain on the West
Fork of Piney of No. 261 dated the 30th
day of March 1836. BEGINNING on a White
pine & blackgum on the bluff running North
fifty five degrees East 160 poles to a
Stake; then North forty five degrees West
200 poles to a Stake; then South 45 East
160 poles; then to the beginning.
Surveyed the 13th day of February 1838.
         Jesse Thompson, S.R. County
Robert Monteith & Robert Roberson
         S.C.C.
A. Gear, Marker
         Scale 100 equal parts to one inch

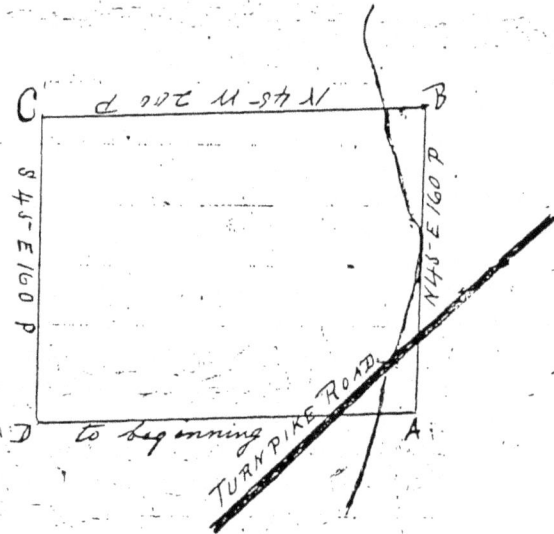

ALEXANDER GEAR   (page 123)

State of Tennessee, Rhea County
In pursuance of an entry made
by Alexander Gear in Said County
of No. 271, and dated the 16th
day of May 1836 for 3000 acres
on Waldens Ridge a Spur of Cumberland Mountain on the waters
of Clear Creek. BEGINNING on a
Chestnutoak, black[oak] and
hickory the begining corner of
James Montgomerys one hundred
acre entry near a clift or ledge
of rocks; running South thirty
degrees West two hundred and
Seventy two poles to a branch
and Chalybeate Spring in the
branch; then crossing another
branch at three hundred poles in
all four hundred and forty two
poles to a hickory and Spanish
oak; then North Sixty degrees
West Seven hundred and Sixty two

Scale 100 equal parts to an inch

poles crossing a West fork of Piney to a Stake; then North thirty degrees East
Seven hundred Sixty two poles to a Stake; then South Sixty degrees East Seven
hundred and Sixty two poles to a Stake; then South thirty degrees West three
hundred and twenty poles to a Stake the beginning. Surveyed the 13th day of
February 1837.   Jesse Thompson, Surveyor of Rhea County
Robert Monteith & Robert Roberson, S.C.C.; A. Gear, Marker

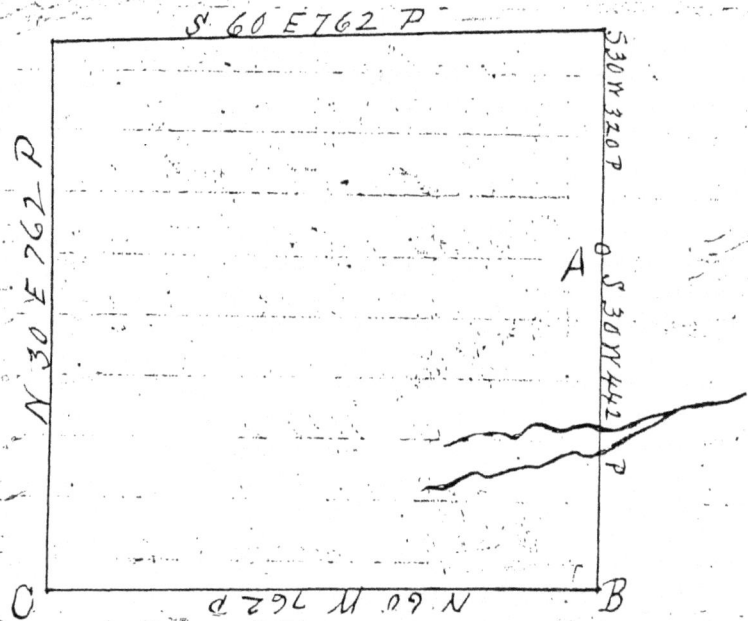

ROBT. QUALLS   (page 124)

State of Tennessee, Rhea County
In pursuance of an entry made by William B.
Smith in Said County of No. 202 and dated
the 17th day of November 1832 for four hundred
acres of land on Waldens Ridge a Spur of Cumberland Mountain. BEGINNING at a blackoak in
the waters of Brush Creek a fork of Sale Creek
on the East Side of an entry made by William
B. Smith the 20th day of August 1832, running
North forty five degrees East 96 poles to a
branch in all three hundred poles to a hickory
and two blackoak trees; then North forty five
degrees West two hundred and thirtees poles
and a half to a Stake, then South forty five
degrees West three hundred poles to a Stake;
then to the beginning. Surveyed the 10th day
of February 1837.
Jesse Thompson, Surveyor for Rhea County
Gatewood Qualls & William Greer, S.C.C.
Henry Miller, Marker
The above certificate of entry is transferred
by assignment by William B. Smith the enterer
to Robert Qualls, and he authorized to obtain
the grant in his own name.

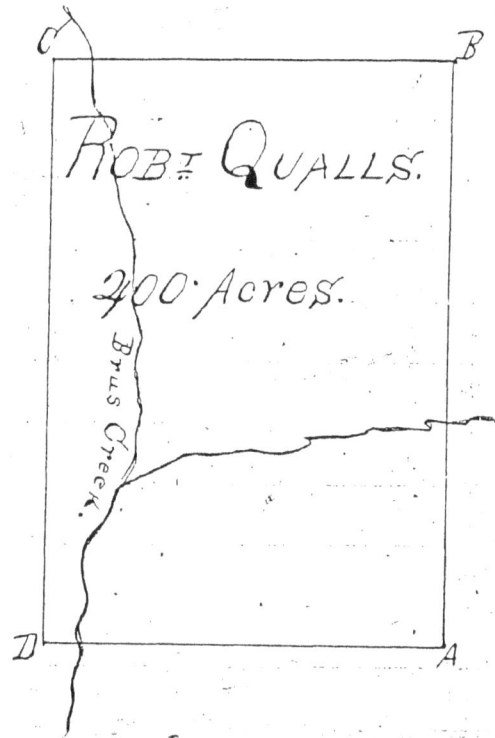

Scale 100 parts to 1 inch

JOHN McCLENDON   (page 125)

State of Tennessee, Rhea County
In pursuance of an entry made by John Ganson of No. 204
for 70 acres dated the 19th day of December 1832, and
transferred by assignment to John McClendon dated the
31 day of December 1832, I have Surveyed for the Said
McClendon the Said 70 acres of land. BEGINNING on a
Whitepine tree on the South Side of the West fork of
Whites Creek running due West forty two poles to a
maple near Sweenys line; then South ten degrees East
one hundred and thirty nine poles to a chestnutoak
tree; then North Seventy five degrees East 119 poles
to a gum tree corner of Archibald D. Paul Survey of
150 acres; then North thirty one degrees West thirty
five poles to John Garrisons line, then with his line
North eighty four degrees West forty two poles to a Whiteoak and Service tree
Garrisons corner, then North fifteen degrees West twenty poles to the beginning,
and by virtue of a deputation to me given by Crispien E. Shelton Surveyor for
Said County, I have Surveyed the above 70 acres of land on Waldens Ridge lying in
Said County of Rhea on the West fork of Whites Creek. Surveyed the 19th day of
May 1834.   Jesse Thompson, Deputy Surveyor R.C.
Hardy Crews & John F. Paul, S.C.C.

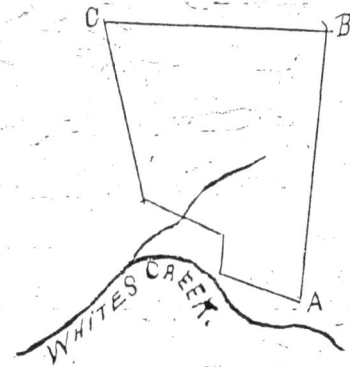

Scale 100 parts to the inch

P.L. PHARRIS   (page 126)

State of Tennessee, Rhea County
In pursuance of an entry made by Peter L. Pharris, Gatewood Qualls, & Henry Miller

in Said County for 5000
acres of land of No. 282
and dated the 2 day of
February 1837.
BEGINNING on a hickory
tree near the corner of
a tract of land entered
by Clark on the waters
of Brush Creek a fork
of Sale Creek running
North twenty degrees
East three hundred and
twenty poles to two
Whiteoaks & hickory,
then North Seventy de-
grees West Seven hundred
and Seventy eight poles
to a blackoak and post-
oak on a ridge; then
South twenty degrees
West fifteen hundred
and forty two poles to
a Stake; then South
Seventy degrees East
Seven hundred and Seven-
ty eight poles to a
Stake; then North twenty
degrees East twelve hun-
dred and twenty poles to
the beginning.
Surveyed the 10 day of
February 1837.
    Jesse Thompson,
        Surveyor of
        Rhea County
James Hilton
William Greer   S.C.C.
Henry Miller, Marker

Scale 200 parts to the inch.

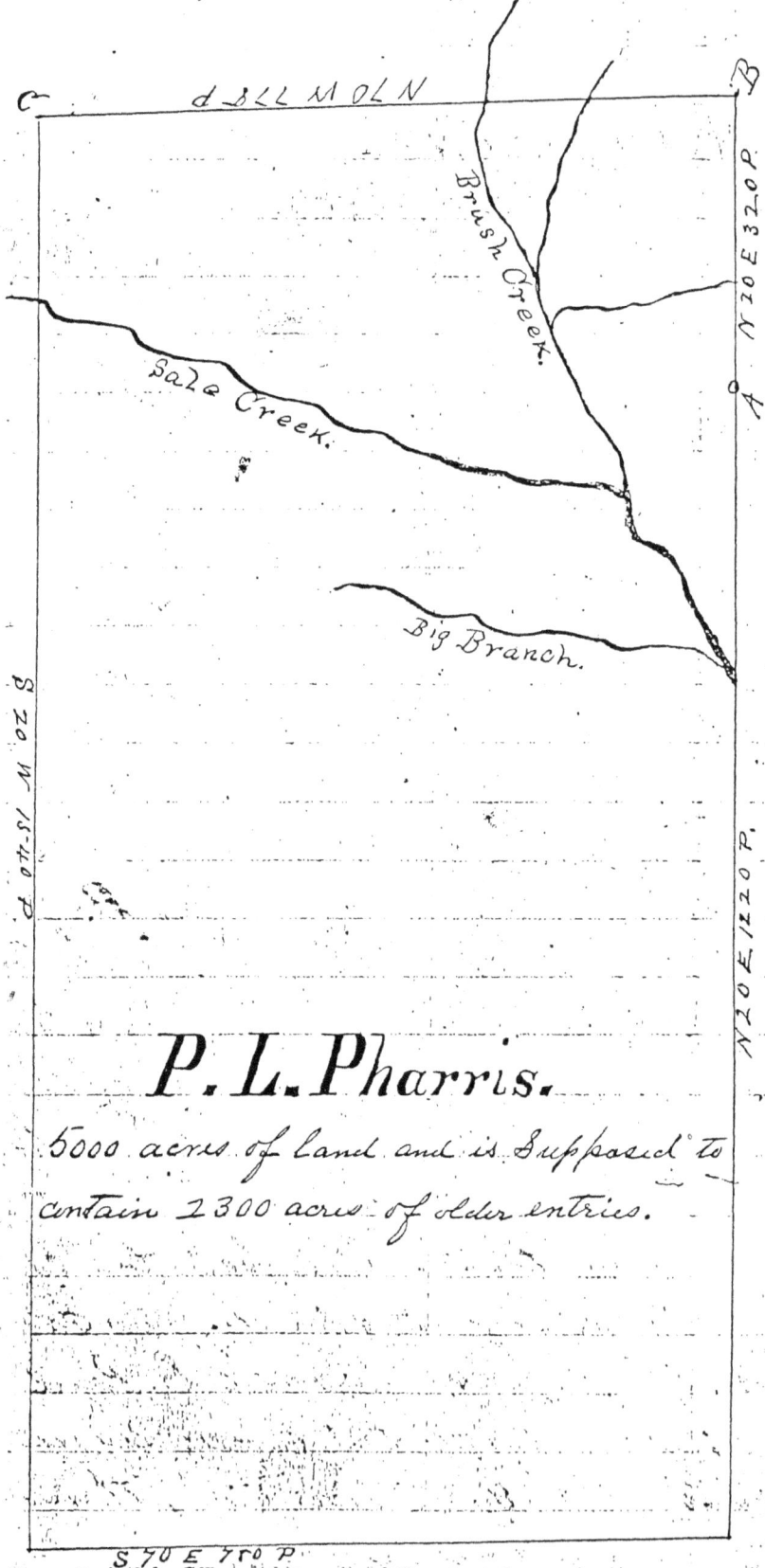

P. L. Pharris.

5000 acres of land and is Supposed to
contain 2300 acres of older entries.

JOB ROMINES (page 127)

State of Tennessee, Rhea County
By virtue of an entry made by Job
Romines in Said County of No. 127
and dated the 17th day of June
1830 for 400 acres of land on
Waldens Ridge on the waters of
Richland Creek on both sides of
Ragsdales turnpike road.
BEGINNING on the South Side of
Said road on a Chestnutoak and
two Sowerwood trees near the bank
of a branch runing North twenty
degrees West one hundred and
Ninety four poles to the turnpike road in all two hundred and
forty poles to a hickory and
chestnutoak trees; then South
Seventy degrees West two hundred
and Sixty Seven poles to a blackoak & postoak; then South twenty
degrees East two hundred and forty
poles to a Stake crossing the road

Scale 100 parts to an inch

106 poles; then North Seventy degrees East two hundred and Sixty Seven poles to
the beginning. Surveyed the 9th day of February 1837.
        Jesse Thompson, Surveyor R.C.
Charles Pickett & James Hilton, S.C.C.   David Ragsdale, Marker

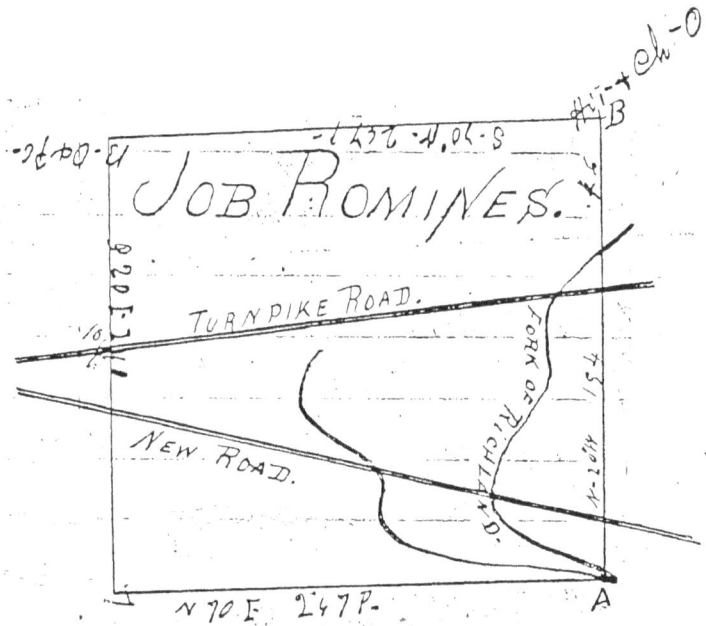

HALEY AND KIMBROUGH (page 128)

State of Tennessee, Rhea County
By virtue of an entry made by Joseph Kimbrough & John Haley in the Entry Takers
office of Said County for five thousand acres of land of No. 248 and dated the
14th day of August 1835, and by virtue of Said entry I have Surveyed the Said
5000 acres lying and being in Said County. BEGINNING on the Northwest corner of
a tract of land now the property of Joel Long by purchase from the heirs of
(blank) Stewart (page 129)
runing South twenty degrees West Sixty poles to a postoak Supposed to be near
the line of a 19000 acre Survey granted by the State of North Carolina to Stockley
Donelson; thence South thirty degrees West with Said line Six hundred and eighty
poles to a Stake in Jesse Thompsons field; then South fifty four degrees West
three hundred and twenty poles to a blackjack tree on the Side of what is called
the Shinbone Ridge; then South fifty degrees West two hundred and Sixteen poles
to a Sycamore tree on a branch of Vans Creek; then South fifty Nine degrees West
one hundred and Sixty three poles to a postoak; then South thirty Six degrees West
two hundred and eighty poles to a Stake oak & blackgum tree; then North fifty two
degrees West one thousand Six hundred and fifty poles to a Stake; then North
thirty eight degrees East one thousand Six hundred and eighty poles to a Stake;
then South fifty two degrees East one thousand Six hundred and fifty poles to the
beginning, containing in the bounds as is Supposed 12,300 acres of older entries
and interference of grants from the State of North Carolina and bounded as is
Supposed by the 19000 acre tract and runing on Waldens Ridge for Compliment.
Surveyed the 23rd day of February 1837.
        Jesse Thompson, Surveyor of R.C.
Mark Bean & John Able, S.C.C.

NOTE— The plat below has been reduced so that it will fit on the page. An inch
scale was added to the upper right corner. B.J.B.

_ 200 equal parts to an inch.

HALEY AND KIMBROUGH

6000. acres but contains as is supposed 12300 acres of
older entries.

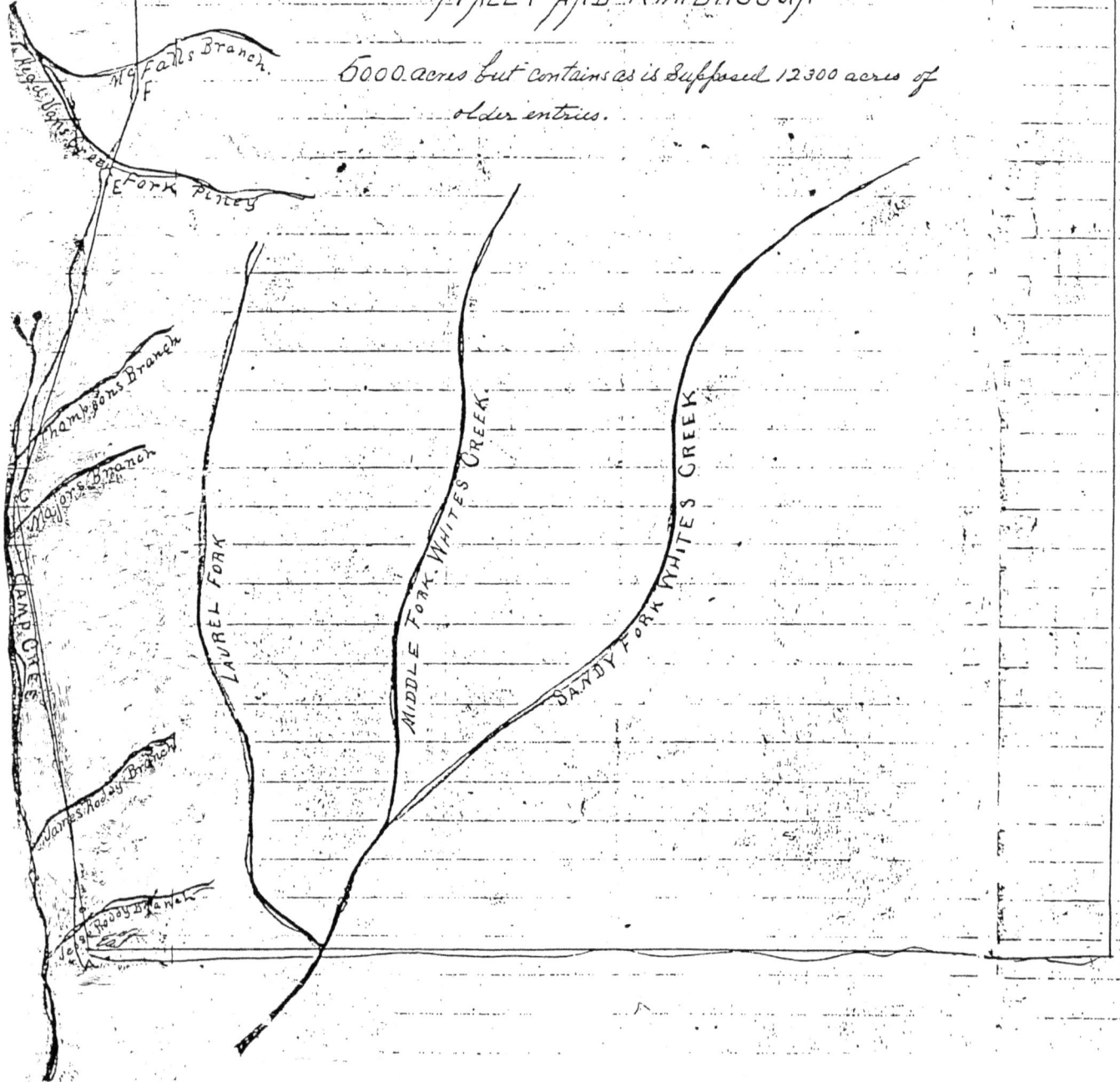

McFalls Branch
F

E Fork Piney

Thompsons Branch

McFork Branch

CAMP CREEK

LAUREL FORK

MIDDLE FORK WHITES CREEK.

SANDY FORK WHITES CREEK

James Roddy Branch

John Roddy Branch

NOTE— The plat below has been reduced so that it will fit on the page. An inch
scale was added to the upper left corner. B.J.B.

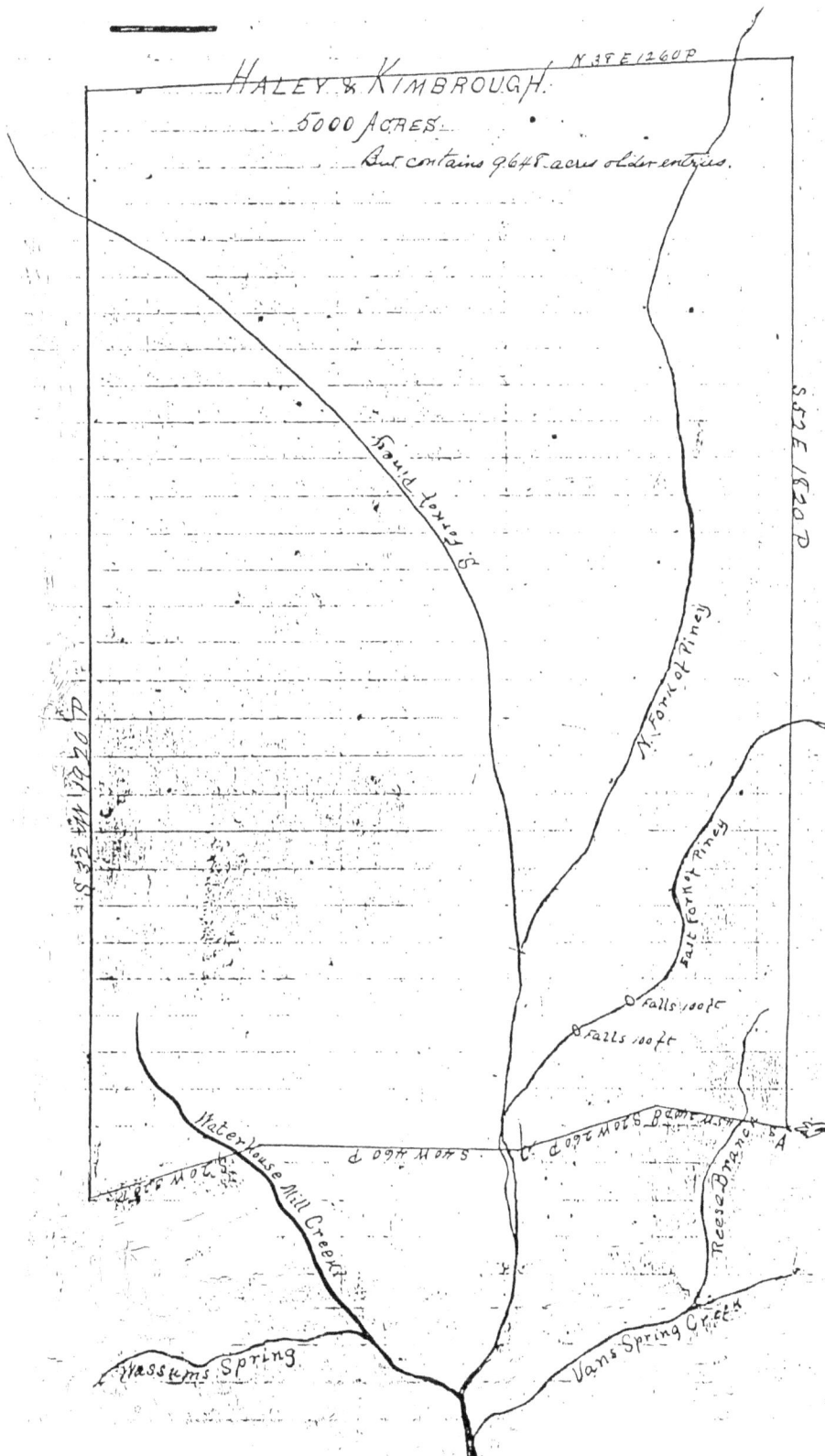

68

HALEY & KIMBROUGH   (page 131)

By virtue of an entry made by Joseph Kimbrough & John Haley in the Entry Takers
office for Said County for 5000 acres of land of No. 249 and dated the 14th day
of August 1835 and by virtue of Said entry I have Surveyed the Said entry of
5000 acres lying and being in Said County. BEGINNING on a whiteoak and blackgum
tree being the South West corner of Entry No. 248 for 5000 acres and Supposed to
be on the line of 19000 acres granted by the State of North Carolina to Stokely
Donelson, and runing South forty five degrees West two hundred and forty poles to
two Small pines on the Shinbone Ridge; then South twenty degrees West two hundred
and Sixty poles to a chestnutoak on a Sluice of Piney River; then South forty degrees West four hundred and Sixty poles to a pine tree on Said ridge; then South
twenty degrees West three hundred and twenty poles to a pine & blackoak on the
Side of the Said Ridge; then North fifty two degrees West nineteen hundred and
twenty poles to a Stake; then North thirty eight degrees East twelve hundred and
Sixty poles to a Stake; then South fifty two degrees East eighteen hundred and
twenty poles to the beginning, containing as is Supposed 9648 acres of older en-
trys and interferences of grants from the State of North Carolina, and bounded as
is Supposed by the 19000 acre tract and runing on Waldens Ridge for compliment
including the forks of Piney and what is called the big falls on the East fork.
Surveyed the 24th day of February 1837. Jesse Thompson, S.R. County
Mark Bean & John Abel, S.C.C.   John Haley, Marker

GATEWOOD QUALLS   (page 132)

State of Tennessee, Rhea County
By virtue of Entry No. 275 dated
6th September 1836, I have Surveyed for Gatewood Qualls two
thousand acres of land in Rhea
County on Waldens Ridge on the
waters of Sale Creek.
BEGINNING on a redoak & hickory
at the foot of the mountain &
on the line of the 19000 acre
tract; then up the mountain
North thirty East with the line
of the 19000 acre along the foot
of the mountain Six hundred and
forty poles to a dogwood & hickory marked "W" on the line of
the 19000 acre tract; then North
Sixty West five hundred poles to
the line of David Ragsdales 800
acre tract; then with his line
and the line of Robert Qualls
1500 acre tract S 30 West Six
hundred and forty poles to a
Stake; then South 60 East five
hundred poles to the beginning.
Surveyed by me this 21 day of
October 1836. Richard Waterhouse
          Deputy Surveyor
John Smallwood & Alex Wilson, S.C.C.   NOTE- Reduced to fit page. B.J.B.

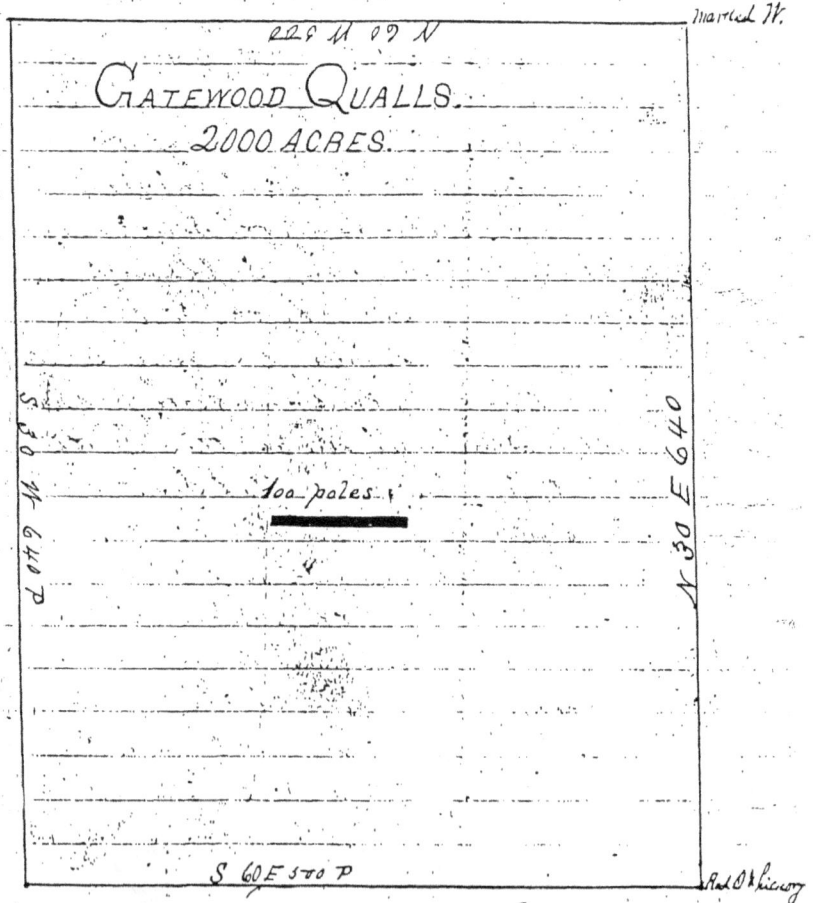

GATEWOOD QUALLS
2000 ACRES.
100 poles

A. GEAR   (page 133)

State of Tennessee, Rhea County
By virtue of an entry of No. 283 dated the 14th day of February 1837 for 5000
acres made by Alexander Gear in Said County on Waldens Ridge of Cumberland Mountain. BEGINNING near the line of Said Gears 3000 acre entry on a double chestnut
and hickory trees running N Sixty degrees West eight hundred and ninety poles
crossing Polecat fork of Piney at 300 poles and the West fork at 660 poles in all
890 poles to a double chestnut and hickory; then South thirty degrees West twelve
hundred and fifty poles to a Stake, then South Sixty degrees East eight hundred
and ninety poles to a Stake; then North thirty degrees East twelve hundred and
fifty poles to the beginning, containing as is Supposed 1953 acres of older en-
trys held by the heirs of Richard G. Waterhouse, Orville Paine & others lying on
the head waters of Richland Creek & Piney. Surveyed the 8th day of March 1837.
            Jesse Thompson, Surveyor R. County
Jacob Gear & Robert Robertson, S.C.C.   Alexander Gear, Marker

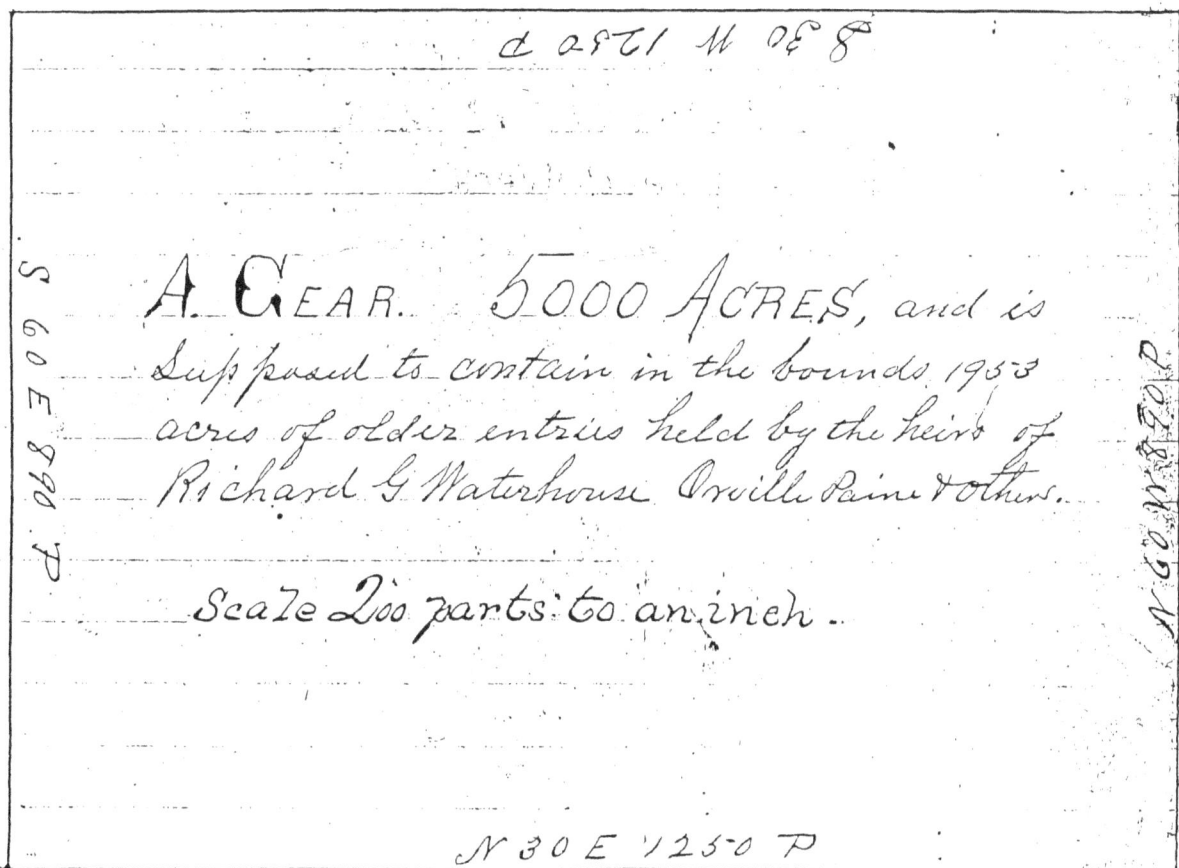

ROBERT QUALLS   (page 134)

State of Tennessee, Rhea County
By virtue of entry No. 239 dated 3rd day of November 1834, I have Surveyed for
Robert Qualls fifteen hundred acres of land on Waldens Ridge in Said County on
the waters of Sale Creek and Richland Creek. BEGINNING on a blackoak and Whiteoak corner to Clarks 400 acres tract; then North thirty East 120 poles to a hickory; then North thirty East 430 poles to a whiteoak marked "W" corner to David
Ragsdales 800 acre tract; then with his line North Sixty West five hundred poles

to a Stake; then South thirty West five hundred and forty poles to a Stake;
then South Sixty East along the line of Clarks 400 acre track of land in all
four hundred poles to the begining. Surveyed by me the 20 day of October 1836.
   Richard Waterhouse, Deputy Surveyor
John Smallwood & Franklin Ragsdale, Chain Carriers; Gatewood Qualls, Marker

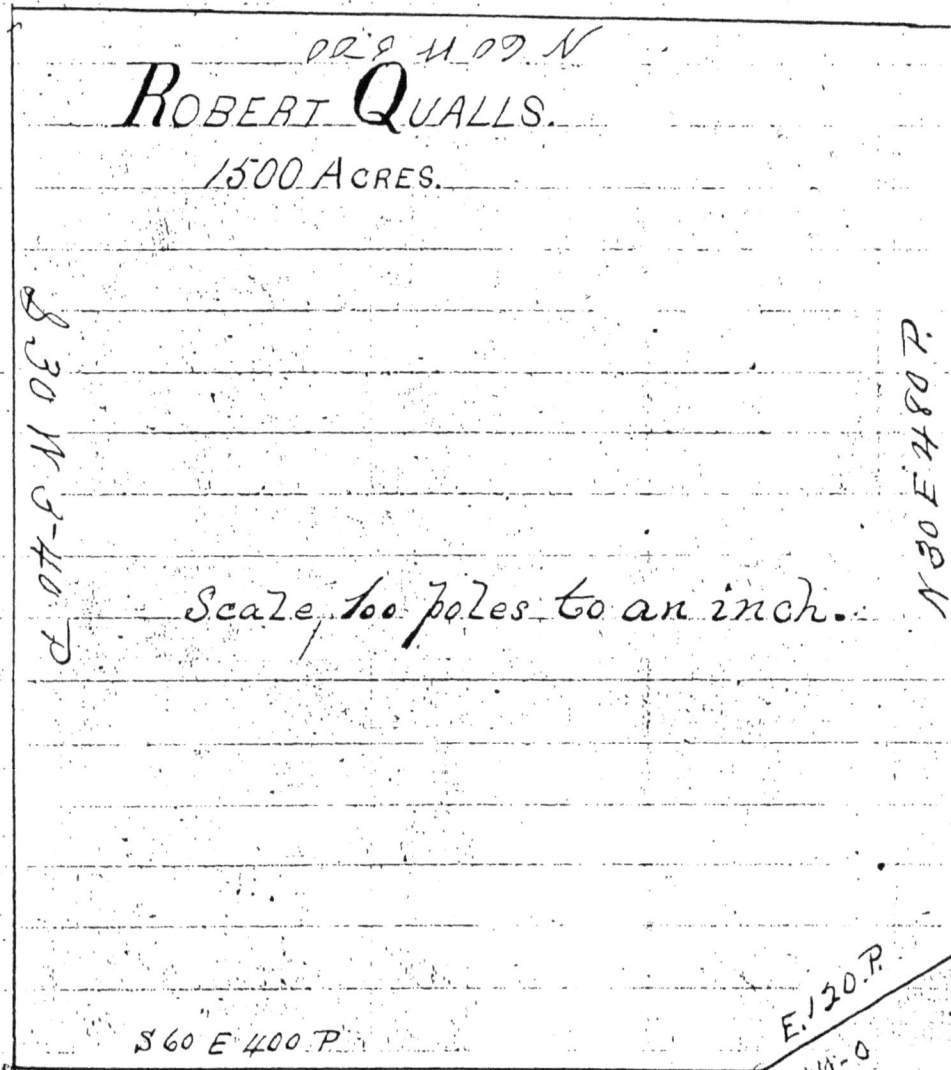

ROBERT ROBERTSON   (page 135)

State of Tennessee, Rhea County
By virtue of an entry made by Robert Robertson in Said County for 5000 acres No.
284 and dated the 14 day of February 1837.   BEGINNING on a double Chestnut and
hickory the Northwest corner of Alexander Gears 5000 acre entry No. 283, running
North thirty degrees East three hundred and twenty poles to three blackoak trees
crossing a laurell branch at 121 poles and crossing the turnpike road at 238
poles; then North Sixty degrees West Seven hundred and twenty five poles to a
Stake; then South thirty degrees West fourteen hundred and fifty poles to a Stake;
then South Sixty degrees East Seven hundred and twenty five poles to a Stake; then
North thirty degrees East eleven hundred and thirty poles to the begining, includ-

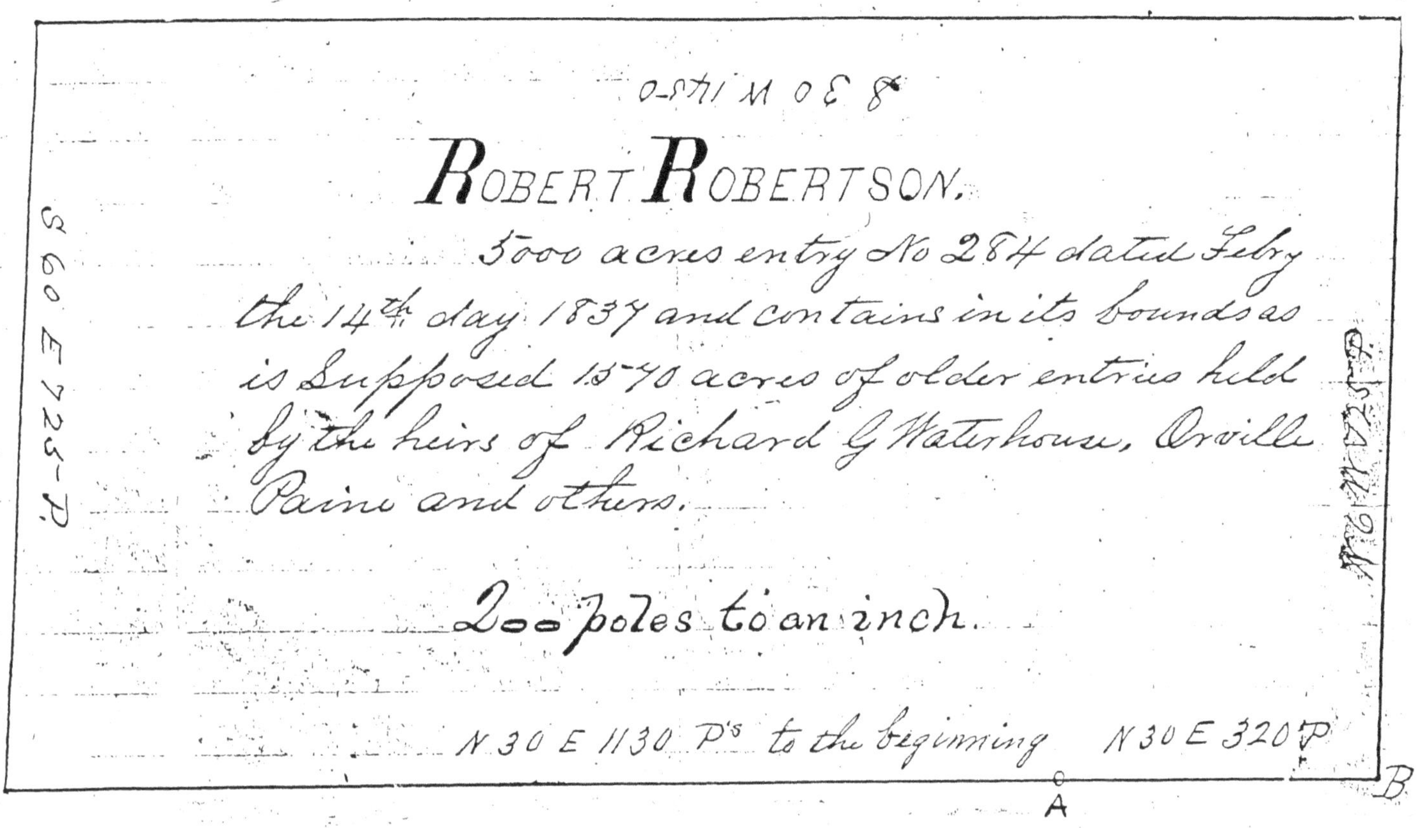

(plat, handwritten survey)

S 30 W 1450

ROBERT ROBERTSON.

5000 acres entry No 284 dated Febry the 14th day 1837 and contains in its bounds as is Supposed 1570 acres of older entries held by the heirs of Richard G Waterhouse, Orville Paine and others.

200 poles to an inch.

N 30 E 1130 P's to the beginning   N 30 E 320 P

S 60 E 725 P

A

B

ing in its bounds as is Supposed 1570 acres of older entries held by the heirs of Richard G. Waterhouse, Orville Paine & others on the waters of Piney & Richland Creek. Surveyed the 8th day of March 1837.
        Jesse Thompson, Surveyor R. County
Jacob Gear & Alexander Gear, S.C.C.   Robert Robertson, Marker

WM GREER   (page 136)

State of Tennessee, Rhea County
By virtue of an entry of No. 279 and dated the 26 day of October 1936 for 2000 acres of land in Said County by William Greer on the Mountain on the waters of Richland Creek. BEGINING on a blackoak the Southwest corner of David Ragsdales 800 acre entry runing South [N written in] thirty degrees East with Said Ragsdales line two hundred and fifty five poles to two postoaks crossing a branch at 120 poles, then North Sixty degrees W nine hundred and forty two poles to a Stake; then North [South written over North] thirty West five hundred & ten poles to a Stake; then South Sixty degrees East Nine hundred and forty two poles to a Stake; then South thirty degrees East two hundred and fifty five poles to the beginning. Surveyed the 11th day of February 1837. Jesse Thompson, Surveyor R. County
Henry Miller & Gatewood Qualls, S.C.C.   William Greer, Marker

NOTE- Plat is on top left of next page.

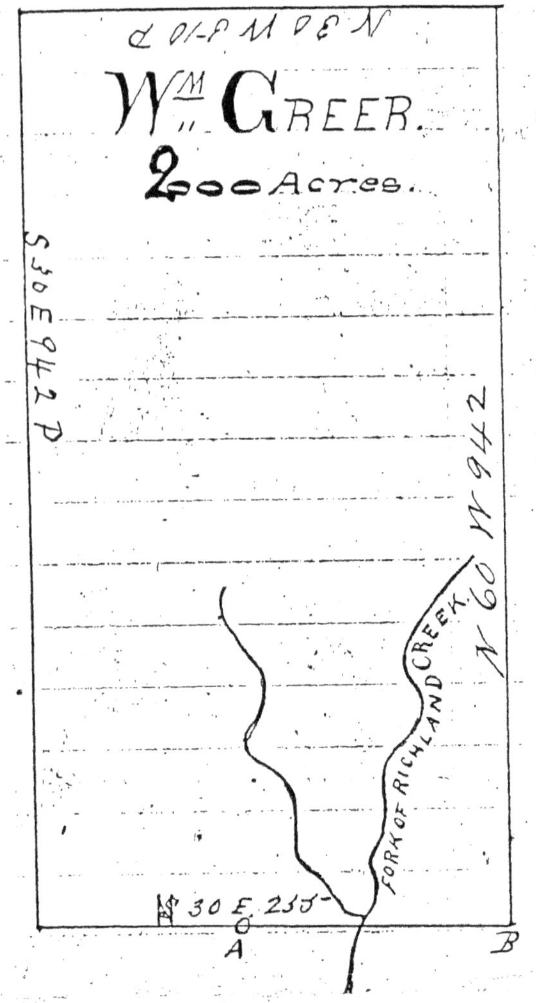

Scale 200 poles to an inch

O. PAINE

State of Tennessee, Rhea County
Pursuant to an entry made by Orville Paine
in the Entry Takers   (page 137)
office for Said State & County for one
thousand acres of land on Waldens Ridge of
Cumberland Mountain in Rhea County filed and
recorded 15th January 1831, I have Surveyed
for said Orville Paine one thousand acres of
land. BEGINNING corner to grant No. 16143
issued by the State of Tennessee on the 26th
day of Sept. 1829 to Orville Paine for 640
acres of land; thence North forty five West
along the line of Said grant 320 poles to a
Stake; thence South 34 W 160 poles to the
Laurel fork of Richland Creek; thence down
Said Creek as it meanders to include the
large falls of Said Creek; thence South 60
East 240 poles to the top of the clift of
what is called the big mountain; thence North
30° E along Said Clift of Said mountain 640
poles to the begining. Surveyed 23rd March
1837.   John Locke, S.D.S.
William Silvey & Bird Paine, S.C.B.

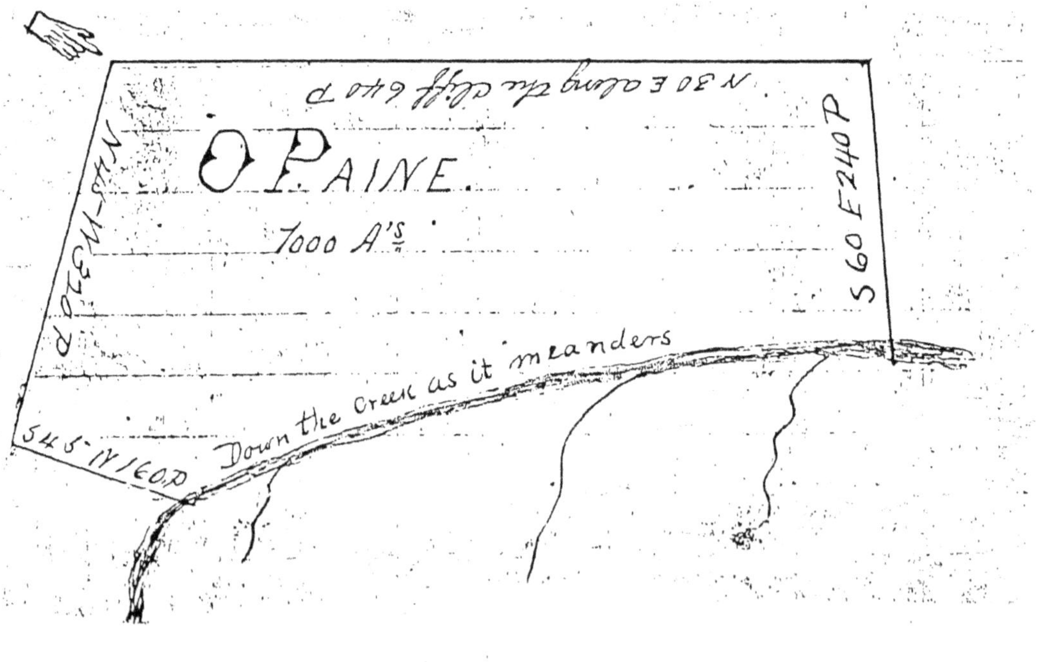

WM SILVEY

State of Tennessee, Rhea County
Pursuant to an entry made by William Silvey in the Entry   (page 139)
Takers office for said County and State for 5000 acres of land on Waldens Ridge
of Cumberland Mountain in Rhea County, dated, filed and issued the 23 day of
February in the year 1837, I have Surveyed for Said William Silvey 3227 acres.
BEGINNING on the Northeast or Second corner of grant No. 16143 granted by the
State of Tennessee to Orville Paine on a Stake near three marked hickorys Standing on the top of the clift; thence along the top of the clift North thirty degrees East one thousand poles to three hickory and two blackoak trees; thence
North eighty three degrees West crossing the polecat fork at four hundred poles
to the bridge fork of Piney at three hundred and twenty poles in all eleven hundred and eighty eight poles to a Stake; then South Seven degrees West two hundred poles crossing Browns fork of Piney to a large blackoak & four Small hickorys

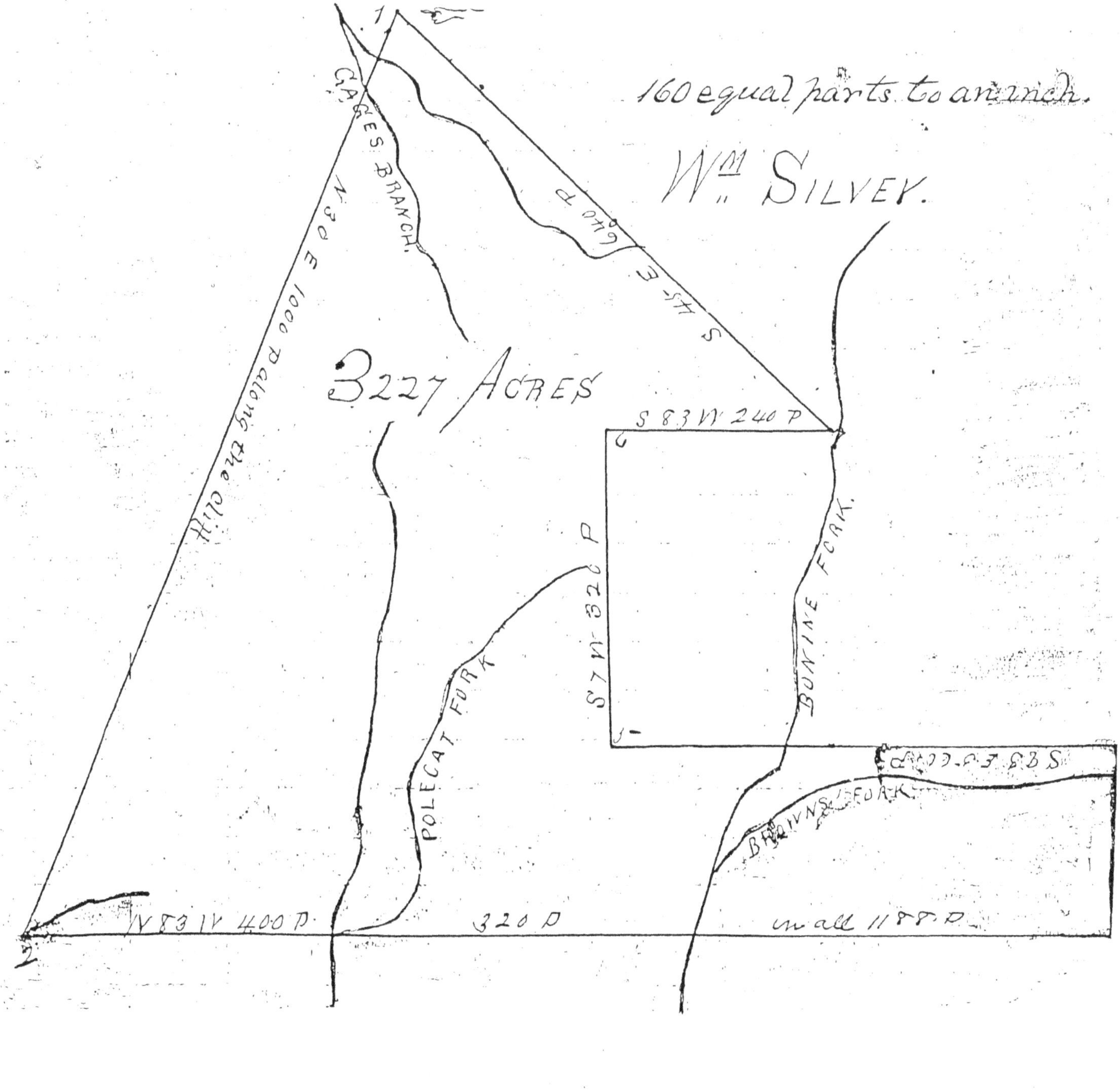

the third or Northwest corner of grant No. 16153 granted by the State of Tennessee to Said Orville Paine; thence with the lines of grant No. 16153 and No. 16152 South eighty three degrees East five hundred & Sixty poles to a Stake; thence with the line of Said grant No. 16152 South Seven degrees West three hundred and twenty poles to two chestnuts and three blackoaks corner to Said grant; thence North eighty three degrees West two hundred and forty poles to five hickory Saplins near Bonines branch and begining corner to Said grant; thence South forty five degrees East three hundred and twenty poles to two whiteoaks and two blackoaks third corner to grant No. 16143; thence South forty five degrees East with the line of Said grant three hundred and twenty poles to the beginning. Surveyed the 21 day of March 1837.   John Locke, S.D.S.
Orville Paine & Bird Paine, S.C.B.

(page 139)

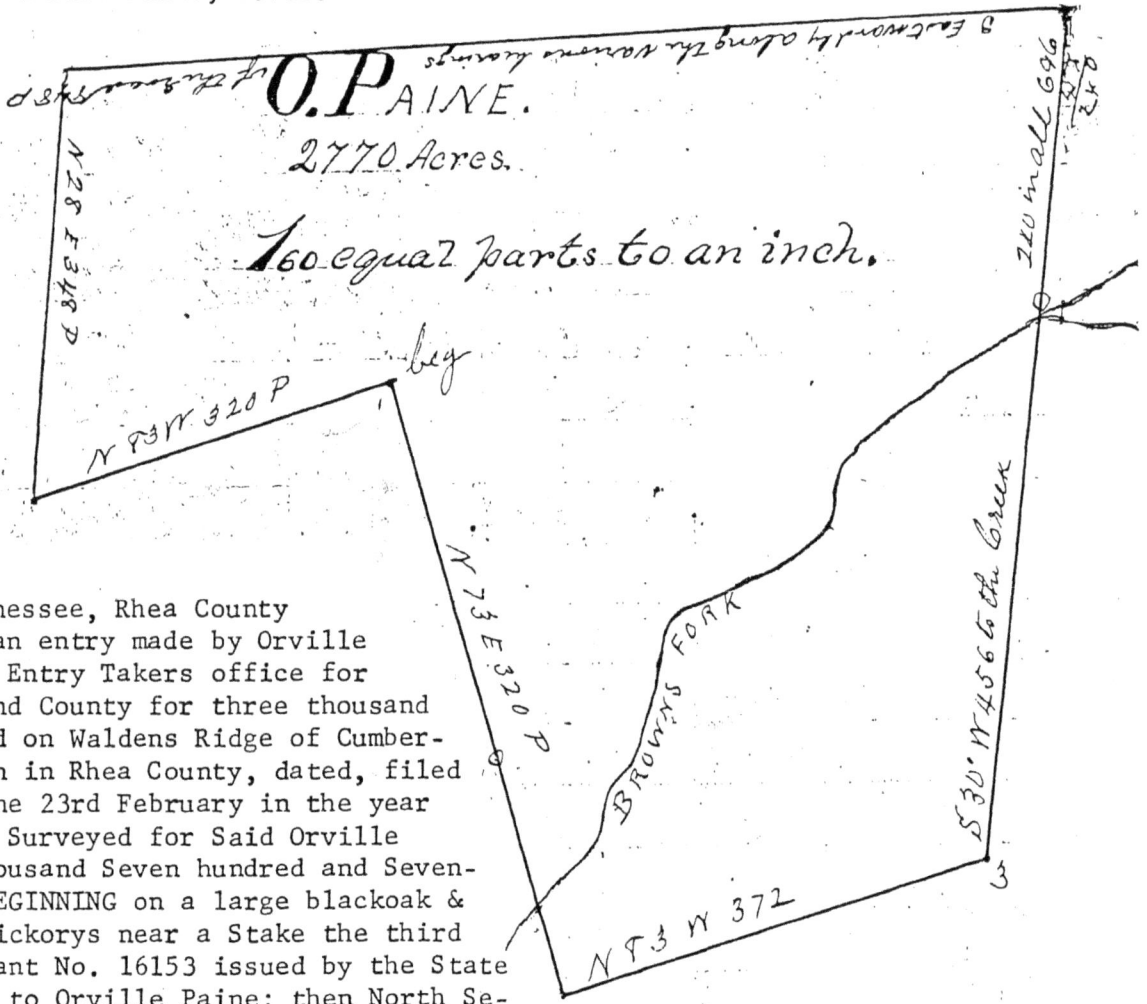

O. PAINE

State of Tennessee, Rhea County
Pursuant to an entry made by Orville
Paine in the Entry Takers office for
Said State and County for three thousand
acres of land on Waldens Ridge of Cumberland Mountain in Rhea County, dated, filed
and issued the 23rd February in the year
1837, I have Surveyed for Said Orville
Paine two thousand Seven hundred and Seventy acres. BEGINNING on a large blackoak &
four small hickorys near a Stake the third
corner of grant No. 16153 issued by the State
of Tennessee to Orville Paine; then North Seven East crossing Browns fork of Piney two hundred poles to a Stake; then North eighty three W three hundred and Seventy two poles to a Stake; thence South thirty West crossing Browns fork of Piney at 456 poles Same course continued in all Six hundred and ninety Six poles to a blackoak, hickory, blackgum and two whiteoaks on Paines Road; then with the different bearings of Said road reduced to a Straight line eight hundred and forty eight poles to five large Spanishoaks; thence North twenty eight East three hundred and forty eight poles to five hickory Saplings begining corner of grant No. 16153; thence with the line of Said grant North eighty three West three hundred and twenty poles to a Stake; thence with the line of Said grant North

(page 140)

Seven East three hundred and twenty poles to the begining. Surveyed the 22nd
March 1837.   John Locke, S.D.S.
William Silvey & Bird Paine, S.C.B.

JESSE THOMPSON

State of Tennessee, Rhea County
Pursuant to an entry made by Jesse Thompson of No. 206 in
the entry takers office for Said County, and dated and
filed the 4th day of February 1833 for 400 acres of land
in Said County on the Side of Waldens Ridge on the waters
of Whites Creek & joining my old Survey for 640 acres.
BEGINNING on a chestnut tree near a bluff of rocks and to
include a Mineral Spring, runing with or near the first
bluff of rocks as you assend the mountain South fifty degrees W two hundred poles to a Stake at the foot of the
bluff of rocks near Thompsons trace,
Then South forty degrees West three
hundred and eighty poles to a
Stake, then South fifty five
degrees East one hundred and
twenty poles to Stake on the
line of a 19000 acre Survey
granted by the State of North
Carolina to Stockley Donelson;
thence with Said line three hundred and Seventy poles to the
line of a 640 acre grant from
North Carolina to Ephraim Dunlap and with Said line due North
one hundred and twenty poles;
thence due East one hundred and
fifty poles to Peter Majors line;
thence with his line fifty five
poles to a Stake; thence with
the line of David M. Roddys 100
acre Survey to the begining, and
by virtue of a deputation to me
given by Crispien E. Shelton,
              (page 141)
I have Surveyed the Said entry
of 400 acres as called for in
Said entry bounded part by natural
boundarys and older titles.
Surveyed the 10th day of October 1835.
        Jesse Thompson, Deputy Surveyor for Rhea County
Absolum L. Thompson & Nathaniel Gillam, S.C.B.

Scale 100 poles to an
inch

JESSE RODDY JR.

State of Tennessee, Rhea County
Pursuant to an entry made by Jesse Roddy Jun. in the Entry office of Said County
for 100 acres of land on the Side of Waldens Ridge of Cumberland Mountain in
Rhea County, filed and recorded 13 day of January 1833. I have Surveyed for Said

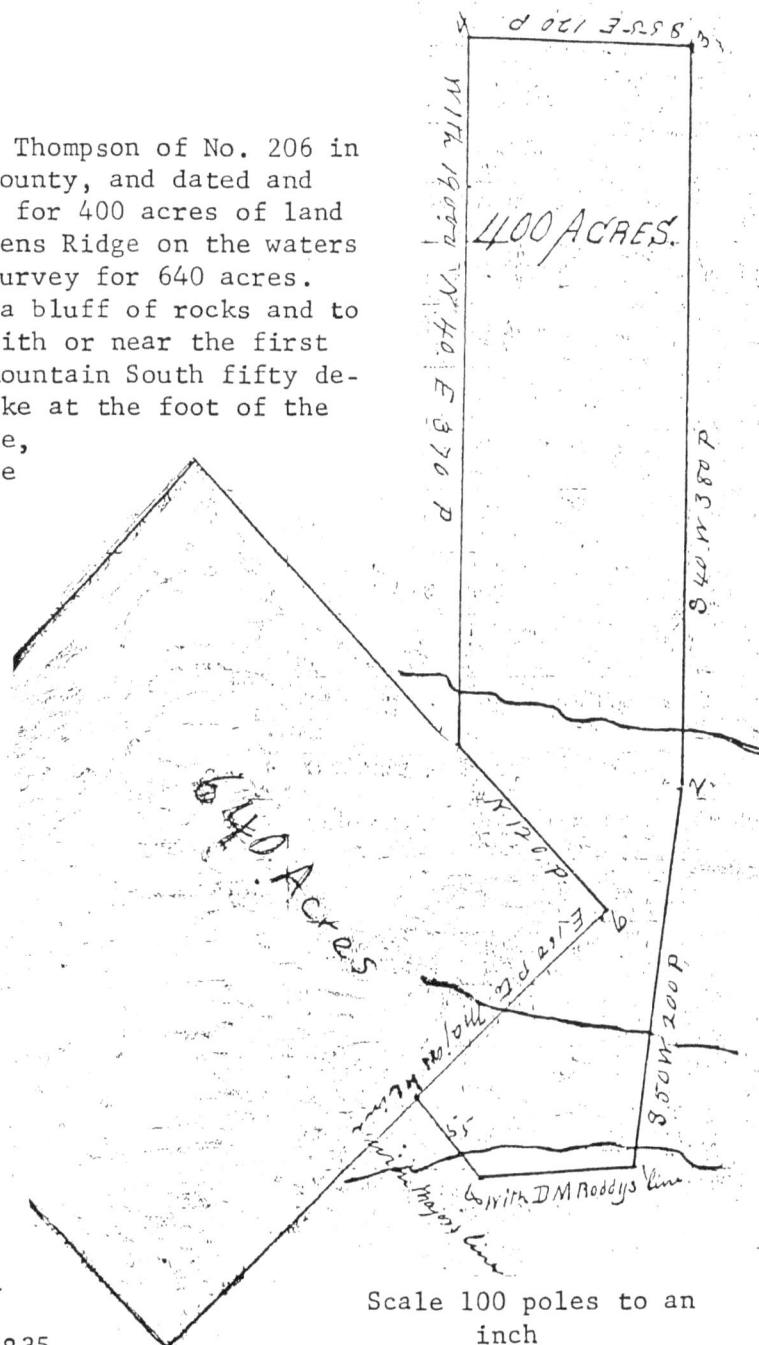

Jesse Roddye Jun. 100 acres of land begining on a whiteoak
and dogwood near a drain runing South thirty five degrees
West 180 poles to a Spanishoak, Sowerwood and blackgum;
then North fifty five degrees West 90 poles to a Stake;
then North thirty five degrees East 180 poles to a Stake;
then to the beginning. Surveyed the 22 day of March 1837.
        Jesse Thompson, Surveyor of Rhea County
Jesse Roddye Sen. & James Roddye, S.C.C.
Jesse Roddye Jun., Marker

                                Scale 100 parts to the inch

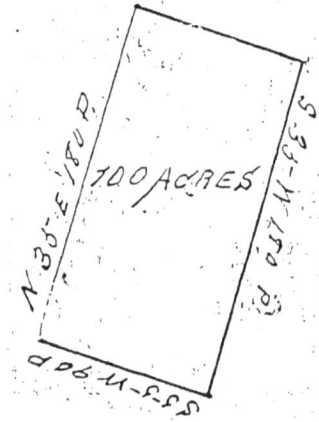

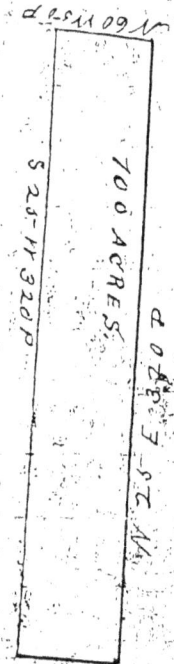

HENRY COLLINS

State of Tennessee, Rhea County
By virtue of an entry made by Henry Collins in the Entry
Takers office for Said County for 100 acres of land on the
waters of Richland Creek and on the Side of Waldens Ridge
of No. 258 and dated the 3rd day of February 1830.
BEGINNING on a postoak and three dogwoods marked as pointers
on Said Collins upper line, running North twenty five degrees
East three hundred and twenty poles with the Supposed line of
the 19000 acre (page torn)   (page 142)
agreed on by Richard Waterhouse & others to a Stake, then
North Sixty degrees West fifty poles to a Stake near a large
clift of rocks; then South twenty five degrees West three
hundred and twenty poles to a Stake; then South Sixty degrees
East fifty poles to the beginning. Surveyed the 6th day of
(page torn) 1837.   Jesse Thompson, S.R.C.
Robert Locke & John Ferguson, S.C.B.

                                        Scale 100 parts
                                          to the inch

W.B. GORDON

State of Tennessee, Rhea County
In pursuance of an entry made in the
Entry Takers office of Rhea County by
William B. Gordon of No. 171 for 320
acres of land on Waldens Ridge and waters of Piney & Whites Creek and dated
the 2nd day of November 1831.
BEGINING on two whiteoaks marked W.B.G.
on a ridge runing North 36° East twenty
Six poles to a Stake on John S. Nelsons
line; then East one hundred and forty
two poles to a chestnut Nelsons corner;
then North one hundred and Sixty poles
to a whiteoak & hickory Nelsons corner;
then South forty five degrees East two
hundred and eighty poles to a whiteoak
near the wagon road; then South thirty
Six degrees West two hundred poles to a
Stake; then to the beginning.
Surveyed the twenty eighth day of Sept 1833.
Thompson Daniel & John Harvey, S.C.B.

                    Scale 100 parts to one inch

                    Jesse Thompson, Deputy Surveyor
                              for Rhea County

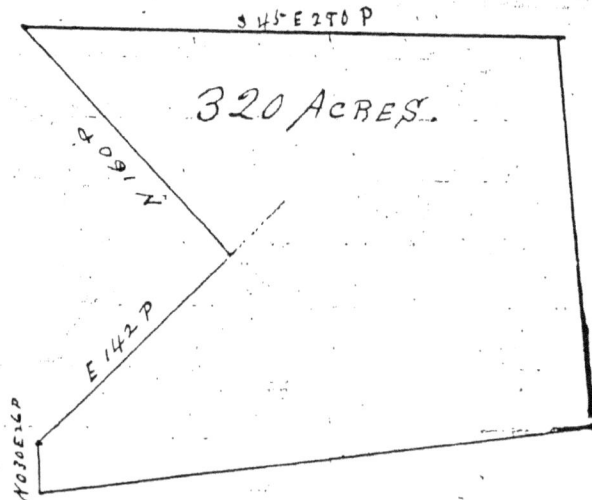

SWAN & GARNER   (page 143)

State of Tennessee, Rhea County
By virtue of an entry made in the Entry Takers office
of Rhea County for 200 acres of land on Waldens Ridge
of No. 72 dated the 4th day of September 1827.
BEGINNING on the waters of Sandy Creek a fork of
Whites Creek on a forked dogwood and Spanishoak running North thirty degrees West one hundred and Sixty
poles to a whiteoak; then North Sixty degrees East
two hundred poles to a Stake; then South thirty degrees East one hundred and Sixty poles to a Stake;
then to the beginning. Surveyed the 11th day of
November 1835.   Jesse Thompson, S.R.C.
Silas Ivy & Allen Luper, S.C.C.

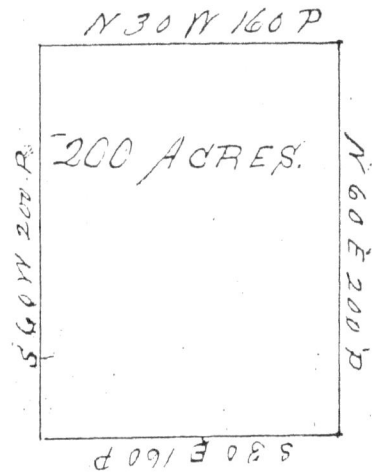

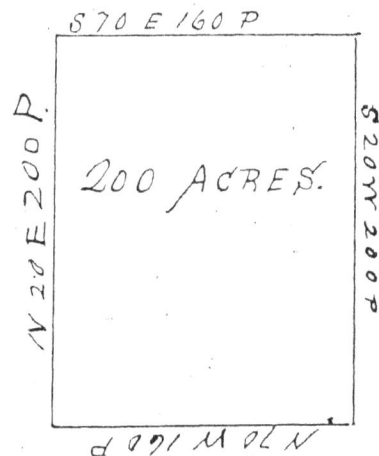

100 equal parts to one inch

GARNER AND SWAN

State of Tennessee, Rhea County
In pursuance of an entry made in the Entry Takers office of Said County of No. 73 dated the 4th day of
September 1827 for 200 acres of land by William Garner and Thomas B. Swan, I have Surveyed the Said two
hundred acres on waters of Otter Creek. BEGINNING
on two chestnutoaks trees runing South Seventy degrees East one hundred and Sixty poles to a whiteoak
and dogwood and blackgum; then South twenty degrees
West two hundred poles to a whiteoak; then North
Seventy degrees West one hundred and Sixty poles to
a Stake; then North twenty East to the beginning.
Surveyed 11th day of November 1835.
        Jesse Thompson, S.R.C.
Silas Ivy & Allen Luper, S.C.C.

100 equal parts to 1 inch

JAMES MONTGOMERY   (page 144)

State of Tennessee, Rhea County
By virtue of an entry made in the Entry Takers office of
Said County of No. 263 dated the 29th day of April 1836
for 100 acres of land by James Montgomery on the waters
of Clear Creek. BEGINNING on a chestnutoak, blackoak,
and hickory at the foot of the ledge of rocks, runing S
thirty degrees West one hundred poles to a blackoak
Standing on a ledge of rocks; then South Sixty degrees
East one hundred poles to a Stake on the line of the
19000 acre Survey; then North thirty degrees East with
Said line one hundred and Sixty poles to a Stake; then
North Sixty degrees West one hundred poles to a Stake;
then South thirty degrees West Sixty poles to the beginning. Surveyed the 22nd day of September 1837.
        Jesse Thompson S.R.C.
Henry Henry & Harvey Montgomery, Sworn C.C.

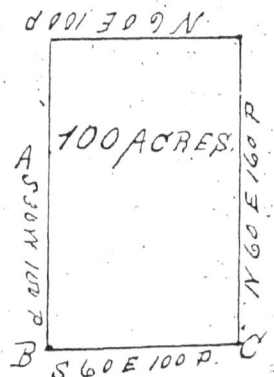

100 equal parts in 1 inch

M. THOMPSON

State of Tennessee, Rhea County
In pursuance of an entry made in the Entry Takers office of Said Rhea County of No. 255
dated the 11th day of December 1835 for 200
acres of land by Moses Thompson, I have Surveyed the Said 200 acres. BEGINNING on Nelsons and Gordons corner on two whiteoaks
running East five poles to the line of Cirus
Waterhouse 170 acre; then due North with Said
line Sixty two poles to Waterhouses corner;
then one hundred & Six poles to Garrison Creek
one hundred and Six poles to Coal Creek in
all two hundred and twenty two poles to two
Small whiteoaks and   (page 145)
blackgum on the line of Waterhouse 421 acre
entry, then North thirty degrees West with
Said line to a blackoak marked "W" on David
Knoxes trace Seventy four poles; then North
Seventy deg. West eighty eight poles to
three hickorys; then North Sixty deg. West
fifty Seven poles to two whiteoaks; then
South thirty deg. West thirty one poles to a
whiteoak and dogwood; then South twenty deg.
East one hundred and fifty two poles to two

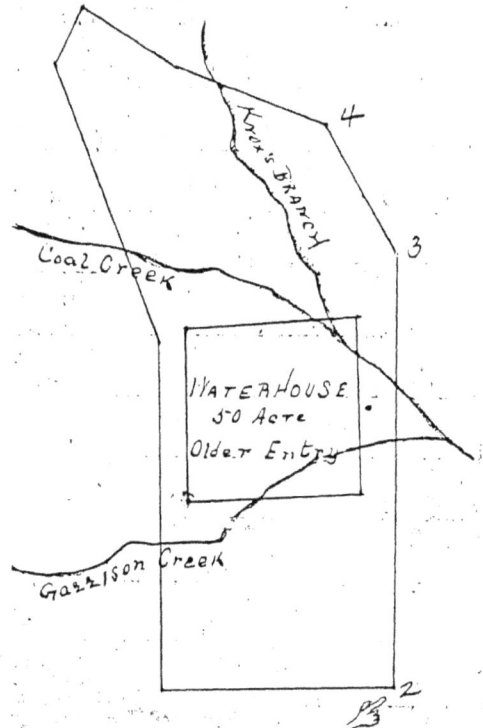

100 equal parts to the inch

hickory trees, then due South crossing Garrisons fork of Whites Creek one hundred
and eighty poles to John Nelsons line, then East to the begining. Surveyed the
3rd day of October 1837.   Jesse Thompson, S.R.C.
Samuel Dudley & Moses Thompson, S.C.B.

JAS. C. BEAN

State of Tennessee,
        Rhea County
In pursuance of an entry
made by James C. Bean of
No. 293 and dated Sep-
tember 19th 1837 for
1000 acres of land
on the side
of Waldens
Ridge.
BEGINNING
on an old
poplar Stump and
Small Sycamore Sup-
posed to be the be-
ginning of the Nine-
teen Thousand acre
Survey; thence S 42° W
417 poles to the beginning
corner of an entry made by
John Haley

(page 146)

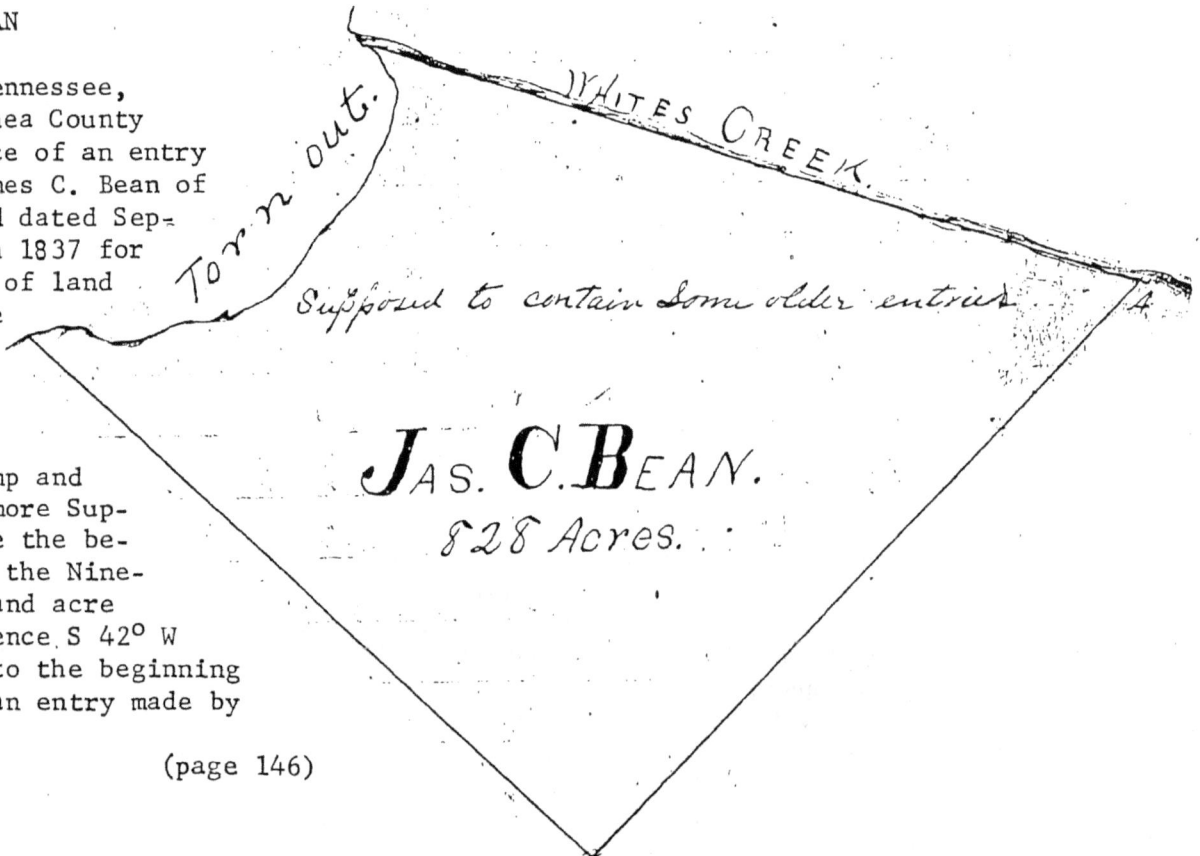

and Joseph Kimbrough No. 248; thence North 48° West 401 poles crossing a Small creek to a blackoak; thence N 80° E 132 poles to a blackoak near the North bank of a Small creek; thence due North 70 poles to Whites Creek; thence with Said Creek to the beginning. Surveyed the 29th day of January 1838.

      Alfred Collins, S.R.C.

Samuel Dotson & James C. Bean, S.C.C.   Jesse Thompson, Marker

WM. COMPTON (page 146)

State of Tennessee, Rhea County
In pursuance of an entry made by William Compton of No. 294 and dated February 12th 1838
for 100 acres of land. BEGINNING on a poplar
tree on a path that runs along the back valley
South 60° East 22 poles to a Small Sassafras
on the top of the Shinbone Ridge; thence North
30° East along the top of the Shinbone 234
poles to a Small blackjack near a blackjack
corner of Robert Mitchell; thence North 60°
West crossing the Valley 60 poles to chestnut tree on the Side of the Mountain; thence
South 25° West with a line of Henry Collins
entry No. 258, 234 poles to a Stake on Said
Collins line, thence South 60 East 18 poles
to the beginning. Surveyed February 13th
1838.   Alfred Collins, S.R.C.
Peter W. Miller & Isaac Thompson, S.C.C.
William Compton, Marker

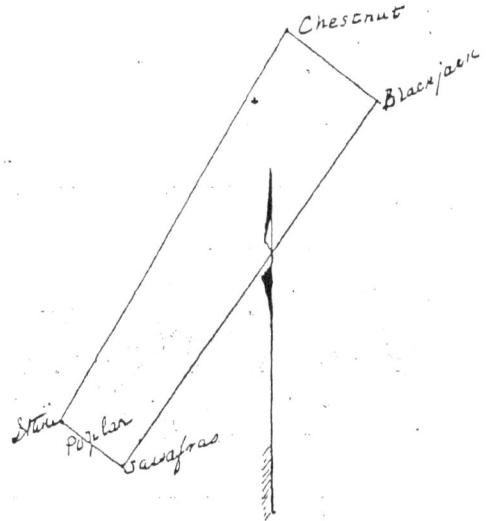

Scale 100 poles to the inch

RICHARD WALKER (page 147)

State of Tennessee, Rhea County
In pursuance of an entry made by Richard Walker of No. 281 & dated January 18th
1837 for five hundred acres of land lying on the face of the mountain and on the

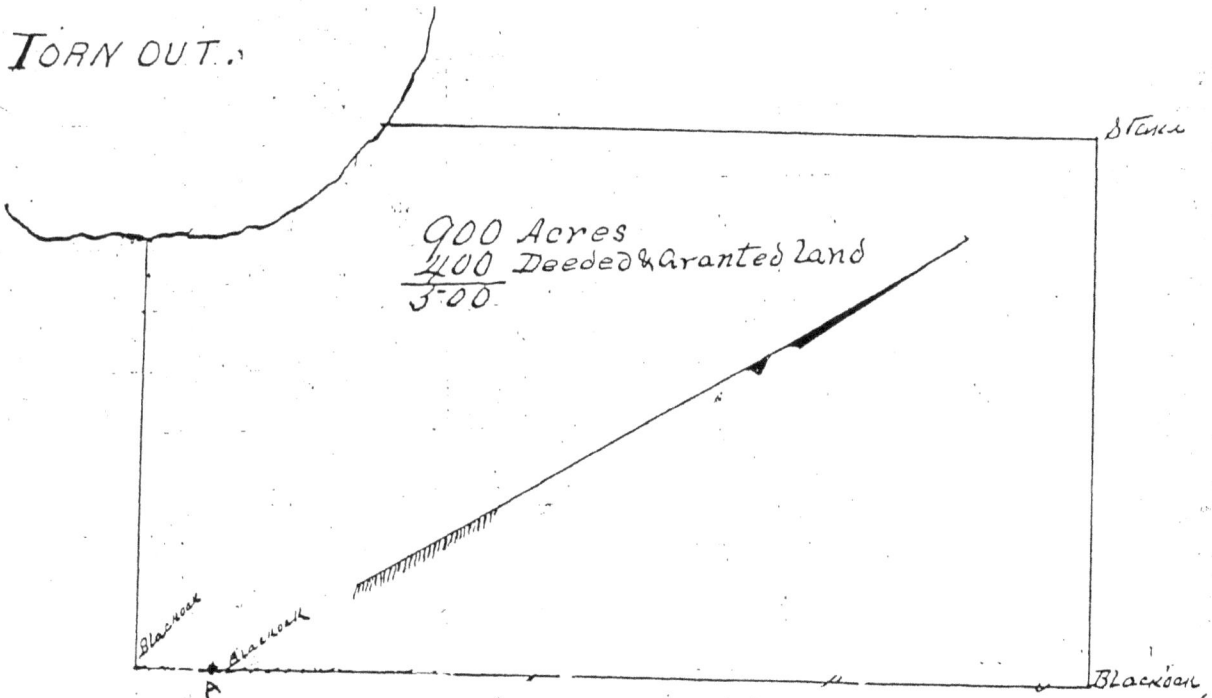

TORN OUT.

900 Acres
400 Deeded & Granted land
5·00

head of Clear Creek. BEGINNING on a large blackoak at the foot of the mountain; thence South 30 West with a Supposed line of the 19000 acre Survey 32 [poles] to a blackoak bush; thence North 60 West 284½ poles to a blackoak at the foot of the mountain; thence South 30 West with the foot of the mountain and a Supposed line of the 19000 acre Survey crossing Clear Creek 474 poles to the beginning. Surveyed February 10th 1838.   Alfred Collins, S.R.C.
Jesse Rector & Alexander Houlpk, S.C.C.   Richard Walker, Marker

G.W. BLACK

(page 143)

State of Tennessee, Rhea County
In pursuance of an entry made by George W. Black of number 296 and dated March 31st 1838 for one hundred acres of land in Said County in district number 4 at the foot and on the Side of Waldens Ridge on the head waters of Clear Creek. BEGINNING on a postoak in a hollow; thence North Seventy degrees West Sixty poles to a hickory on the Side of the Mountain; thence North twenty degrees East crossing Beaties turnpike road at eighty Six poles in all one hundred & Seventy eight poles to a chestnutoak on the Side of the mountain; thence South Seventy degrees East ninety poles to a Stake, thence South twenty degrees West one hundred and Seventy eight poles to a Stake; thence North Seventy degrees West twenty poles to the beginning. Surveyed April 9th 1838.
        A. Collins S.R.C.
Henry H. Miller & Charles Thurman, S.C.C.   G.W. Black, Marker

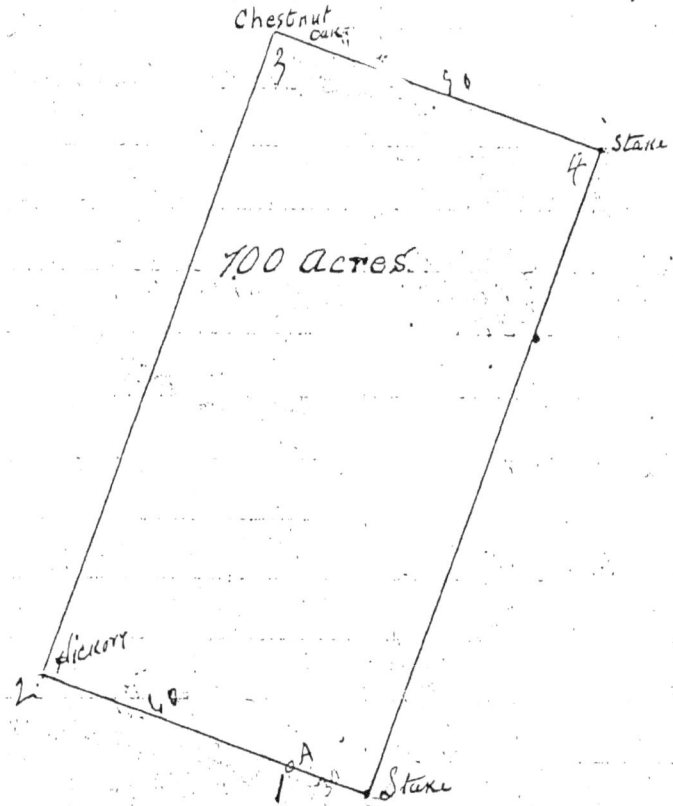

Z. REED

(page 149)

State of Tennessee, Rhea County
In pursuance of an entry made by Zebulon Reed of No. 298 and dated April 21st 1838 for 46 acres of land in Said County on the Side of Waldens Ridge lying on the branch above Howertons Mill. BEGINNING on an oak tree corner to Mandy E. Howertons; thence North 60° East 18 poles to a postoak; thence North 26° East 40 poles to a Blackjack and redoak; thence North 66 West 36 poles to a pine; thence North 74 West 26 poles to a chestnutoak; thence North 71 West 40 poles to a Stake; thence South 41 West 40 poles to a chestnutoak; thence South 22 East 40 poles to a poplar; thence South 80½ East 16 poles to two blackoaks; thence South 54 East 48

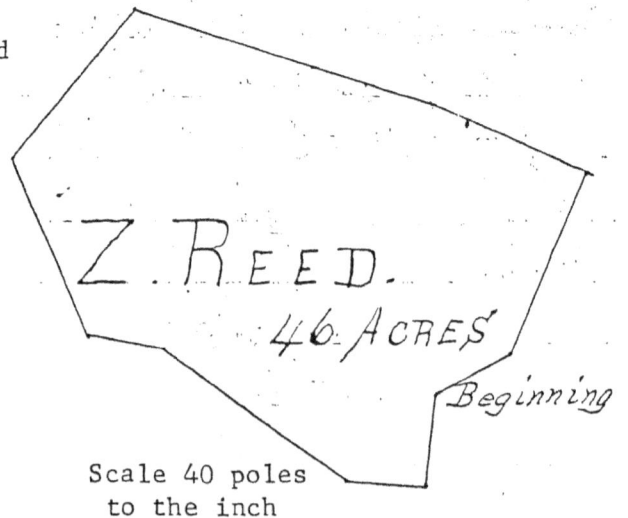

Scale 40 poles
to the inch

poles to a hickory bush; thence South 87 East 16 poles to a hickory on M. Howertons line; thence with his line to the beginning. Surveyed 21st 1838.

Alfred Collins, Surveyor of Rhea County

James P. Collins & Henry Collins, S.C.C.   Zebulon Reed, Marker

ORVILLE PAINE

By virtue of an entry made by Orville Paine in the Entry Takers office in Rhea County dated & issued the 28 day March in the year 1837, I have Surveyed for Sd Orville Paine two hundred and Sixty acres of land lying and being in Rhea County Tennessee on Waldens Ridge of Cumberland Mountain on the waters of Richland Creek.

BEGINNING on a hickory, whiteoak & 2 blackoaks corner to grant No. 16143 issued by the State of Tennessee on the 26th   (page 150) September 1829 to Said Orville Paine for 640 acres; thence South 30° West along the top of the mountain 320 poles to a Stake; thence South 60 East crossing Gages Branch 160 poles to a Stake on the top of the first or little mountain; then along the top of the Sd first or Little Mountain North 30 East 200 poles to 3 Spanishoaks & Sowerwood corner to Franklin & Newton Lockes land; thence with the line of Sd Lockes grant No. 54 West to the beginning. Surveyed 29th March 1837. Jesse Thompson, Surveyor for Rhea County by his Special Deputy John Locke William Silvey & Bird Paine, Sworn C.B.

THOMAS IVES

By virtue of an entry made by Thomas Ives in the Entry Takers office in Rhea County dated and issued the 28th day of March in the year 1837, I have Surveyed for Said Thomas Ives 3500 acres of land lying and being in Rhea County Tennessee on Waldens Ridge of Cumberland Mountain on the waters of Richland Creek. BEGINNING on Blackoak, hickory, blackgum and two whiteoaks on the South Side of Piney trace and corner to Said Paines entry of No. 286; thence South 30° West 749 poles to a Stake; thence South 60° East 749 poles to a Stake, thence North 30° East 749 poles to a Stake; thence North 60° West to the beginning. Surveyed 29th March 1837. Jesse Thompson, Surveyor for Rhea County by his Special Deputy John Locke William Silvey & Bird Paine, S.C.B.

82

JESSE RODDYE SEN   (page 151)

State of Tennessee, Rhea County
In pursuance of an entry made by Jesse Roddye
Senior of No. 291 and dated March 24th 1837 for
200 acres of land. BEGINNING on a Spanishoak
on the top of the pine ridge; thence South 13°
West 41 poles to a pine; thence South 33° West
33 poles to a blackgum; thence South 174 poles
to a blackoak on Jesse Roddys line, thence West
with his line 169 poles to a Stake; thence
North 24° East 320 poles to a whiteoak beginning corner to Jesse Roddy Junr 100 acre tract;
thence South 52 East 83 poles to the beginning.
Surveyed August 4th 1838.
Alfred Collins, Surveyor for Rhea County
Joseph Long & Jesse Roddy Junr, S.C.B.

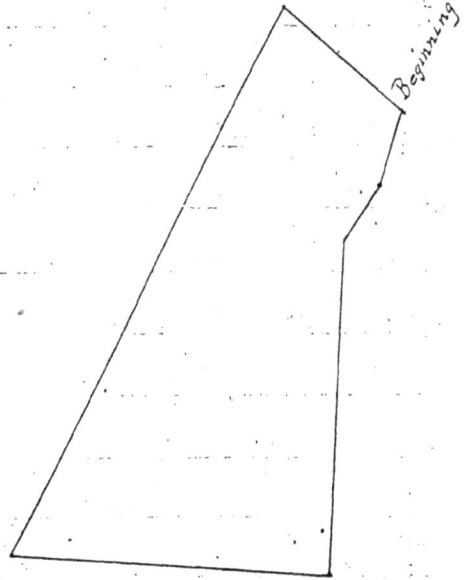

Scale 100 poles to the inch

JAS. RODDY

State of Tennessee, Rhea County
In pursuance of an entry made by
James Roddy of No. 292, and dated
March 30th 1837 for 300 acres of
land. Beginning on the Side of
Waldens Ridge on Jesse Roddy Juniors
corner; thence South 35° West Suposed
to Haleys line 180 poles, thence with
his line North 52 West 85 poles to a
Stake; thence North 35 East 480
poles to Whites Creek; thence down
Said Creek 100 poles to Joseph Longs
line; thence with a conditional line
between Said Long and Roddy (as follows) South 50° West 30 poles to a
Whiteoak; thence South ?

(page 152)
West 116 poles to a Chestnut; thence
South 62 West 20 poles to a Stake;
thence South 28 West 120 poles to a
blackoak on Jesse Roddy Jun. line
which ends this conditional line between Long & Roddy, thence with Said
Jesse Roddys line North 55 West 46
poles to the beginning. Surveyed
August 4th 1838.   Alfred Collins
          Surveyor for Rhea County
Joseph Long and Samuel Edmondson,
          S.C.B.

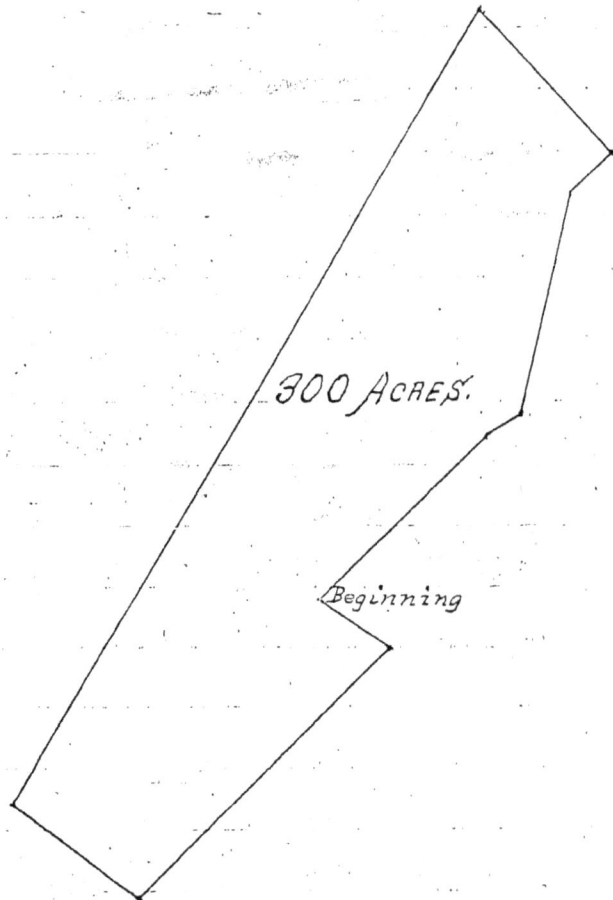

Scale 100 poles to the inch

JNO. HALEY   (page 152)

State of Tennessee,
          Rhea County
In pursuance of an entry
made by John Haley of
No. 226 and dated 3rd
February 1834 for 300
acres of land on the wa-
ters of Piney Creek North
of Gordons Road.
BEGINNING on a Spruce pine
on the bluff of Cowpen
branch a West fork of Pi-
ney; thence South 40° West
76 poles to a Maple & a

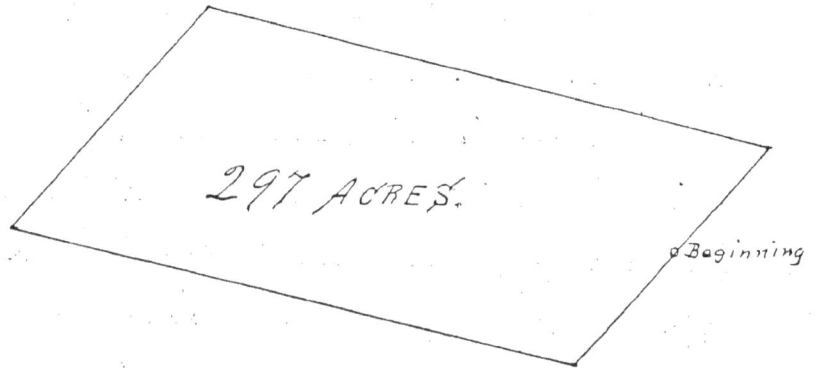

297 ACRES.

Beginning

Scale   100 poles to the inch

hickory pointer; thence North 80° West 308 poles to two hickorys; thence North
40 East 154 poles to a Stake, thence South 80° East 308 poles to a large pine
marked E; thence South 40° West 78 poles to the beginning. Surveyed August 2nd
1838.   Alfred Collins, Surveyor for Rhea County
Pleasant Hedgecoth and John Green, S.C.B.

JNO. HALEY

State of Tennessee, Rhea County
In pursuance of an entry made by John
Haley of No. 225 and dated 3rd February
1834 for 300 acres of land on the waters
of Piney Creek. BEGINNING at a Stake
North of   (page 153)
Allen Loopers house on his line, a chestnut and two pines marked as pointers;
thence South 80 West 143 poles to a Stake
a Postoak, hickory and blackoak pointers;
thence North 70 West 100 poles to a
chestnut on Elijah Prices East line;
thence with his line North 22 West 118
poles to a Spanishoak; thence North 40
East crossing Basan Creek at 26 poles
in all 44 poles to a large whitepine on
the Side of a ridge; thence North 18
West 200 poles to a Spanishoak; thence
South 80 East 288 poles to a Whiteoak, a
double chestnutoak pointer; thence South
45 West 145 poles to a Stake corner to
William Gibson; thence with his line due

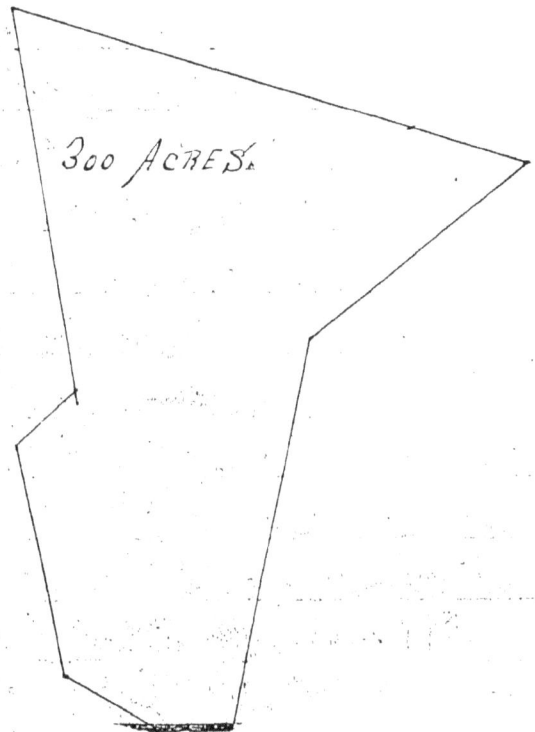

300 ACRES.

South 208 poles to a postoak; thence North 80 East 143 poles to a Stake; thence
South 2 poles to the beginning. Surveyed Aug. 2nd 1838.
          Alfred Collins, Surveyor for Rhea County
Pleasant Hedgecoth & John Green, S.C.B.

E.G. HALEY

State of Tennessee, Rhea County
In pursuance of an entry made by E.G. Haley of No. 299 and dated August 1st 1838

84

for 1100 acres of land being in Rhea County   (page 154)
on Cumberland Mountain. BEGINNING on a double hickory a whiteoak, Pine, hickory
marked as pointers on the Southwest Side of Crab Orchard Creek about 3/4 of a
mile below the junction of Fall Creek; thence South 40° West 285 poles to a large
pine marked E; thence North 80 West 308 poles to a Stake; thence South 40 West
154 poles to two hickorys; thence North 80 West 89 poles to a Spanishoak and a
whiteoak pointer; thence North 18 West 176 poles to a pine and blackoak; thence
North 75 East 152 to a yellow pine and pine pointers; thence North 22 West 18
poles to a Chestnut corner of E.G. Haley; thence with his line North 50 East 198
poles to a Stake 3 blackoaks and one chestnutoak marked as pts.; thence North 30
West 86 poles to a chestnut; thence North 60 East 102 to a dogwood and hickory;
thence a Strait line to the beginning. Surveyed August 4th 1838.
                          Alfred Collins, S.R.C.
Pleasant Hedgecoth and John Greer [sic], S.C.B.

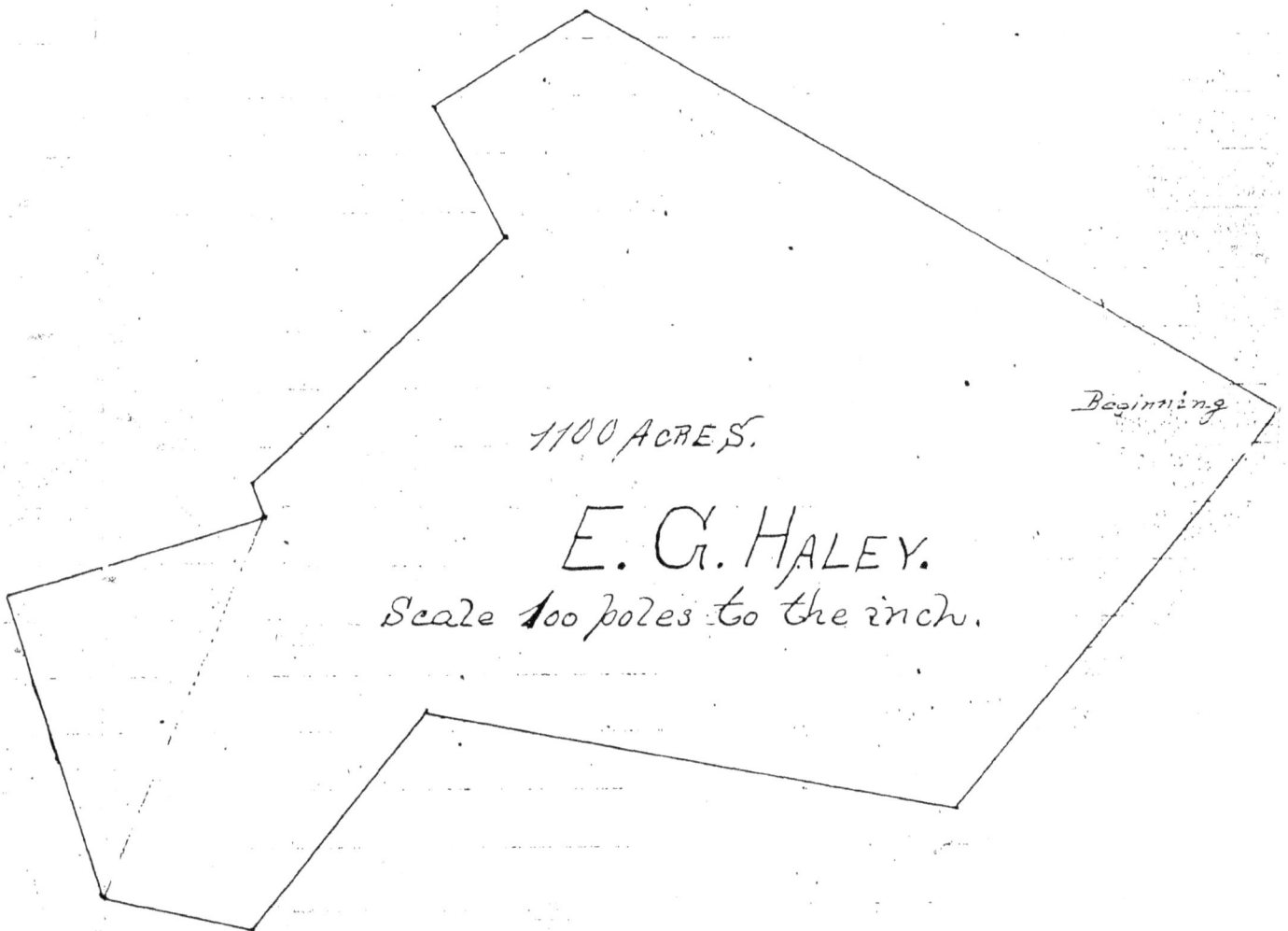

1100 ACRES.

E. G. HALEY.
Scale 100 poles to the inch.

J.B. INLOW

State of Tennessee, Rhea County
In pursuance of an entry made by John B. Inlow of No. 266 and dated May 13th 1836
for 5000 acres of land exclusive   (page 155)
of all legal prior claims in Rhea County Tennessee on Waldens Ridge. BEGINNING
on a hickory and two black oaks marked as pointers in the line between Rhea and
Bledsoe Counties and where the Southern line of Joseph G. Smiths five Thousand
acre Survey crosses Said County line and running North 30° East with the County
line crossing Several branches and a creek at 640 poles the line all 660 poles
to a blackoak; thence South 60 East 1320 poles to a Stake; thence South 30 West
660 poles to a Stake; thence North 60 West 1320 poles to the beginning. Surveyed
29th August 1838.   Alfred Collins, Surveyor for Rhea County
David Schoolfield, Richard Schoolfield, William Pepper, & William T. Webb, S.C.B.

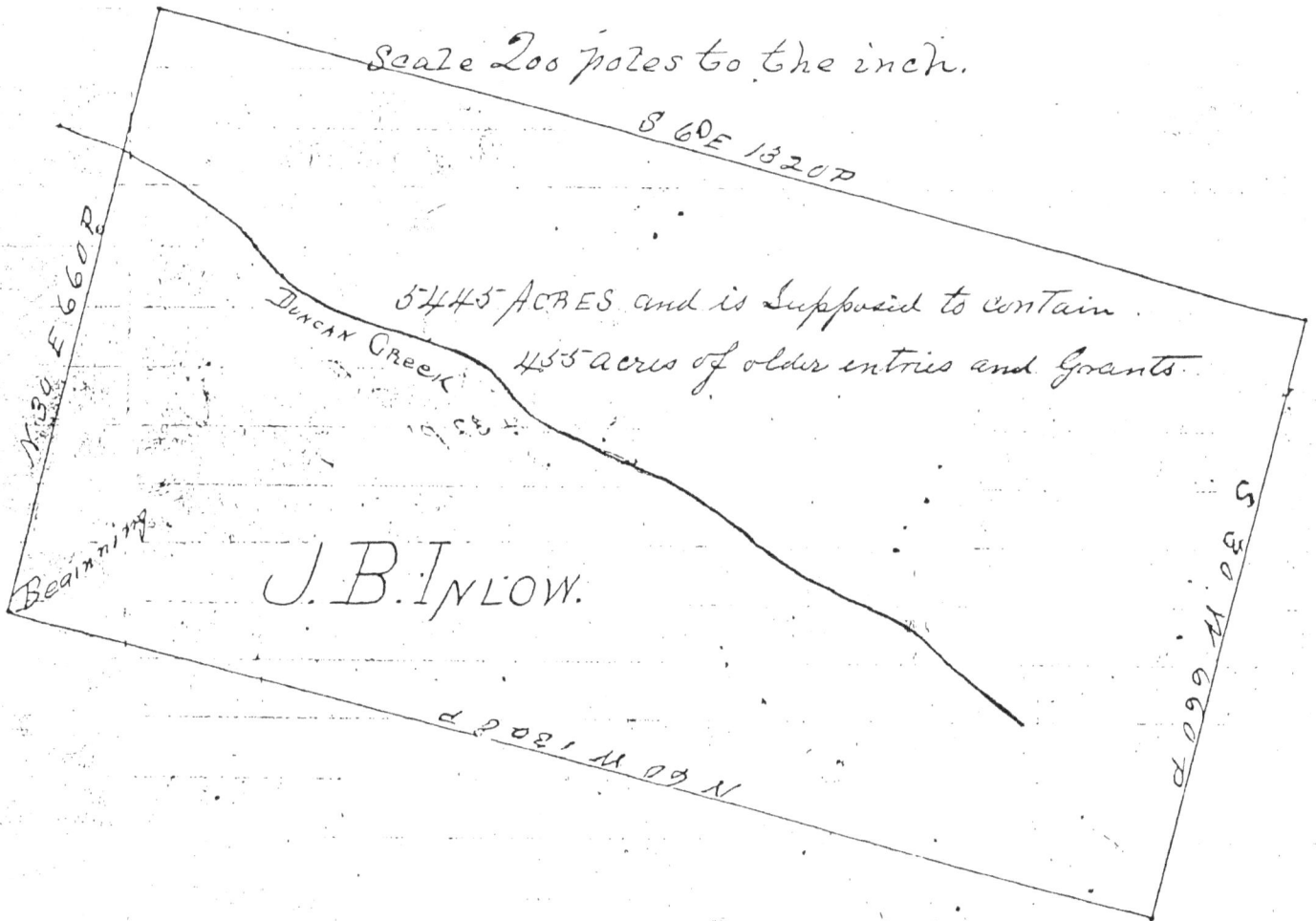

E.C. RICE

State of Tennessee, Rhea County
In pursuance of an entry made by Elijah C. Rice of No. 267 and dated 13th May
1836 for 5000 acres of land exclusive of all prior legal claims in Rhea County
on Waldens Ridge adjoining a five thousand acre entry in the name of John B.
Inlow. BEGINNING on a   (page 156)
blackoak tree it being the Northwest corner of an entry made by John B. Inlow and
running North 30° East with the line between Rhea and Bledsoe County crossing

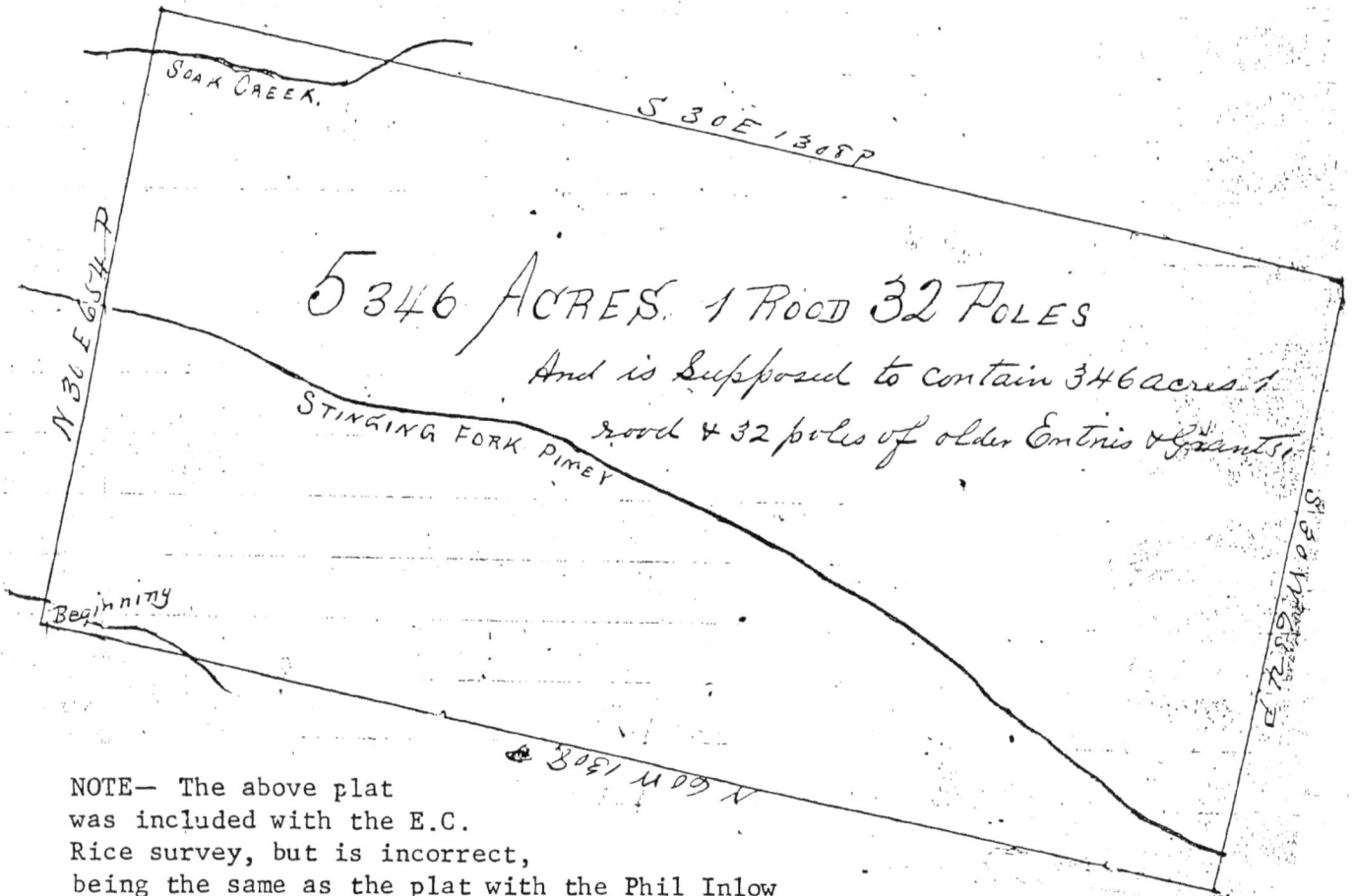

5 346 ACRES. 1 ROOD 32 POLES

And is Supposed to contain 346 acres 1 rood & 32 poles of older Entries & Grants

SOAK CREEK.

S 30 E 1308 P

N 30 E 654 P

STINGING FORK PINEY

Beginning

N 60 W 1308

NOTE— The above plat
was included with the E.C.
Rice survey, but is incorrect,
being the same as the plat with the Phil Inlow
survey (on next page).

several branches and Duscan Creek at 440 poles in all 660 poles to a whiteoak a
hickory and two chestnutoaks marked as pointers; thence South 60 East 1320 poles
to a Stake; thence South 30 West 660 poles to a Stake; thence North 60 West 1320
poles to the beginning. Surveyed August 29th 1838.
                    Alfred Collins, Surveyor for Rhea County
David Schoolfield, Richard Schoolfield, William Pepper & William T. Webb, S.C.B.

PHIL INLOW

State of Tennessee, Rhea County
In pursuance of an entry made by Phillip Inlow of No. 268 and dated May 13th
1836 for 5000 acres of land exclusive of all prior legal claims in Rhea County on
Waldens Ridge adjoining a five thousand acre entry in the name of Elijah C. Rice.
BEGINNING on a whiteoak, a hickory and two chestnutoaks marked as pointers, it
being the Northwest corner of the entry made by Elijah C. Rice and running
                                                        (page 157)
North 30 East with the line between Rhea and Bledsoe counties crossing a creek at
30 poles the Stinging fork of Piney at 334 poles and Soak Creek at 620 poles in
all 654 poles to a redoak and three whiteoaks marked as pointers; thence South 60
West 1308 poles to a Stake; thence South 30 West 654 poles to a Stake; thence
North 60 West 1308 poles to the beginning. Surveyed August 30th 1838.
                    Alfred Collins, Surveyor for Rhea County
David Schoolfield, Richard Schoolfield, William Pepper, & William T. Webb, S.C.B.

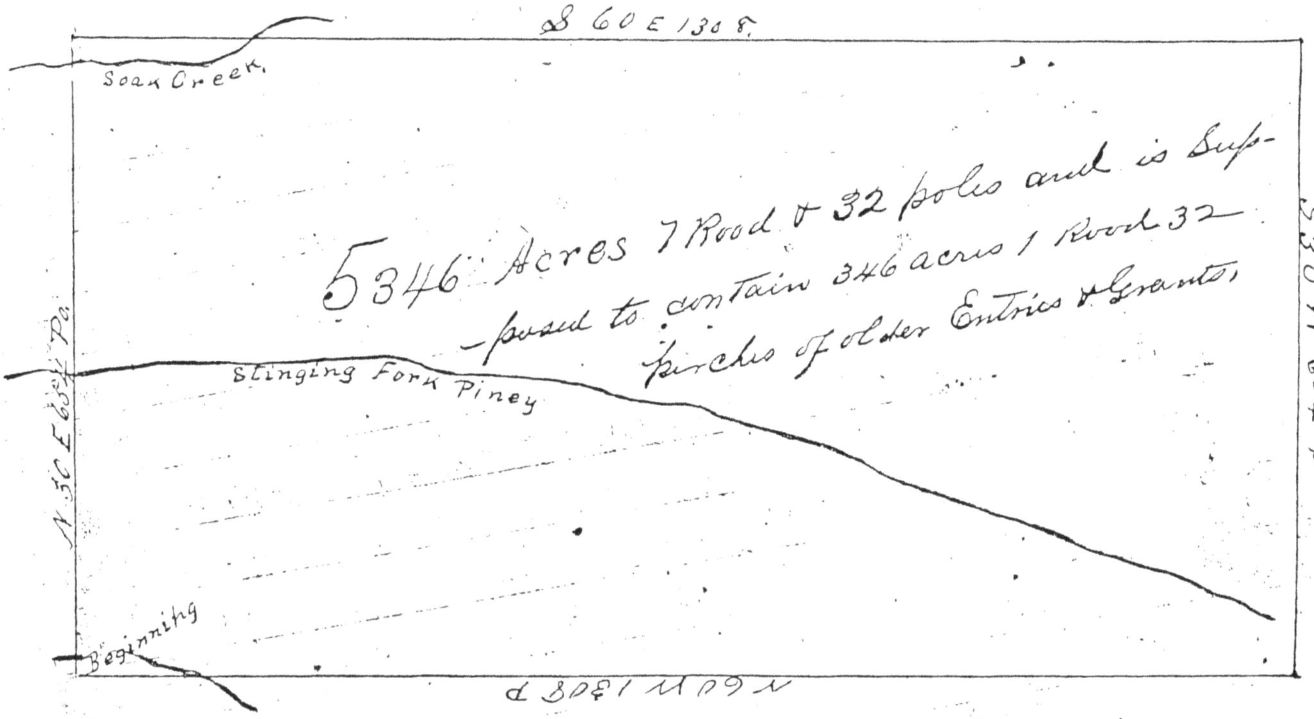

S 60 E 130 P

Soak Creek.

5346 Acres 7 Rood & 32 poles and is Sup-
-posed to contain 346 acres 1 Rood 32
perches of older Entries & Grants,

Stinging Fork Piney

N 30 E 654 P

S 30 W 654 P

Beginning

N 60 W 1308 P

PHIL. INLOW.
Scale 200 poles to the inch.

N 60 E 1320 P

5-44-5- ACRES.
And is Supposed to contain 445 acres of older entries & Grants.

N 30 E 660 P

S 30 W E 60 P

Beginning

N 60 W 1320 P

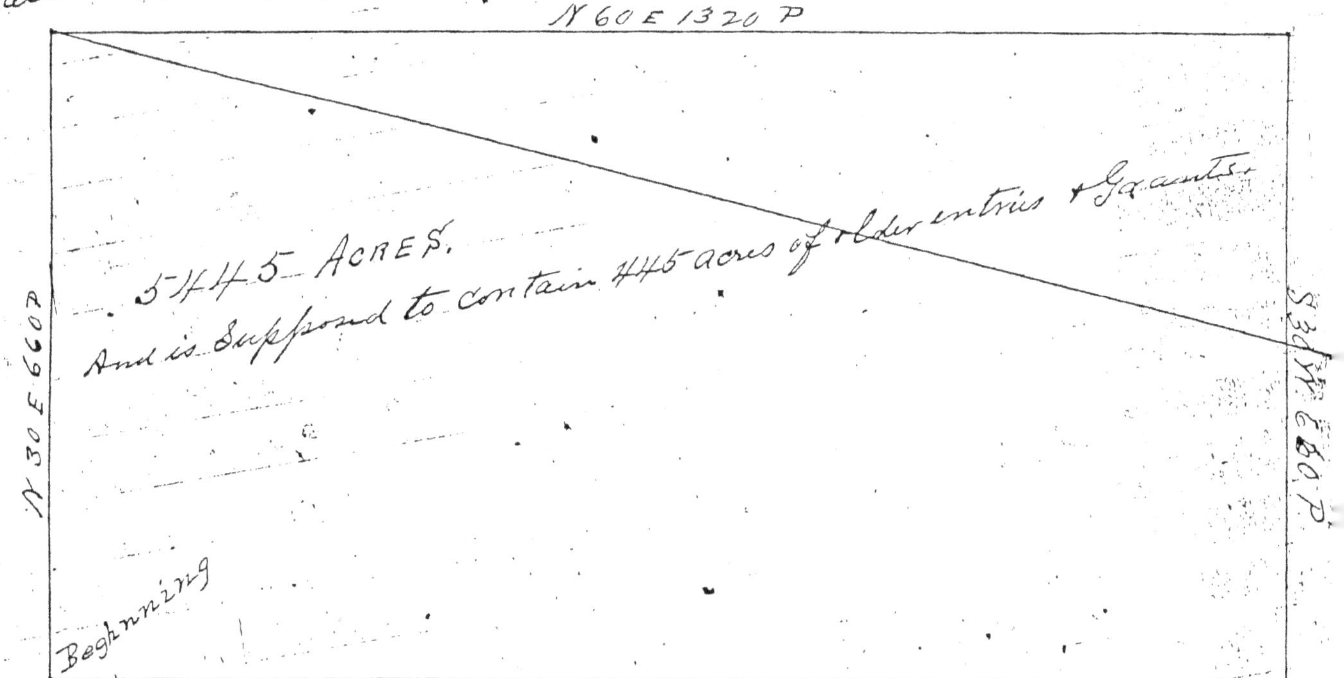

WM FAULKNER.
Scale 200 poles to the inch.

WM FAULKNER [sic]   (page 157)

State of Tennessee, Rhea County
In pursuance of an entry made by William Falkner [sic] of No. 269 and dated May
13th 1836 for 5000 acres of land exclusive of all prior legal claims in Rhea
County on Waldens Ridge. BEGINNING on a redoak and three whiteoaks marked as
pointers it being the North West corner of a certain five thousand acre entry in
the name of Phillip Inlow and running North 30 East with the line between Rhea
and Bledsoe   (page 158)
counties crossing Several branches 660 poles to a Stake; thence South 60 East
1320 poles to a Stake, then South 30 West 660 poles to a Stake; thence North 60
West 1320 poles to the beginning.   Surveyed August 30th 1838.
          Alfred Collins, Surveyor for Rhea County
David Schoolfield, Richard Schoolfield, William Pepper & William T. Webb, S.C.B.

VAL. HOUPT   (page 158)

State of Tennessee, Rhea County
In pursuance of an entry made by
Valentine Houpt of No. 297 and
dated April 3rd 1838 for 300
acres of land in Rhea County.
BEGINNING on Richard Walkers line
at a blackoak tree; thence with
his line North 30 East 103 poles to
a blackoak corner to Said Walkers;
thence with another line of Said Walker North 60 West 250 poles to a Stake;
thence North 23 East 85 poles to a Stake;
thence South 70 East with a line of George
W. Black 250 poles to a Stake; thence South
9 West 30 poles to a blackgum, thence South
70 E 108 poles to a Stake on John Condley
line; thence with his line South 30 West
212 poles to a large poplar corner to Said
Condley, Robert Fergusons heirs and others;
thence N 60 W 106 poles to the beginning.
Surveyed September 29th 1838.
Alfred Collins, Surveyor for Rhea County
Jesse Houp & Alexander Houp, S.C.B.
Valentine Houp, Marker

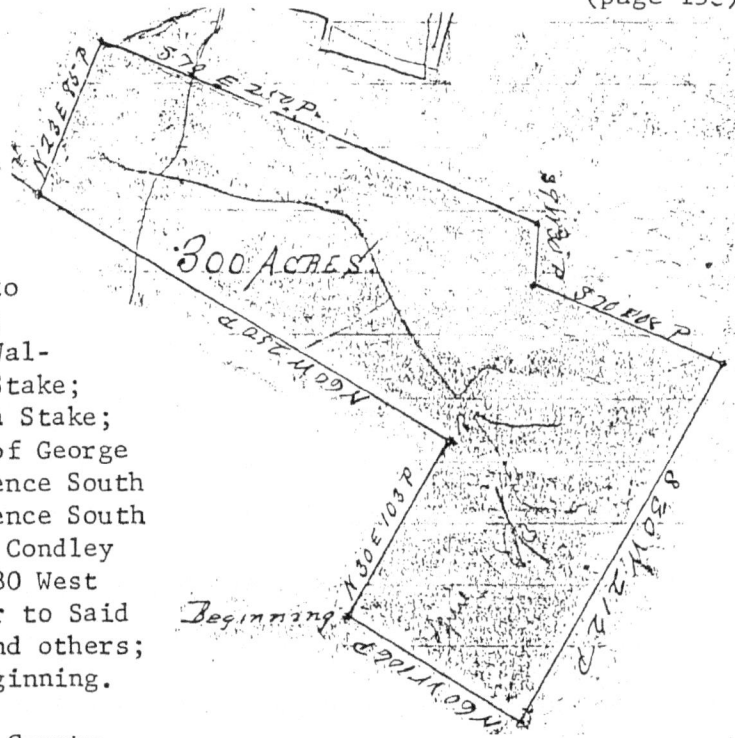

Scale   100 poles to the inch

JOHN CONDLEY   (page 159)

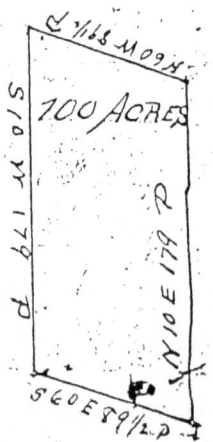

State of Tennessee, Rhea County
In pursuance of an entry made by John Condley of No. 300, and
dated October 5th 1838 for 100 acres of land in Rhea County.
BEGINNING on a large poplar marked "C" in a hollow near a Spring;
thence North 10° East 179 poles to a Small blackoak two Whiteoaks
and a redoak marked as pointers, thence North 60 West 89½ poles
to a Stake, thence South 10 West 179 poles to a Stake; thence
South 60 East 89½ poles to the beginning. Surveyed October 6th
1838.   Alfred Collins, Surveyor for Rhea County
James Pearce and George Black, C.B.   Henry Collins, Marker

100 poles to the inch

ALLEN LOOPER ET ALS

State of Tennessee, Rhea County
In pursuance of an entry made by
Allen Looper, Gilbert Looper,
Jesse Brumble and Duncan Cox of
No. 257 and dated January 29th
1836 for 300 acres of land in Rhea
County, I have this day Surveyed
for James Preston Assignee of
James [sic] Looper, Gilbert Looper,
Jesse Brumble and Duncan Cox the
Said three hundred acres of land.
BEGINNING on a Chestnut tree on
the North Side of Bear Creek on

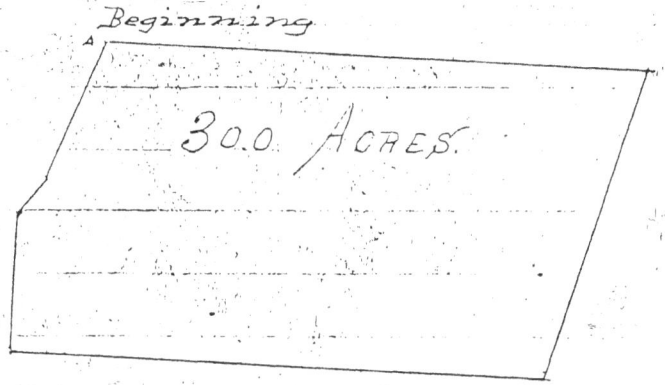

Scale   100 poles to the inch

Said Allen Loopers lower end line of one hundred and fifty acre Survey near Said
Jesse Brumbles beginning corner of one hundred acre Survey; thence South 25° West
80 poles to a chestnut; thence South 37° West 20 poles to a Cucumber; thence
South 3° West 68 poles to a chestnut, thence due East 287½ poles to a whiteoak;
thence North 17½ East 164 poles to a Stake; thence due West 287½ poles to the
beginning. Surveyed   (page 160)
August 1st 1838.   Alfred Collins, Surveyor for Rhea County
Joseph Long & William Cox, S.C.B.

HANNAH HOYT [sic]

State of Tennessee, Rhea County
In pursuance of an entry made by Edmund Howerton of No. 274
and dated August 19th 1836 for one hundred acres of land in
Rhea County, I have this day Surveyed for Hannah Hoit [sic]
assignee of Said Howerton one hundred acres of land.
BEGINNING on a blackoak and postoak marked as a corner on
Micajah Howertons line and corner to James A. Darwin, thence
North 24° East 200 poles to a Stake two postoaks and a black-
oak marked as pointers; thence North 66° West 100 poles to a
pine on the first bench of the mountain; thence South 24°
West 200 poles to a Stake; thence South 66° East 100 poles
to the beginning. Surveyed November 10th 1838.
          Alfred Collins, Surveyor for Rhea County
Henry Weidenhoffer & Stephen Hoit, S.C.B.

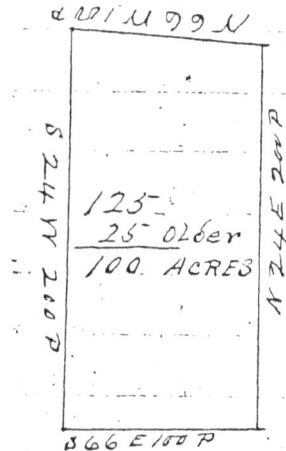

100 poles to the inch

JESSE RODDY, SR.

State of Tennessee, Rhea County
In pursuance of an entry made by Jesse
Roddye [sic] Sen. of No. 301 and dated Nov.
7th 1838 for 300 acres of land in Rhea
County. BEGINNING on a maple tree on a
branch near the foot of the mountain; thence
due East crossing a Creek at 180 poles in
all 267 poles to a postosk and two hickorys
marked as   (page 161)
pointers; thence due South 253 poles to two
redbud bushes; thence North 55 West 219
poles to a whiteoak in the lane; thence

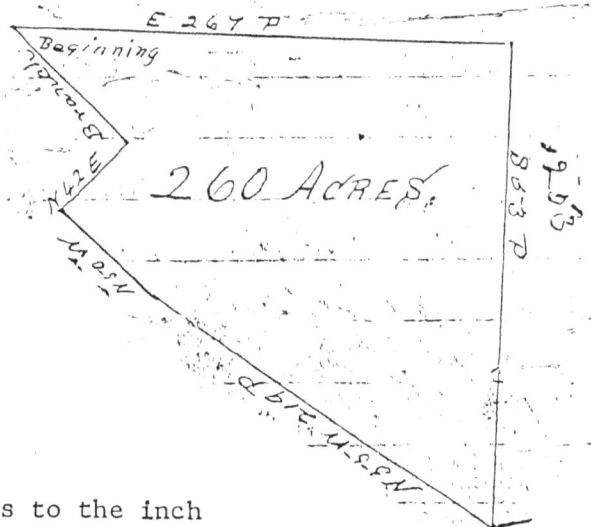

100 parts to the inch

North 50 West 67 poles to two Walnuts; thence North 42 East 51 poles to a white-oak at a branch; thence with the branch to the beginning. Surveyed November 19th 1838. Alfred Collins, Surveyor for Rhea County
Jesse Roddy Jr. & Wiat Wright, S.C.B.

RICHD. WATERHOUSE (page 161)

State of Tennessee, Rhea County
In pursuance of an entry made in the Entry Takers office for Rhea County in the State of Tennessee by Richard Waterhouse of No. 235, and dated the 4 day of September 1834 for one thousand acres and by virtue of a deputation to me given by Alfred Collins, Surveyor for Rhea County in the State of Tennessee, I have Surveyed for the Said Richard Waterhouse on Piney River in Rhea County and State of Tennessee one thousand acres of land. BEGINNING on a white-oak corner of a 230 acre tract called the Paul tract and a
(page 162)
tract granted by the State of Tennessee to T.B. Rice on the Northeast Side of Piney River at the Shutin on Piney; then with a line of Said 500 acre tract S 45 W 100 poles crossing Piney River to 2 chestnuts and a Small gum corner to Said 500 acre tract; then South 20 W 500 poles to a Stake on the line of Robert Ferguson, Samuel B. Ferguson, Thomas Ferguson & Levi W. Ferguson 1000 acre tract; then with their line S 45 E 300 poles to a Stake their corner on the line of the 19000 acre tract; then with a line of Said tract N 30 E 500 poles to Piney River; then up Piney River as it meanders 300 poles to the beginning.

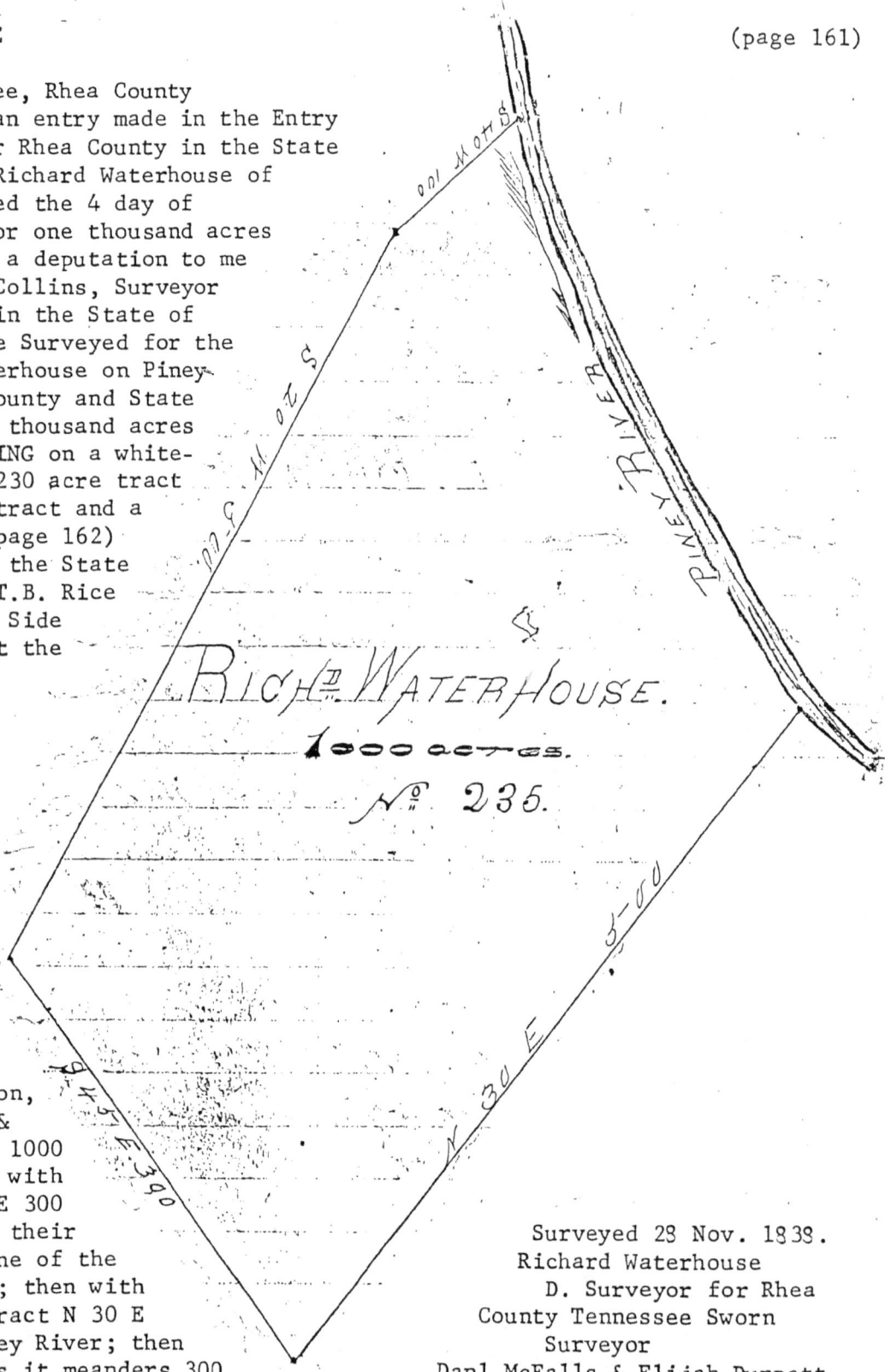

Rich.ᴰ Waterhouse. 1000 acres. N.º 235.

Surveyed 28 Nov. 1838.
Richard Waterhouse
D. Surveyor for Rhea County Tennessee Sworn Surveyor
Danl McFalls & Elijah Dunpett, C.C.

E. BREWER   (page 162)

State of Tennessee, Rhea County
In pursuance of an entry made by Eli Brewer of No. 254
and dated 3rd December 1835 for one hundred acres of
land in Rhea County on Waldens Ridge of Cumberland
Mountain on the waters of Whites Creek. BEGINNING on
a blackgum corner to George Gillespie; thence North 25
East with his line 159 poles to a Stake on Smiths line;
thence with his line due West 57 poles to a blackgum;
thence South 28 West with Mondays line 253 poles to a
Stake; thence due East 70 poles to a Stake; thence
North 25 East 94 poles to the beginning.
Surveyed November 22nd 1838.
        Alfred Collins, Surveyor for Rhea County
Elijah Brewer & Pleasant Brewer, S.C.B.

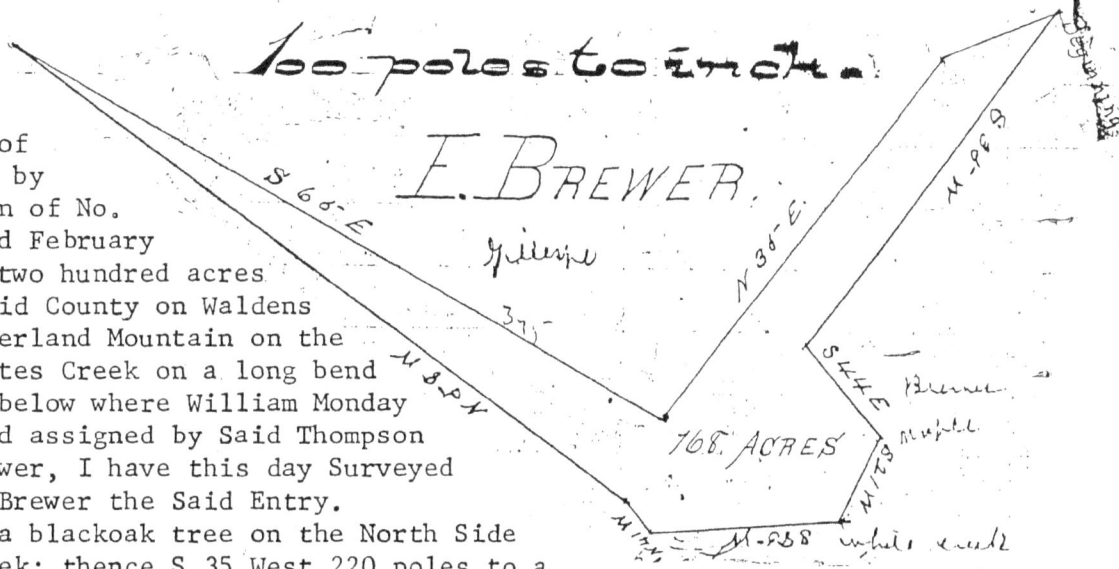

100 poles to the inch

E. BREWER   (page 163)

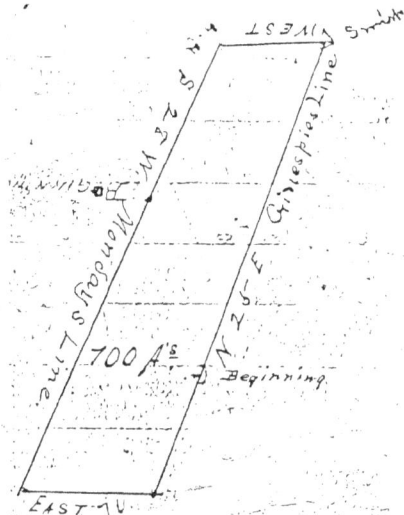

State
of Tennessee,
Rhea County
In pursuance of
an entry made by
Jesse Thompson of No.
208, and dated February
6th 1833 for two hundred acres
of land in Said County on Waldens
Ridge of Cumberland Mountain on the
waters of Whites Creek on a long bend
of the Creek below where William Monday
now lives, and assigned by Said Thompson
to Elijah Brewer, I have this day Surveyed
for the Said Brewer the Said Entry.
BEGINNING on a blackoak tree on the North Side
of Whites Creek; thence S 35 West 220 poles to a
Stake; thence South 44 East with a line of Elijah Brewer 60 poles to a maple;
thence South 21 West 52 poles to a pine, blackoak and whiteoak on the bluff of
Whites Creek; thence South 85 West with the Creek 100 poles to a blackoak;
thence North 41 West 24 poles to a pine; thence North 58 West with a bluff of
Whites Creek 375 poles to Gillespies line; thence with his line S 65 East 375
poles to a Stake at or near Gillespies corner; thence North 35 East with another
line of Said Gillespie 240 poles to Redwines line; thence with his line to the
beginning. Surveyed November 21st 1838.
        Alfred Collins, Surveyor for Rhea County
Joseph Winfield & Eli Brewer, S.C.B.

E. BREWER   (page 164)

State of Tennessee, Rhea County
In pursuance of an entry made by Jesse Thompson of No. 161 and dated September
25th 1831 for two hundred acres of land in Said County on Waldens Ridge of Cumberland Mountain on both sides of Whites Creek and assigned by Said Thompson to

to William Smith, and then assigned by
Said Smith to Elijah Brewer, I have this
day Surveyed for Said Brewer the Said
entry. BEGINNING on a Chestnut, a hickory and a maple marked as pointers on
the South bank of Whites Creek; thence
South 40 West 253 poles to a Stake;
thence North 50 West 126½ poles to a
Stake, thence North 40 East 253 poles
to a Stake; thence South 50 East 126½
poles to the beginning.
Surveyed November 21st 1838.
Alfred Collins, Surveyor of Rhea County
Joseph Winfield & Eli Brewer, S.C.B.

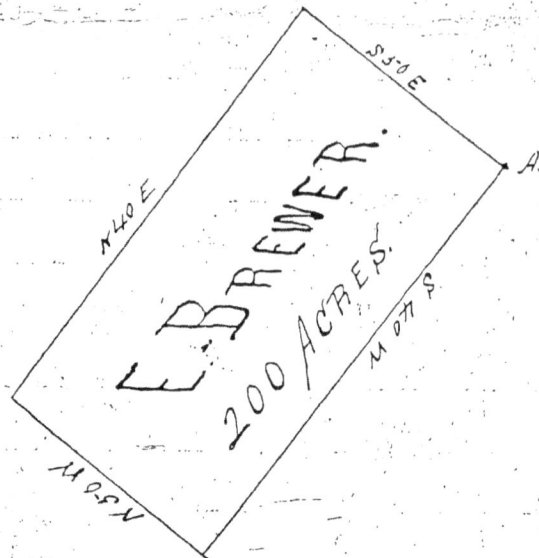

JOSEPH WINFIELD

State of Tennessee, Rhea County
In pursuance of an entry made by Joseph
Winfield of No. 205 and dated January 21st
1833 for four hundred acres of
land in Said County on Waldens
Ridge of Cumberland Mountain
on the waters of Whites Creek.
BEGINNING on two hickorys corner to William Monday; thence
due South 180 poles to a Stake
a blackgum, Sowerwood and
Chestnut marked as pointers;
thence due West 355½ poles to
a Stake; thence due North 180
poles to a Stake; thence due
East 355½ poles to the beginning. Surveyed
                    (page 165)
November 22nd 1838.
        Alfred Collins, Surveyor for Rhea County
Pleasant Brewer & Elijah Brewer, S.C.B.

100 poles to an inch

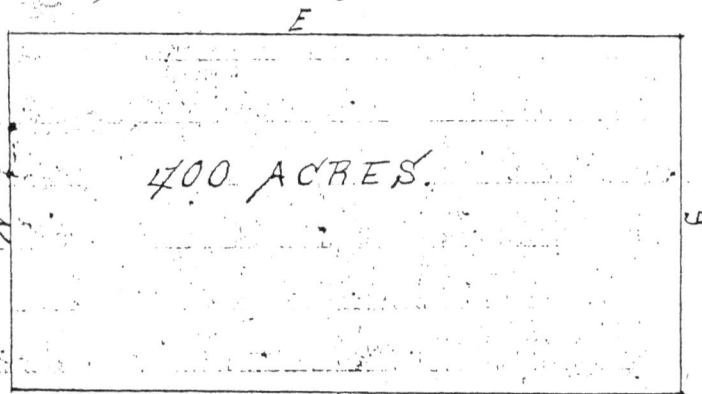

100 poles to an inch

REBECCA DAVIS

State of Tennessee, Rhea County
In pursuance of an entry made by Rebecca Davis of No.
256 and dated January 23rd 1836 for fifty acres of land
in Said County at the foot and on the Side of Waldens
Ridge. BEGINNING on a whiteoak and dogwood in a hollow;
thence North 45 East 102 poles to a dogwood and redoak;
thence North 45 West 78 1/3 poles to a Stake on the Side
of the mountain; thence South 45 West 102 poles to a
Stake; thence South 45 East 78 1/3 poles to the beginning.
19th 1838.   Alfred Collins, Surveyor for Rhea County
William T. Gillenwaters and James Roddy, S.C.B.

100 to inch

Surveyed November

J.M. BEATY

State of Tennessee, Rhea County
In pursuance of an entry made by
John M. Beaty of No. 229 and dated
22nd April 1834 for three hundred
acres of land in Said County on
Waldens Ridge a Spur of Cumberland
Mountain on a creek known by the
name of Duscan fork of Piney River.
BEGINNING at a pine tree marked JMB
on the North Side of a Steep ridge
and South of Said Creek, and running South 82 East 309 2/3 poles to
a Stake; thence North 8° [plat has
80°] East 155 poles to a Stake;
thence North 82 West 309 2/3 poles to a Stake; thence South 8° [sic] West 155
poles to the beginning. Surveyed November   (page 166)
26th 1838.   Alfred Collins, Surveyor for Rhea County
George Oxier & James Stephens, S.C.B.

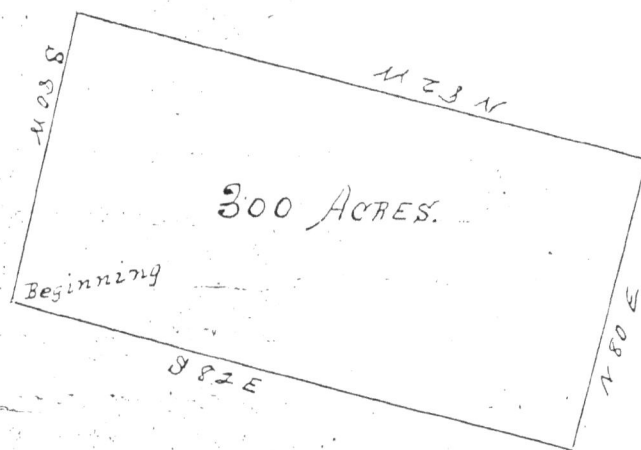

300 ACRES.

100 poles to the inch

B. HOLLOWAY

State of Tennessee, Rhea County
In pursuance of an Entry made by Burton Holloway of No. 165 and dated October 18th 1831 for
two hundred acres of land in Said County on
Waldens Ridge of Cumberland Mountain on the
waters of Whites Creek on the South Side of
Said Creek. BEGINNING on a Small postoak two
chestnuts and a blackgum marked as pointers
it being the Southwest corner of Major Holloways four hundred acre entry; thence with his
line North 30 East 247 poles to a double
Chestnut; thence South 63 East 130 poles to a
Stake; thence North 63 West 130 poles to the
beginning. Surveyed November 23rd 1838.
Alfred Collins, Surveyor for Rhea County
William Bennett & William H. Seay, S.C.B.

200 ACRES.

100 poles to an inch

M. HOLLOWAY

State of Tennessee, Rhea County
In pursuance made by Major Holloway of No. 159 and dated September 3rd 1831 for
four hundred acres of land in Said County on Waldens Ridge of Cumberland Mountain on the waters of Whites Creek on the South Side of Said Creek

(page 167)

BEGINNING on a Spanishoak tree it being the South East corner of Bert L. Stephens
two hundred acre tract; thence with Said Stephens line due North 140 poles to a
Stake on William Bennetts line; thence with his line North 50 East 114 poles to
a Chestnutoak on William H. Seays line; thence South 60 East 217 poles to a
Stake; then South 30 West passing Burton Holloways corner at 13 poles in all 260
poles to a postoak bush; thence a Straight line to the beginning. Surveyed November 23rd 1838.   Alfred Collins, Surveyor for Rhea County
William Bennett & William H. Seay, S.C.B.

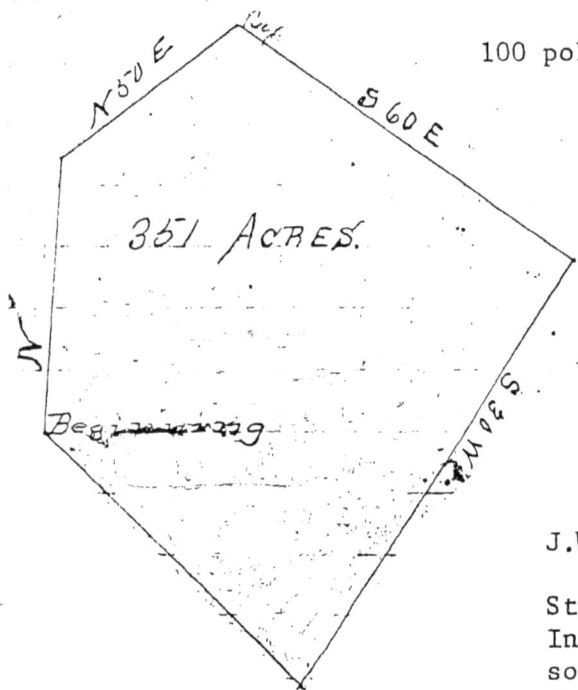

100 poles to an inch

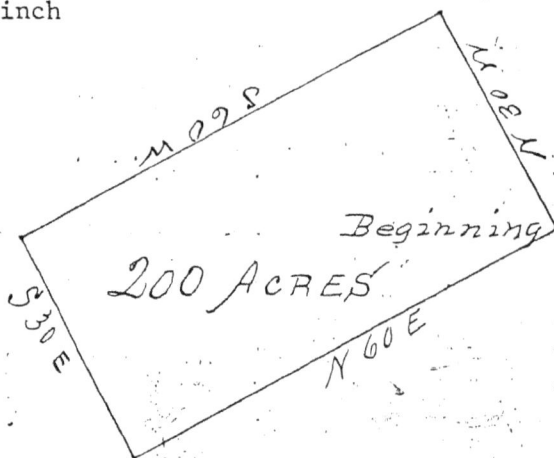

N 30 E

S 60 E

351 ACRES.

S 30 W

Beginning

S 60 W

N 30 W

200 ACRES

S 30 E

Beginning

N 60 E

J.W. THOMPSON (page 167)

State of Tennessee, Rhea County
In pursuance of an entry made by James W. Thompson of No. 195 and dated September 17th 1832
for two hundred acres of land in Said County on
Waldens Ridge of Cumberland Mountain on the head waters of Clear Creek. BEGINNING
on a Spanishoak, a hickory and blackoak marked as pointers; then North 30 West
127 poles to a Stake, three blackoaks and a postoak marked as pointers; thence
South 60 West 252 poles to a Stake; thence South 30 East 127 poles to a Stake;
thence N 60 East 252 poles to the beginning. Surveyed November 28th 1838.
     Alfred Collins, Surveyor for Rhea County
Josep Brown & Robert Ferguson, S.C.B.

JAMES W. THOMPSON [JOSEPH M. THOMPSON] (page 168)

State of Tennessee, Rhea County
In pursuance of an entry made by James W. Thompson of
No. 196 and dated September 17th 1832 for Seventy five
acres of land in Said County on Waldens Ridge of Cumberland Mountain on the waters of Piney on both sides
of Beatys turnpike road and assigned to Joseph M.
Thompson and I have this day Surveyed the Same for
Said Joseph M. Thompson. BEGINNING on a large Chestnut tree near the road, thence North 45 West 80 poles
to a Stake; thence North 45 East [150 poles, thence
South 45 East] 80 poles to a whiteoak at the bend of
the road; thence South 45 West 150 poles to the beginning. Surveyed November 28th 1838.
     Alfred Collins, Surveyor for Rhea County
Robert Ferguson & Joseph Brown, S.C.B.

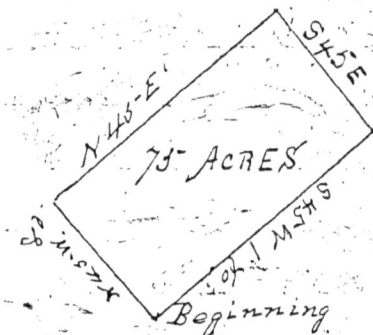

N 45 E

S 45 E

75 ACRES

N 45 W

S 45 W

Beginning

100 poles to the inch

JAMES FERGUSON

State of Tennessee, Rhea County
In pursuance of an entry made by James Ferguson of No. 277, and dated October
1st 1836 for one thousand acres of land in Said County on Waldens Ridge of Cumberland Mountain on the waters of Piney River and Clear Creek and assigned to
Robert Ferguson, I have this day Surveyed for the Said Robert Ferguson the Said
tract of land (page 169)

95

BEGINNING on a white pine corner to Fergusons
one thousand acre Survey on the Southeast
bank of Piney River; thence with a line
of Said Ferguson South 45 East 360 poles
to a Supposed line of the nineteen
thousand acre Survey; thence South
15 West with a Supposed line of the
nineteen thousand acre Survey 444½
poles to a Stake; thence North 45
West 360 poles to a Stake; thence
North 15 East 444½ poles to the
beginning. Surveyed November
28th 1838. Alfred Collins, S.R.C.
Thomas Thompson & Joseph Brown,
        S.C.B.

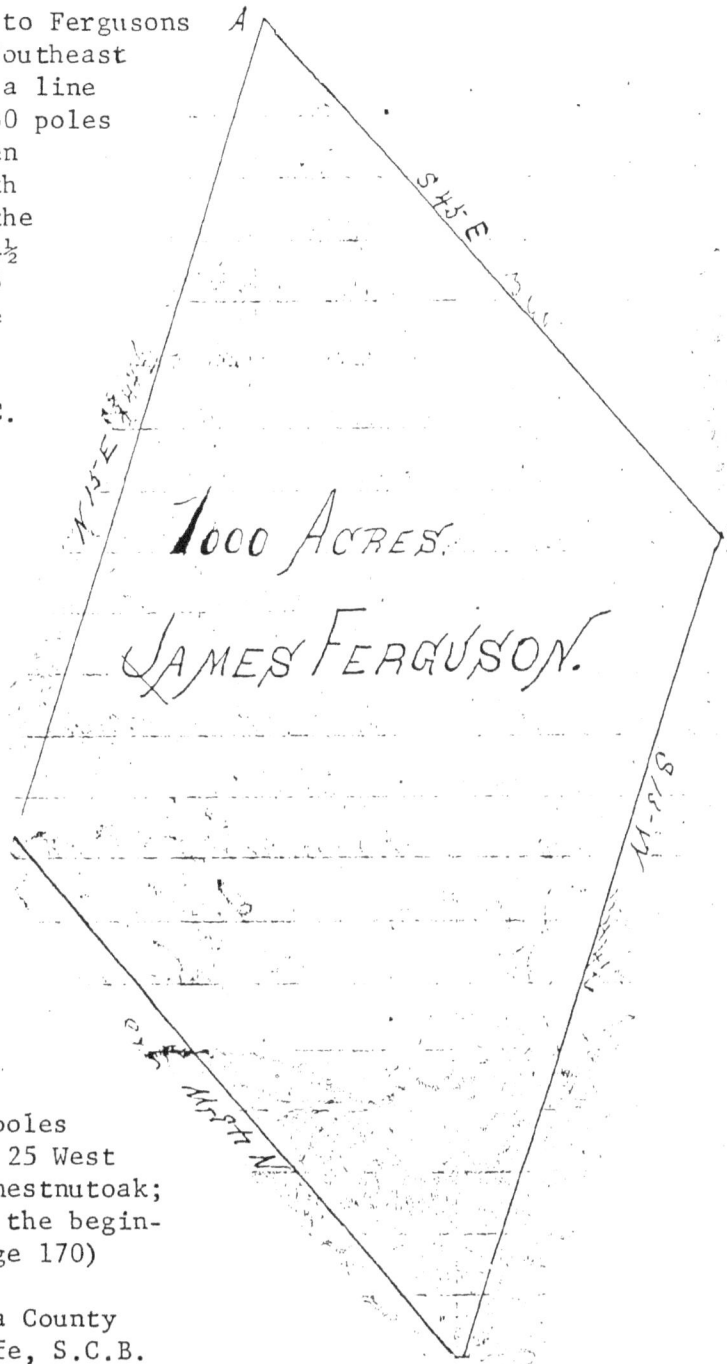

ZEB. REED

State of Tennessee, Rhea County
In pursuance of an entry made
by Zebulon Reed of No. 250
and dated August 31st 1835
for twenty five acres of
land in Said County on
the Side of Waldens
Ridge a Spur of Cumber-
land Mountain and lying
on the branch above
Micajah Howertons Mill.
BEGINNING on a whiteoak tree
corner to Said Micajah and
Edmond Howertons; thence North
25 East 45 poles to a Stake, a
blackoak and a postoak marked as
pointers; then North 65 West 89 poles
to a double chestnut; then South 25 West
45 poles to two hickorys and a Chestnutoak;
thence South 65 East 89 poles to the beginning.   (page 170)
Surveyed November 29th 1838.
Alfred Collins, Surveyor for Rhea County
Joseph L. Hoit & Henry Weidenhoffe, S.C.B.

1000 Acres.
James Ferguson.

ZEB. REED.
25 Acres.

CORNELIUS HARRIS

State of Tennessee, Rhea County
In pursuance of an entry made by Cornelius
Harris of No. 162 and dated September 28th
1831 for 200 acres of land in Said County on
Waldens Ridge on the waters of Whites Creek
and assigned to Pleasant Brewer, I have this
day Surveyed for the Said Brewer the Said
tract. BEGINNING on the South Side of the
Camp Branch on a blackoak tree; thence running due North 160 poles to a Stake two

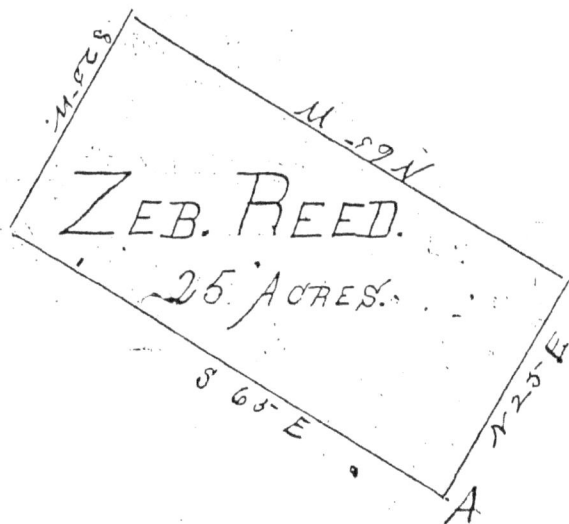

chestnuts a postoak and a hickory marked as pointers; thence due West 200 poles to a blackgum; thence due South 160 poles to a blackoak, whiteoak and chestnut; thence due East 200 poles to the beginning. Surveyed November 22nd 1838. Alfred Collins, Surveyor for Rhea County Elijah Brewer & Eli Brown, S.C.B.

100 poles to an inch

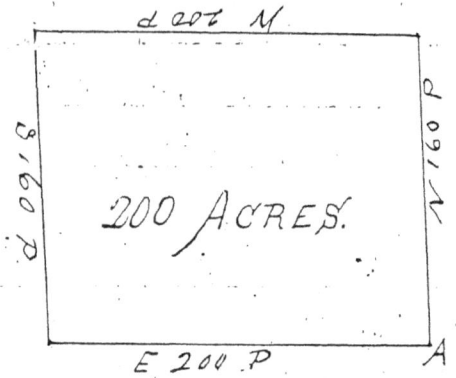

Plat diagram: "200 ACRES." with bearings N 200 P, S 160 P, N 160 P, E 200 P, corner A

WM. KENT

State of Tennessee, Rhea County
In pursuance of an entry made by William Kent
(page 171)
of No. 307 and dated December 8th 1838 for one thousand acres of land in Said County on the waters of Sale and Richland creeks. BEGINNING on two postoaks corner of a two thousand acre entry made by William Greer and on the line of an eight hundred acre Survey of David Ragsdale near Ragsdales old turnpike road; thence North 60 West crossing a branch at 320 poles in all 400 poles to two postoaks and a hickory; thence North 30 East 400 poles to a postoak redoak and hickory; thence South 60 East crossing a Creek at 100 poles in all 400 poles to three whiteoaks and a chestnut; thence South 30 West 400 poles to the beginning. Surveyed December 10th 1838. Alfred Collins, Surveyor for Rhea County Henry A. Shelton & Gatewood Qualls, S.C.B.

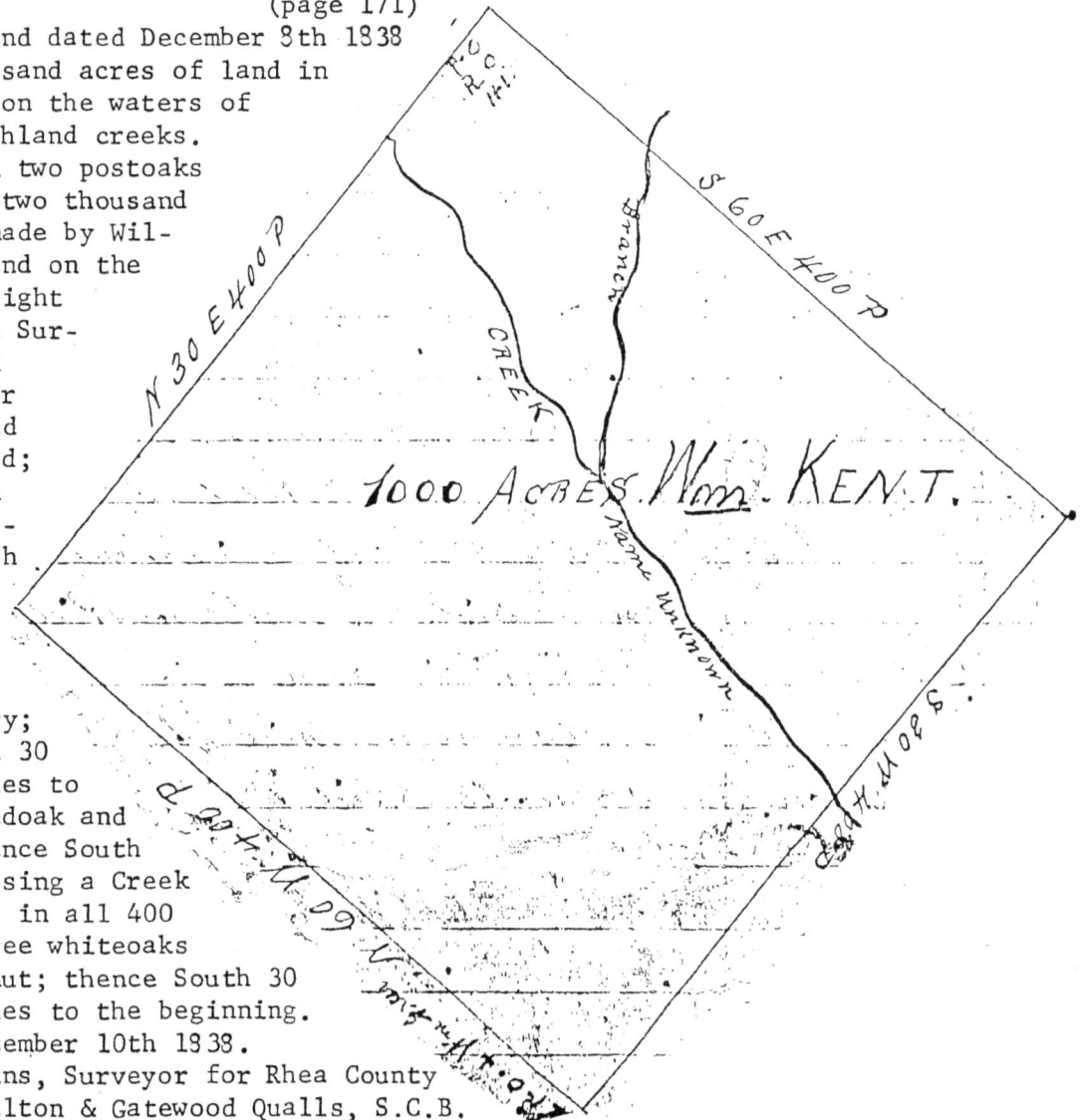

Plat diagram: "1000 ACRES. Wm. KENT." with bearings N 30 E 400 P, S 60 E 400 P, S 30 W 400 P, N 60 W 400 P; showing Creek, Branch, and "Name unknown" water course

W.O. KENT

State of Tennessee, Rhea County
In pursuance of an entry made by Stephen Hoit of No. 308 and dated December 8th
1838 for one thousand acres of land in Said County, I have Surveyed for William
O. Kent assignee of the Said Hoit the Said tract. BEGINNING at the Southwest
corner of an entry made [by] William Kent on two postoaks and a hickory; thence
North 60 West crossing   (page 172)
Teage Creek at 80 poles in all 400 poles to three postoaks on the County line;
thence with Said line North 30 East crossing Polebridge Creek at 224 poles and
Ragsdales upper turnpike road at 236 poles in all 400 poles to two hickorys;
thence South 60 East 400 poles to a postoak, redoak and hickory; thence South
30 West 400 poles to the beginning. Surveyed December 11th 1838.
        Alfred Collins, Surveyor for Rhea County
Henry A. Shelton & Gatewood Qualls, S.C.B.

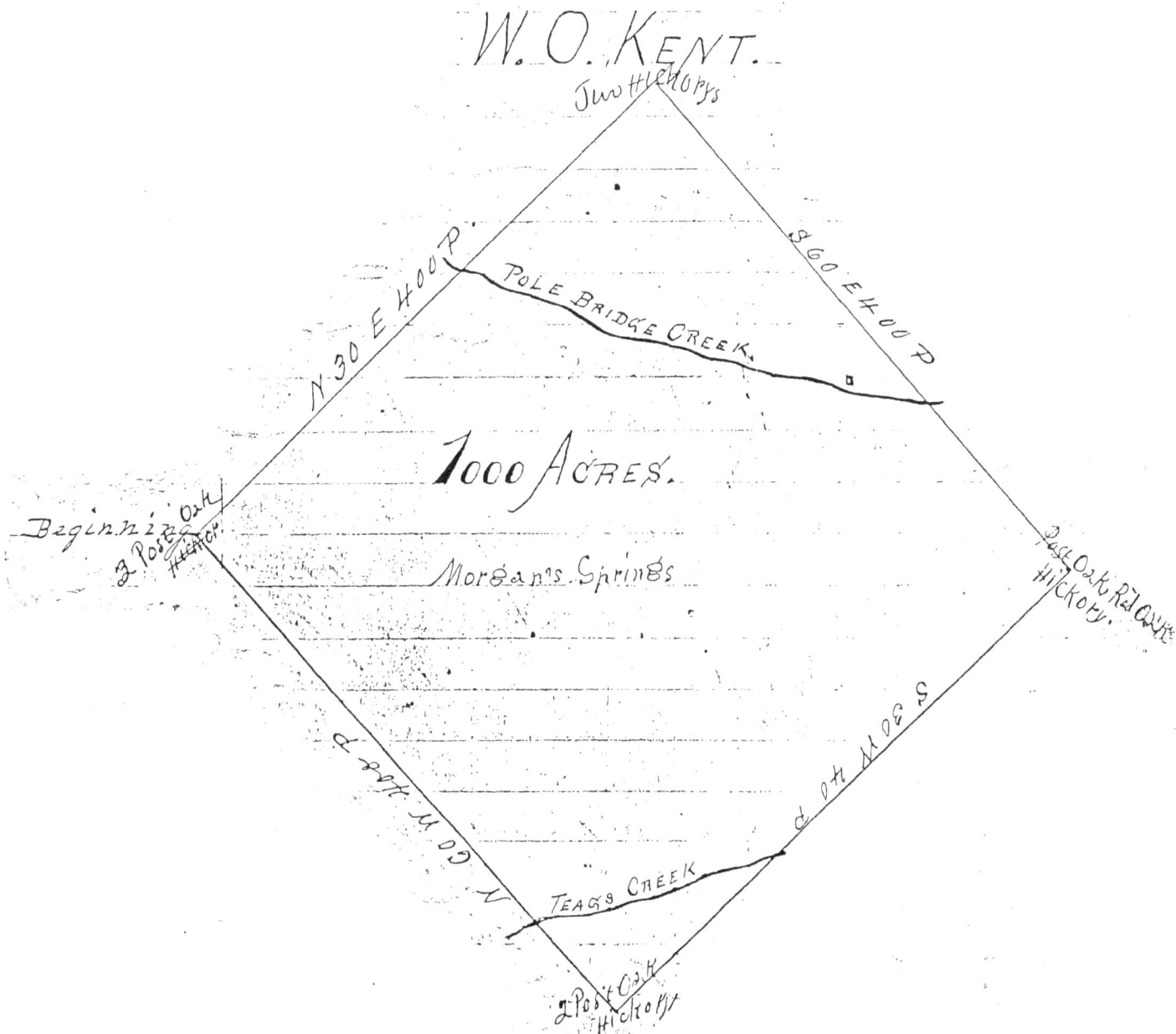

W.O. KENT   (page 172)

State of Tennessee, Rhea County
In pursuance of an entry made by William O. Kent of No. 309 and dated December
8th 1838 for one thousand acres of land in Said County on the waters of Richland
Creek. BEGINNING at or near the County line on two hickorys and a postoak it
being the Northwest corner of an entry made by Stephen Hoyt; thence North 30 East
with the County line crossing a Spring branch at 102 poles and a South fork of
Richland Creek at 190 poles and a Spring branch at 343 poles in all 400 poles to
two postoaks; thence South 60 East 400 poles to a blackoak and redoak and postoak;
thence South   (page 173)
thirty West 400 poles to a postoak, redoak and hickory; thence North 60 West 400
poles to the beginning. Surveyed December 11th 1838.
        Alfred Collins, S.R.C.
Henry A. Shelton & Gatewood Qualls, S.C.C.

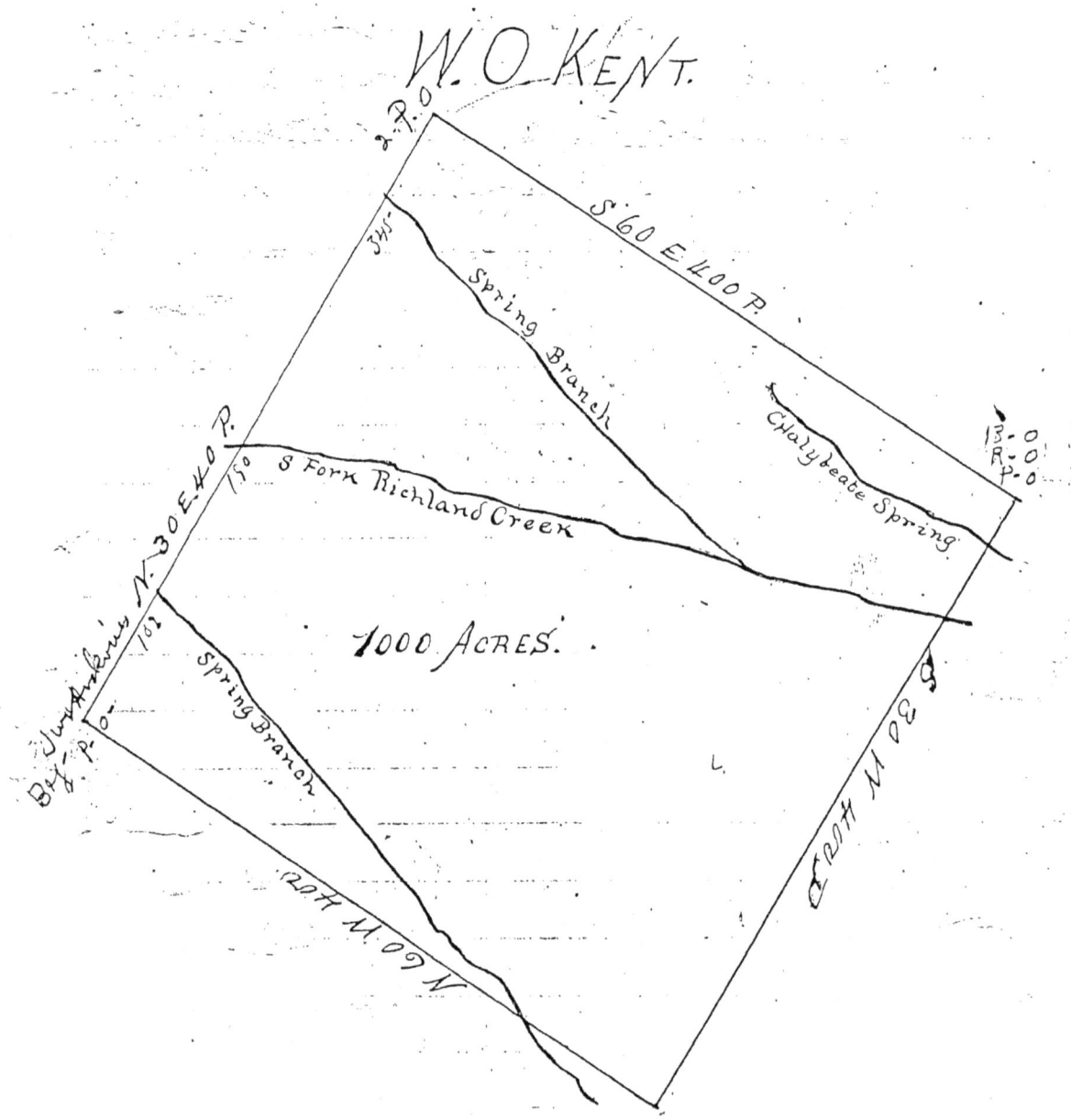

W.O. KENT   (page 173)

State of Tennessee, Rhea County
In pursuance of an entry made by Joseph L. Hoyt of No. 310 and dated December 8th
1838 for one Thousand acres of land in Said County, I have Surveyed for William
O. Kent assignee of Said Hoyt the Said tract. BEGINNING on the line of Bledsoe
& Rhea Counties at the North West corner of an entry made by William O. Kent on
two postoaks on the side of a ridge; thence N 30 E crossing a large Creek at 260
poles in all 400 poles to a postoak and hickory; thence S 60 East 400 poles to a
hickory and blackoak; thence South 30 West 400 poles to a blackoak redoak and
postoak; thence North 60 West 400 poles to the beginning. Surveyed December 11th
1838.   Alfred Collins, S.R.C.
Henry A. Shelton & Gatewood Qualls, S.C.B.

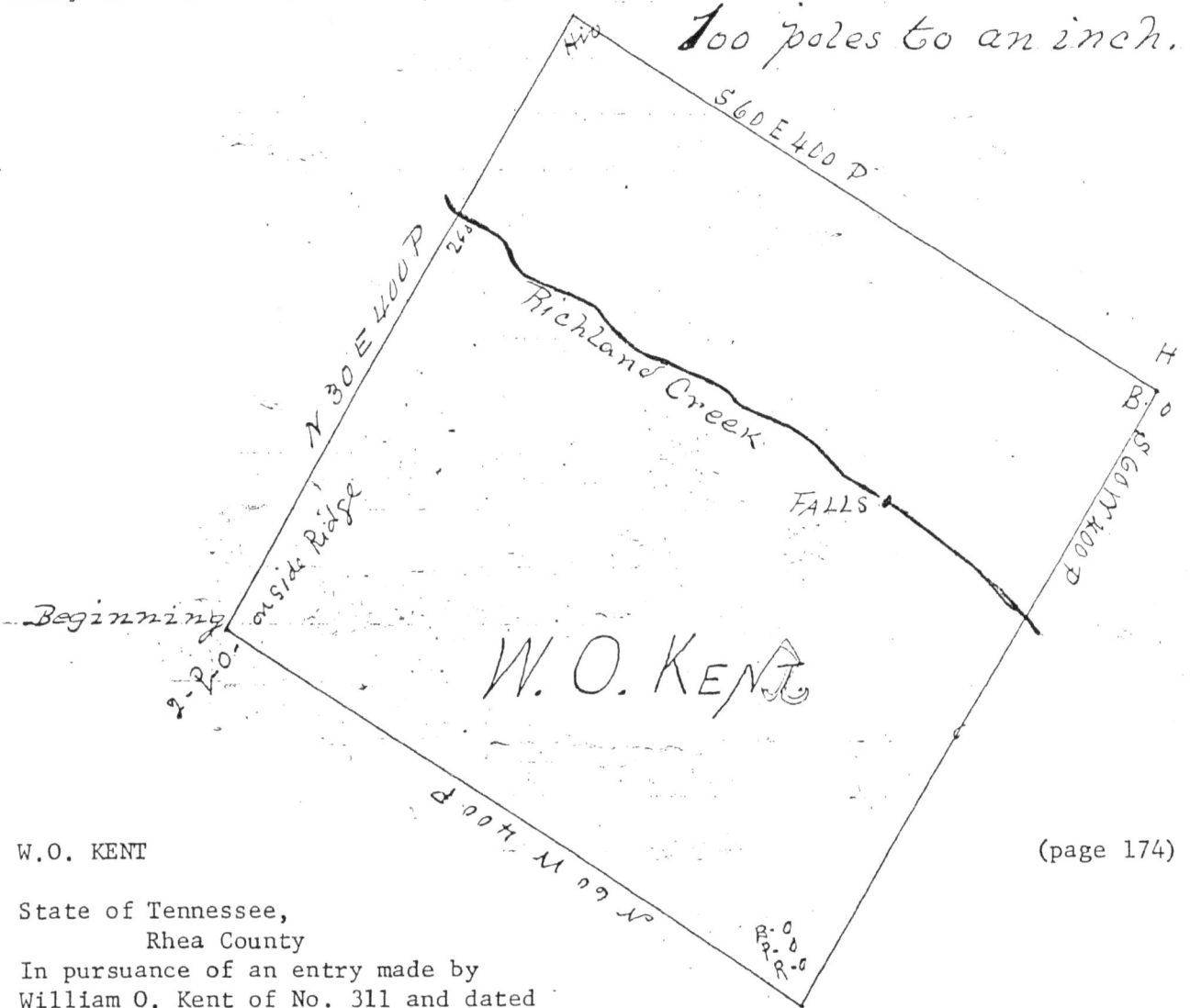

100 poles to an inch.

S 60 E 400 P

N 30 E 400 P

Richland Creek

FALLS

H. B. S 60 M 400 P

Beginning

onside Ridge

2-P.O.

W. O. KENT

N 60 W 400 P

B.O. P.O. R.O.

W.O. KENT   (page 174)

State of Tennessee,
          Rhea County
In pursuance of an entry made by
William O. Kent of No. 311 and dated
December 8th 1838 for one thousand acres of land in Said County. BEGINNING on
the line of Rhea and Bledsoe Counties at the northwest corner of an entry made
by Joseph L. Hoyt on a postoak and hickory; thence North 30 East crossing a
Creek at 130 poles and a Spring branch at 370 poles in all 400 poles to a hickory, blackoak and Whiteoak; thence South 60 East along a Spring branch 400
poles to two postoaks and a redoak; thence South 30 West crossing a branch at
180 poles in all 400 poles to a hickory & blackoak; thence North 60 West 400
poles to the beginning. Surveyed December 11th 1838.

Alfred Collins, Surveyor for Rhea County
Henry A. Shelton & Gatewood Qualls, S.C.B.

100 poles to inch.

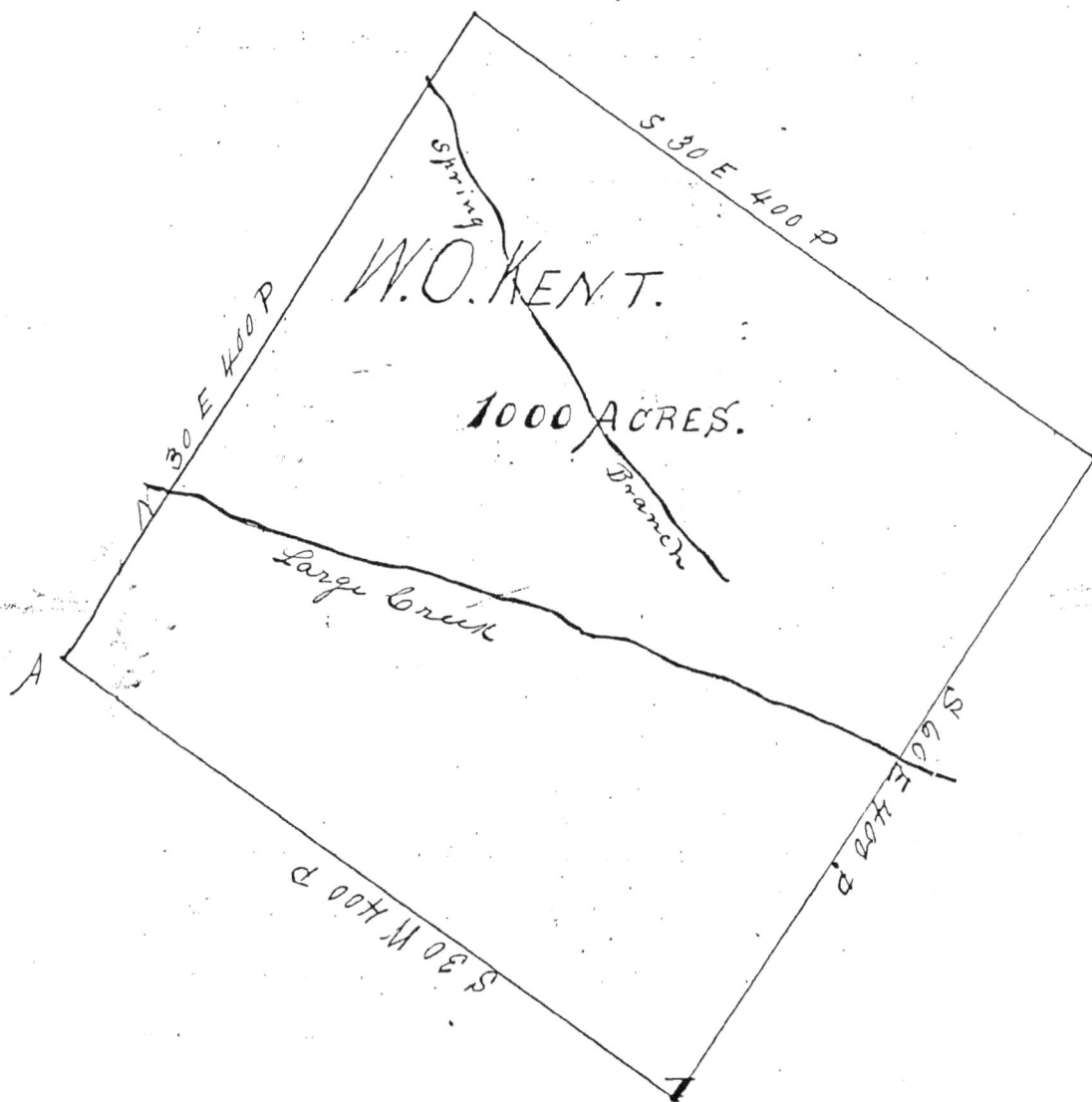

W. O. KENT.

1000 ACRES.

S 30 E 400 P

N 30 E 400 P

Spring

Branch

Large Creek

A

S 30 W 400 P

S 60 E 400 P

H. WEIDENHOFFER   (page 175)

State of Tennessee, Rhea County
In pursuance of an entry made by Henry Weidenhoffer of No. 312 and dated December
8th 1838 for one thousand acres of land in Said County, I have Surveyed for William O. Kent assignee of Said Weidenhoffer the Said tract. BEGINNING on the
Northeast corner of an entry made by William O. Kent on two postoaks and a redoak;
thence South 30 West crossing a branch at 180 poles and Paines turnpike at 220
poles in all 400 poles to a blackoak and hickory; thence South 60 East 400 poles
to a Stake; thence North 30 East 400 poles to a Stake; thence North 60 West 400
poles to the beginning. Surveyed December 12th 1838. Alfred Collins, S.R.C.
Henry A. Shelton & Gatewood Qualls, S.C.B.

100 poles to an inch.

H. WEIDENHOFFER.

N FORK

1000 ACRES.

RICHLAND

N 60 W 400 P
S 30 W 400 P
N 60 W 400 P
S 30 E 400 P
S 60 E 400 P

A

C

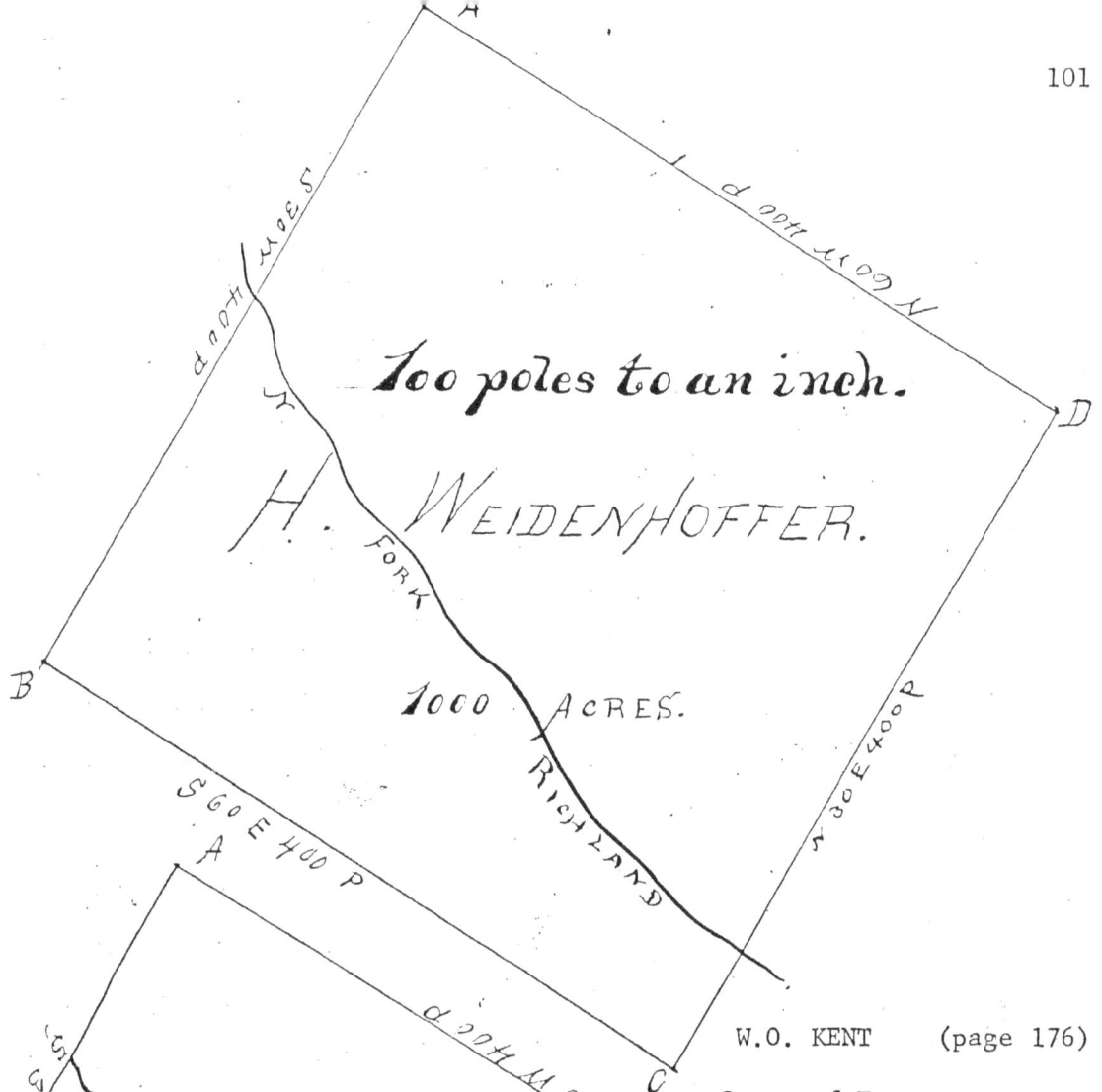

W.O. KENT. (page 176)

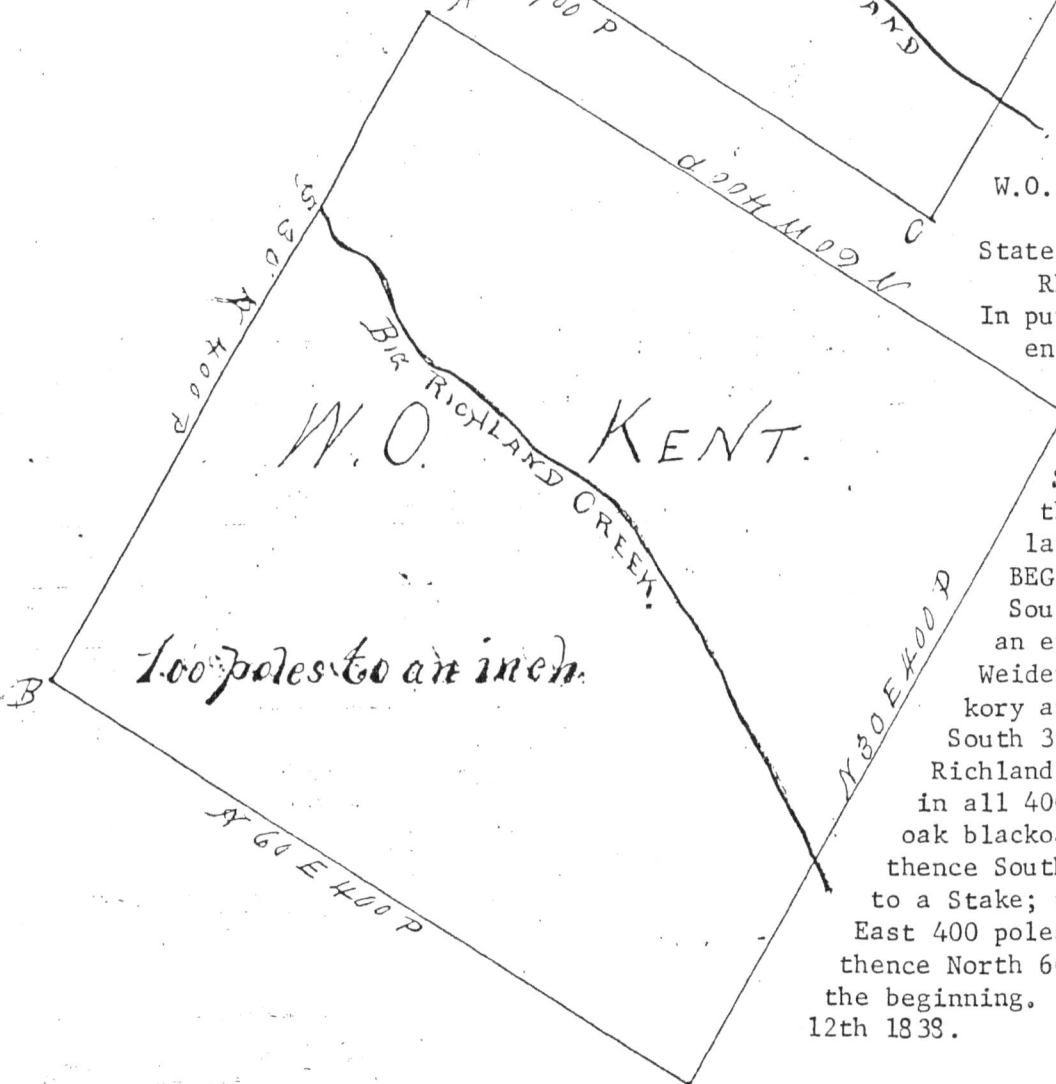

W. O. KENT.

BIG RICHLAND CREEK

100 poles to an inch.

S 30 W 400 P
N 30 E 400 P
N 60 E 400 P

B

State of Tennessee,
Rhea County
In pursuance of an
entry made by Wil-
liam O. Kent of
No. 313 and
dated December
8th 1838 for one
thousand acres of
land in Said County
BEGINNING on the
Southwest corner of
an entry made by Henry
Weidenhoffer on a hic-
kory and blackoak; thence
South 30 West crossing
Richland Creek at 104 poles
in all 400 poles to a redoak blackoak and postoak;
thence South 60 East 400 poles
to a Stake; thence North 30
East 400 poles to a Stake;
thence North 60 West 400 poles to
the beginning. Surveyed December
12th 1838.

Alfred Collins, S.R.C.
Henry A. Shelton & Gatewood Qualls,
       S.C.B.

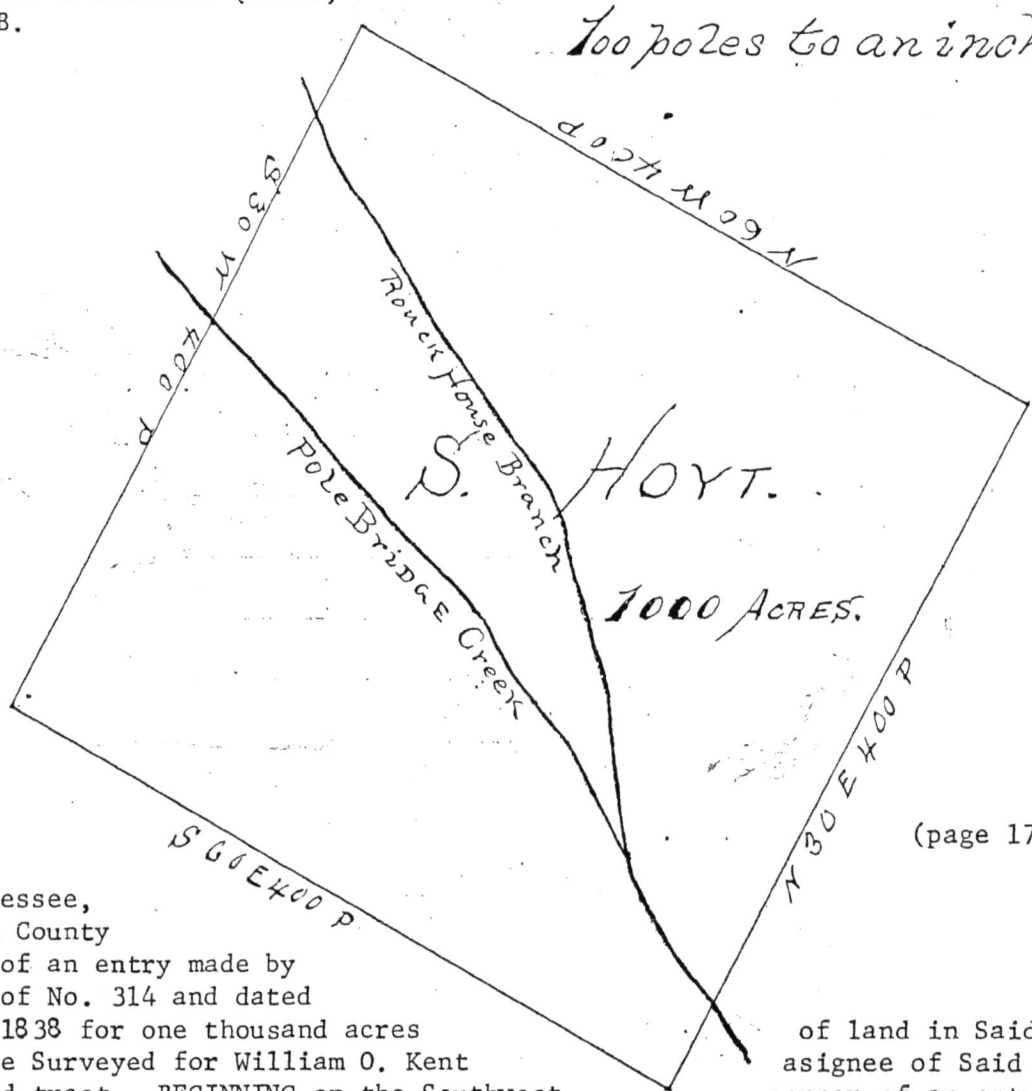

100 poles to an inch.

N 60 W 400 P

S 30 W 400 P

Rock House Branch

Pole Bridge Creek

S. HOYT.

1000 ACRES.

N 30 E 400 P

S 60 E 400 P

S. HOYT   (page 177)

State of Tennessee,
        Rhea County
In pursuance of an entry made by
Stephen Hoyt of No. 314 and dated
December 8th 1838 for one thousand acres   of land in Said
County, I have Surveyed for William O. Kent   asignee of Said
Hoyt, the Said tract. BEGINNING on the Southwest   corner of an entry
made by William O. Kent on a blackoak, redoak and   postoak; thence
South 30 West crossing Rockhouse branch at 38 poles and Polebridge Creek at 140
poles in all 400 poles to a postoak, redoak and hickory; thence South 60 East 400
poles to three whiteoaks and a Chestnut; thence North 30 East 400 poles to a
Stake; thence North 60 West 400 poles to the beginning. Surveyed December 12th
1838.   Alfred Collins, S.R.C.
Henry A. Shelton and Gatewood Qualls, S.C.B.

W.O. KENT   (page 178)

State of Tennessee, Rhea County
In pursuance of an entry made by William O. Kent of No. 315 and dated December
8th 1838 for one thousand acres of land in Said County. BEGINNING at the Southeast corner of Gatewood Qualls two thousand acre Survey on a Blackoak and hickory;
thence with his line N 60 W 430 poles to a Stake; thence South 23 West 280 poles
to the Hamilton County line; thence with Said line South 35 East 510 poles to two
large poplars a whiteoak and Beach Near a Small branch; thence North 23 East crossing a Cylebiate [sic] Spring at 180 poles in all 500 poles to the beginning.
Surveyed December 13th 1838.   Alfred Collins, S.R.C.
Henry A. Shelton and Gatewood Qualls, S.C.B.

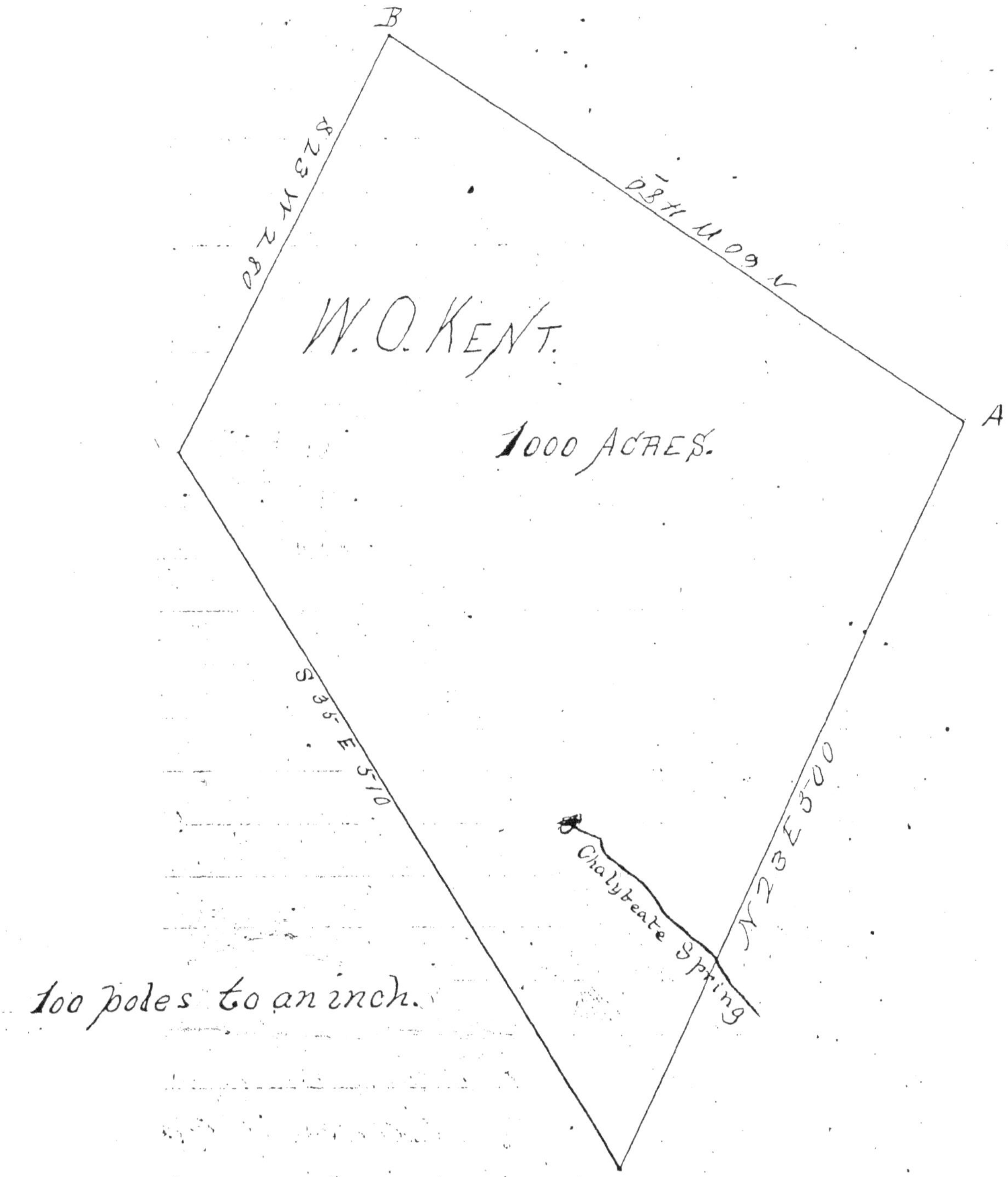
B
A
S 23 W 280
N 60 W 480
W. O. Kent.
1000 Acres.
S 35 E 570
N 23 E 500
Chalybeate Spring
100 poles to an inch.

B.H. THROOP [sic] (page 179)

State of Tennessee, Rhea County
In pursuance of an entry made by Benjamin H. Throup [sic] of No. 317 and dated December 10th 1838 for three thousand two hundred acres of land in Said County. BEGINNING on the Northeast corner of an entry made by William O. Kent at three large Whiteoaks and double chestnut running thence South 62 East crossing the windings of a Creek three times in forty poles the S.E. fork of Richland at 420 poles in all 640 poles to a Stake on a point of land known as buzzard point; thence North 30 East 960 poles to a Stake near Paines turnpike road; thence North 62 West 640 poles to a Stake; thence South 30 West 960 poles to the beginning. Surveyed December 13th 1838. Alfred Collins, Surveyor for Rhea County
Henry A. Shelton & Gatewood Qualls, S.C.B.

200 poles to an inch.

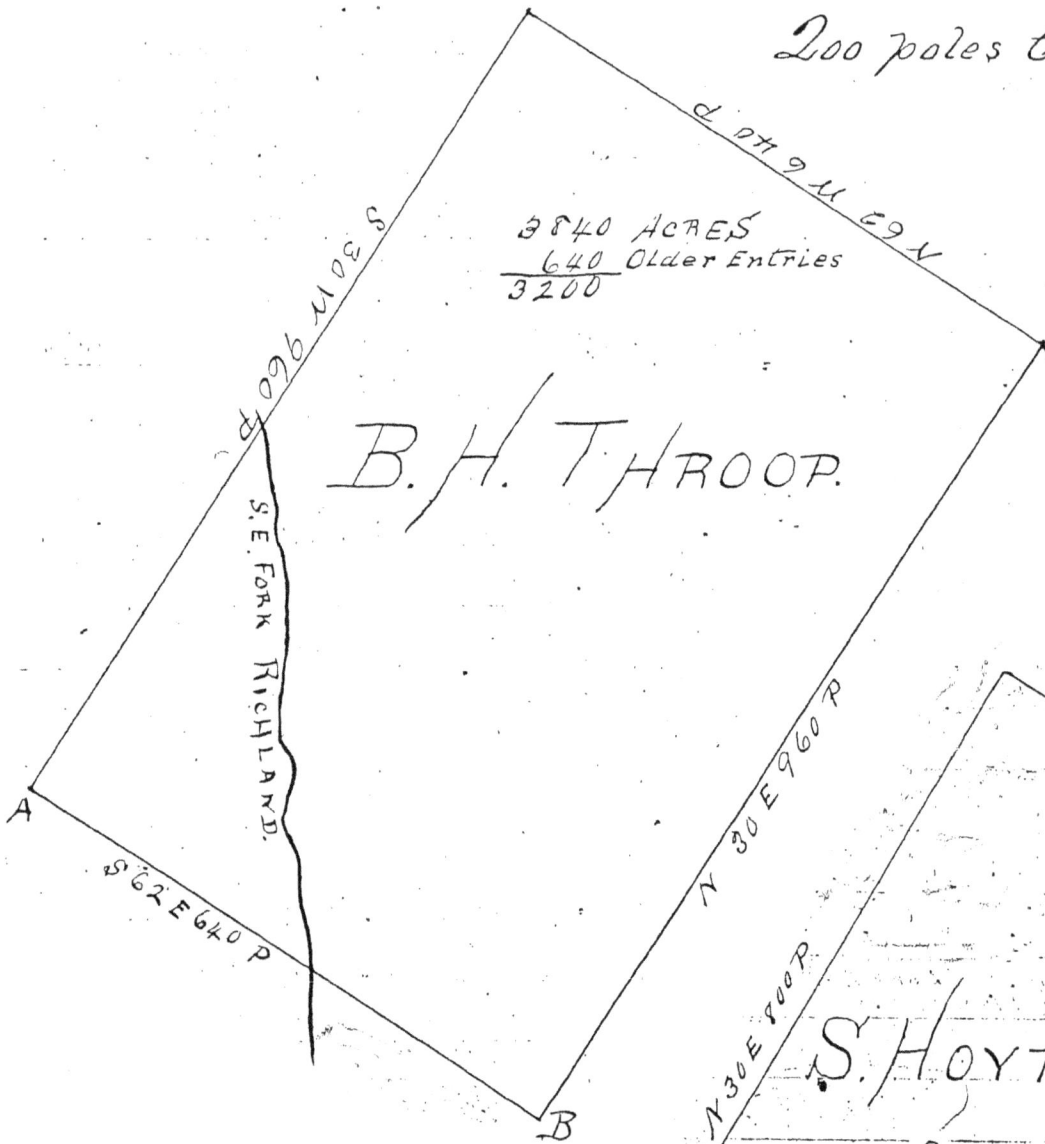

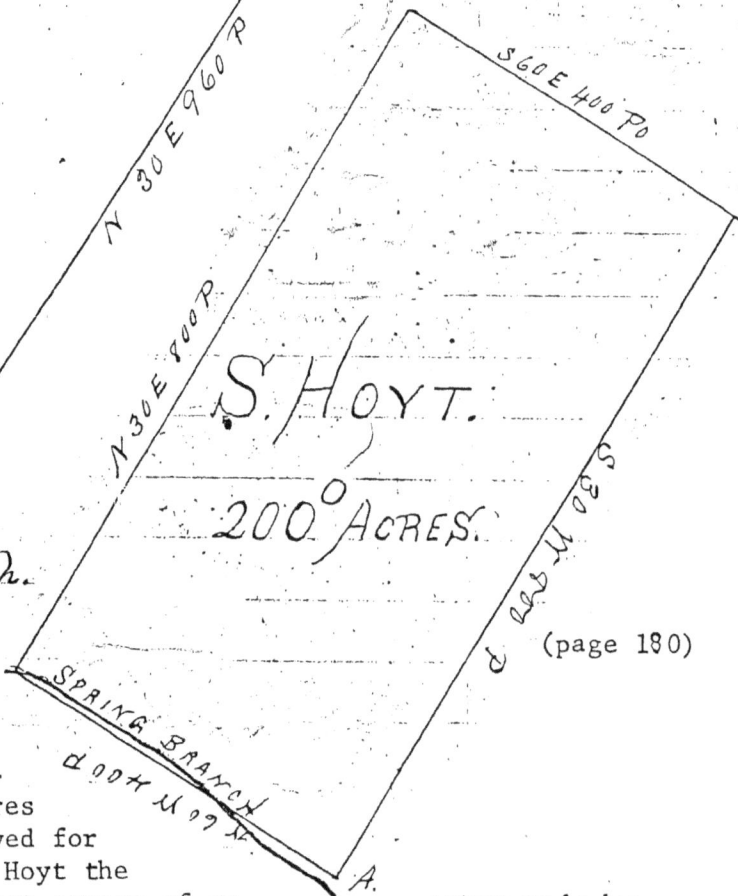

N 63 W 960 P

3840 ACRES
640 Older Entries
3200

B.H.THROOP.

S 30 W 960 P

S.E. Fork Richland.

N 30 E 960 P

A

S 62 E 640 P

B

200 poles to an inch.

S 60 E 400 Po

N 30 E 800 P

S. HOYT.

200 ACRES.

S 30 W 800 P

SPRING BRANCH

N 60 W 400 P

A

(page 180)

S. HOYT

State of Tennessee, Rhea County
In pursuance of an entry made by
Stephen Hoyt of No. 318 and dated De-
cember 10th 1838 for two thousand acres
of land in Said County, I have Surveyed for
William O. Kent assignee of the Said Hoyt the
Said tract. BEGINNING on the Northwest corner of an entry made by
Henry Weidenhoffer for one thousand acres on a redoak and two postoaks, thence
North 60 West along a Spring branch 400 poles to a hickory, blackoak and white-
oak on the County line, between Rhea and Bledsoe Counties; thence with Said line
North 30 East crossing Several branches 800 poles to a Stake, thence South 60
East 400 poles to a Stake; thence South 30 West 800 poles to the beginning.
Surveyed December 13th 1838.   Alfred Collins, Surveyor for Rhea County
Henry A. Shelton & Gatewood Qualls, S.C.B.

GATEWOOD QUALLS

State of Tennessee, Rhea County
In pursuance of an entry made by Gatewood Qualls of No. 316

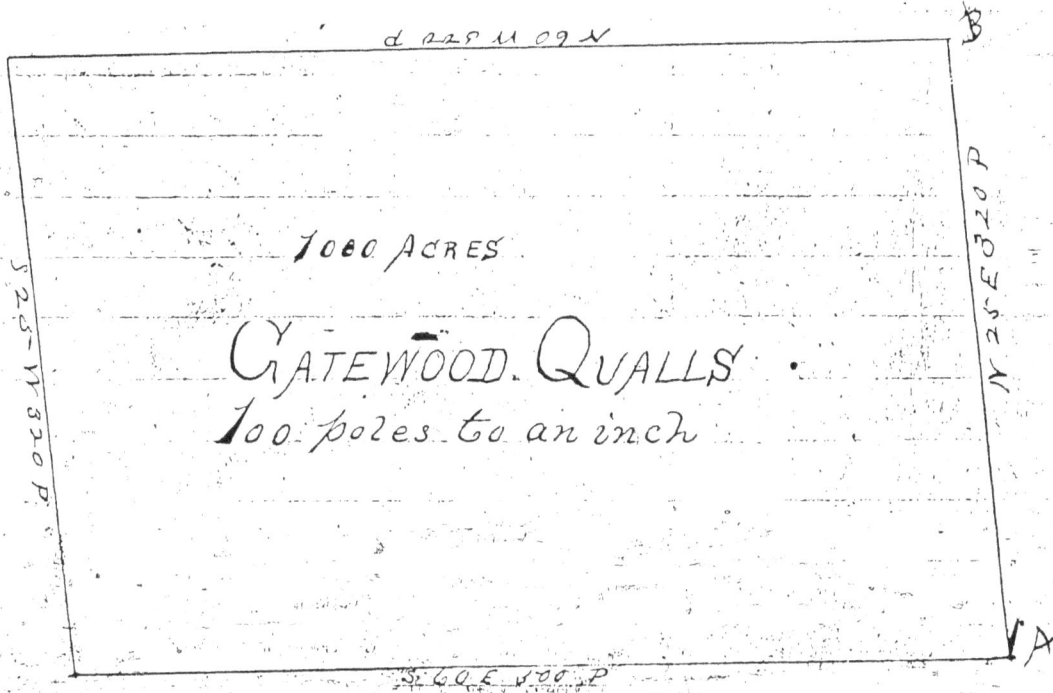

(page 181)

and dated December 8th 1838 for one thousand acres of land in Said County.
BEGINNING on Said Qualls two thousand acre Survey on a dogwood and hickory thence
North 25 East 320 poles to a chestnut dogwood and postoak near James Stewarts
line; thence North 60 West 500 poles to a Stake on David Ragsdales line; thence
South 25 West 320 poles to a Stake; thence South 60 East 500 poles to the begin-
ning. Surveyed December 13th 1838. Alfred Collins, Surveyor for Rhea County
Henry A. Shelton & William O. Kent, S.C.B.

H.A. SHELTON

State of Tennessee, Rhea County
In pursuance of an entry made by Henry A. Shelton of No. 319 and dated December
10th 1838 for three Thousand acres of land in Said County. BEGINNING on two
postoaks corner to William Kents one thousand acre entry and on David Ragsdales
line; thence with his line South 30 West 254 poles to a large forked blackoak
near a pond; thence South 60 East with another line of Said Ragsdale 10 poles to
a chestnut corner to Robert Qualls fifteen hundred acre Survey; thence with his
line South 30 West 340 poles to a blackoak; thence North 60 West 60 poles

(page 182)

to a whiteoak, poplar and hickory on a line of a five thousand acre Survey of
Henry Miller and others, thence with their line North 20 East 80 poles to two
Whiteoaks and a hickory; thence with another line of Said Survey North 70 West
778 poles to the County line, thence North 33½ East 640 poles to three postoaks; thence South 60 East 800 poles to the beginning. Surveyed December 13th
1838. Alfred Collins, Surveyor for Rhea County
Gatewood Qualls & William O. Kent, S.C.B. (Plat on following page)

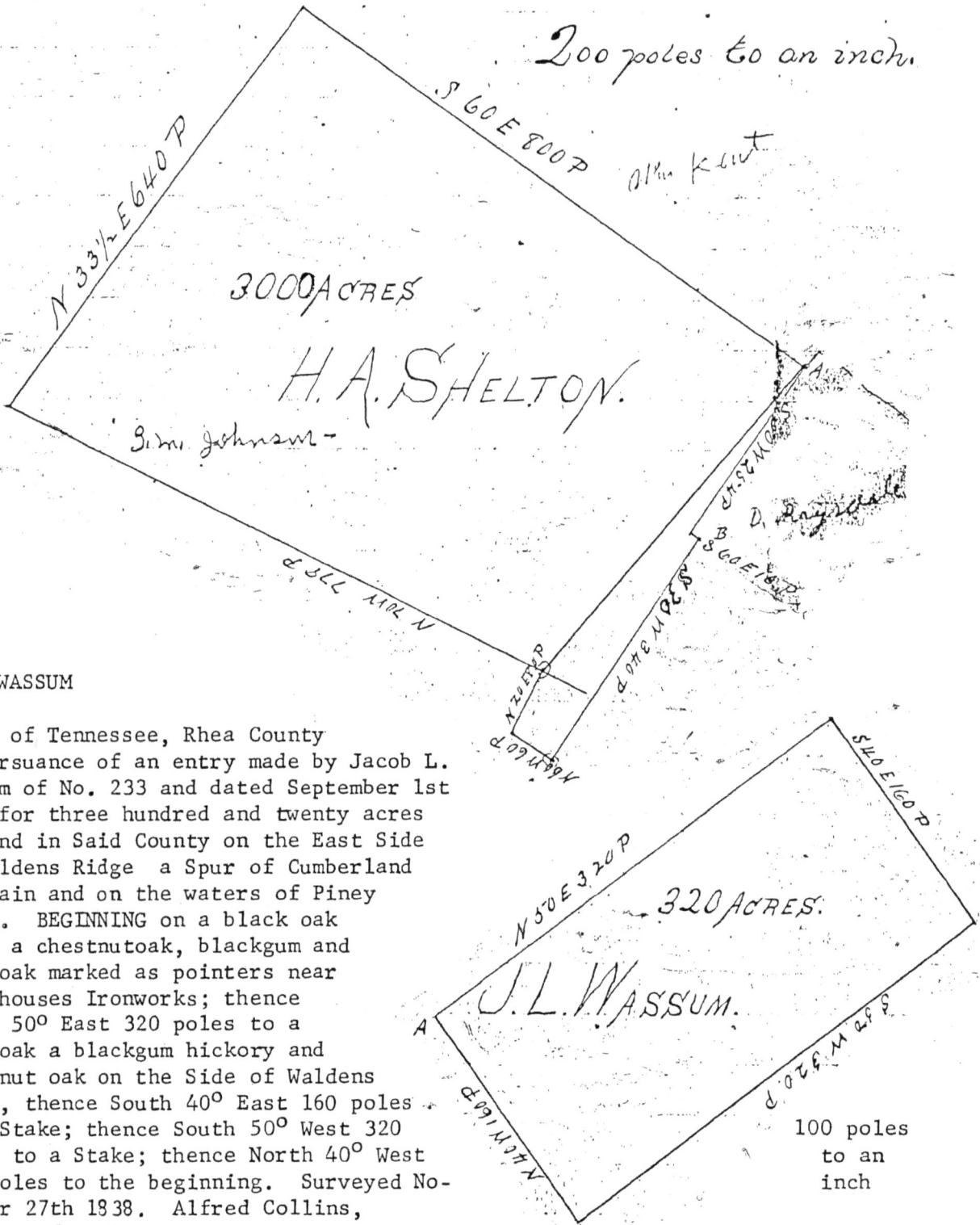

200 poles to an inch.

N 33½ E 640 P

S 60 E 800 P

3000 ACRES

H. A. SHELTON.

G. M. Johnson –

N 40 W 778 P

S 60 E 1160 P

S 30 W 320 P

320 ACRES.

J. L. WASSUM.

N 50 E 320 P

S 40 W 320 P

N 40 W 160 P

100 poles
to an
inch

J.L. WASSUM

State of Tennessee, Rhea County
In pursuance of an entry made by Jacob L.
Wassum of No. 233 and dated September 1st
1834 for three hundred and twenty acres
of land in Said County on the East Side
of Waldens Ridge a Spur of Cumberland
Mountain and on the waters of Piney
River. BEGINNING on a black oak
tree, a chestnutoak, blackgum and
blackoak marked as pointers near
Waterhouses Ironworks; thence
North 50° East 320 poles to a
blackoak a blackgum hickory and
chestnut oak on the Side of Waldens
Ridge, thence South 40° East 160 poles
to a Stake; thence South 50° West 320
poles to a Stake; thence North 40° West
160 poles to the beginning. Surveyed November 27th 1838. Alfred Collins,
Surveyor for Rhea County
Joseph Garrison & Eli Ferguson, S.C.B.

J.L. WASSUM   (page 183)

State of Tennessee, Rhea County
In pursuance of an entry made by Jacob L. Wassum of No. 234 and dated September
1st 1834 for three hundred and twenty acres of land in Said County on the East
side of Waldens Ridge a Spur of Cumberland Mountain and on the waters of Piney
River. BEGINNING on a blackoak tree, blackgum, hickory and chestnutoak; thence

North 44 East 320 poles to a blackoak tree; thence South 40 East
160 poles to a Stake; thence South 44° West 320 poles to a
Stake; thence North 40° West 160 poles to the beginning.
Surveyed November 27th 1839.
Alfred Collins, Surveyor for Rhea County
Joseph Garrison & Eli Ferguson, S.C.B.

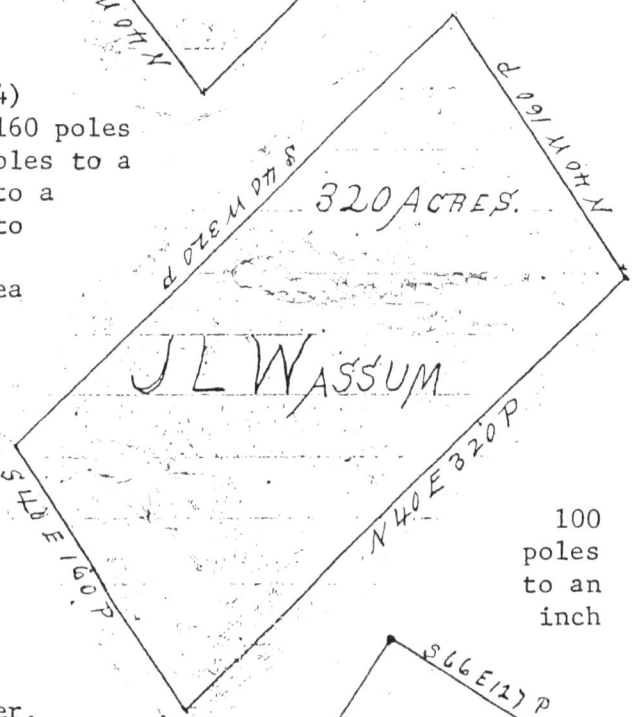

J.L. WASSUM

State of Tennessee, Rhea County
In pursuance of an Entry made by
Jacob L. Wassum of No. 236 and
dated September 4th 1834 for
three hundred and twenty
acres of land in Said
County on the East Side of Waldens
Ridge a Spur of Cumberland Mountain
and on the waters of Piney River.
BEGINNING on a blackoak tree it being
the Northwest corner of entry No. 284
made by Jacob L. Wassum and

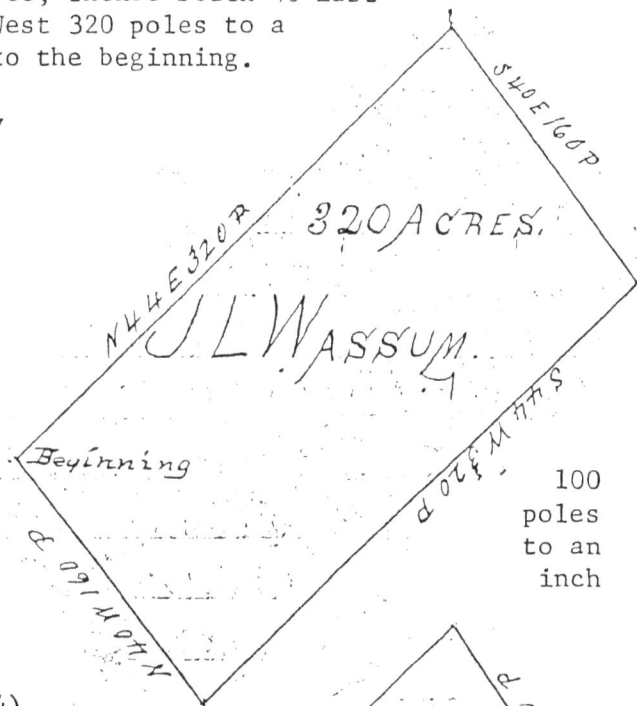

(page 184)

running with Said entry South 40° East 160 poles
to a Stake; thence North 40° East 320 poles to a
Stake, thence North 40° West 160 poles to a
Stake; thence South 40° West 320 poles to
the beginning. Surveyed November 27th
1938. Alfred Collins, Surveyor for Rhea
County.
Joseph Garrison & Eli Ferguson, S.C.B.

D. McFALLS

State of Tennessee, Rhea County
In pursuance of an entry made by
Daniel McFalls of No. 325 and dated
January 17th 1839 for two hundred
acres of land in Said County on Waldens Ridge of Cumberland Mountain on
Cove Creek a fork of Piney Creek or River.
BEGINNING on a White pine on the North Side
of Cove Creek; thence South 27° West 202
poles to a small hickory, three chestnut trees
marked as pointers; thence North 63 West 127
poles to a Whiteoak maple and Sowerwood;
thence North 27 East 252 poles to two birch
and two dogwood trees, thence South 63 East
127 poles to the beginning.
Surveyed February 2nd 1839.
Alfred Collins, Surveyor for Rhea County
Samuel Holloway & John Dunlap, S.C.B.

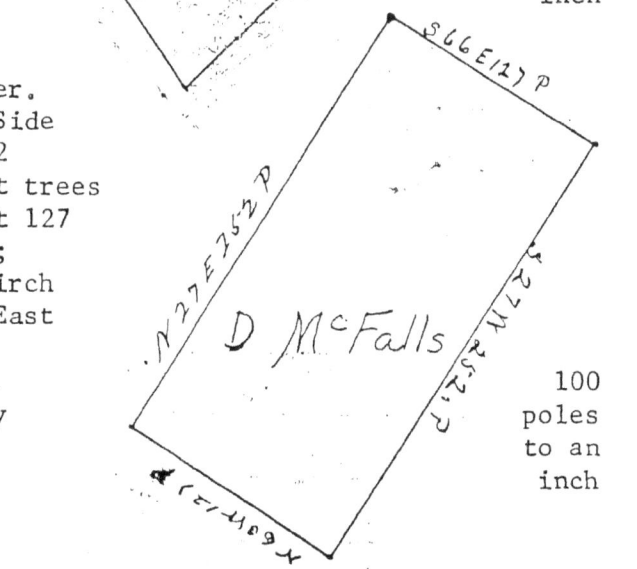

320 ACRES.
J L Wassum.
N 44 E 320 P
S 40 E 160 P
S 44 W 320 P
N 40 W 160 P
Beginning
100 poles to an inch

320 ACRES.
J L Wassum
S 40 W 320 P
N 40 W 160 P
N 40 E 320 P
S 40 E 160 P
Beginning
100 poles to an inch

D McFalls
S 66 E 127 P
N 27 E 252 P
S 27 W 202 P
N 63 W 127 P
100 poles to an inch

108

G.W. BIRDETT

State of Tennessee, Rhea County
In pursuance of an entry made by George W.
Birdet [sic] of No. 320 and dated December
17th 1838 for three hundred acres of land
in Said County on the Side of Waldens
Ridge a Spur of Cumberland Mountain.
BEGINNING on a Pine

(page 185)

tree corner to Hannah Hoyt on the first
bench of the mountain; thence due West
100 poles to three hickorys at a large
Clift of the mountain; thence with the
clift North 40° East 320 poles to a
double chestnut and hickory; thence
South 75° East 120 poles to a
hickory and Sycamore at the foot
of the mountain; thence South 26° West

100
poles
to an
inch

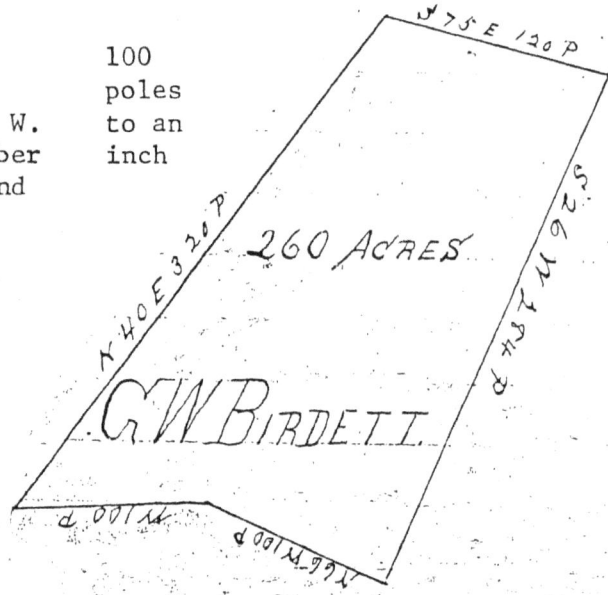

284 poles to a Stake, two postoaks and a blackoak marked as pointers corner to
Hannah Hoyt; thence with her line North 66 West 100 poles to the beginning.
Surveyed January 27th 1839. Alfred Collins, Surveyor for Rhea County
Anderson Walker & Zachariah Compton, C.B.

SAML. DUDLEY

State of Tennessee, Rhea County
In pursuance of an entry made by Samuel Dudley
of No. 326 and dated February 2nd 1839 for
thirty Seven acres of land in Said County on
Waldens Ridge of Cumberland Mountain on the
waters of Piney Creek or River. BEGINNING on
a whiteoak tree near Rices line marked S.D.;
thence South 55 East 57 poles to a whiteoak
and dogwood; thence North 31 East 89 poles to
a Blackgum, thence North 47 West 73 poles to
a Sowerwood, hickory and blackgum; thence a
Straight line to the beginning.
Surveyed February 2nd 1839.
Alfred Collins, Surveyor for Rhea County
Calvin Dudley & Doctor Dudley, S.C.B.

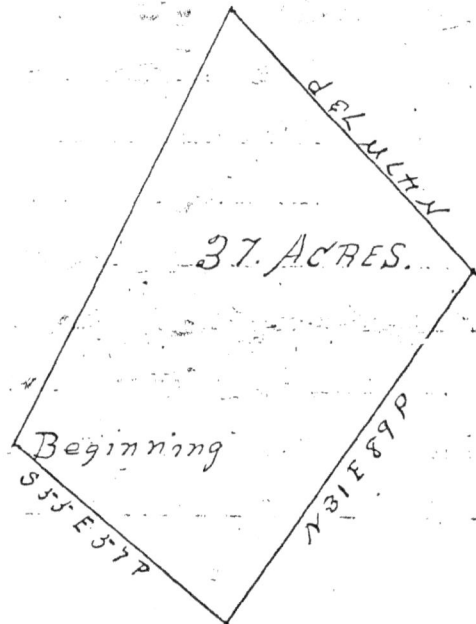

40 poles to an inch

R.H. DYER

(page 186)

Stste of Tennessee, Rhea County
In pursuance of [an entry] made by Robert H. Dyer of No. 327 and dated May the
20th 1839 for 100 acres of land in Said County on Waldens Ridge of Cumberland
Mountain. BEGINNING on a Whiteoak and double chestnut; Thence South 30° West 100
poles to a blackoak; then North 61 West 80 poles to a postoak on Dolans line;
then with his line North 15 West 150 poles to a hickory; then North 35 East 68
poles to a Blackoak and Whiteoak; then South 66 East 14 poles to a Chestnut; then
North 20 East 40 poles to a double whiteoak; then South 70 East 20 poles

R.H. DYER

Plat labels:
- S 66 E 14 P
- N 35 E 68 P
- N 20 E 40 P
- S 70 E 20 P
- S 31 W 120 P
- S 35 E 85 P
- N 15 W 120 P
- S 60 E 76 P
- N 59 W 85 P
- DOGWOOD

R.H. Dyer.
50 poles to an inch.

100 ACRES.

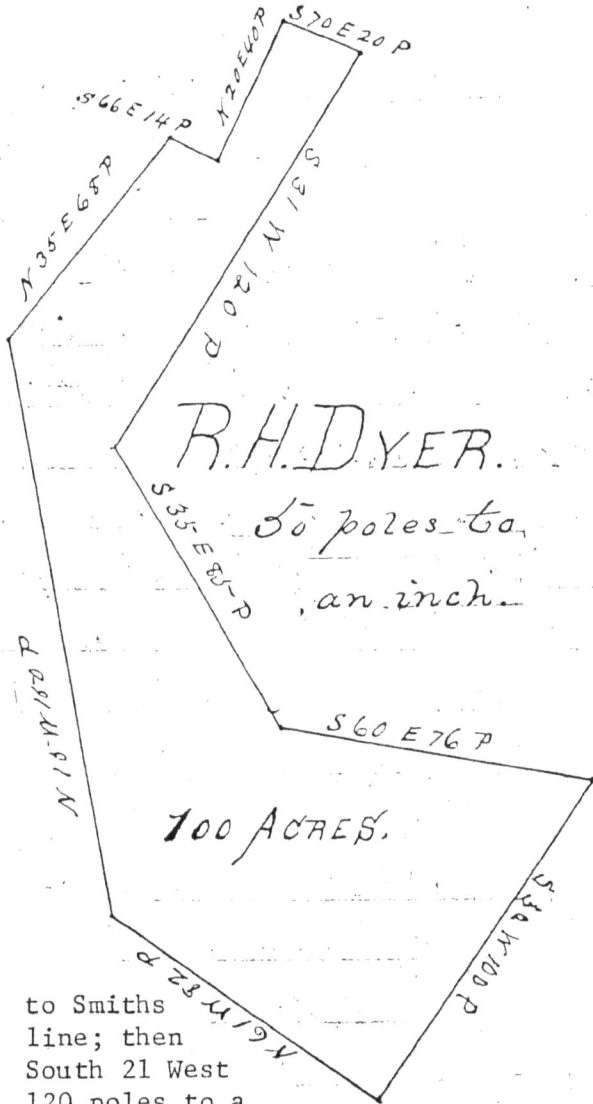

to Smiths
line; then
South 21 West
120 poles to a
hickory; then South 59 East 85 poles
to a hickory; then South 60 East 76
poles to the beginning. Surveyed May
20th 1839. Alfred Collins,
    Surveyor for Rhea County
John Johnson & Joseph J. Dyer, S.C.B.

D. McFALLS

100 poles to inch.

Plat labels:
- DOGWOOD
- McNESH
- S 3 E 920 P
- Straight line to the beginning

D. McFalls.
1280. ACRES.

A

(page 187)

D. McFALLS

State of Tennessee,
Rhea County

In pursuance of an en-
try made by Daniel Mc-
Falls of No. 324 and da-
ted January 17th 1839 for
twelve hundred and eighty
acres of land in Said
County. BEGINNING on the
South side of a pond at the
top of the mountain on Johnsons
fork of Piney on a chestnut
marked A.H. then with the bluff
North 8 West 48 poles to a redoak
Hickory and dogwood on the bluff then with the bluff North 59 West 74 poles to
a Chestnutoak; then with the bend of the bluff North 77 West passing a blackoak
at 190 poles in all 360 poles to a Stake Supposed to a bluff of Canebrake fork;
then South 3 East 920 poles to a Stake; then a Straight line to the beginning.
Surveyed November 28th 1839. Alfred Collins, Surveyor for Rhea County
Jonas Likens & Isaac Likens, S.C.B.

(NOTE— The plat above for D. McFalls tract was reduced to fit the page and a
one-inch scale added to the upper right corner)

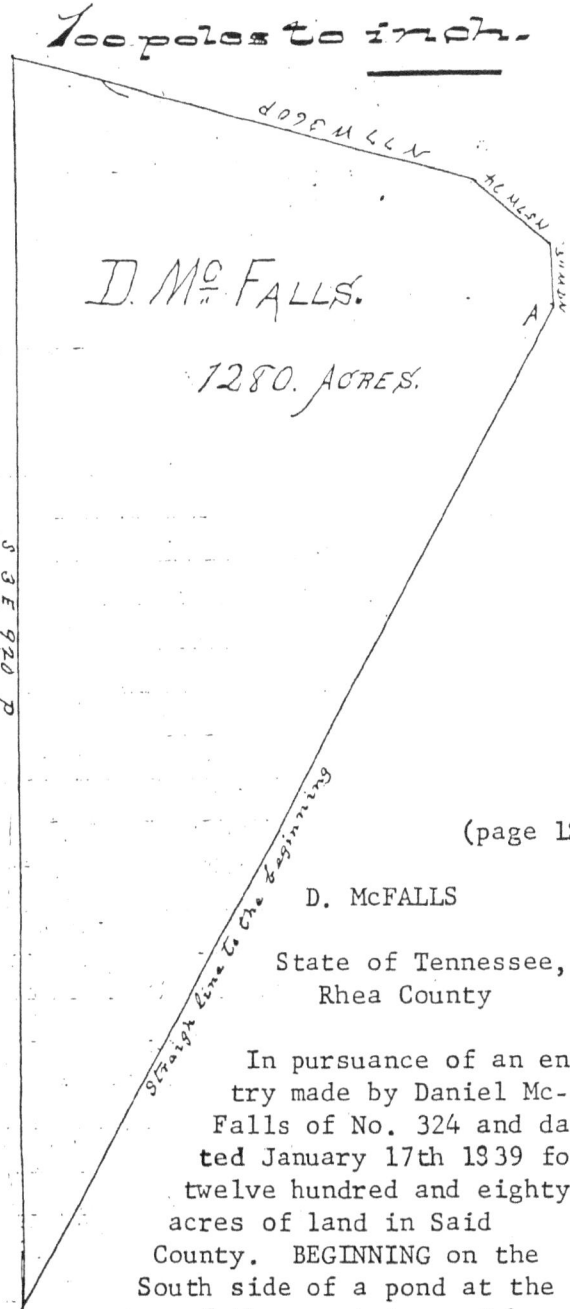

110

A. COLLINS (page 138)

State of Tennessee,
            Rhea County
In pursuance of an
entry made by
Alfred Collins
of No. 329 and
dated January
17th 1840 for two
thousand acres of
land in Said County
on Waldens Ridge of
Cumberland Mountain and
on the waters of Piney
River. BEGINNING on a
whiteoak, two chestnutoaks
and a hickory marked as pointers
on a line of a 5000 acre Survey of
John B. Inlows then with his line
North 60 West 420 poles to a whiteoak and
double chestnut near the County line between
Rhea and Bledsoe Counties; then with the County
line South 30 West 360 poles to two postoaks near
Beatys Road then South 60 East 900 poles to a Stake near
then North 30 East 360 poles to a Stake on Said Inlows Survey; then with a line
of the Same North 60 West 480 poles to the beginning. Surveyed January 18th 1840.
            Alfred Collins, Surveyor for Rhea County
James P. Collins & James Pearce, C.B.

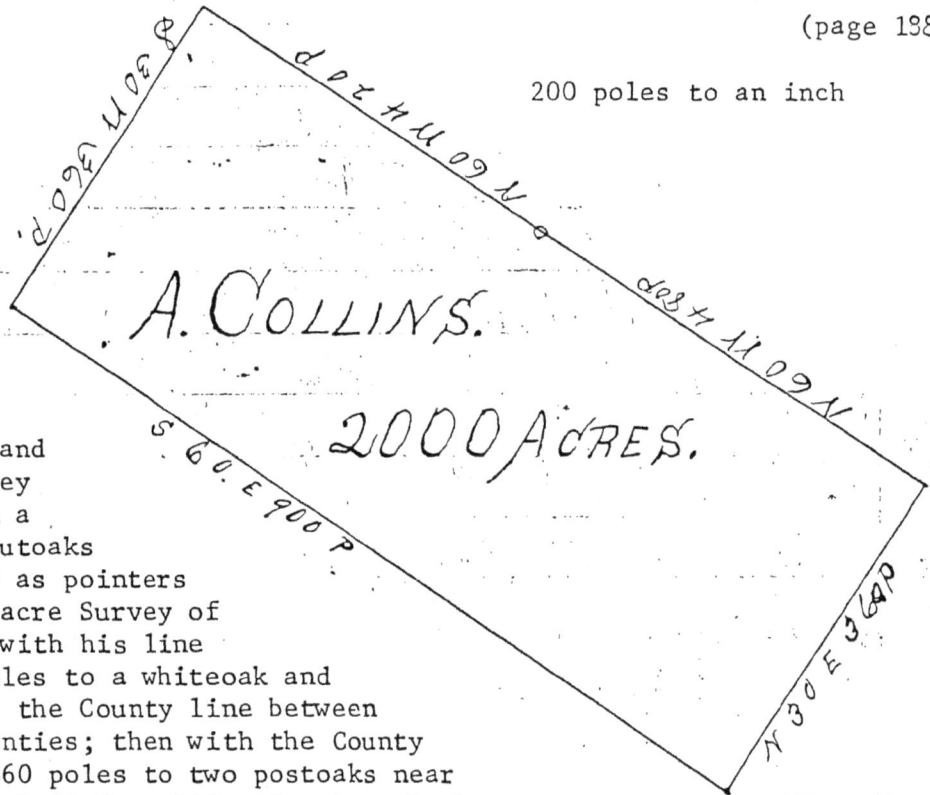

200 poles to an inch

A. COLLINS.

2000 ACRES.

Piney River

B. BENSON (page 139)

State of Tennessee, Rhea County
By virtue of an entry made by
Barclay S. Benson No. 328 and
dated November 25th 1839 for
300 acres of land in Said County
on Waldens Ridge and on the waters of Richland Creek.
BEGINNING on a hickory near a
Chalibeate Spring between the
roads leading from Ragsdales
turnpike to Pikeville & McMinn-
ville and running as follows;
thence N 80° W 100 poles to a
postoak marked "B"; thence S 20°
W 100 poles to a large Redoak on
an old line; thence S 60° E 240
poles to a Small postoak on a
Small drean [sic]; thence N 45°
E 126 poles to a hickory; thence
N 12° W 21 poles to a chestnut
corner to an old entry; thence
with the line of Said entry N 17°

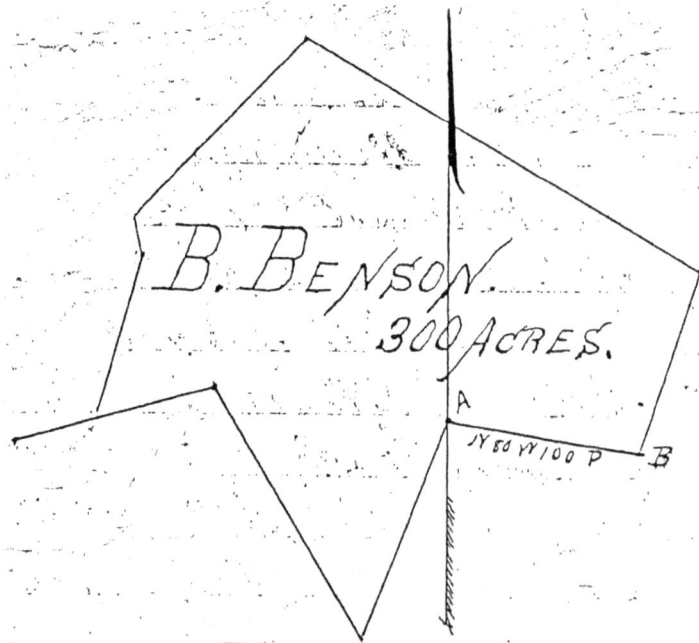

B. BENSON.
300 ACRES.

100 poles to the inch

E 85 poles to a hickory; thence N 72° E 24 poles to a Stake; thence S 75° W 82½ poles to a Stake; thence N 32° W 150 poles to a postoak; thence S 22 W 122 poles to the beginning. Surveyed April 6th 1841.

William H. Bell, Surveyor for Rhea County
Joshua Riddle & G.W. Morgan, C. Bearers

JNO DUNLAP

State of Tennessee, Rhea County
By virtue of an entry No. 332 made in the Entry Takers office on the 16th Sept 1841 for Rhea County in the State of Tennessee by John Dunlap by virtue of his occupant right and by virtue of a deputation from Wm H. Bell the County Surveyor for Said Rhea County, I have Surveyed for John Dunlap three hundred and

(page 190)

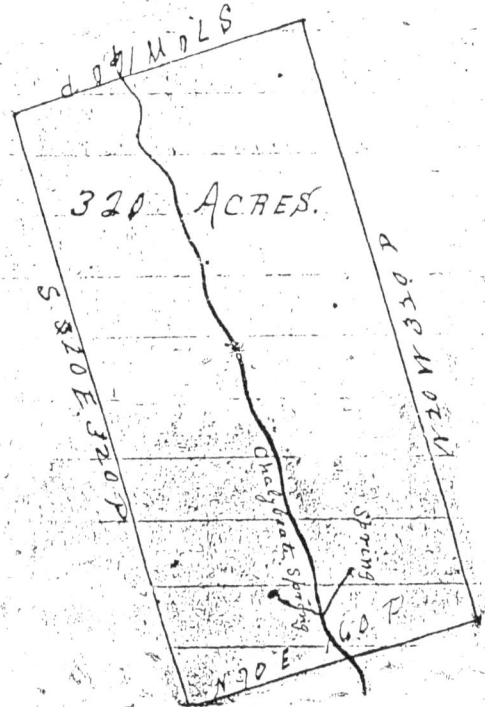

twenty acres of land in Said County of Rhea on Waldens on both sides of Cove Creek in an oblong including two Springs and the house and improvements where Said Dunlap now lives. BEGINNING on a Spruce pine marked A on the Northeast Side of Said Cove Creek near the Spring; thence N 20 W 320 poles; thence S 70 W crossing the Creek 160 poles; thence S 20 E 320 poles; thence N 70 E crossing Sd Creek below the Spring to the beginning. 18th September 1844.

Wm H. Bell, Surveyor for Rhea County, by his deputy Richard Waterhouse
John Dunlap & Jacob Dunlap, C.C.

JAS. LOYD

State of Tennessee, Rhea County
By virtue of an entry No. 339 dated the 16th November 1843 and certified to me I have Surveyed for James Loyd the original enterer 1000 acres of land lying and being on Waldens Ridge on the waters of Brush and Ragsdales Creeks. BEGINNING on a postoak marked J.L. near Snows corner; running thence South 45 East 112 poles to a postoak corner; thence North 45 East 500 poles to a Spruce pine and hickory and Sowerwood pointers on the brink of Ragsdales Creek; thence North 45 West 320 poles to a double postoak corner; thence South 45 West 500 poles to a large blackoak; thence South 45 East 208 poles to the beginning.
Surveyed the 21st November 1843
Wm H. Bell, Surveyor for Rhea County
A. Loyd & R. Loyd, Chain bearers

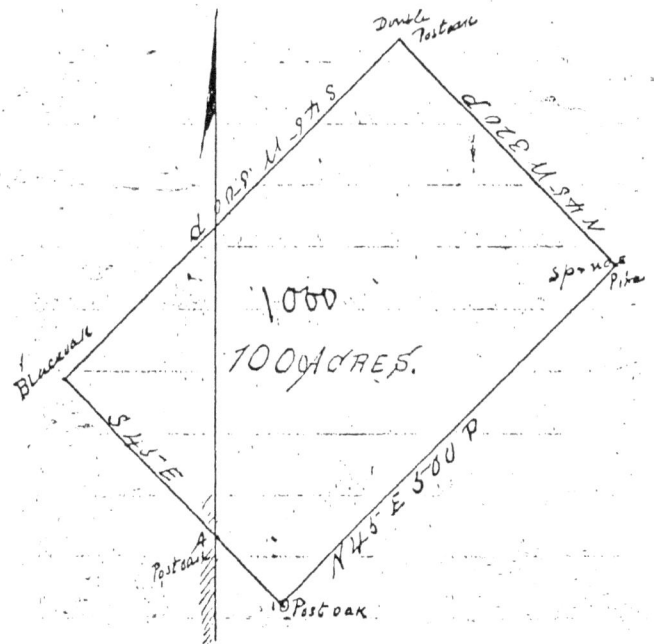

200 poles to the inch

John Loyd, Marker

A.J. BOLINGER (page 191)

In virtue of an entry made by A.J. Bollinger [sic]
in the Entry Takers office for the County of
Rhea and State of Tennessee on the 12th Feb.
1845 I have this day Surveyed for Bollinger
1000 acres of land lying and being in
Said County on Wallins Ridge on the
waters of Piney River. BEGINNING on
two whiteoaks on the preston old path
East of the Stock road and adjoining
Warrens line running thence South 45 degrees East 210 poles to a blackoak and 2
whiteoaks; thence South 45 West crossing the
Stock road at 22 poles and passing the corner
of an old Survey marked J.A.D. at 106 poles in
all 400 poles to 5 blackgums; thence North 45 East
400 poles to a cluster of Small dogwoods near a large
rock at the edge of an old field; thence South 45 East 190 poles to the beginning.
Surveyed the 18th day of February 1845.

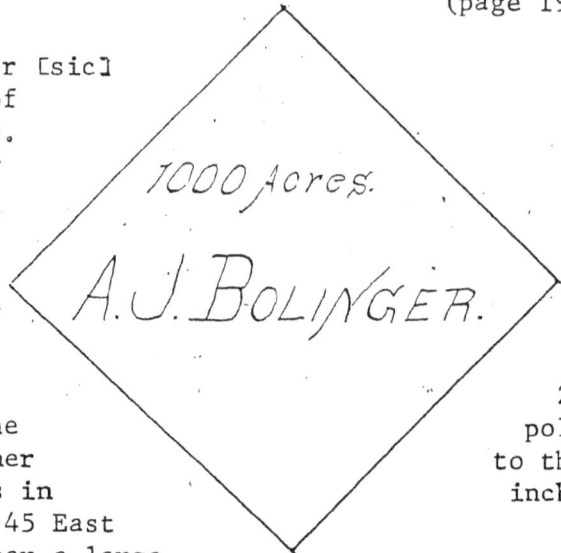

1000 Acres.
A.J.BOLINGER.

200
poles
to the
inch

　　　Wm H. Bell, Surveyor for Rhea County by his deputy Jesse P. Thompson
Richard Wablord & J. Boyd, C. bearers　　　　J. Bollinger, Marker

J.H. BOLINGER (page 192)

State of Tennessee,
　　　Rhea County
In pursuance of an entry
made by J.H. Bolinger in
the Entry Takers office
for Rhea County dated 7th
November 1846.and No. 347
and certified to me I have
this day Surveyed for the
Said Bolinger 9380 acres
of land including 4380
older entries or more.
BEGINNING on a Stake near
a rock branded I.H.B.
running thence due East
588 poles to a Stake;
thence due North 844 poles
to a rock branded I.H.B.
and Some blackjacks marked
as pointers on the brow of
the mountain; thence North
45 West 640 poles to a
Stake; thence West 500
poles to a Stake; thence
South 45 West 590 poles to
a Stake; thence South 418
poles to a Stake; thence
South 45 East 310 poles to
2 whiteoaks on Warrens line;
thence South 60 East to the

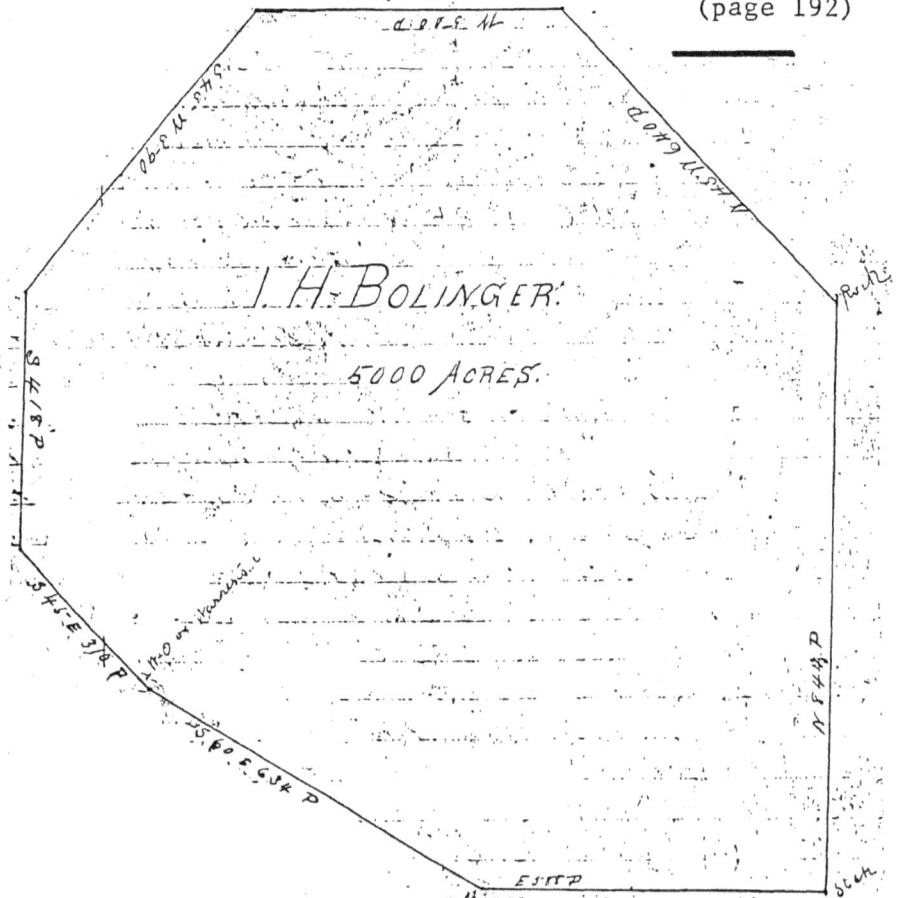

I.H.BOLINGER.
5000 Acres.

(NOTE— The above
plat was reduced to fit
the page. One inch scale
added in upper right corner)

beginning. Surveyed 13th Feb. 1846.
Wm H. Bell, Surveyor for Rhea County
Saml Brown, R.? Gatlett(?), &
        H.H. Bolinger, C.C.

(NOTE— Plat of Bolinger tract
was reduced to fit page; one
inch scale added)

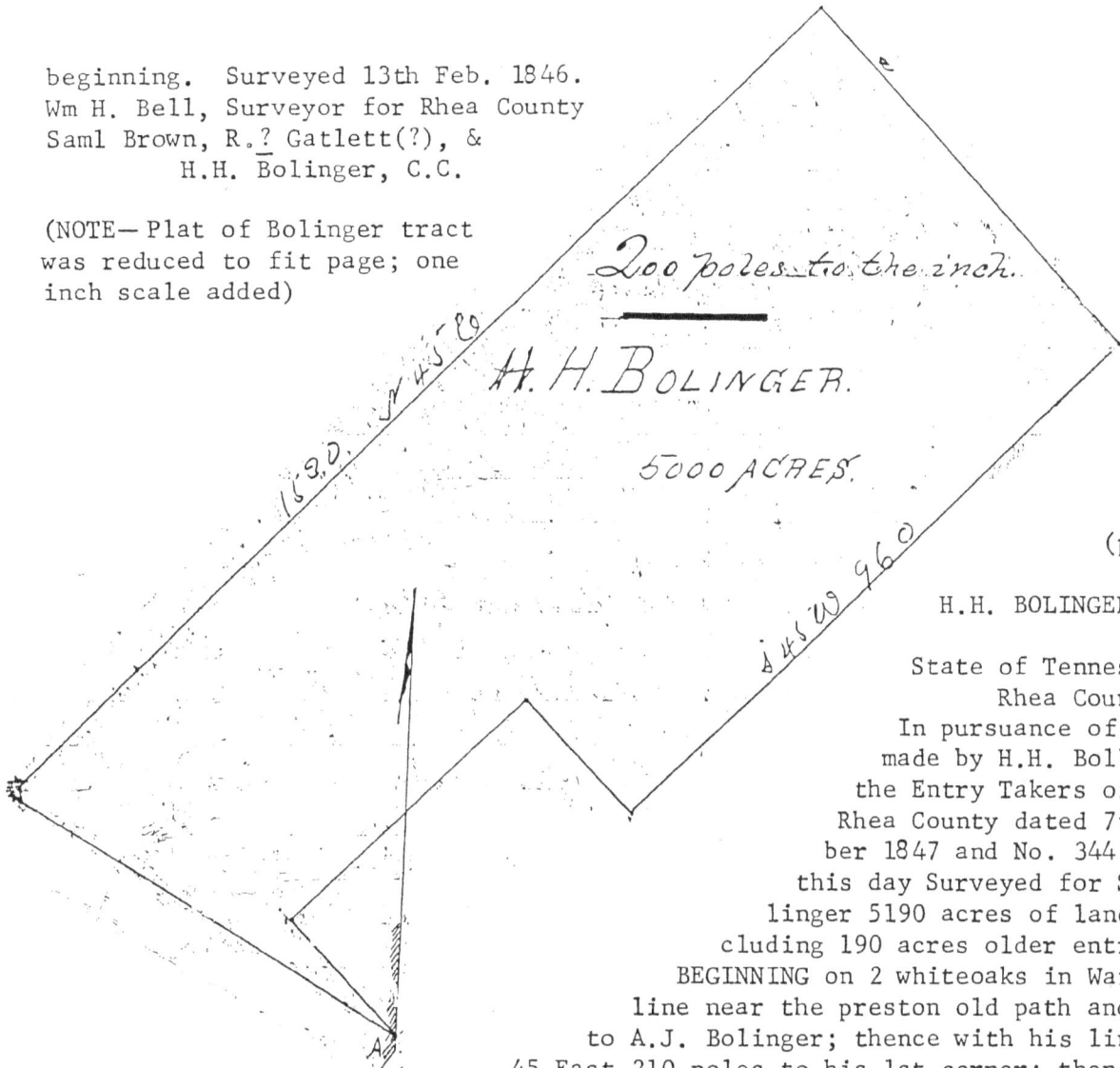

200 poles to the inch.

H. H. BOLINGER.

5000 ACRES.

(page 193)

H.H. BOLINGER

State of Tennessee
Rhea County
In pursuance of an entry
made by H.H. Bollinger in
the Entry Takers office for
Rhea County dated 7th November 1847 and No. 344 I have
this day Surveyed for Said Bollinger 5190 acres of land including 190 acres older entries.
BEGINNING on 2 whiteoaks in Warrens
line near the preston old path and corner
to A.J. Bolinger; thence with his line South
45 East 210 poles to his 1st corner; thence South
45 West 400 poles to his 2nd corner; thence with his line North 45 West 210 poles
to a chestnut and 2 whiteoaks in Said line; thence South 45 West crossing a ford
of Piney 960 poles to 3 whiteoaks and a gum; thence South 45 East 634 poles to a
Stake; thence North 45 East 1530 poles to a Stake near a rock branded H.H.B.;
thence North 60 West to the beginning. Surveyed 16th Feb 1847.
      W.H. Bell, Surveyor for Rhea County
Reese & George Guthrie, C.Bs   F. Bolinger, Marker

W.H. HARRIS   (page 194)

State of Tennessee, Rhea County
By virtue of an entry made in the Entry Takers office of Rhea County of No.
(blank) and dated the 1st day of March 1845 for two hundred acres of land on
Waldens Ridge of Cumberland Mountain by William H. Harris, I have Surveyed the
Said 200 acres of land. BEGINNING on a blackoak near the Alloway Branch and on
the line of a 640 acre Survey of Waterhouse running North 30 East 100 poles
crossing the Alloway Creek at 80 poles to a pine & blackoak on the bluff of Said
Creek; thence North 68 West 280 poles to a blackoak and hickory; thence South 30
West 166 poles crossing the Alloway Creek at 120 poles to two Small hickorys;
thence South 68 East 200 poles to the line of Waterhouses tract; thence North 30
degrees East 66 poles to his North corner, thence South 68 East with his line to
the beginning. Surveyed the 11th February 1848.

WASSON AND ORME

State of Tennessee, Rhea County
Pursuant to an entry made in the
Entry Takers office of Said County
of No. 350 and dated the first day
of March 1847 for two thousand
acres of land by E.E. Wasson and
Shiloh Arm [sic] on Waldens Ridge
of Cumberland Mountain on the waters of Piney River and by virtue
of Said entry made as aforesaid,
I have Surveyed the Said two thousand acres of land. BEGINNING
                    (page 195)
on a redoak on the side of a ridge
near a large rock on the North side
of the Stinging fork of Said Creek
runing North 21 East 220 poles to a
large Chestnut and Seven blackgum
pointers on the bluff of Soky Creek; thence North 84 East along the bluff of Sd
Creek 288 poles to a Spanishoak; and pine Chestnut and blackgum pointers; thence
a direct line to the deep hollow and down Said hollow to Piney River, thence up
Said river with the meanders thereof to the mouth of Duskins; thence up Said
Duskins with the meanders thereof 640 poles to a Stake thence a direct line to
the begining. Surveyed the 2nd day of September 1848.
William H. Bell, Surveyor, By his Deputy Jesse P. Thompson
John Thurman & S.P. Orme, Sworn Chain Carriers

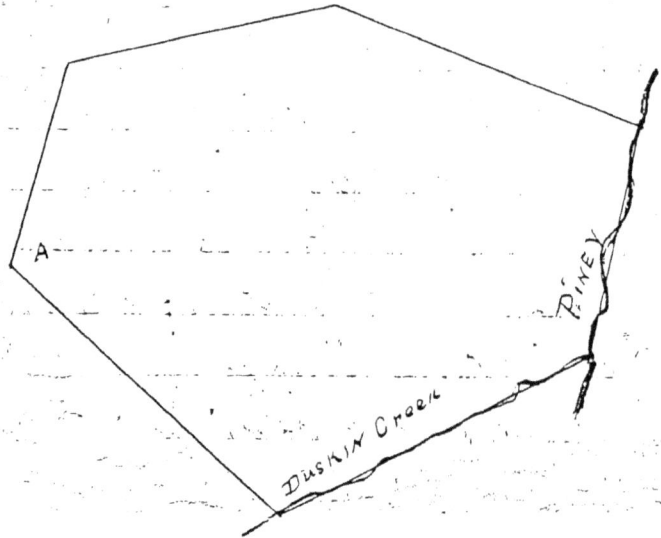

200 poles to the inch

W.G. SHORT

State of Tennessee, Rhea County
By virtue of an entry made in the Entry Takers Office of Said County by Washington
G. Short of No. 355 and dated the 9th day of November 1848 for two thousand acres
of land on Waldens Ridge of Cumberland Mountain. BEGINNING on a Whitepine on the
bank of Basin Creek near Gibsons Saw Mill running due South crossing Gordons Road
at 320 poles in all 420 poles to a Maple and Spanishoak on the bank of Orter
Creek; thence down Said Orter Creek with the meanders thereof to Whites Creek;
thence down Whites Creek with the meanders thereof to the mouth of Piney; thence
up Said Piney with the meanders to Fall Creek; thence up Said Fall Creek to the
mouth of Basin; thence up Said Basin Creek to the beginning containing 2000 acres
more or less. Surveyed the 24th Nov. 1848.
        Franklin Locke, Surveyor, by his Deputy Jesse P. Thompson
Joseph Parker & Zebedy Brown, C.C.

JNO. DUNLAP   (page 196)

State of Tennessee, Rhea County
By virtue of an entry made in the Entry Takers office of Rhea County of No. 357
and dated the 19th day of March 1846 by Dennis McClendon for 300 acres of land on
Waldens Ridge of Cumberland Mounrain and on the waters of Piney River and trans-
ferred by assignment to John Dunlap, I have Surveyed the Sd 300 acres of land.
BEGINNING on a large whiteoak on the head of the North prong of the pine branch,
runing South 25 West 306 poles to a Spanishoak on a branch and on the bluff of
Johnson Fork of Piney; thence down Said Johnsons Fork to the mouth of the Pine

Branch; thence up Said branch & the North prong of the Same to the begining containing 300 acres be the Same more or less. Surveyed (blank) January 1849.
     Franklin Locke, Surveyor by his deputy Jesse P. Thompson
John Dunlap & Jacob Dunlap, Sworn Chain Carriers

N.B.

Following will be found the copies of five surveys which have been So badly torn
and defaced as to make it impossible to copy them entire, but the best that can
be done has here been presented.   Young Colville, Transcriber
Aug. 6th 1880

JNO. GRASHAM   (page 197)

State of Tennessee, Rhea County
Pursuant to an entry made in the Entry Takers office of Rhea County of No. [353]
and dated the 6th day of September 1847 for 1000 acres of land by John Grasham
on Waldens Ridge of Cumberland Mountain on the waters of Whites Creek. . . .d
entry I have Surveyed for the . . . Said one thousand acres of land . . . at the
mouth of Basin . . . the mouth of the Long . . . to Elijah Haleys line . . . the
line of Gibsons . . .d Gibsons to . . . said Gibsons line 180 poles . . . on . . .
So 80° East 188 poles to a . . . gum and whiteoak pointers; thence No 47° E . . .
to a hickory on Greers line; thence with his line . . . East 20 poles to his corner; thence No 73° E 2° poles to Brumels line; thence North 80° E 162½ poles to a
blackoak; thence to the beginning. Surveyed the 2nd February 1849.
     Franklin Locke, Surveyor By his Deputy Jesse P. Thompson
John Matlock & Henry Lowry, S.C. Carriers

RICHD. PLUMLEE

State of Tennessee,
    Rhea County
In pursuance of an entry
made in the Entry Takers
office for Rhea County
in the State of Tennes-
see by Richard Plumlee &
Joseph Thompson of No.
380 on . . .

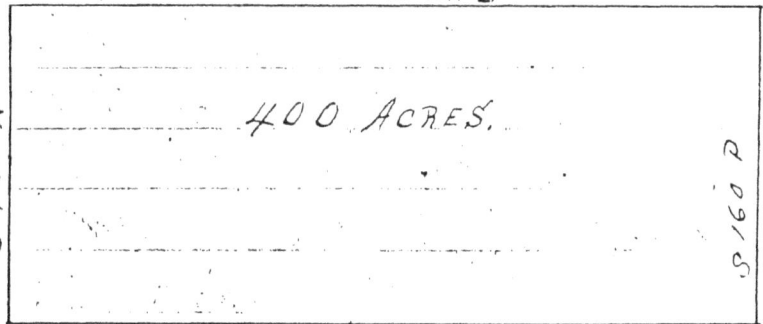

  100 poles to the inch

J.W. CLIFT   (page 198)

State of Tennessee, Rhea County
In pursuance of an entry made in the Entry Takers office for Rhea County, Tennessee . . . deputation given by F . . . . . . Surveyor for Rhea County & State of
Tennessee, I have Surveyed for the Said . . . Tennessee 5000 acres of land on
Waldens Ridge of Cumberland Mountain. BEGINNING on a rock marked A a hickory and
2 Spanishoaks marked . . . on the North East bank of said Richland Creek at the
foot of Waldens Ridge; thence North 46 East . . . poles to a pine; thence North
44 West 1200 poles to a Stake; then South 46 West 1000 poles to a Stake; then
South 44 East 1200 poles to a Stake; then North 46 East 500 poles to the beginning. Surveyed 24th August 1849. James W. Clift, D.S. for Rhea County
. . . . . . & . . . . . . S.C.C.   (Plat on next page)

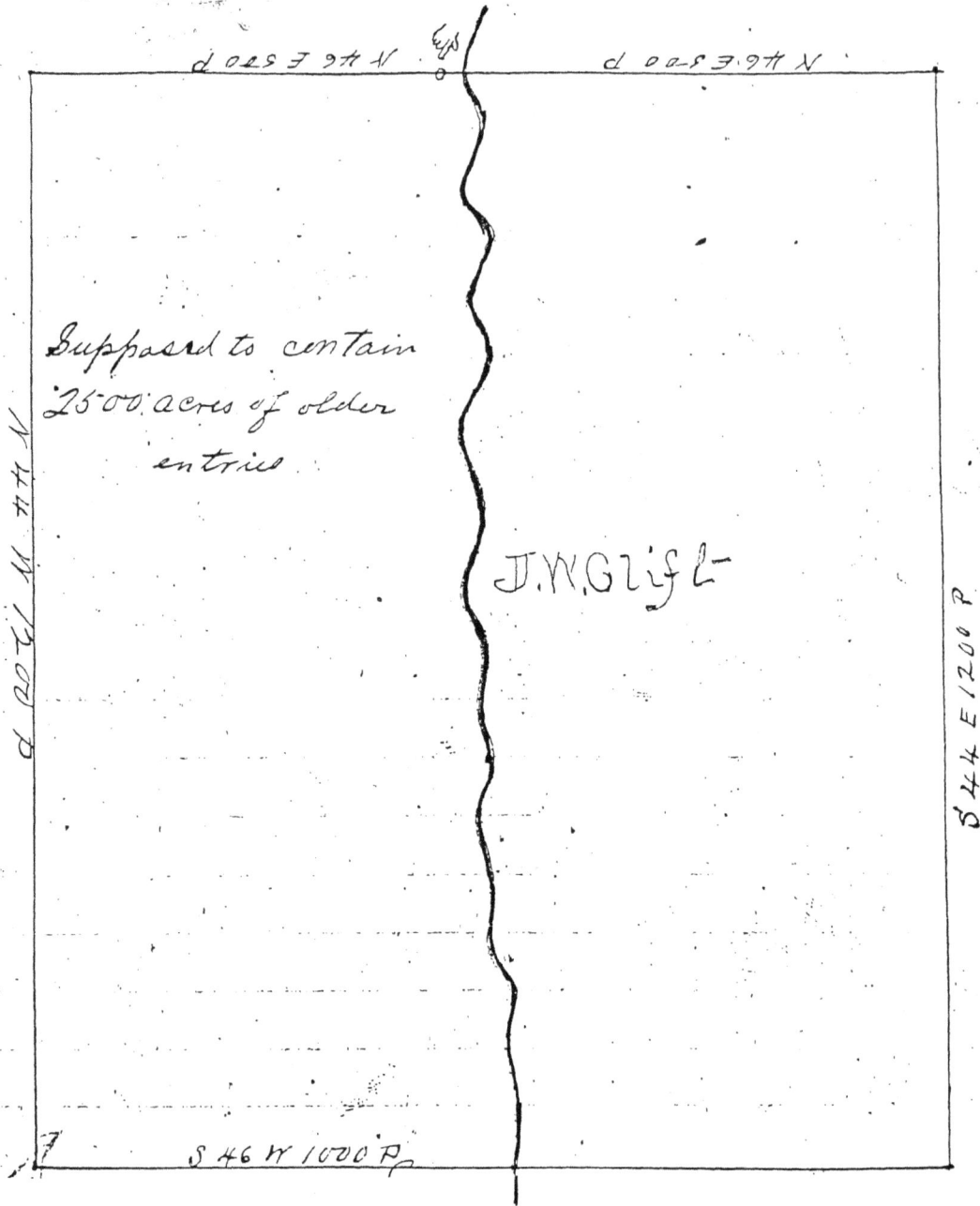

116

Supposed to contain
2500 acres of older
entries

N 46 E 520 P

N 46 E 500 P

S 44 E 1200 P

N 44 W 1200 P

J.W.Glift

S 46 W 1000 P

J. HENDERSON

State of Tennessee,
Rhea County
In pursuance of an
entry made in the
Entry Takers of-
fice for Rhea
County in the
State of Tennes-
see . . . . .

100 poles to
an inch

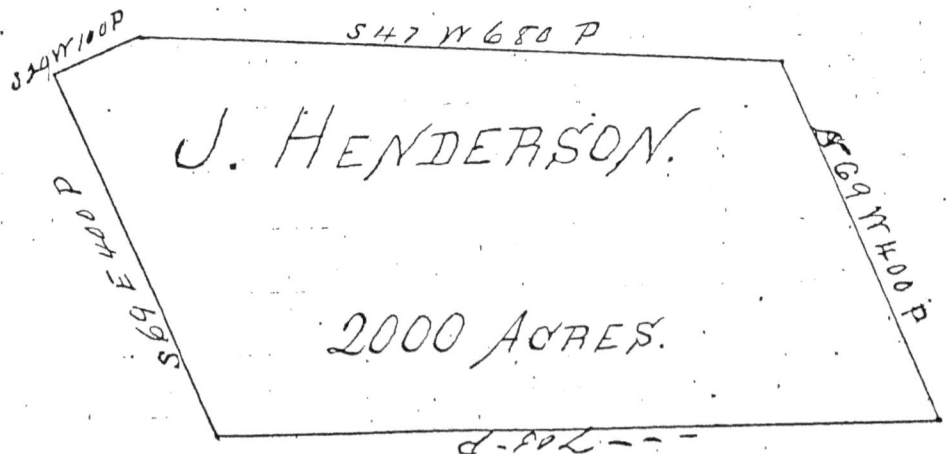

S 47 W 680 P

S 44 W 100 P

J. HENDERSON.

2000 ACRES.

S 69 E 400 P

S 69 W 400 P

D. PLUMLEE   (page 199)

State of Tennessee, Rhea County
In pursuance of an entry made in the Entry Takers
office for Rhea County in the State of Tennessee by
Daniel Plumlee of No. 379 dated the 20th of May 1852
for three hundred acres of land I have Surveyed for
the Said Daniel Plumlee 169 acres on Waldens Ridge
of Cumberland Mountain in the County of Rhea and State of Tennessee.   BEGINNING
on a Whiteoak the North corner of a 200 acre tract formerly owned by Thomas
Riddle on the North Side . . . branch of Sale Creek; thence South 62 West 172
poles to a blackoak; thence South 28 E 134 poles to a postoak on Stones line;
thence with his line North 35 East to a hickory Stones corner, thence with his
line South 55 East 108 poles to a blackoak; thence North 24 East 27 poles to a
Whiteoak & Maple Thos. Riddles corner; thence with Riddles line to the beginning.
Surveyed the 1st day of March 1854.   . . . .
Charles P. Thompson & . . . Johnson, S.C.C.

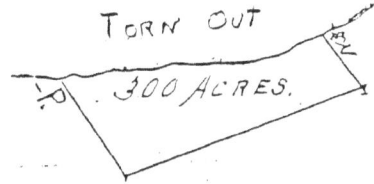

MORGAN AND PICKETT   (page 200)

State of Tennessee, Rhea County
In pursuance of an entry made in the Entry Takers office for
Rhea County and State of Tennessee by Washington Morgan &
P.M. Pickett of No. 399 dated 15 October 1856 for 1000 acres
of land on Waldens Ridge and waters of Richland Creek, I have
Surveyed for Washington Morgan & R.F. McDonald assignee of
P.M. Pickett 400 acres more or less bounded as follows.
BEGINNING on two Postoaks the North West corner of an entry
made by David Ragsdale; thence N 30 East 612 poles to two
chestnut oaks on the clift of Polebridge Creek; thence down
Said Clift to 2 chestnuts oaks corner of E.H. Morgan; thence
with Said Morgans line S 41 W 72 poles to Said Morgans beginning corner; thence S 49 E 56 poles to a Stake; thence a
Short distance to the N West corner of an entry made by James
Stewart; thence with Said Stewarts line S 45 W 450 poles to
said Stewarts corner; thence with the Same till it comes to
the line of said Ragsdales; thence with Said Ragsdales line to
the beginning.   (page 201)
                Surveyed 20th August 1857.
                    R.F. McDonald, Deputy Surveyor
                        David Morgan & George Morgan,
                            Sworn C.C.

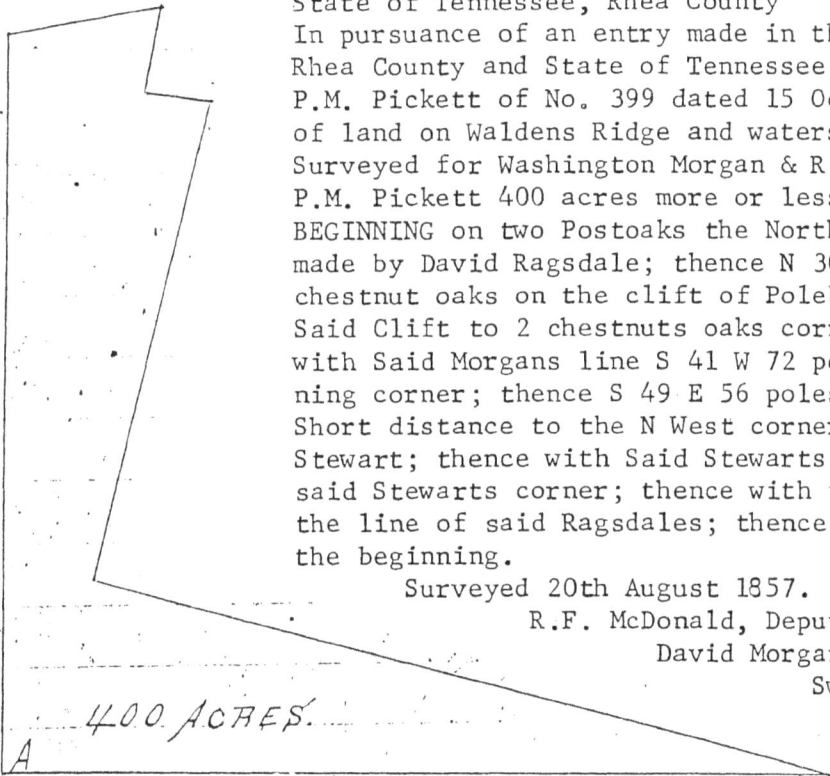

B.F. BRIDGEMAN

State of Tennessee, Rhea County
In pursuance of an entry No. 397 and dated 25th
day of January 1856 and to me directed, I have
this day proceeded to Survey for Said Bridgeman
45 acres of land on Waldens Ridge and the waters
of Richland Creek adjoining the land of Said
Bridgeman, J.M. & W.J. Rigsby and James Skillen
bounded as follows. BEGINNING on a Stake the

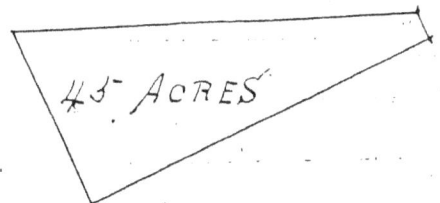

Northwest corner of a 100 acre tract of Said Bridgeman; thence N 15 W 79 poles
to a blackoak on the line of James Skillen; thence with Said Skillens line S
82 E 170 poles to Said Skillen South East corner; thence to Bridgemans North
East corner thence N 75 W 160 poles to the begining. Surveyed 20th August 1857.
     R.F. McDonald, Deputy Surveyor   [no C.C. listed]

P.M. PICKETT

State of Tennessee, Rhea County
In pursuance of an entry No. 386 and
dated 21 July 1854 and to me directed
I have this day proceeded to Survey
for the Said Pickett a certain parcel
or tract of land in Said Rhea County
lying on Waldens Ridge and on the
waters of Richland Creek, adjoining
the land entered by David Ragsdale.
BEGINNING on and bounded as fol-
                    (page 202)
lows begining on a Chestnutoak
marked with the letter A Standing on
the clift of Cranmores Cove; thence
N 60 W 24 poles to David Ragsdales
South corner; thence the Same course
with Ragsdales line 200 poles to a
Stake a postoak and redoak pointers;
thence S 30 W 400 poles to two chestnut; thence S 30 E 260 poles to a
Chestnutoak on the clift of Cranmores
Cove; thence with the Clift to the
beginning. Surveyed 11th March 1856.
R.F. McDonald, Deputy Surveyor
James McDonough & George Morgan,
          C. Carriers
W. Morgan, Marker

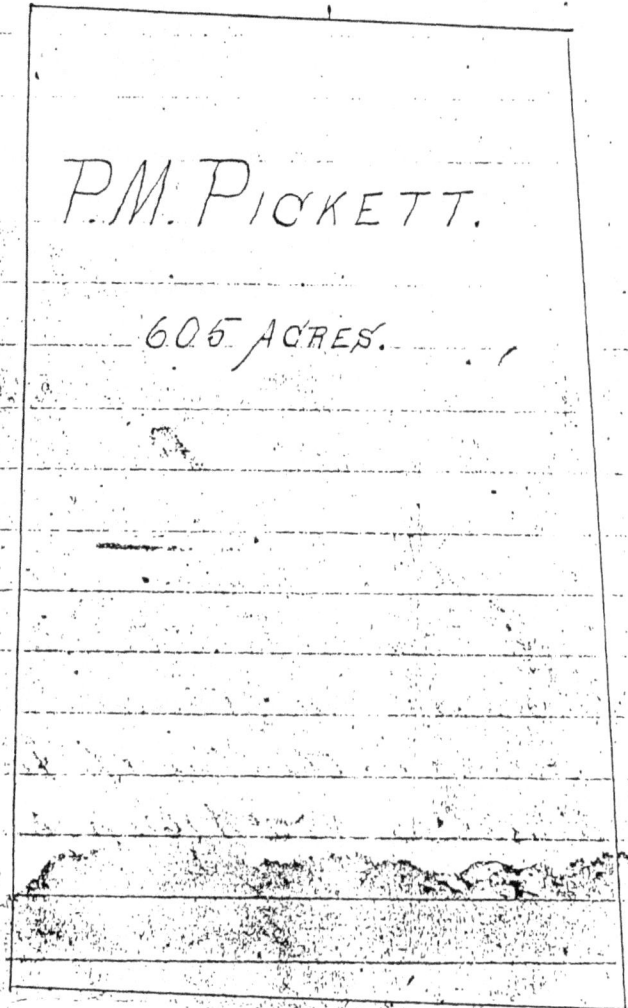

P.M. PICKETT.

605 ACRES.

J.M. & W.J. RIGSBY

(page 202)

State of Tennessee, Rhea County
In pursuance of an entry No. 393 dated the 25th July 1855, I have this day pro-
ceeded to Survey for J.M. & W.J. Rigsby a parcel or tract of land in Rhea County
on Waldens Ridge and on the waters of Richland and Brush Creek and joining B.F.
Bridgeman, James Skillen, T. Reese & Benjamin Riggs. BEGINING & bounded as fol-
lows: beginning on two postoaks the Northwest corner of 200 acre tract of B.F.
Bridgeman; thence N 15 W with Bridgeman line 100 poles to a hickory & blackoak
Said Bridgemans corner; thence Same course 79 poles to 3 Blackoaks on the line of
James Skillen thence with Skillens line N 82 W 164 poles to a Stake and pointers
Skillens corner; Same course continued 32 poles to a Stake on Thomas Rees line;
thence with Said Rees line South 130 poles to a hickory Rees corner, Same course
continued 106 poles to a Whiteoak & two hickorys on the line of Plumlee; thence

(page 203)

with Said Plumlys line N 80 E 162 poles to a Stake Plumlys corner thence S 10 E
174 poles to 2 hickory on the line of Bridgeman & Rigsby; thence with Bridgeman
& Rigsbys line N 75 E 111 poles to 2 postoaks their beginning corner; thence N 15
W with their line 160 poles to the begining containing 405 acres.
                R.F. McDonald, Deputy Surveyor
J.I. Riddle & Charles Morgan, C. Carriers & Marker

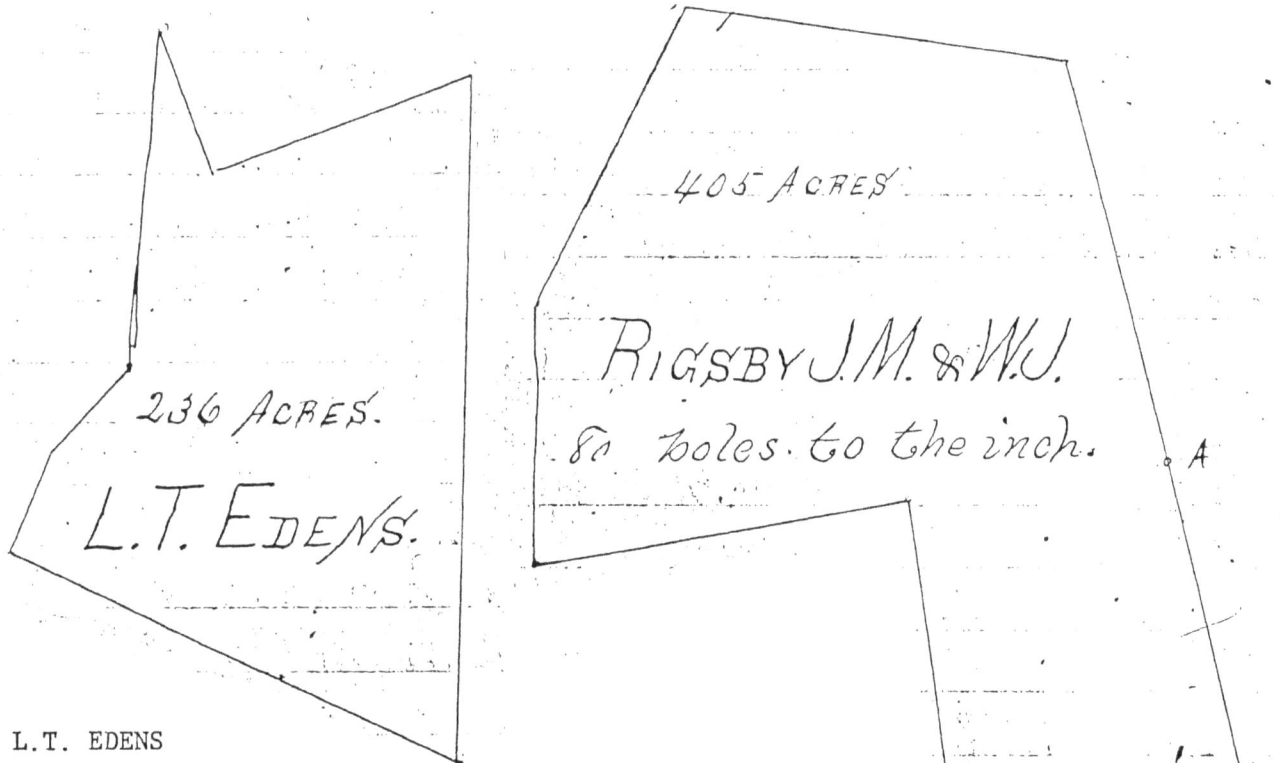

236 ACRES.
L.T. EDENS.

405 ACRES.
RIGSBY J.M. & W.J.
80 poles to the inch.
A

L.T. EDENS

State of Tennessee, Rhea County
In pursuance of an entry No. 396 and dated the 20 day of
March 1836 and to [me] directed, I have this day proceeded
to Survey for L.T. Edens a certain tract or parcel of [land]
on the waters of Brush Creek and on Waldens Ridge beginning
and bounded as follows: BEGINNING on two chestnut oaks and
marked with letter A and standing on the clift of Gilbreaths branch and on the
line of an entry made by Edmund Bean; thence West 116 poles to a hickory Said
Beans corner; thence North 63 poles to a whiteoak E. Hickmans corner; thence S
26 W 14 poles to a blackoak Said Hickmans corner; thence West 60 poles to a
Stake; thence S 34½ East 27 poles to the corner of a 77 acre tract entered by
Russel & others; thence with Said Russels line S 45 W 46 poles to 2 postoaks,
thence S 45 E 210 poles to 2 Blackgums a chestnut oak on the clift of Cranmore
Cove; thence to the begining containing 236 acres. Surveyed 25th March 1856.
                R.F. McDonald, Deputy Surveyor
Wm Rigsby & E.P. Williams, Sworn Chain Carriers

E.H. MORGAN   (page 204)

State of Tennessee, Rhea County
In pursuance of an entry No. 373 and dated the 4th day of September 1851 and to
me directed, I this day Surveyed for E.H. Morgan a certain piece or tract of land
in Rhea County lying on Waldens Ridge and on the waters of Richland Creek and adjoining the land of Washington Morgan, begining and bounded as follows:

BEGINNING on a blackoak on a pile of flat rocks on the South side of Tyners Creek and near Everetts cowford; thence S 49 E 278 poles to a pine hickory and chestnut on the West line of Said W. Morgan and on the West Side of Richland Creek; thence with the line of Said Morgan N 10 W 90 poles to Said Morgans begining corner thence S 80 E 100 poles to a blackgum Said Morgans corner, thence S 10 E 160 poles to the corner of Said Morgan near Richland Creek; thence down the bluff of Said Creek to Buzzard Point; thence up the bluff of Hendersons Creek to a point that runing S 41 West will run to the beginning containing by estimation 300 acres. Surveyed 22 March 1856. R.F. McDonald, Dpty Surveyor James McDonough & William Morgan, Sworn Chain Carriers; W. Morgan, Marker

J.I. RIDDLE

State of Tennessee, Rhea County
In pursuance of an entry No. 388 and dated 23rd day of October 1854 and to me directed I have this day proceeded to Survey for Joshua I. Riddle a certain parcel or tract of land lying on Waldens Ridge and on the waters of Richland

(page 205)

Creek and adjoining the lands of Charles Morgan and the Said Riddle & others begining and bounded as follows: BEGINING on a Chestnut tree corner of Said Riddle 50 acre Survey and also corner of a 200 [acre] Survey of Charles Morgan, running with Said Morgans line S 39 E 130 poles to a postoak marked with W.M. and continuing the Same course 40 poles more to a Stake and three hickorys marked as pointers; thence S 48 E 140 poles to a double blackoak; thence N 60 W 164 poles to a postoak; thence N 26 West 86 poles to a Spanish oak; thence N 6 E 214 poles to a blackoak near the South Side of Washington Morgans turnpike road, thence N 26 W 315 poles to the center of Polebridge Creek opposite 2 blackoaks; thence up Said Creek as it meanders to a Sweetgum Standing in center of Said Creek; thence Soo(?) W 200 poles to a Stake; thence S 72 E 35 poles to the beginning containing 600 acres. Surveyed 4th day of November 1854.
                    R.F. McDonald, Deputy Surveyor
William Rigsby & Charles Morgan, Sworn C.C.

B.F. BRIDGEMAN

State of Tennessee, Rhea County
In pursuance of an entry No. 389 and dated 30th January 1855 and to me directed, I have this day proceeded to Survey for B.F. Bridgeman & William Rigsby a certain parcel or tract of land in Said County lying on Waldens Ridge and on the waters of Brush Creek and adjoining the lands of Said Bridgeman and R.P. Loyd and bounded as follows: BEGINNING on two postoaks the Southwest corner of Said Bridgemans 200 acre tract; thence S 75 W 121 poles to a blackoak on the line of Said Loyd; thence with the Same S 50 E 216 poles to a postoak & blackoak; thence No 40 E 231 poles (page torn)

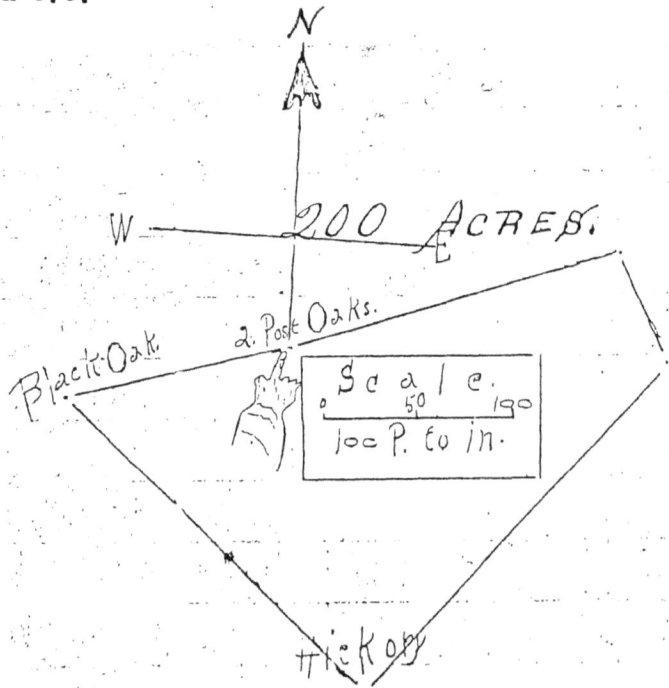

(page 206)

hickorys; thence N 26 W 60 poles to a Stake 2 whiteoaks and blackoak pointers Said Bridgemans corner; thence with the line of the Same S 75 West 200 poles to the

beginning containing 200 acres.   R.F. McDonald, Deputy Surveyor
Pleasant Snow & L.P. Loyd, Sworn Chain Carriers

J.M. BURWICK   (page 206)

State of Tennessee, Rhea County
By virtue of an entry made in the Entry Takers office of Rhea County of No. 421
and dated 6th day Feby 1860 for 50 acres more or less by John M. Burwick and
transferred by assignment by Said Burwick to the Said M.S. Riddle & Phillip Foust
I have this day Surveyed for the Said Riddle & Foust the following described tract
of land (to wit). BEGINNING on a large blackoak on the Lea path near the foot of
the mountain and corner to Lewis Morgan and running with Said Morgan line N 29
East 136 poles to a Spanishoak on Tuttles line; thence with Said line N 45 W to
the extreme heighth of the mountain thence with the meanders of the top of Said
Mountain to the Lea path; thence down the mountain with Said Lea path to the begining. Surveyed 21st day of April 1862.   Jesse P. Thompson, Surveyor
J.M. Burwick & W.L. Humphrey, Sworn Chain Carriers

S. FERGUSON

State of Tennessee, Rhea County
Pursuant to an entry made in the Entry Takers
office of Said County of No. 412 and dated the
11th day of January 1859 for 500 acres of land
I have Surveyed the following described tract
of land to wit: BEGINNING on a maple corner
to Andrew Wyrick and running N 59 W
                                   (page 207)
229 poles to a blackoak on the top of the
mountain, thence up the meanders of the mountain N 30 E 80 poles to a blackoak; thence
N 25 E 120 poles to a whiteoak; thence East
201 poles to a poplar & Maple at the foot of
the mountain and on the line of the 19000
acre; thence with the foot of Said Mountain
and the line of the 19000 acre tract to the
beginning. Surveyed 17th day of January 1859.
Jesse P. Thompson, Surveyor for Rhea County
John Ferguson & William Upton,
        Sworn Chain Carriers

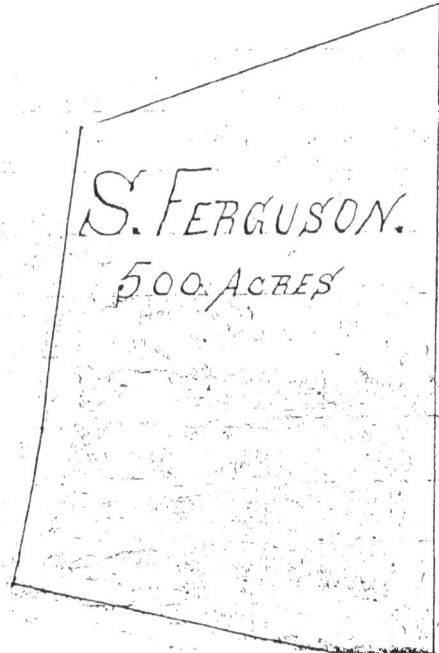

S. FERGUSON. 500 ACRES

ADISON LOCKE

State of Tennessee, Rhea County
By virtue of an entry made in the Entry Takers office of Rhea County of No. 415
and dated 8th day of March 1859 by Addison Locke, I have Surveyed the Said entry. BEGINNING on a white pine on the North side of the Devils or Duskin fork
of Piney and the Northwest corner to entry No. 414 and at the County line run-
ning N 30 E with the County line 1780 poles to Cove Creek; thence down
                                                              (page 208)
Said Creek to Johnsons fork; thence down Said Johnsons fork to Piney; thence up
Said Piney to the Duskin; thence up Said Duskin to the beginning. Surveyed 31
March 1859.   Jesse P. Thompson, Surveyor for Rhea County.
Yancy Loy & J.L. Dunlap, Sworn Chain Carriers   (Plat on following page)

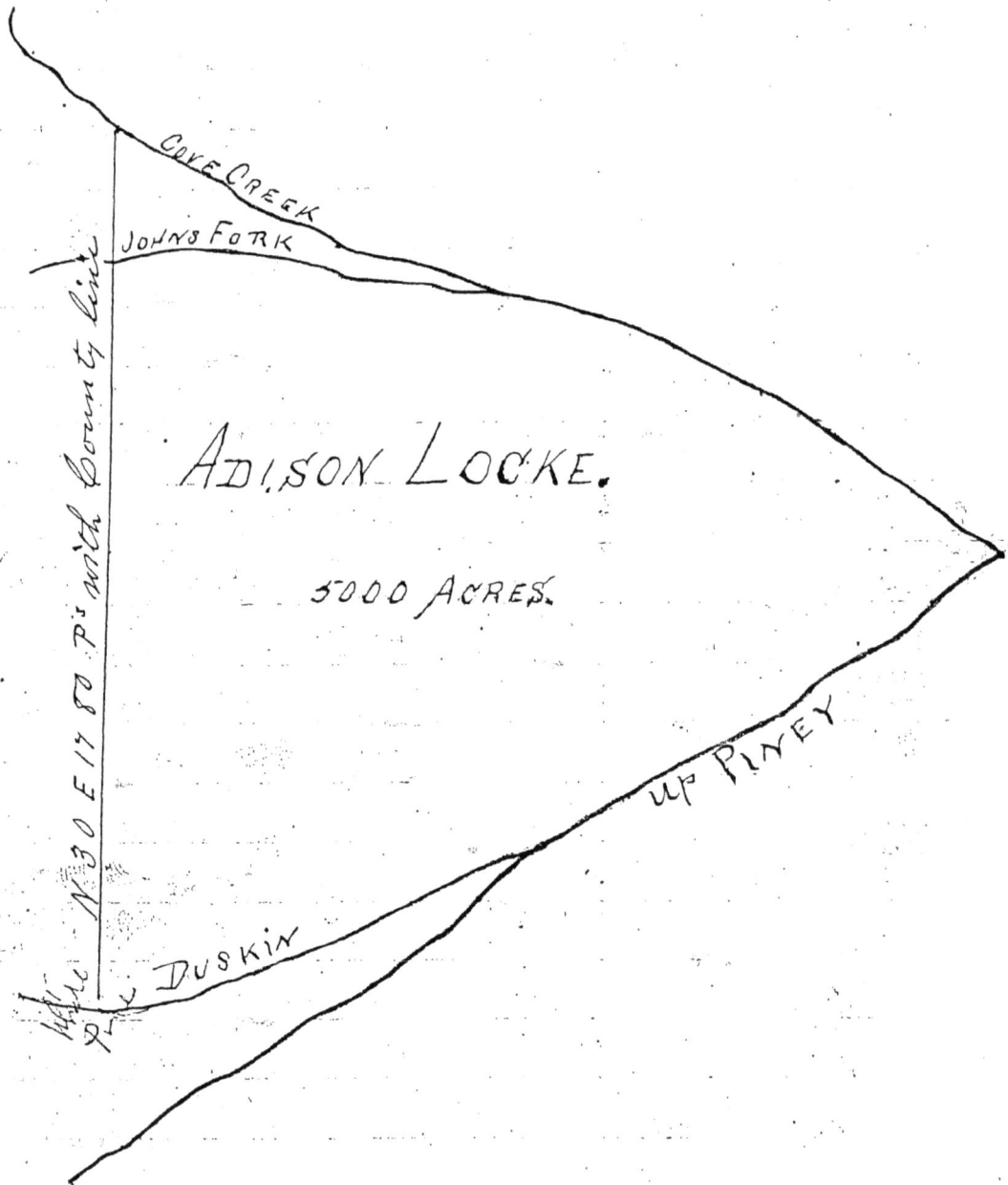

ADISON LOCKE

State of Tennessee, Rhea County
By virtue of an entry made in the Entry Takers office of Rhea County No. 414 and
dated 8th day of March 1859 by Adison Locke, I have Surveyed Said Entry.
BEGINNING on the Southeast corner of entry No. 249 made by Haley & Kimbrough for
5000 acres and running with a line of the Same N 52 W 400 poles to Piney Creek;
thence up Said Piney as it meanders to the mouth of the Duskin fork of Said
Creek; thence up Said Duskin Creek to a White pine near a large rock where the
Rhea County line crosses Said Creek; thence with the County line S 20 W 4320
[poles] to Bumbee [Bumblebee] fork of Said Creek; thence down Said Bumbee as it
meanders to Piney Creek; thence a direct line to the beginning. Surveyed 31st
March 1859.   Jesse P. Thompson, Surveyor for Rhea County
Yancy Loy & Jacob L. Dunlap, S.C.C.

(Plat on following page)

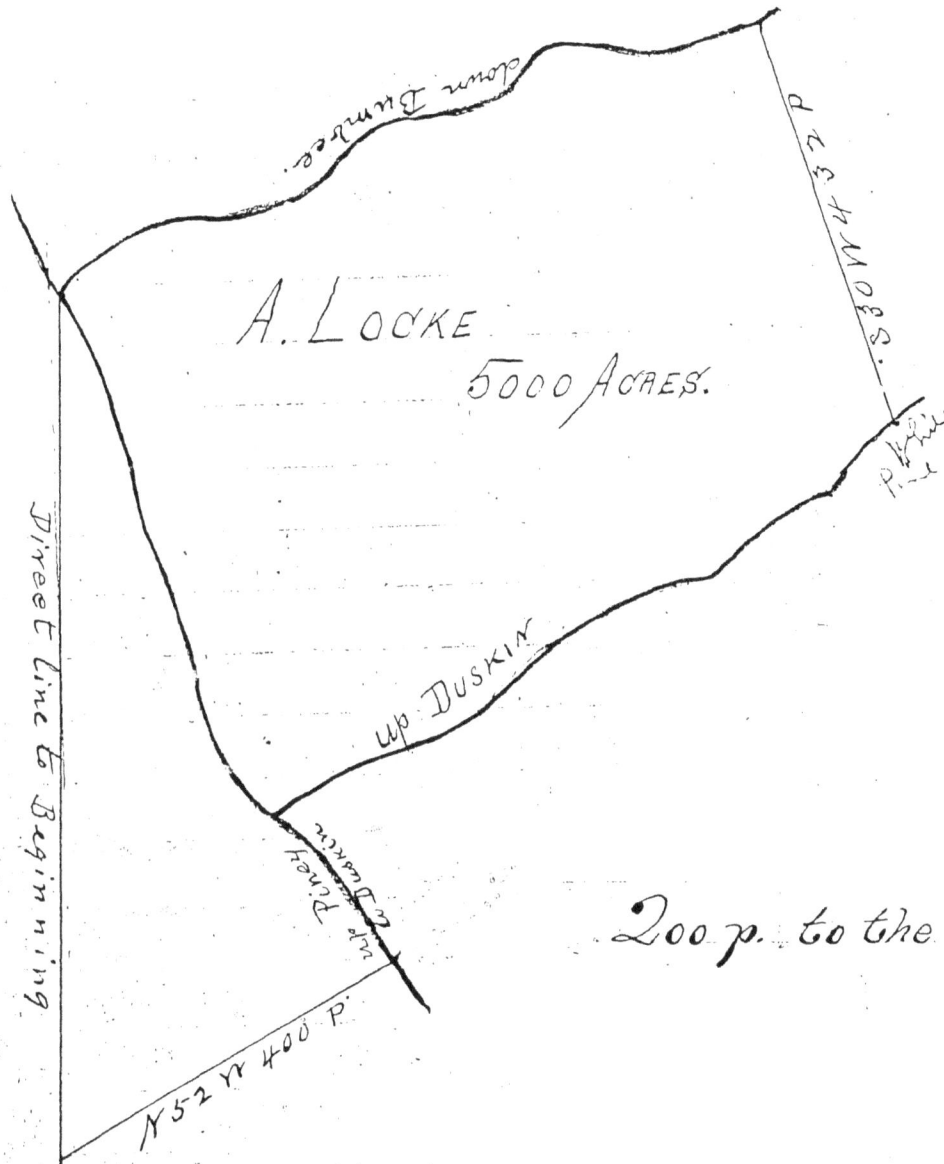

down Duskee.

A. LOCKE
5000 ACRES.

N 30 W 332 p

P. Knob

Direct line to Beginning

up DUSKIN

up Piney

up Duskin

N 52 W 400 P.

2oo p. to the inch.

JAS. NEILL   (page 209)

State of Tennessee, Rhea County
By virtue of an entry made in the entry takers office of Said County of No. 413
dated 19th January 1859 by James Neill for five thousand acres of land. I have
Surveyed for the Said Neill the following tract of land. BEGINING on a Sweetgum
corner to Levi W. and Samuel B. Ferguson on a branch at the foot of the mountain
thence along the foot of the mountain and with the line of the 19000 acre grant
to Piney Creek; thence up Said Piney Creek as it meanders 640 poles above the
mouth of the Pine branch to a point due North from a double dogwood at the top of
the bluff of Said Creek; thence due South passing Said dogwood 920 poles to a
large chestnut; thence East 160 poles to a hickory on a bluff at the top of the
mountain; thence N 50 East to a Stake on the line of the 19000 acre grant at the
foot of the mountain, thence with the line of Said 19000 acre grant to the corner
of James C. Ferguson; thence with his line N 10 E to the beginning. Surveyed the
4th day of February 1859. Jesse P. Thompson, Surveyor of Rhea County
Robert Ferguson & William McCully, Sworn C.C.   (Plat on following page)

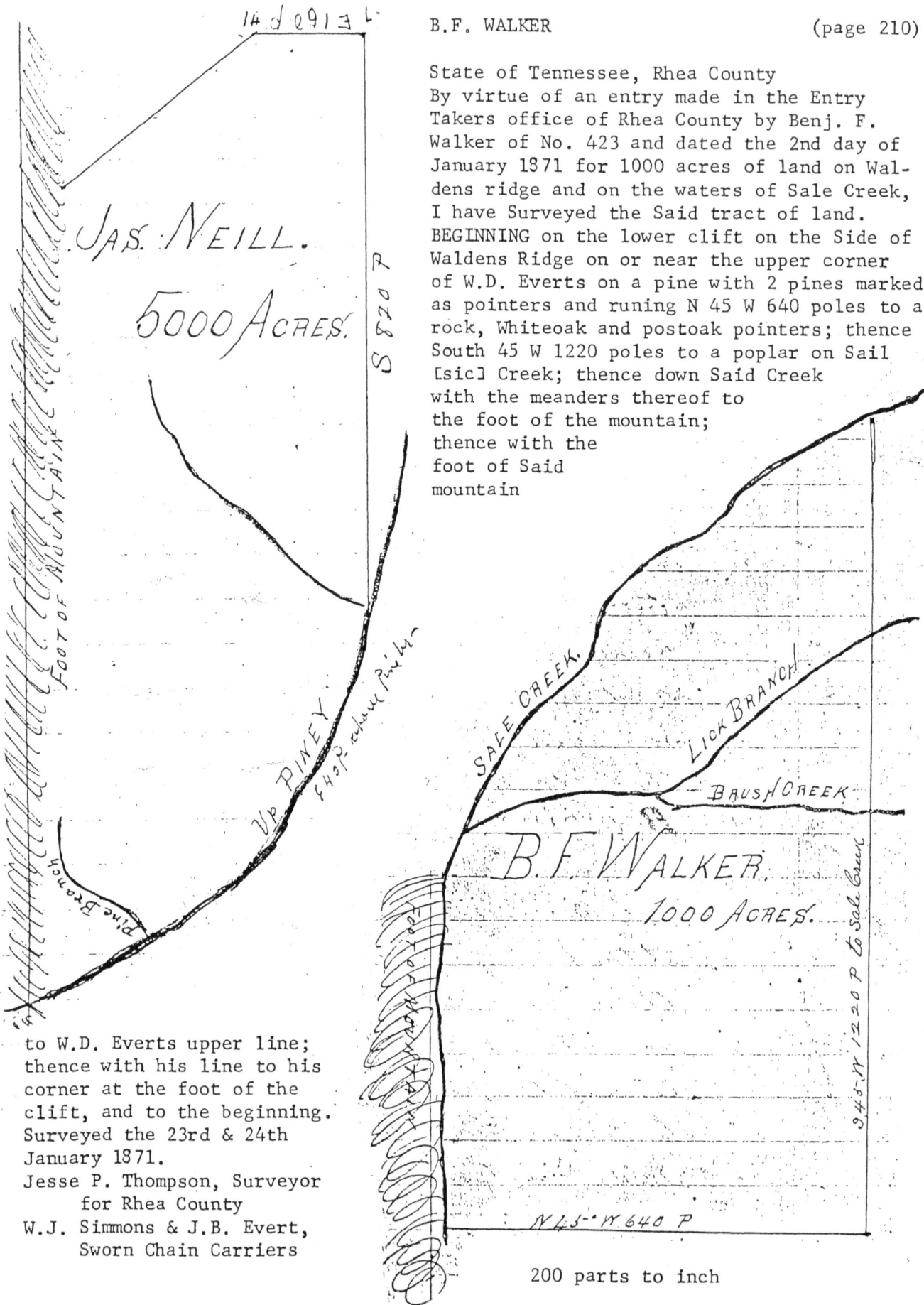

JAS. NEILL.

5000 ACRES.

FOOT OF MOUNTAINE

Pine Branch

Up PINEY

640 P down Piney

S 820 P

14 d 0913 L

E 160 P

B.F. WALKER   (page 210)

State of Tennessee, Rhea County
By virtue of an entry made in the Entry
Takers office of Rhea County by Benj. F.
Walker of No. 423 and dated the 2nd day of
January 1871 for 1000 acres of land on Waldens ridge and on the waters of Sale Creek,
I have Surveyed the Said tract of land.
BEGINNING on the lower clift on the Side of
Waldens Ridge on or near the upper corner
of W.D. Everts on a pine with 2 pines marked
as pointers and runing N 45 W 640 poles to a
rock, Whiteoak and postoak pointers; thence
South 45 W 1220 poles to a poplar on Sail
[sic] Creek; thence down Said Creek
with the meanders thereof to
the foot of the mountain;
thence with the
foot of Said
mountain

SALE CREEK.

LICK BRANCH

BRUSH CREEK

B.F. WALKER.

1000 ACRES.

S45-W 1220 P to Sale Creek

N 45° W 640 P

to W.D. Everts upper line;
thence with his line to his
corner at the foot of the
clift, and to the beginning.
Surveyed the 23rd & 24th
January 1871.
Jesse P. Thompson, Surveyor
      for Rhea County
W.J. Simmons & J.B. Evert,
Sworn Chain Carriers

200 parts to inch

W.P. WRIGHT   (page 211)

State of Tennessee, Rhea County
By virtue of an entry No. 424 and
dated 25th January 1871 made by
W.P. Wright for 250 acres of land
on Waldens Ridge and on the waters
of Richland Creek, I have Surveyed
for the Said W.P. Wright the following described tract of land, to wit:
BEGINING on Thomas Walkers East corner on a double blackoak, a blackoak
and hickory marked as pointers, and
runing with Loyds line N 69 W 200
poles to a Stake postoak & 2 blackoaks
marked as pointers; thence North cros-   100 poles to the inch
sing Morgans turnpike road at 100 poles
in all 200 poles to a Stake postoak hickory and two blackoaks pointers; thence S
69 W 30⅞ poles to a Stake on Thomas Walkers; thence with Said Walkers line to the
begining. Surveyed 21st day of November 1872.
        Jesse P. Thompson, Surveyor for Rhea County
Thomas Walker & J.M. Walker, Sworn Chain Carriers

M.S. RIDDLE

State of Tennessee, Rhea County
By virtue of an entry made in the entry takers office
of Said County of No. 429 and dated 10th day of February 1873 by Milo S. Riddle and transferred by him
to Mary O. Riddle and H.D. Riddle, I have Surveyed
for the Said Mary O. Riddle and H.D. Riddle the following described tract of land to wit: BEGINING at
Burwicks corner at the first clift of rock on the
face of the mountain at the Lea path on a blackjack
and blackgum and runing up the mountain with the Lea
path West 34 poles to two small hickorys; thence South 66 West 48 poles to a
chestnut tree; thence N 76 W 86 poles to a Stake & postoak at the top of the
mountain Sup-   (page 212)
posed to be on Morgans line; thence with Morgans line and near the top of the
mountain to B.F. Walkers line; thence with Said Walkers line S 45 East to his
beginning corner and Burwicks line; thence with Burwicks line and clift of rocks
to the beginning. Surveyed the 11th November 1873.
        Jesse P. Thompson, Surveyor for Rhea County
William Simons & Hiram Riddle, Sworn Chain Carriers

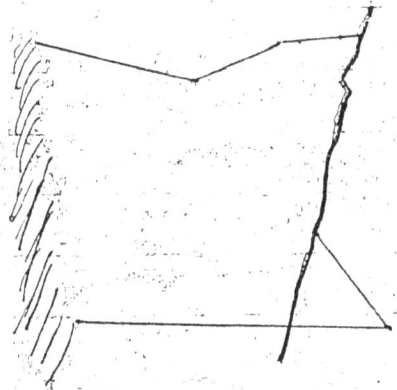

JAS. DEATHERAGE

By virtue of an entry No. 426 made in the entry takers office of Rhea County and
dated the 2nd day of September 1871 by James Deatheridge, the following described
tract of land to wit: BEGINING at a hickory and double chestnut corner to A.
Gears and Robert Robinsons 5000 acre grant and runing with Gears line S 60 E
180 poles to the corner of Said Gears 3000 acre grant; thence with a line of Said
grant North 30 E 222 poles to a Stake on Alfred Collins 2000 acre tract line;
thence with Said Collins line to the line of Robinsons 5000 acre; thence with
Said Robinsons line S 30 West to the beginning. Surveyed 2nd day of September
1871.   Jesse P. Thompson, Surveyor for Rhea County

126

Isaac Jolly & Columbus Deatheridge,
    Sworn Chain Carriers

A. WYRICK

(DEATHERIDGE
TRACT ⟶

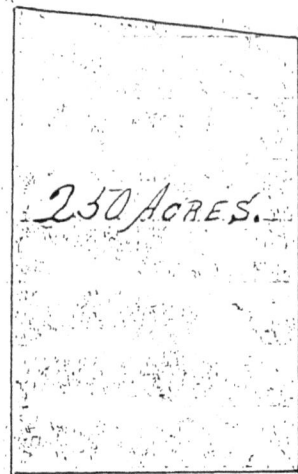

250 ACRES.

State of Tennessee, Rhea County
Pursuant to an entry made in the entry takers office of
Rhea County of No. 431 and dated the 22nd day of September 1873 by Alfred Wyrick and Said entry being transferred by assignment to J.L. Wassum & Stephen Cawood, I
have Surveyed for Said Wassum & Cawood the following
described tract   (page 213)
of land to wit: BEGINNING at a
Maple corner to William Wyrick
land and Solomon Wyrick grant and
runing with Solomon Wyricks line
S 57 E 30 poles to a postoak Stump
on the top of the Shinbone ridge;
thence with Said Wyricks line and
the top of Said ridge S 30 W 46
poles to a blackjack; thence S 29
W 6 poles to a chestnutoak; thence
S 53 W 16 poles to a redoak; thence
S 15 W 16 poles to a hickory at the

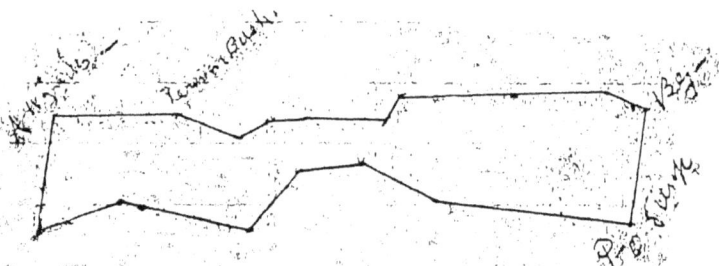

narrows; thence with Henry Millers line S 29 E 12 poles to a Stake Spottedoak
pointers South 8 E (blank) poles to a redoak on top of Shinbone ridge; thence
with the top of Said ridge S 34 W 30 poles; thence S 8 E 18 poles; thence S 16 W
5 poles to a Stake on W.T. Gasses line; thence with Said Gasses N 60 W 31 poles
to a Stake on Andrew Wyricks line; thence with Said Wyricks line N 22 E 32 poles
to persimon bush; thence N 41 E 10 poles, thence N 39 E 8 poles North 18 poles,
N 15 E 10 poles, N 22 E 23 poles, N 44 W 6 poles; thence N 30 E 38 poles to a
blackgum; thence N 47 E to the beginning. Surveyed 20th November 1873.
                                    Jesse P. Thompson
William Wyrick & Alfred Wyrick, Sworn Chain Carriers

J.W. HUGHES

State of Tennessee, Rhea County
By virtue of an entry in the entry takers office of Said County of
No. 428 and dated the 4th day of November 1872 by Joshua Riddle
and transferred by assignment to John W. Hughes, I have Surveyed
for the Said John W. Hughes 150 acres of land more or less on
Waldens Ridge.   BEGINNING on two chestnut trees at the top of the
clift of Said mountain and Supposed to be on Tuttles line, and
running N 65 W 18 poles to a Stake on the line of Ragsdales 100
acre tract; thence with the line of Said tract ? 30 W 188 poles to
a whiteoak corner to Morgans 600 acre Survey; thence S 60 East 26
poles to a chestnutoak on the top of the mountain (last line torn)
                              (page 214)
meanders of the top of Said mountain to the beginning. Surveyed
12th January 1873.   Jesse P. Thompson, Surveyor for Rhea County
Joshua Riddle & Hiram Riddle, Sworn Chain Carriers

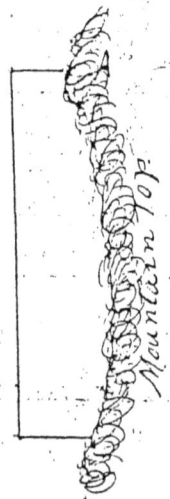

Otter Creek

Down Whites Creek,

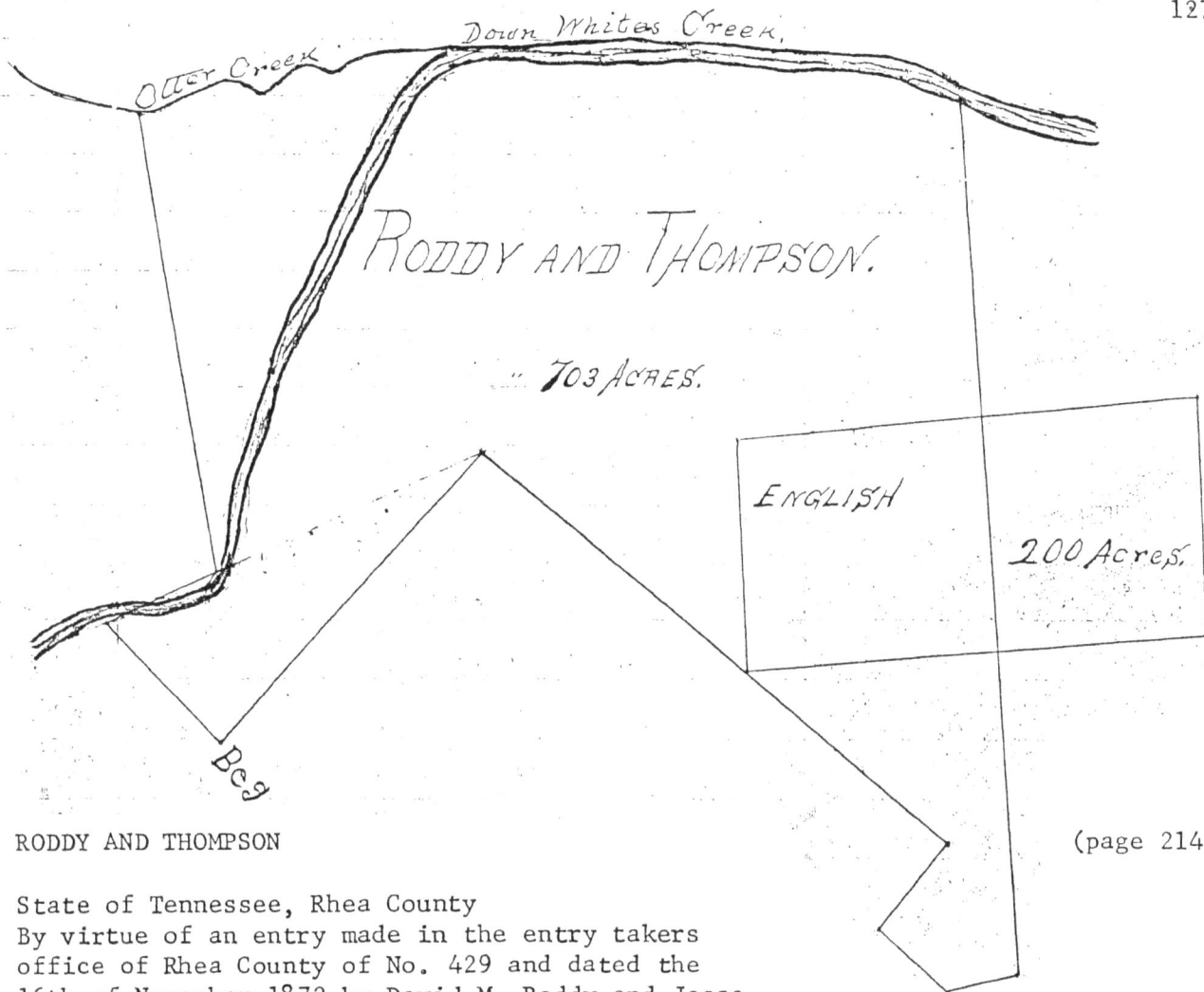

RODDY AND THOMPSON.

703 ACRES.

ENGLISH

200 Acres,

Beg

RODDY AND THOMPSON   (page 214)

State of Tennessee, Rhea County
By virtue of an entry made in the entry takers
office of Rhea County of No. 429 and dated the
16th of November 1872 by David M. Roddy and Jesse
P. Thompson for 400 acres more or less, I have
Surveyed for Said Roddy & Thompson Said Entry. BEGINING on a Spanishoak and Blackgum where the Haley & Kimbrough line of a 5000 acre tract crosses the line of a
600 acre tract granted to W.G. English and runing with the line of Haley & Kimbrough N 52 W crossing Whites Creek to a Stake; thence to the South corner of an
entry made by James Bundren for 300 acres; thence with Said Bundrens line North to
Otter Creek; thence down Said Otter Creek to Whites Creek; thence down Said Creek
as it meanders to the corner of James C. Beans 1000 acre tract; then with Said
Beans line South 474 poles to his Stake corner; thence with Said Beans line Southwest to Fullingtons line; thence (last line torn) line to the line of English 600
                                                                      (page 215)
acre tract; thence with English line N 45 E to his corner on the bank of Little
Laurel; thence with the closing line of English N 45 W 262 poles to a pine his
begining corner; thence with the first line of Said tract S 45 W 200 poles to the
begining. Surveyed 6 May 1873. Jesse P. Thompson, Surveyor for Rhea County
W.F. Thompson & John Pryor, Sworn Chain Carriers

SMITH AND WEST

State of Tennessee, Rhea County
By virtue of an entry made in the entry takers office of Said County of Rhea by
George W. Smith and W.T. West of No. 444 and dated 15th day of January 1875 for
400 acres of land on Waldens Ridge on the waters of Sandy Creek, I have Surveyed
for Said Smith & West the following described boundary of land to wit: BEGINING

at a hickory & blackgum & chestnut pointers and runing N 15 W
44 poles to a blackoak on William Mondays old line; thence
with Said Mondays line N 30 E
214 poles to James Lodens line;
thence with Said Lodens line
West 116 poles to his corner
chestnut and whiteoak pointers;
thence with another line of Lodens land North 140 poles to a
hickory corner; thence S 84 W
114 poles to 2 blackgums on
Waterhouses line; thence S 18 W
162 poles to a Small whiteoak
on the bank of Sandy Creek;
thence down Said creek as it
meanders to the line of Mathis
400 acre tract; thence with the
line of Said 400 acre tract
S 62 E 290 poles to the beginning. Surveyed Jan 15th 187?
Jesse P. Thompson,
    Surveyor for Rhea County
Isaac L. Baker & Robert Smith,
    Sworn Chain Carriers

402 ACRES
SMITH AND WEST.

WALKER, THOMPSON & PYOTT

(page 216)

State of Tennessee, Rhea County
By virtue of an entry made in the Entry
Takers office of Rhea County for 4000
acres of land more or less of No. 433
and dated 30 day of October 1873 by
John P. Walker, Jesse P. Thompson and
J.I. Pyott, I have Surveyed for the
Said Walker, Thompson, and Pyott the
following boundary of land to wit:
BEGINNING on a persimon on the old
County line between Rhea and Hamilton
Counties at the foot of the mountain
on the West Side of Harts turnpike road
and runing N 13° E crossing Sale Creek
at 61 poles in all 127 poles to a poplar tree at Spring branch; thence N 18°
E 33 poles to a large poplar tree;
thence N 25° E crossing Walkers turnpike at 8 poles in all 50 poles to a
whiteoak; then N 34° E 23 poles to a
poplar and pine pointer at the foot of
the mountain; thence along the foot of
Said mountain with the meanders thereof to Whites Creek; thence up Said
Whites Creek to the Cumberland County
line; thence with Said County line to

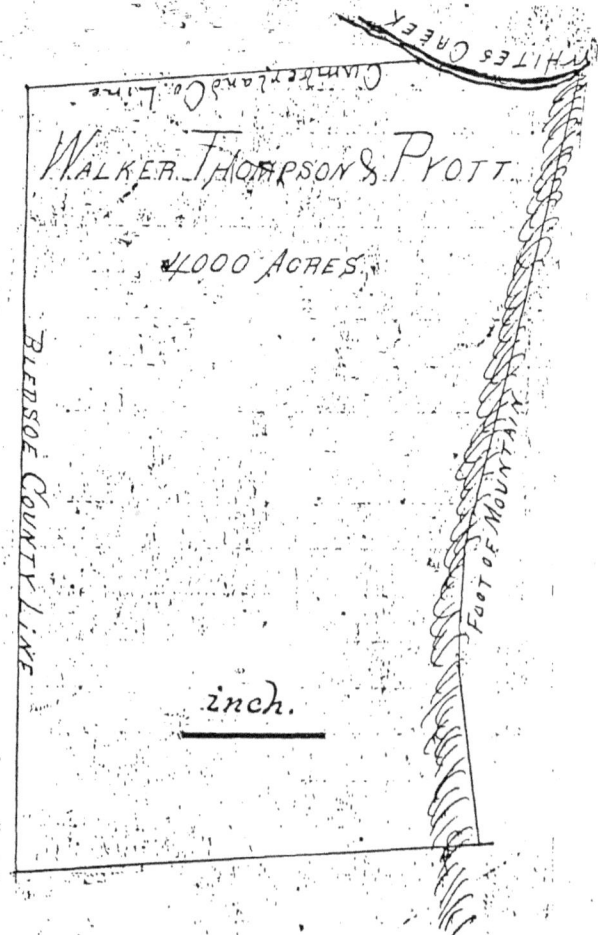

WALKER THOMPSON & PYOTT.
4000 ACRES
Cumberland Co. Line
WHITES CREEK
BLEDSOE COUNTY LINE
FOOT OF MOUNTAIN
inch.

the Bledsoe County line between Rhea and Bledsoe
Counties to the Hamilton County line; thence
with Said Hamilton and Rhea County line to the
beginning, excluding all older valid grants
within Said bounds. Surveyed 14th November 1873
Jesse P. Thompson, Surveyor for Rhea County
James M. Fann & G.W. Fann, Sworn Chain Carriers

(missing)   (page 217)

(missing)   (page 218)

WM. BURWICK   (page 219)

State of Tennessee, Rhea County
In pursuance of an entry No. 400 dated the 5th
day of Novr. 1856 and to me directed, I have
this day Surveyed for Wm Burwick 300 acres of
land more or less in Rhea County on the Side
of Waldens Ridge on the waters of Sale Creek
& Gilbreaths branch bounded as follows to wit:
BEGINING on two Sowerwood & chestnutoak on
the bank of Gilbreaths branch; thence along
the foot of Said ridge N 53° E 61 poles to a
blackoak; thence N 30° E 161 poles to a hickory; thence N 42° E 80 poles to a Whiteoak;
thence N 32° E 88 poles to a whiteoak; thence
N 21° E 120 poles to a whiteoak marked H and
blackoak marked M; thence the Same course 105
poles to a Sowerwood; thence N 29° E 62 poles
to a Stake in Lea path; thence N 55 W 100
poles more or less to the first clift; thence
along the top of Said clift to the corner
clift of Gilbreath; thence South 53° W to Said
branch; thence down with the meanders of Said
branch to the beginning. Surveyed the 15th
day of February 1857. R.F. McDonald,
                          Deputy Surveyor
[no Chain Carriers listed]

MORGAN & GREGORY   (page 220)

State of Tennessee, Rhea County
In pursuance of an Entry made by Charles Morgan
& Thomas Gregory No. 434 dated the 14th day of
December 1874 for 200 acres more or less of
land in said County, I have Surveyed for Said
Morgan & Gregory the following agreeable to
their Entry. BEGINNING on a postoak redoak &
hickory at Swaffords Salting ground & corner
of a 1000 acre Survey owned by S.J.A. Frazier
and with Said Fraziers line N 60 W 240 poles
to Polebridge Creek Whiteoak & blackgum pointers; thence down Polebridge Creek with the

300 ACRES.

WM. BURWICK

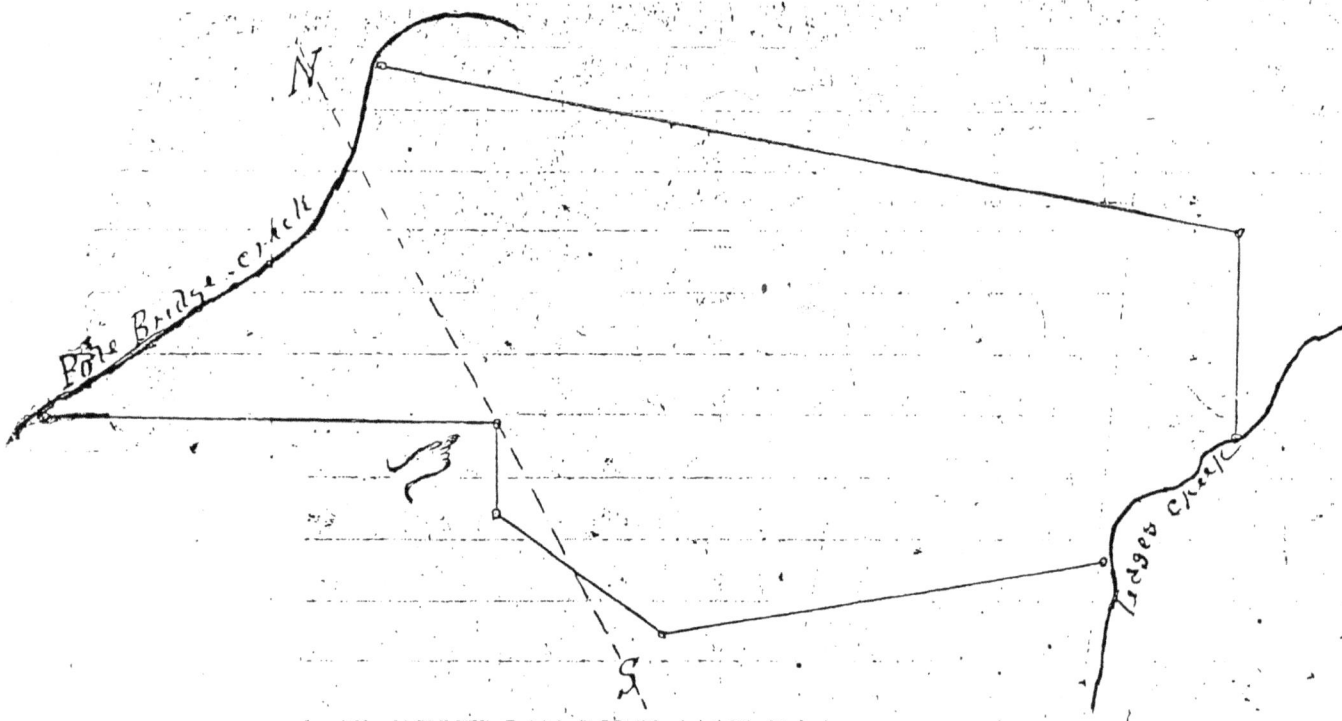

meanders to the Barger line to a Spruce pine & blackgum, thence with the Sd Barger
line S 50° E 466 poles to a Hickory bush hickory & Postoak Pointer on a line of
a 400 acre Survey made by W. Morgan & R.F. McDonald, thence with their line S 30°
W 106 poles to Teauges Creek a Hickory sasafras and Whiteoak pointers, thence up
the meanders of Said Teauges Creek to a Spruce pine and maple on Bensons line,
thence With Bensons line N 70° W 238 poles to a blackoak near a mud hole in the
Kiuka Road corner of J.I. Riddles 600 acre Survey, thence with Said Riddle Survey
N 26° W 111 poles to a rock and two Postoak pointers on the line of Said S.J.A.
Frazier, thence with the Sd Frazier line N 30 E 48 poles to the beginning, Con-
taining 600 acres. Surveyed Sept. 10, (bottom line torn) R.F. McDonald

J.B. SMITH

(page 221)

State of Tennessee, Rhea County
By virtue of an Entry made in the Entry Takers office for the County of Rhea and
State of Tennessee of No. 425 dated the 31st day of March 1871 by Jackson B.
Smith, I have this day Surveyed for the said J.B. Smith the following described
boundary of land, to wit: BEGINNING on a Spruce Pine on the North bank of Sandy
Creek, two Holly's marked as pointers, and running North 54 poles to a Pine,
Black Oak and White Oak pointers on the line of Brewers 190 acre grant at the top
of the Bluff of said Creek; thence with the line of Brewers 100 acre tract to the
line of Gillespies and Smiths 1200 acre grant, thence with the line of said 1200
acre tract to a Sowerwood and Chestnut corner to said tract and the same Course
Continued North 64° West 54 poles to a Stake on the line of William Mondays 200
acre Entry; thence with the line of said 200 acre tract to a Hickory corner to
George Smiths land, thence with Said Smiths line to his pine knot corner and the
same course continued to Sandy Creek, thence down said Creek as it meanders to
the beginning. Surveyed the 10th January 1873.
                    Jesse P. Thompson, Rhea County Surveyor
Robt Smith & Elijah Hayes, Chain Carriers
(plat on following page)

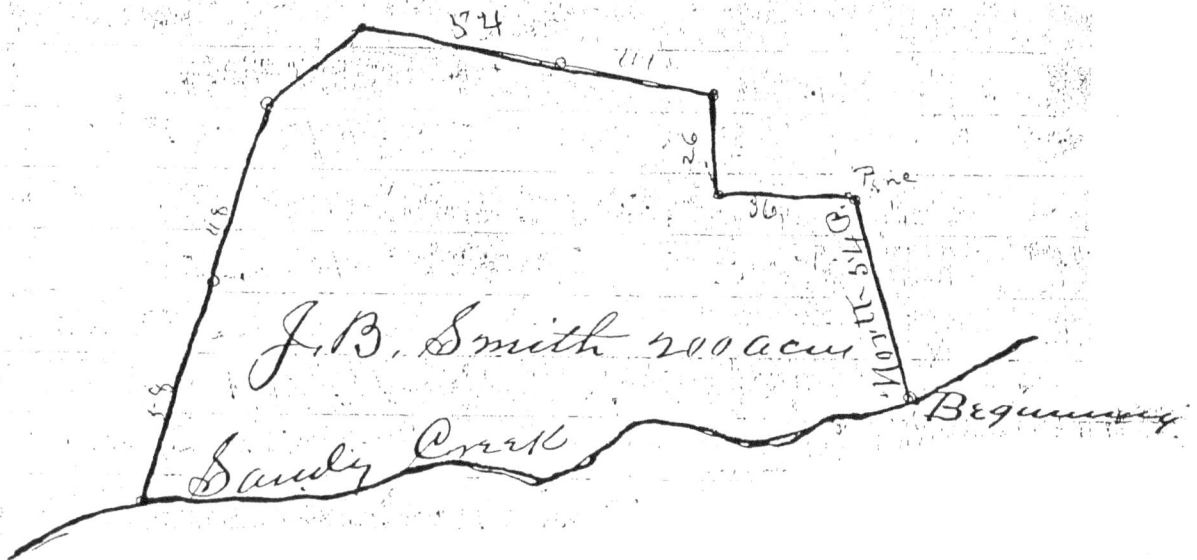

B.F. SHELOW & CO.   PROCESSIONING

State of Tennessee, Rhea County
Surveyor's Office, December 13th 1880
In pursuance of the following notice to wit. Mr. N.Q. Allen take notice that on
the 15th day of December next and Succeeding days if necessary we will proceed
to establish the lines of our lands South and West Heiskell's Gap in the 1st,
9th & 12th Civil Districts of Rhea County in pursuance and . . . with Section
2020 to 2024 . . . (last line is ragged)   (page 223)
inclusive of the Code of Tennessee commencing Said processioning on a white oak
on the east side of Piney River Known as the beginning Corner of T.B. Rice 500
acre Survey this 15th Nov. 1880.   B.F. Shelow & Co.
One copy of Said notice was posted at the Court House door in Washington, one at
each of the voting precincts in the 1st, 9th & 12th Civil Districts of Said
County. Also to the following persons to wit: V.C. & N.Q. Allen, agents and At-
torney's of Lowe heirs, Luke M. Heiskell, S.P.C. & R.M. Roberson, David Roberson,
Catherine Roberson, Alex Montgomery, Wm Ward, Franklin Waterhouse, Jno R. Neil,
Jesse P. Thompson, John M. Holloway, W.D. Holloway, W.S. Holloway, R.L. Gass(?)
Guardian &c, S.H. Holloway, R. Holloway, S.J. Wheeler, W.P. Roddy, Thos. Ingle
(?) & wife Vann(?), Moses F. Thompson & wife Olivia(?), Masa Scarbrough, Chester
Foster(?), Samuel Pyott, Leander Foster, J.L. McPherson, Riley Edington, A.J.
Jolley, H.C. Stebins, E.F. Waterhouse, --- (last line ragged)

                                                                   (page 224)
Waterhouse, Cyress Waterhouse, Alice Waterhouse, Darius Waterhouse, Callie Waterhouse and Ucled Waterhouse Jun, The Claimants or agents of the Claimants of the
adjoining lands which notice was proven before me by the affidavits of E.F. Waterhouse and W.F. Shelow and acknowledged by the Messers Allens, and E.F. Waterhouse to have been served and acknowledged twenty days before the Said 15th day
of December 1880.
        I R.F. McDonald Surveyor of the County & State aforesaid did on the
Said 15th day of December 1880 (and continued the said Survey from day to day
completing the Same on the 18th day of Decr 1880)   Survey and establish the
lines of the lands lying South and West of Heiskell's Gap belonging to the said
B.F. Shelow, J.D. Roberts, Wm F. Sanks, David E. Rees, E.L. Carpenter, W.P. Darwin and W.T. Gass in accordance with and in pursuance of Sections 2020, 2021,
2022, 2023, & 2024 inclusive of the Code of Tennessee, Commencing Said proces-

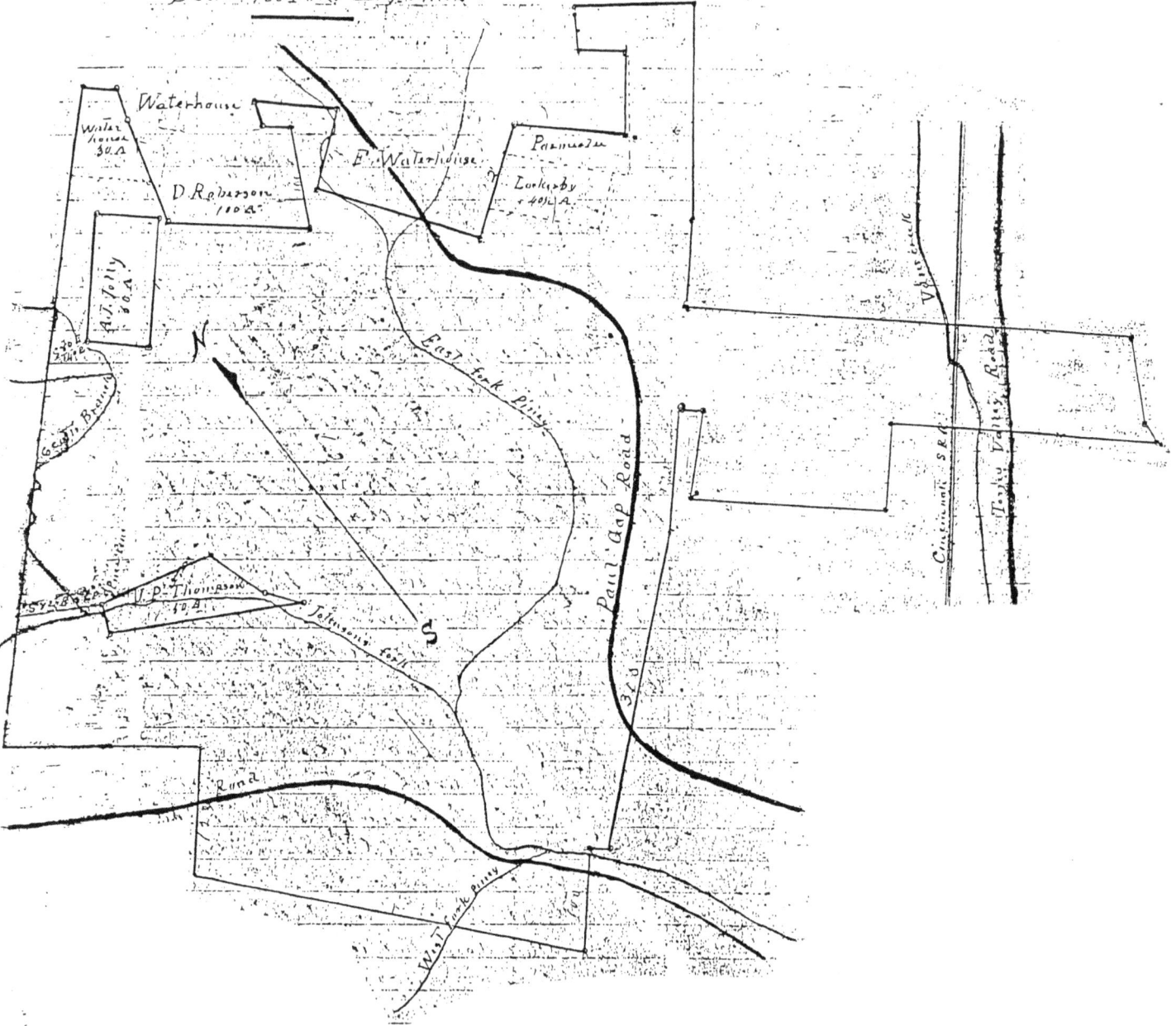

sioning Survey on a Whiteoak marked W on N.E. side of Piney river at the Shutin,
it being the beginning corner of a 500 acre tract known as the T.B. Rice Survey
and beginning corner of a 1000 acre tract known as the Richard Waterhouse Survey
and running with the line of S.H. Holloway S 56½° E 23 poles to a pile of rocks
chestnut oak blackgum and four small pines marked as pointers corner of said
Holloway and beginning corner of a 320 acre tract formerly belonging to J.L.
Wassum, thence with the lines of Said Holloway and Alex Montgomery N 50° E the
variation of the needle making the proper degree N 51½° E 310 poles to a pine
stump and rocks piled (torn edge) around it two chestnut oaks and black gum
pointers, thence N 44° E now N 45½° E with the line of said (last line ragged)

(page 225)

Wheeler 122 poles to a pile of Rocks Chestnut hickory and blackgum pointers corner to Said Wheeler, thence with a line of Said Wheelers S 47½° E 49 poles to a
white oak and hickory pointer corner to Said Wheeler's, thence with the line of
Said Wheeler S 47½° W 84 poles to a stake two blackgums and hickory pointers corner of said Wheelers and on a line of Masa Scarbrough, thence with the lines of
said Scarbrough, N.Q. Allen, W.D. Holloway and W.T. Gass S 47½° E 196 poles to a
black walnut corner of S.J. Wheeler and a line of the Said W.T. Gass, thence
with a line of Said Wheelers N 44½° E 84 poles to a stake in a lane, thence a
line of Said Wheelers S 47½° E crossing the center of the C.S.R.R. at 63½ poles
Vanns Creek at 82 poles Valey Road at 108 poles in all 170 poles to a postoak,
thence with the line of F. Waterhouse S 48° E 97 poles to a rock and two postoak pointers corner of Said Waterhouse and on a line of Wm Ward, thence with
the line of said Ward N 03° E 21 poles to a rock and postoak pointer corner to
said Ward, thence with Said Wards line N 30° E 84 poles to a rock 2 P.O. &
blackjack pointers on said Wards line and corner to L.M. Heiskell, thence with
the line of Said Heiskell N 47½° W crossing the Tennessee Valley road at 137
poles the C.S.R.R. at 176½ poles and Vanns creek at 183 poles in all 466 poles
to a Rock and a large chestnut pointer on the face or side of the mountain
corner to Said Heiskells, thence with a line of Said Heishell N 45½° E 84 poles
to blackoak marked XX   P.O. pointer marked W, thence with the line of said
Heiskell and S.P.C. & R.M. Roberson N 41½° E 208 poles to a pile of Rocks and
Spanish oak pointer, thence N 50° W 119 poles to a large blackoak on the top of
Waldens ridge or mountain, thence S 40 W 9½ poles to a large chestnut Blk gum
and redoak pointers corner H.C. Stebins, thence with the line of said Stebins
S 31° W 34 poles to a pile of   (page 226)
Rocks Redoak Postoak & Sourwood pointers, thence S 50° E 47 poles to two black
oak, thence S 41½° W 80 poles to a rock 3 blackoak pointers two marked X North
E corner of the T.B. Rice 2000 acre Survey, thence with the line of said 2000
acre Survey N 47½° W 115 poles to a rock Blk gum Hickory & W.O pointers on the
line of Franklin Waterhouse, thence with the line of said Waterhouse S 54 W 112
poles to a rock & chestnut Marked II, thence with an other line of Said Water=
house N 36° W 172 poles to 4 Rocks blackgum marked R.W. and whiteoak and dogwood
pointers, thence with an other line of said Waterhouse N 54° E 86 poles to a
stake on the line of the said Rice 2000 acre survey, thence with the line of the
same N 47½ W 84 poles to a rock two whiteoaks & chesnut pointers on the line of
a 50 acre survey of the said Waterhouse, thence with his line S 21½° W 26 poles
to a Blk gum his corner and on a line of D. Robersons 100 acre tract, then with
lines of Said Robersons S 56½° E 27½ poles to a rock and whiteoak 2 P.O & 2 W.
O marked as pointers, thence S 31½° W 102 poles to a blackoak, thence N 56½° W
144 poles to a Whiteoak and two whiteoak pointers, then N 18° E 102 poles to a
chestnut corner of F. Waterhouse, thence with his line N 21½° E 27½ poles to the
line of the said 2000 acre Rice Survey, thence N 47½° W 32 poles to a rock and
whiteoak marked X Redoak & dogwood pointers, then S 46½ W crossing Ferrin branch
at 226 poles Scott Branch at 295 and passing a Beechtree Marked Dec. 18, 1880 at
395 poles Scotts Branch again at 397½ poles Same Branch again at 410 poles
Same branch 428 poles Same branch again at 459 Johnsons fork   (page 227)
of Piney at 581 poles in all 640 poles to a rock two whiteoaks and hickory
pointers, thence S 43½ E 152 poles to a rock and two Sourwood pointers on the
line of Said T.B. Rice 500 acre Survey, thence with a [line] of said 500 acre
Survey S 42° W to the North West corner of Said Survey, then S 38 E 400 poles to
two chestnuts and blackgum, then N 42 E crossing Piney 100 poles to the Beginning
Containing by Estimation two thousand nine hundred and ninety eight acres.
      R.F. McDonald, Surveyor for Rhea County

N.M. Duncan & W.F. Shelow, Sworn Chain Carriers; J.P. Thompson, Marker
    Certificate issued to Registers office 24th Dec. 1880. R.F. McDonald

F. LOCKE LAND   PROCESSIONING   (page 228)

SURVEY OF F. LOCKE LAND IN RHEA COUNTY, TENNESSEE

State of Tennessee, Rhea County
Office of County Surveyor for Said County, October 6th 1882
In pursuance to the following Notice to wit: Mrs. R.F. Henry & W.R. Henry you are
hereby Notified that on the 6th day of September 1882 & Succeeding days if necessary we will proceed to survey & establish the line of the lands which we lately
acquired by the Will of Mrs. Isabella T. Locke dec'd near the town of Washington
in the 6th Civil District of Rhea County, Tennessee on the north side of the Ten=
nessee River & known as the Franklin Locke lands in persuance of and according
with Section 2020 to 20: inclusive of the Code of Tennessee. We will begin said
processioning survey at the branch on the North side & bank of the Tennessee
River at what is now known as Henrys Ferry. This August 7th 1882.
       G.W. Wilson   Elvira Paine
       S.J.A. Frazier   A. Paine
       Mary Mynatt   Elvina Cunnyngham
       B.K. Mynatt
One copy of said Notice was posted on the Court House door of Rhea County 20 day
previous to said 6th of September 1882 & one copy at the voting place in said
6th Civil District, the following parties had a similar notice served upon them
by the Sheriff of Rhea County to wit: R.F. Henry, W.R. Henry, J.R. Barnett & Mrs.
Rhoda A. Pearce, Guardian of the Minor Heirs of R.C. Mintgomery dec'd, the claimants & agents of the claimants of the adjoining lands which said notice reached
me with the legal & proper order of said Office there on showing the same to have
been served upon said parties more than twenty days prior to said 6th day of
September 1882.
    I E.F. Waterhouse, Surveyor for the County & in the State aforesaid did
on the 6th day of September 1882 (and continued said survey from day to day until
completed) Survey & Establish the lines of the tract of land herein before men-
tioned in accordance   (page 229)
with & in persuance of Section 2020, 2021, 2022, 2023, & 2024 inclusive of the
Code of Tennessee. Commencing Said processioning Survey at the mouth of a branch
on the North side & bank of the Tennessee River at what is now known as Henry's
Ferry, Thence up said branch as it meanders to a large Hackberry on the bank of
said branch where and old fence intersects the same, thence with the old picket
fence North 74° West about 34 poles to the outside fence and the same course continued with an old marked conditional line in all 194 Poles to a stake in the
center of the Washington and Sulphur Springs road, thence with said road North
47° East 6 Poles, thence North 36½° East 22 Poles, thence North 30° East 50 Poles
thence North 29½° East 19½ Poles to a stake in the center of the road opposite a
large Black Oak in the mouth of the lane, thence along the lane With E.F. Waterhouses line North 53½° West 80 Poles to a Black[?] corner to E.F. Waterhouse and
on Montgomerys line, thence with said Montgomerys line South 88½° East to a stake
and Sweet Gum marked A on the South East side of the Washington Road, thence with
another line of Montgomerys North 31½° East 78 Poles to a Wateroak on the long
reach line and in the edge of Pond, thence with said long reach line North 1½°
East about 45 Poles to Montgomerys Rock corner near a sink Spring and the same
course continued in all about 104 Poles to a stake which a corner to tract No. 2,
thence with a line of tract No. 2 South 87½° East 21½ Poles to a red oak and gum
in a sink which is also a corner to tract No. 2, thence with Montgomerys line

South 36½° East 26 poles to a Postoak, thence South 77½° East 53½ Poles to a Postoak, thence South 42½° East with Montgomerys line to the River, thence down the River as it meanders [to] the Beginning Containing by estimation 416 acres more or less. The above is the description of tract No. 1 Isabella T. Lockes Land.

The following is a discription of tract No. 2 Mrs. Isabella T. Lockes Lands. BEGINNING at a Stake in the center of the Washington and Sulphur Springs road also a corner to tract No. 1 running thence north 267 Poles with the back

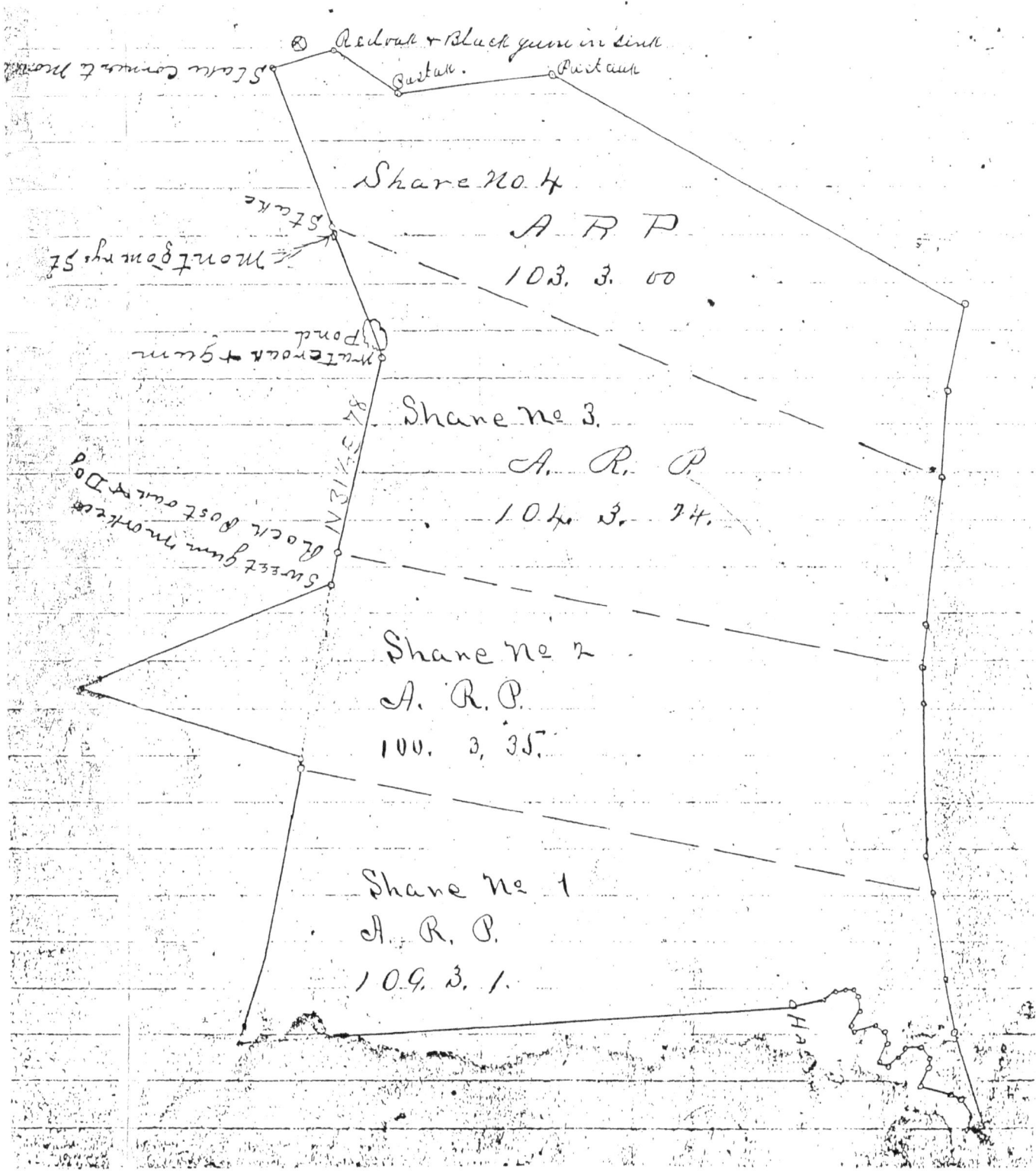

line of the long reach tract to a stake with a red oak and 2 hickory pointers, thence South 88° East 84 Poles to a stake in the Barnett Mill Pond thence South ?1½° West ___?___ (last line ragged) (page 230)

two large marked White oaks (Kellys corner) at 11 poles in all 196 Poles to a stake with a Hickory and red oak Pointers on Montgomerys line, Thence with another line of Montgomerys South 42½° West 96 Poles to a Redoak and Black Gum in a sink a corner to Montgomery and also a corner to tract No. 1, thence with a line of tract No. 1 North 87½° West 21½ Poles to the Beginning Containing by estimation 129 acres more or less.

(page 231)

State of Tennessee, Rhea County   SURVEYORS OFFICE

I, E.F. Waterhouse, Surveyor for said County in said State do certify that the above Plat and discription of the land herein before named and processioned by me to the best of my knowledge is true and correct and is recorded the Surveyors Book in my office on pages 228 etsig. This the 6th day of October 1882.

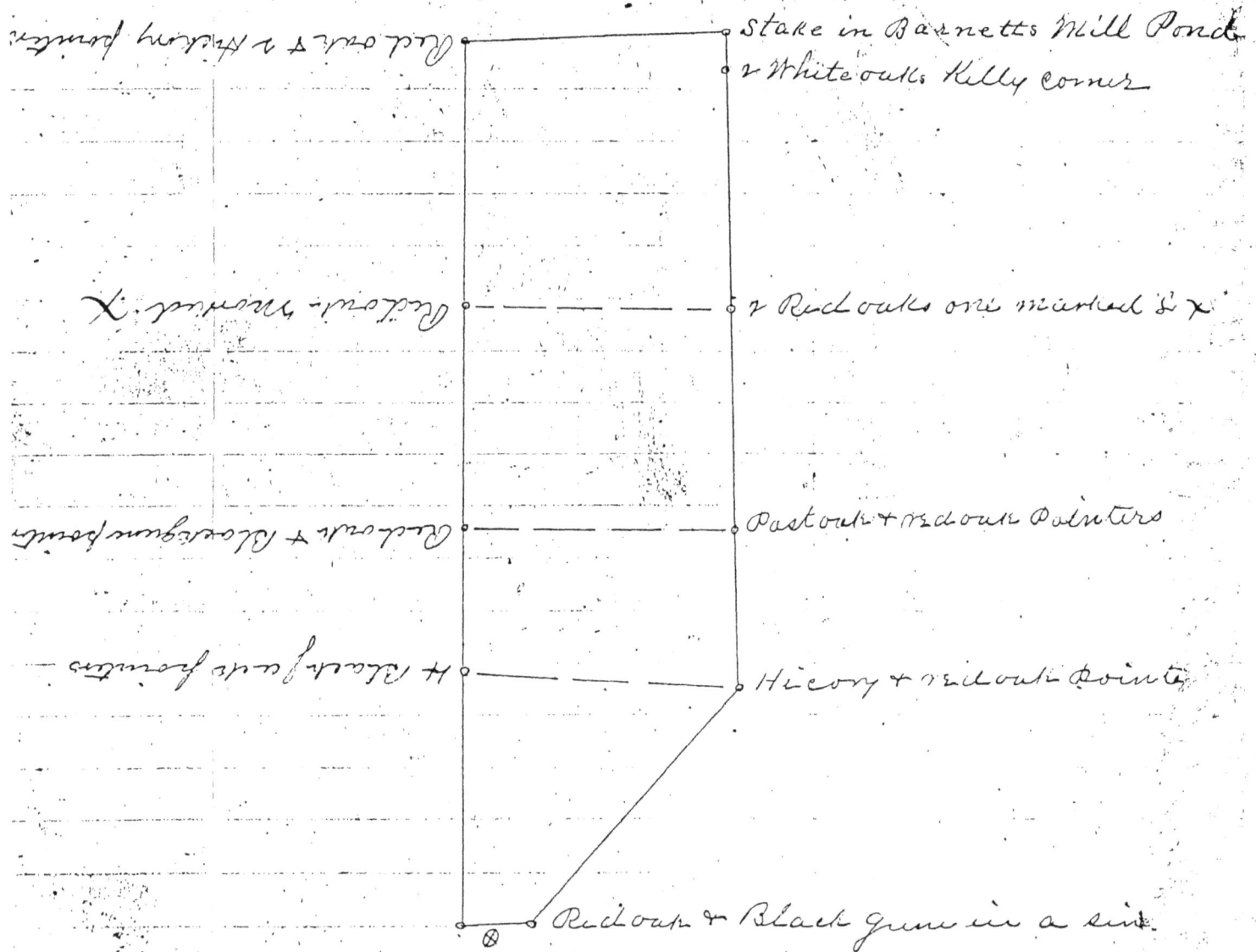

WILLIAM B. GOTHARD   (page 232)

State of Tennessee, Rhea County
By virtue of Special Entry No. 436 made in the Entry
Takers Office of Rhea County, bearing date of April
5, 1889 by William B. Gothard, I have surveyed for
the said Gothard the following described tract of
land. BEGINNING on a Stone marked D.C.I. corner to
the Dayton Coal and Iron Co. Ltd. land standing on
the East side of Dutchmans Nob on the North side of
the Dayton Cove Road running with said road S 87½° W
10 P. and 23 L., N 85° W 22 4/5 Poles to Stone marked
D.C.I., another corner of Dayton Coal and Iron Co.
Ltd. land on the top of Lone Mountain; thence with
the line of heirs of Darious Waterhouse N 8° W 5
poles, N 20° E 12½ poles, N 9° E 6 poles, N
34½° E 26 poles, N 19° E 24 poles, N 9° W 48
poles to Double Pines corner to the Dayton
Coal and Iron Co. Ltd. line; thence with their
line S ½° E 124 poles to the Beginning, Containing by estimation 10 acres more or less.
Surveyed April 24, 1889.
J.L. Daniel, Dept. Sur. R. Co.
Henry O. Nickolds & J. Jones, C.C.

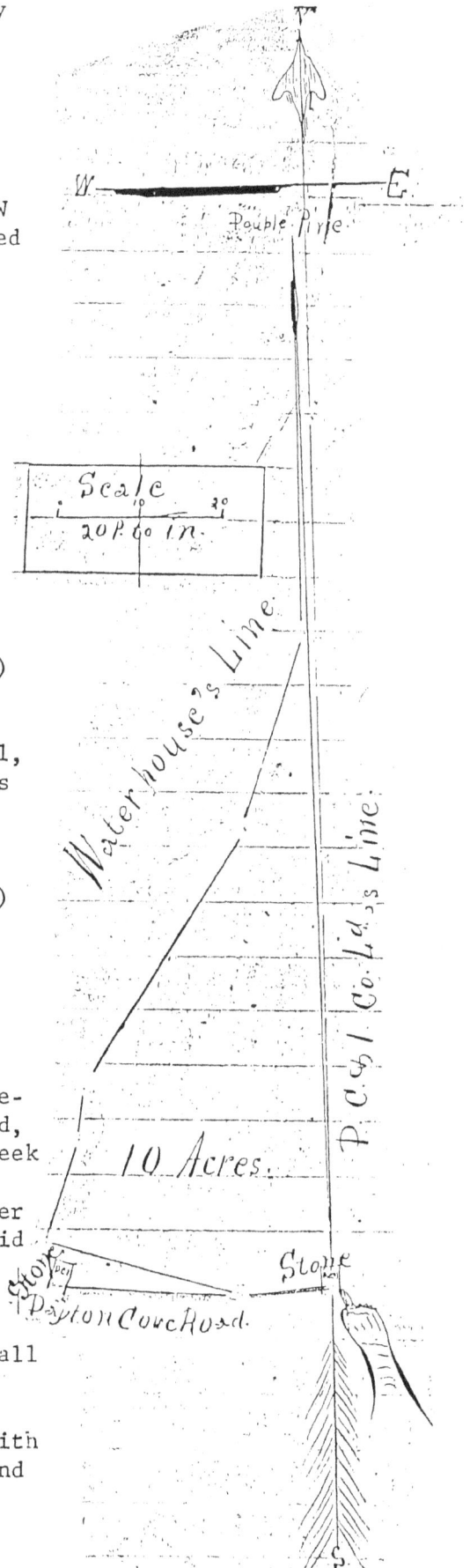

W.M. FOUST   (page 233)

NOTE— No description was recorded for the tract of
W.M. Foust Surveyed on April 23, 1889 by J.L. Daniel,
Deputy Surveyor for Rhea County, although a plat was
included (on following page).

A. PAINE   (page 234)

   PROCESSIONING LANDS OF A. PAINE ON PINEY CREEK

State of Tennessee, Rhea County
Surveyors Office October 27, 1902
In pursuance to the following Notice to wit:
To W.T. Gass, W.P. Darwin, Heirs of John R. Neal, deceased, T.W. Smith, Heirs of John Stanbough deceased,
(blank) Allen, David Weaver, Eli Hayes and Piney Creek
Coal and Land Company: This is to notify you, and
each of you, that I will on the 29th day of September
1902 between the hours of 10 A.M. and 5 P.M., on said
day proceed to procession my lands lying on Waldens
Ridge on the waters of Piney Creek, beginning on a
Postoak in the line of Hayes and Weaver and run and
survey and mark the lines and establish corners to all
my lands in said locality, and continue the survey
from day to day until all of the lines are surveyed
and marked; and you are further notified to bring with
you all title papers and maps you may have to any and

138

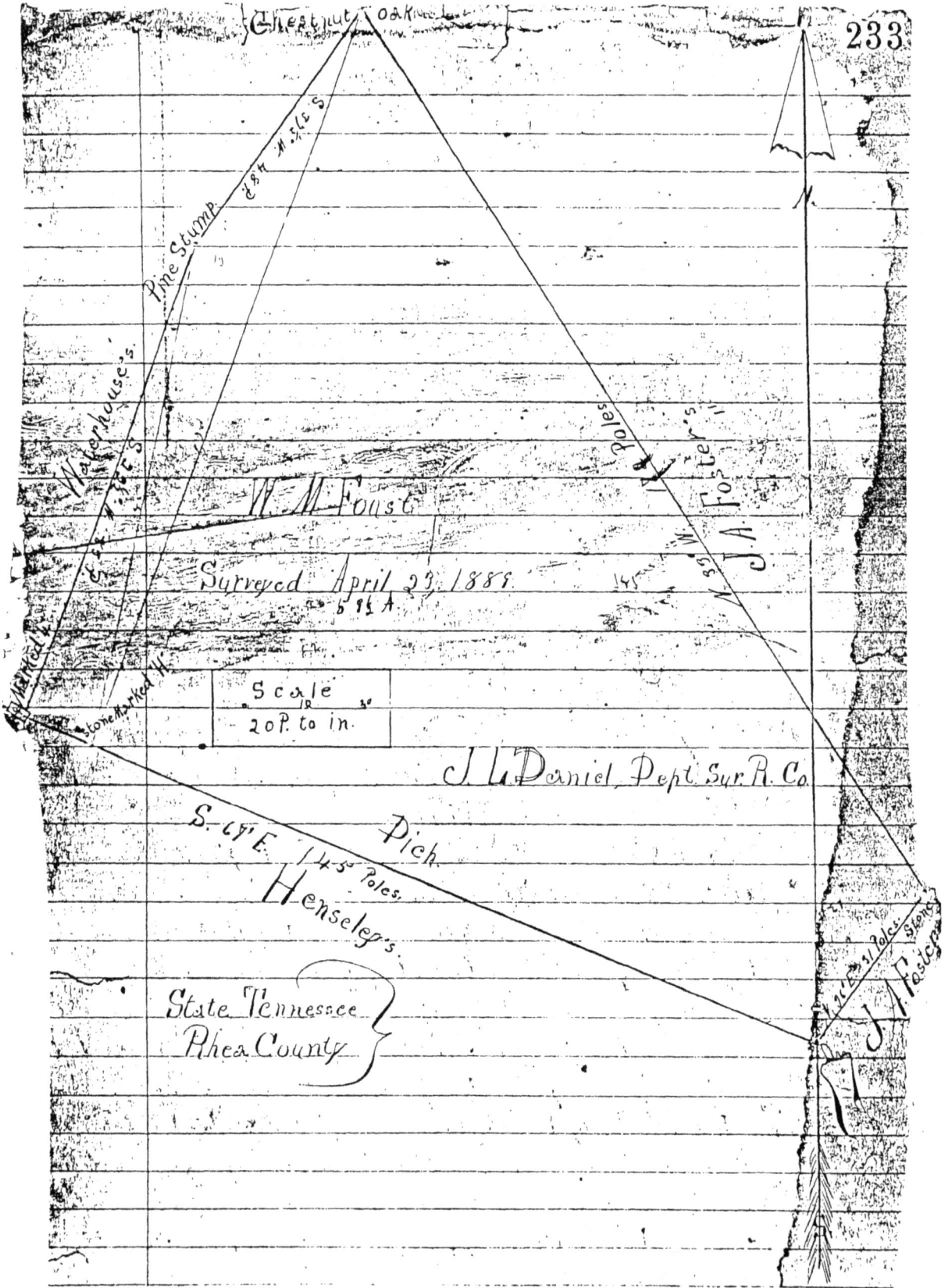

Chestnut Oak

233

Pine Stump

284 N. 51° E.

Waterhouse's

N. 74° Poles

J. A. Foster's

N. 33° W.

145

W. M. Foust

Surveyed April 23, 1888.

594 A.

Stone Marked H

Scale
20 P. to in.

J. L. Daniel, Dept. Sur. R. Co.

S. 69° E. 145 Poles.

Pich.

Henseley's

State Tennessee
Rhea County

J. A. Foster

all of your lands adjoining those of mine.
This September 4th 1902.   A. Paine
            Executed the within notice by personal service on each of the named par-
ties and by leaving a copy of same with ___?___ of the named parties on the 5 and
6 of Sept 1902 and posting at Courthouse and precincts according to _(last line
missing)_   (page 236)
I, J.L. Daniel Surveyor for Rhea County did on the 23 day of September 1902 (and
subsequent days) in accordance to the above Notice, a copy of which I held and
with various copies of Grants and deeds furnished me by said Paine and others,
proceed to rund and survey two tracts of lands claimed by the said A. Paine
lying on Waldens Ridge on the West fork of Piney Creek in persuance to Sections
2020 to 2024, 2827 to 2831 inclusive of the Code: Beginning said Processioning
survey on September 29, 1902 at 1:35 P.M. in the presence of David Weaver, W.P.
Darwin, Cye Henry, A. Paine, Joe Paine, and others, on the N.E. corner of Entry
No. 1 of John Hammels 60 acre tract ___?___ the line of his 100 acre tract now
Weaver tract running thence with the line of the 60 [acre] tract N 66° W crossing Piney Creek at 64 poles at a point where ___?___ bridge had stood and about
2 poles above the end of the present bridge structure, passing Hayes or Quales(?)
fence at 84 poles, crossing _a ?_ road at 170(?) in all 204 poles to a Stone in
the edge of the Hawkins old field, thence N 24° E ___?___ crossing a road at 57
poles in all 165 poles to a pile of stone with Blackgum. Dogwood and Sourwood
pointers with bearings as follows: Blackgum South 11 feet;;(missing)
Dogwood S 35° W 15 feet, Sourwood S 60° W 15 feet _(remainder of page missing)_
                                                              (page 237)
Stone marked "J.S." with pointers(?) on the South bluff of Piney __?__ and running N 45° W (Var _?°_) original __?__ crossing Piney Creek at 30 poles ___?___
small crooked Postoak at 50 poles in all 200 poles to W---tone(?) with two
small Hickories and __?__ Blackoak pointers, N.48° E (Var 3°) passing a Stone
marked "J.S." at 2.84 poles, crossed __?__ at _?_ poles, a marked line at 48
poles in all 10? poles to a Stone in a line supposed to be the South boundary
line of the Joe Smith 500 [or 5000] acre Grant and 4.5 poles East of a ___?___
oak in Smiths , thence with said supposed Smiths line S 56° E crossing the
line __?__ South(?) __?__ corner supposed to be the corner the land of Alfred
Collins 2000 acre Grant _?_ about 118 poles, crossing Piney Creek at ____ poles,
the Public road at 136 poles in all 300 poles to a stone with four Postoak
pointers in said Supposed Smiths line, thence S 42° W crossing the Public road
at 36 poles near Ganaways road, thence crossing a marked line at 575 poles and
crossing Piney Creek at 86 poles and at 1?4 poles in all 154 poles to the
Beginning.
State of Tennessee, Rhea County
The above Plat and description was correct as surveyed by me under the above
Processioning Notice on September 29, 1902 and suceeding days till completed
on October 26, 1902 and is recorded in Surveyors Book Pages 234 to 237 inclusive
And Plat and description issued to the Register on November 12, 1902.
                              J.L. Daniel, Surveyor for Rhea County

NOTE- The plat for the above Survey was spread over two pages (234 and 235)
and is reproduced on the following two pages. The handwriting is very difficult
to read and was further complicated with age spots on page 237. Some words are
completely obliterated and have been indicated above as __?__ . B.J.B.

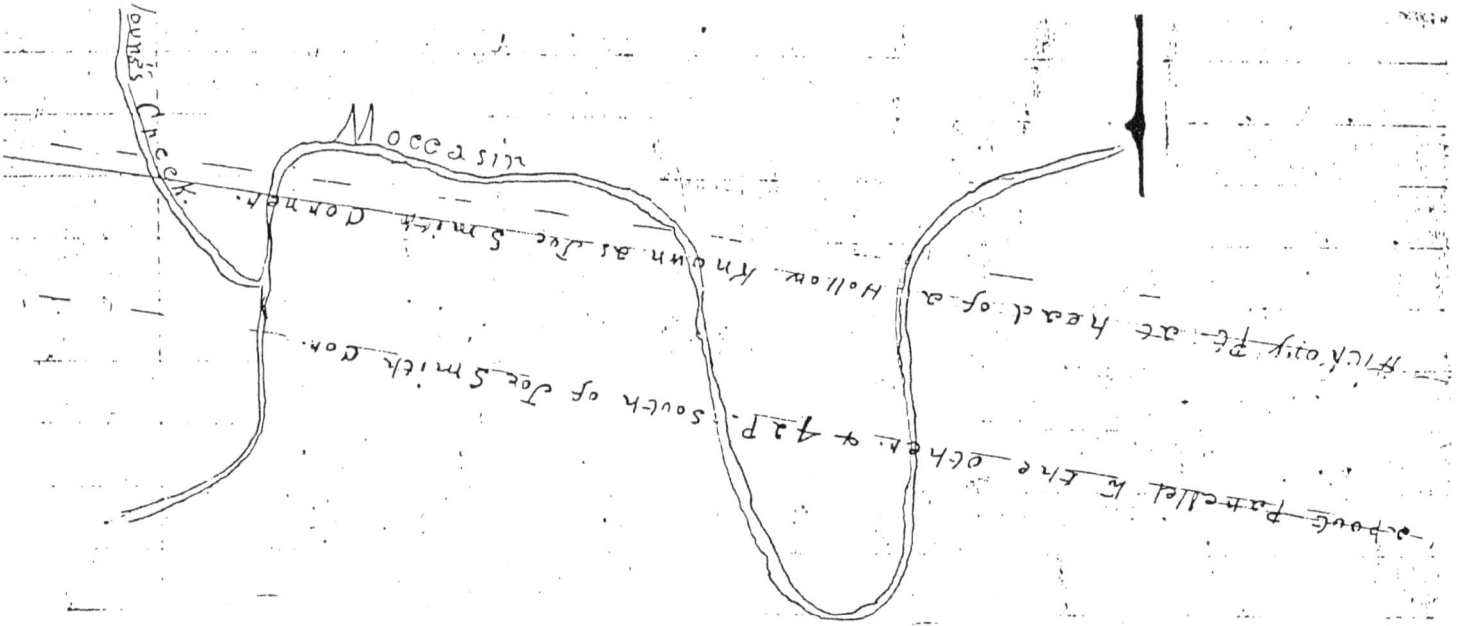

Portion of Plat on page 234 (Lands of A. Paine on Piney Creek)

PROCESSIONING LANDS of A. PAINE ON PINEY CREEK

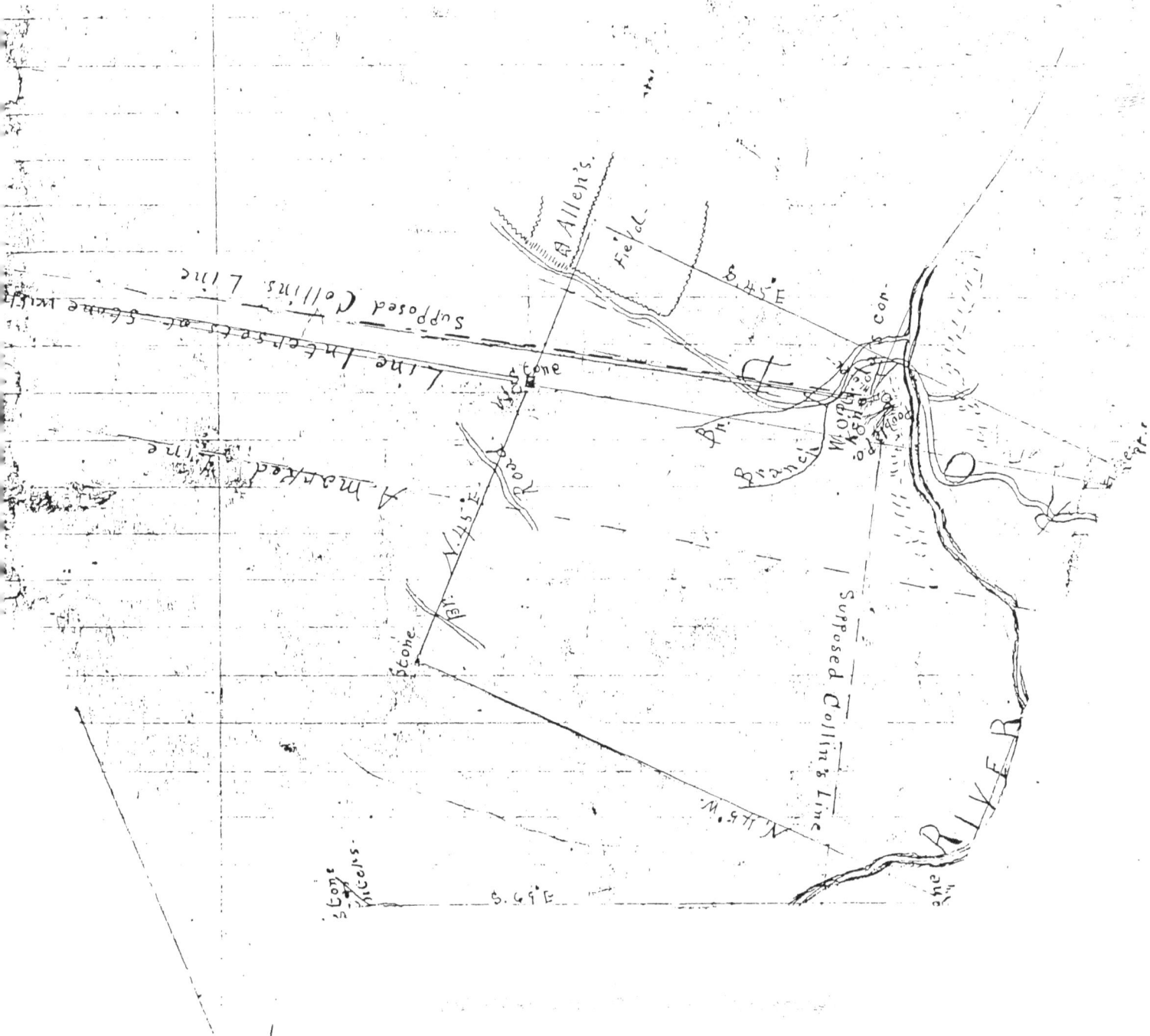

NOTE— bottom half of page missing

Portion of Plat on page 235 (Lands of A. Paine on Piney Creek)

142

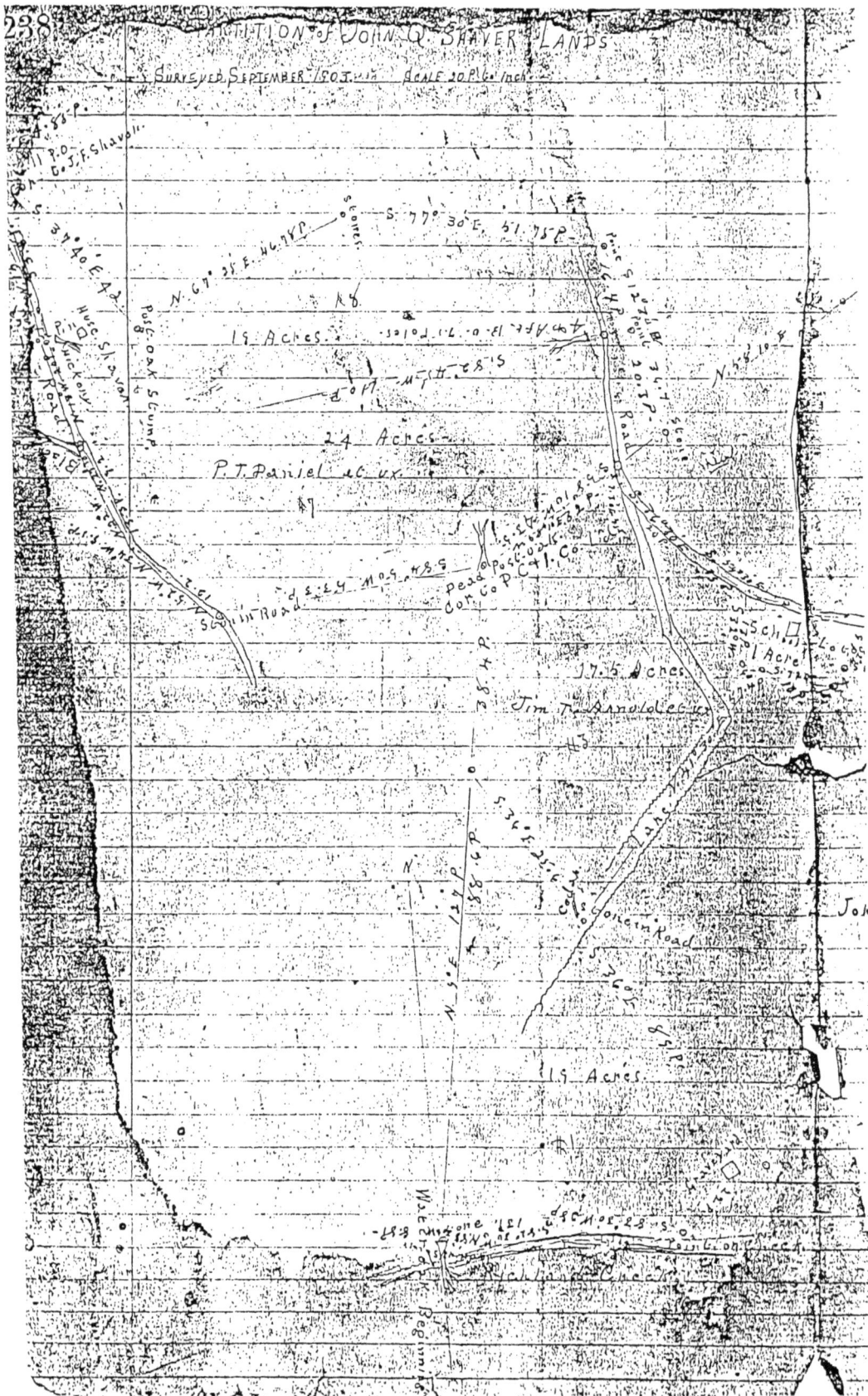

PARTITION OF JOHN Q. SHAVER LANDS

(page 238)

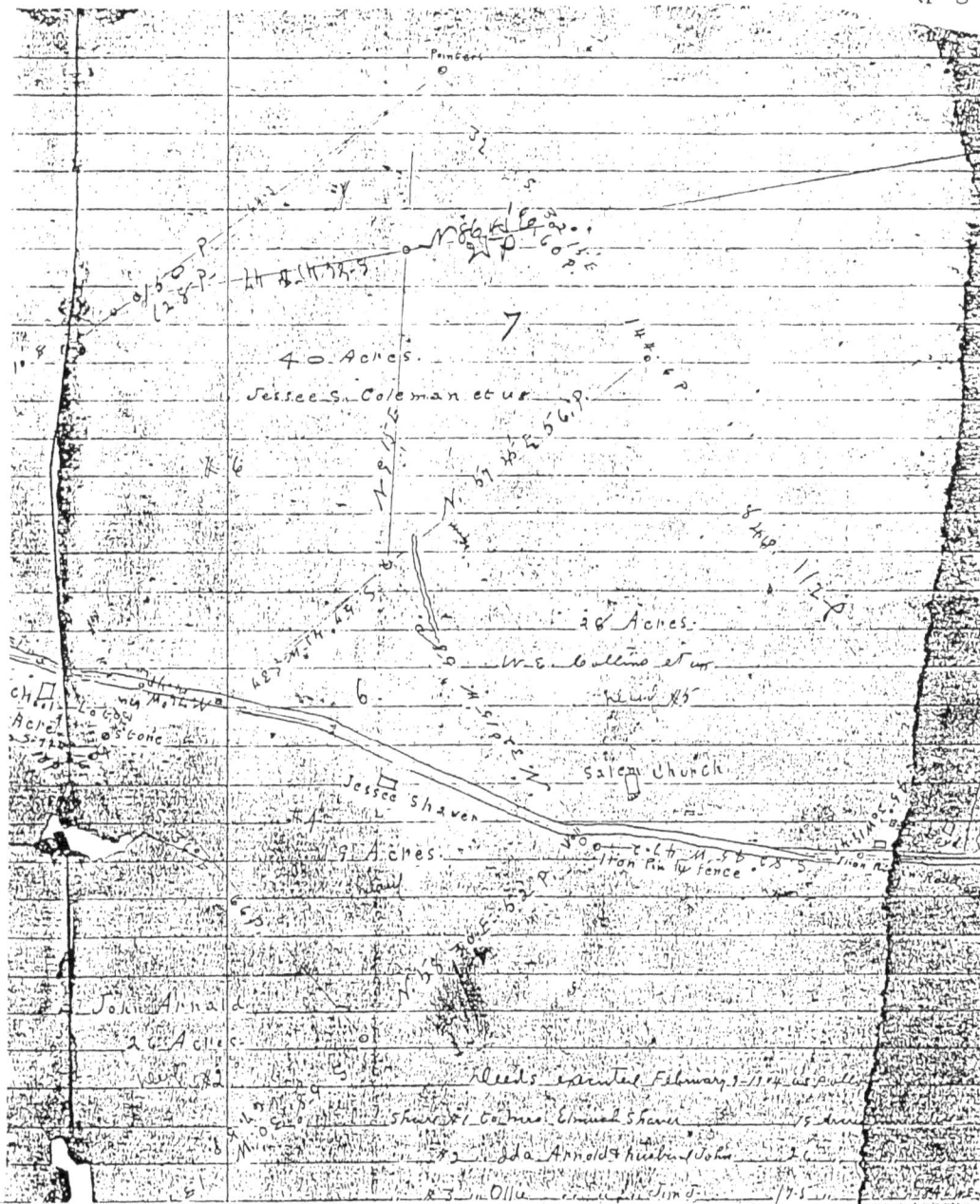

Deeds executed February 9, 1904 as follows:

Share	#1	to Mrs. Elmirah Shaver	19	Acres more or less
"	#2	to Ida Arnold & husband John	26	" " "
"	#3	to Ollie Arnold & husband Jim J.	17.5	" " "
"	#4	to Jesse Shaver	19	" " "
"	#5	to Alice A. Collins & husband W.E.	35	" " "
"	#6	to Delia T. Coleman & husband J.S.	27.5	" " "
"	#7	to Hester Daniel & husband P.J.	22.5	" " "
"	#8	to Huston Shaver	?5	" " "

NOTE: All of Shares Nos. 7 & 8 E. of the road was deeded to Share No. 6 and all of Share #3 east of the __?__ was deeded to Share #5 which was 8.5A making this Share 36.5 A. less 1.5A Salem Church lot. These changes made by agreement of the parties selling to each other these parts. Also Share #8 purches [sic] 6.5A from Share #6 out of the N.E. corner.

240

Schoalfield

Telephone Line

Beginning Patent No 137
Sept 20, 1787 640 A. W.C.

White Walnut Bottom Tract

Com gone

W.O. gone

Scambough

Poplar

Jim Campbell

Lane

Well

Garden

Alley

P.W. Pearce's

Tel. Line

House

Jeff Alley's New Ground

where Bradshaw Lives

original R.O. down

Stake

J.B. SPEARS   (page 241)

State of Tennessee, Rhea County
Surveyors Office, May 23 1904
In pursuance to the following Notice to wit:
To W.T. Gass, R.D. Davis, Agent of John Stanbough Heirs, W.(?) B. Schoolfield,
Love Neal, Peter W. Eberly, Seth Alley, John Alley, Jeff Alley, J.M. Campbell,
P.W. Pearce, John McPherson, and E.F. Waterhouse.
        You are hereby notified that on Monday, May 19th 1904 between the hours
of 10 A.M. and 3 P.M. of said day I will proceed with the County Surveyor J.L.
Daniel to procession my lands lying in the 2nd Dist. of Rhea County, Tennessee,
better known as the "Gass Farm". Beginning the survey on a poplar corner to my
lands and the Stanbough lands   ?   Poplar stands West of the C.N.O & T.P.
Railway and Said Survey will continue from day to day until all the lines of my
farm are rerun and marked and corner stones placed at each corner. You are
further notified to bring with you title papers and maps showing the location
and boundary of your land.
This April the 12th 1904   J.B. Spears
        Come to hand day issued and executed by leaving a true copy of this
Notice with each of the within named parties. April 18, 1904.
                          J.F. Dasson, Constable
                          Serving twelve notices— 86.00
        I, J.L. Daniel, Surveyor for Rhea County, Tennessee did on the 19th day
of May, 1904, and subsequent days in accordance with the above notice which I
had given(?) me and various deeds to the lands of the said J.B. Spears proceeded
to survey said lands in the presence of J.B. Spears, W.T. Gass, Willard Knight,
Charles Esics, P.W. Eberly, Seth Alley, Jeff Alley, J.M. Campbell, P.W. Pearce,
on Monday, May 19, 1904, 11 A.M. Beginning at a large Poplar corner in the lines
of Spears and Stanbough near the foot of the ridge and running with a line of the
said Spears and Stanbough N 60° W Var 3°27'= N 56°33' W pasing   ?   P.O. at
9.5 poles   ?   at 27 poles another(?)   ?   P.O. at 62 poles in all 114 poles
to a Postoak and Stone marked J.S.; then N 28° E Var 2°=N 30° E passing to the
right of house in which R.D. Davis lives at   ?   (page 242)
crossing Spring branch at 90 poles in all 110 poles to a Red oak stump by Stone
marked "J.S." on S.E. side of the road, then N 41° E Va 2°=N 43° E 42 poles to a
Stake on E side of the road near where Sam Neal now lives, then N 26° E Va 2°=
N 25° E 14 poles crossing a hollow to a Stake on a hill side on N. side a road
leading through the field, then N 9° E Va 2°=N 11° E passing about 15 poles to
Right of Love Neals house at 30 poles in all 56 poles to a Stake in Neals field,
then N 8° E Var 2°=N 20° E passing through a berry field at 39 poles in all
124.3 poles to a Stake on the West side of the road, then S 60° E Va 3°=S 57° E
81 poles to a Ash the S.W. corner of Schoolfields farm standing South of a ra-
vine near the South top of the hill, then S 60° E Va 2°=S 58° E at 121 poles we
are about 1.5 poles in Schoolfields field, crossing a ditch at 156 poles
C.N.O & T.P. Ry 155.2 poles, Public road at 187 poles, the American Telephone
Line and Seth Alleys at 244 poles in all 250 poles to a stake in a hollow, then
S 10° W Va 4°=S 14° W passing through Seth Alleys field and passing over his
well at 87.5 poles, crossing the lane near a planted stone at 100 poles in all
233.5 poles to a Stake in J.M. Campbells line which is the line of the old
White Walnut Bottom tract N.C. Patent No. 157, Sept. 20, 1757, then with said
line N 60° W Va 4°=N 56° W 70 poles to a Stake in P.W. Pearces berry field about
5 poles E of the corner field, then S 30° W Va 4°=S 34° W crossing S fence of
berry field at 34.5 poles 4.5 poles E of corner field, crossing the road in a
hollow near the forks of the road at 75 poles, Jeff Alleys berry field fence at
99 poles in all 107 poles to a Stake in Alleys field on hill side, then N 60° W

Va 3°=N 57° W crossing said Telephone line at 10 poles, public road 14 poles, C.N.O & T.P. Ry at 56 poles in all 185 poles to the Beginning.
State of Tennessee, Rhea County
The above plat and descriptions are practically correct and are correctly recorded as surveyed by me as surveyor for Rhea County on Monday, May 19, 1904 and subsequent days until the same was completed on the 14th and is recorded in Surveyors Book on pages 240-1-2 inclusive.   J.L. Daniel, Sur. Rhea Co.

J.L. WIERICK   (page 243)

State of Tennessee, Rhea County
In pursuance to the following Notice:
        To H.L. Eastland Agent &c. You will take Notice that on the 26th day of October 1905 beginning at 10 oclock a.m. I will establish the line adjoining tract owned by your son Mark Eastland of which you have charge as his agent, Situated in 1st Civil district of Rhea Co.mTennessee, the surveying of said line will begin on the top of Muddy Creek Ridge and at a rock called for in my deed to said land, the common rner   (page 244)
corner and Western end of said division line.
        This Sept 30th 1905   J.L. Wierick
I served the within Notice by reading and making known the contents thereof and leaving a copy with H.L. Eastland on this Oct 2, 1905. John Heiskell, Dept. Shff
        I, J.L. Daniel, Surveyor for Rhea County, Tennessee did on the 26th day of October 1905 in compliance to the above notice which I had with me and in the presence of H.L. Eastland, J.L. Wierick, J.C. Locke, J.L. McPherson, Mark Eastland, A.J. Eastland, J.P. Brady, J.H. Pearson, and John Wassom proceed to locate the lines of the said J.L. Wierick adjoining the land of the said Mark Eastland beginning said survey about 10 A.M. on said day and continued the same until completed on Saturday 28. By consent of Eastland and Wierick we first ran a line from the S.W. corner of Eastlands land a corner also to the Broyles land a Blackoak with a Hickory pointer on top of Muddy Creek Ridge and after careful search we were unable to find a Stone which we could identify as a corner stone as called for in the Notice and also which is called for in both Wiericks and Eastlands deed therefore by consent of both parties we began the survey of the line at a Red Elm which is an undisputed common corner to each tract, and ran from this corner first by the Wierick deed on a variation of 1°30' and then ran by the Eastland deed on reverse calls with the same variation but this proved to be to light a variation and on final survey we located the lines as follows beginning on a planted stone near a Spring and common corner of J.L. Wierick, J.H. Pearson and Mark Eastland at the East end of the crossfence between Wierick and Eastland and ran with said crossfence S 77° W Variation 2°30' 36 poles to a Stone; then S 59°30' W 21.8 p. to Said Elm which stands on the S. bank of a branch near Wiericks house below the Spring, then N 7° E to a Stone which we put in   (page 245)
on the W side of said branch; then N 51°31' W 6 poles to a Stone we put up, then N 82°30' W 12 poles to a Stone put up by us, then N 35°30' W crossing a branch at 2 p. and 78 p. a Whiteoak stump at 90 said to have been a line tree; passing
__?__ on the steep hillside in all 186 poles to a Stone by a path with Pine and Blackoak bushes as pointer on top of Muddy Creek Ridge and wish [which] we locate as the corner of said Wierick and Eastland. We also ran Wiericks line along the top of said Ridge S 77°30' E 13 p; N 66°30' E 8.3 p.;nN 8° E 13.0 p; N 59° E 18.5 poles to stones and Hickory and Spotted oak pointer a corner of Wiericks and Pearson.
        The lines run are correctly shown on page 243, the orange colored lines represent the lines as claimed by Eastland; the black lines represent the lines we locate as Wiericks. This October 30, 1905. J.L. Daniel, Surveyor

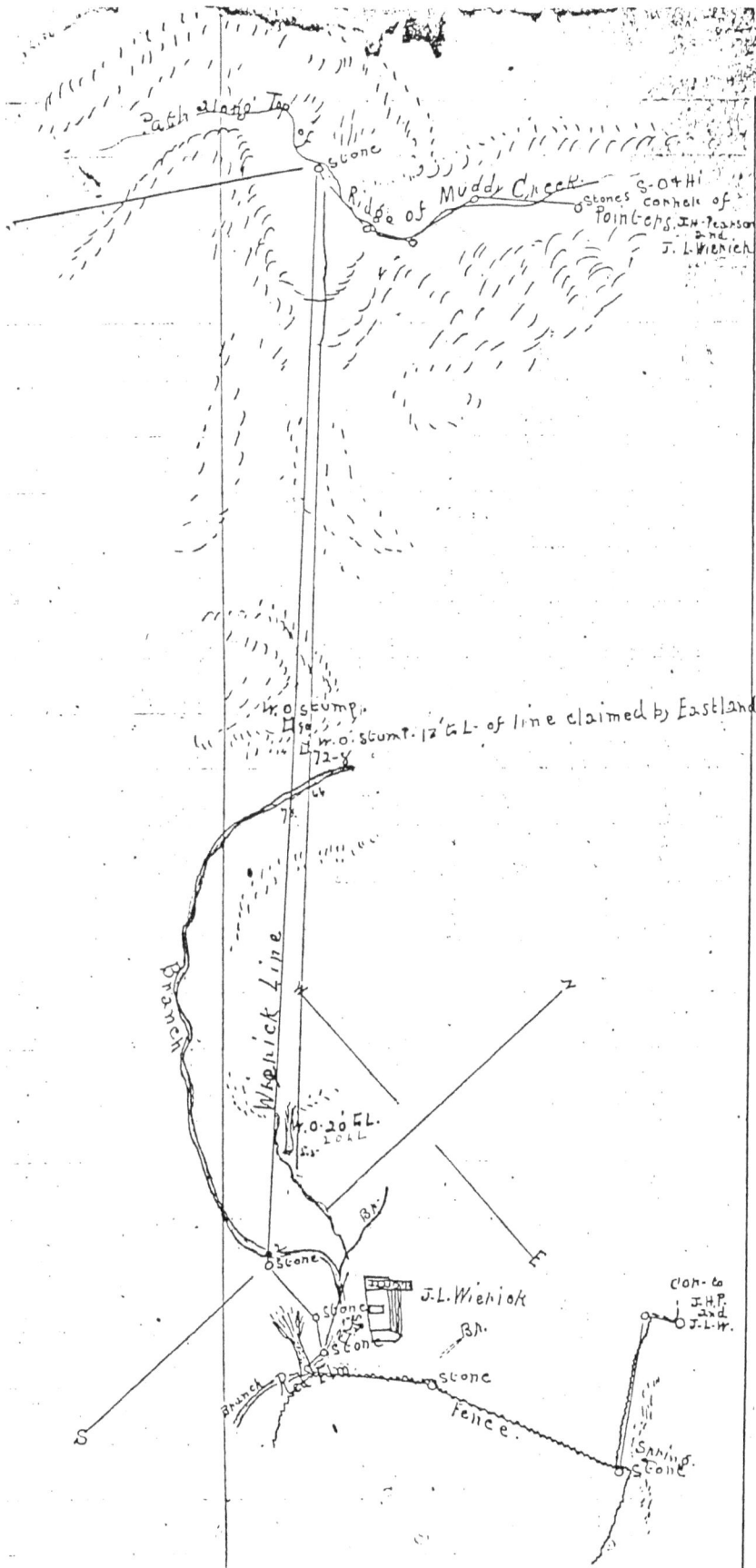

Plat of J.L. Wiericks tract as surveyed in 1905.

148

S 70° 10' E — 204.9

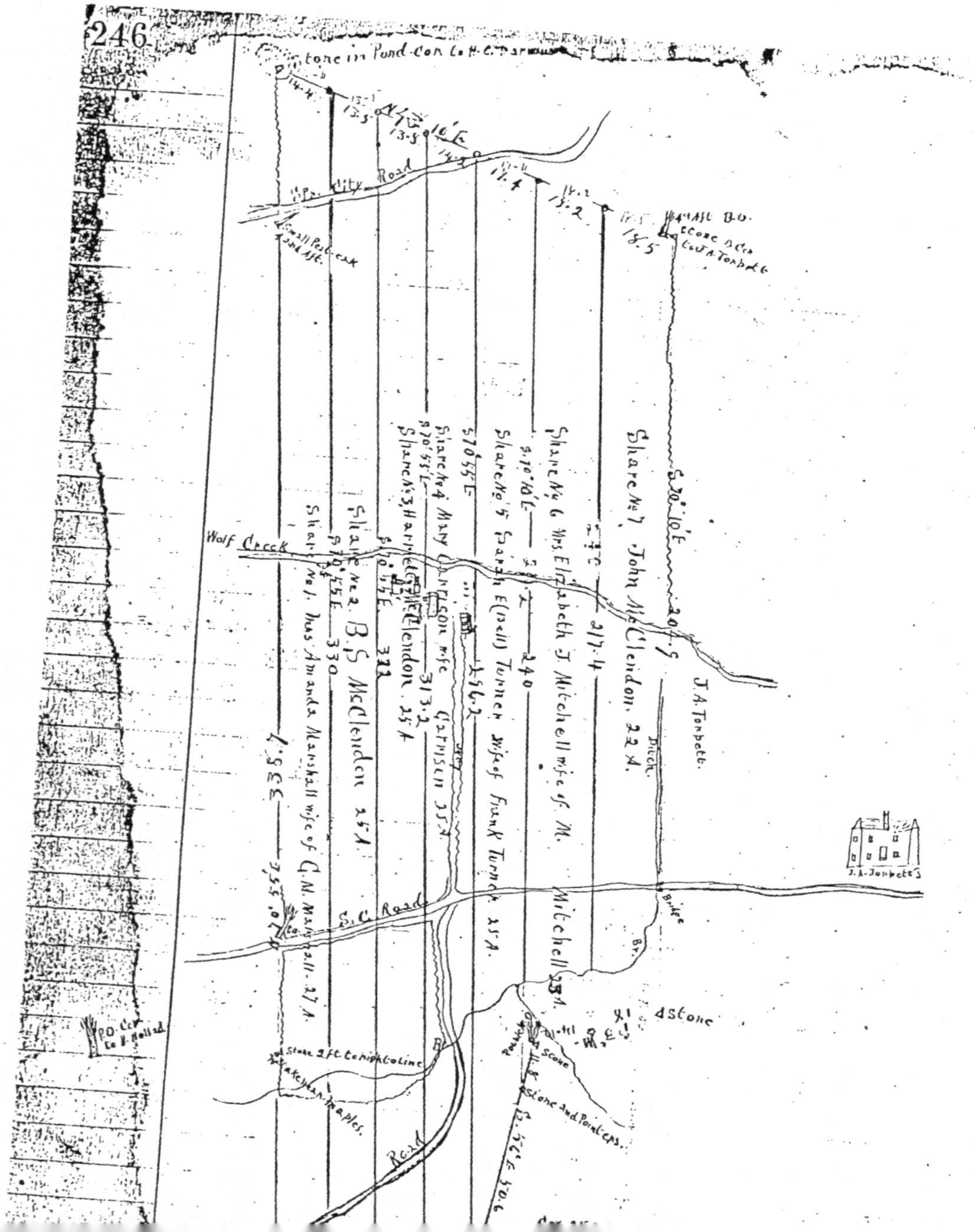

J. A. Torbett.

Ditch.

Bridge

Br.

Share No 7. John McClendon. 22 A.

270 — 217.4

Share No 6 Mrs Elizabeth J. Mitchell wife of M. Mitchell 23 A.

S 70° 10' E — 21.2 — 240

Share No 5 Sarah E (Bell) Turner wife of Frank Turner. 25 A.

S 70° 55' E — 296.2

Share No 4 Mary Garrison wife Garrison 25 A.

S 70° 55' E — 313.2

Share No 3 Harriet McClendon. 25 A.

S 70° 55' E — 322

Share No 2. B. S. McClendon 25 A.

S 70° 55' E — 330

Share No 1. Mrs Amanda Marshall wife of G. N. Marshall - 27 A.

Wolf Creek

S. C. Road

246

WILLIS McCLENDON   (page 247)

State of Tennessee, Rhea County
I certify that the plat on page 246 correctly represents the survey of the Willis McClendon farm lying on Wolf Creek in the Second District as surveyed Oct.
25 to 31, 1906 and partitioned H.C. Darwin, C.R. Holloway and J.A. Torbett,
Executors of Willis McClendon under his Will of April 5, 1906, and each share
is Numbered beginning with the South share and going North consecutively from
No. 1 to No. 7. The roads and Wolf Creek are sketched in approximately except
at the points of intersections of the boundary lines. The corners of the various
shares are designated by stone. At the corner marked "Stake near Maples" a
stone was placed in by agreement of G.M. Marshall and Huse Holland 2 ft. North
of the Stake. The boundary lines are given in the present magnetic bearings,
which shows a Va [Variation] on the South boundary line of 4°05', on West boundary line 2°40', North boundary line of 2°50', and the other lines 3° and 4°.
Weather was clear and cool.   J.L. Daniel, S. of Rhea Co.

A.C. GIBSON   (page 248)

State of Tennessee, Rhea County
Persuance to the following Notice to wit:
To G.H. West, W.C. Bailey, W.H. Rodgers, citizens of Dayton, Rhea County, Tennessee:—
        You are hereby notified that I will on December 10, 1906 at the hour of
2 P.M. proceed to procession the lines of my lot at North side of First Avenue
in Dayton and will begin said survey on the corner of First Avenue and Market
Street it being the S.E. Corner of Lot No. 17 in Block 2 of Tapscotts plan of
Gardenhire Addition of Dayton and we will locate and establish the corners and
lines of my lot which is Lot # 21 in said Block according to my deed and said
plat. You are hereby notified and requested to be present with your deeds and
assist in the proper location of the Lot. This Dec. 10, 1906. A.C. Gibson
        We acknowledge servace on the within Notice and ___?___ the 20 days notice
required to be given by law. This Dec. 10, 1906.   W.C. Baily, W.H. Rodgers
        I acknowledge the receipt of a copy of the within notice and acknowledge
its receipt to have the same effect as if served upon me by the Sheriff twenty
days previous to this date but to have no other or further effect.
        This Dec. 10, 1906   G.H. West

NOTE— No plat or record of the survey was included in the Book.
(blank)   (page 249)

A.A. SNEED   (page 250)

State of Tennessee, Rhea County
In pursuance to the notice below sent out to wit:
To George S. Cooley and Ruben Swafford. I hereby give Notice that I will on
April 2, 1908 between the hours of 8 and 10 O'clock A.M. Procession my lands
by calling the County Surveyor, J.L. Daniel and beginning the Processioning Survey on the corner of Sam Davis and myself in the Waterhouse line on the old
Washington road and continuing the survey from day to day till the corners and
lines of my lands are established and marked. You are each requested to be present and have with you your Title papers and assist in the correct location of
the corners and lines of the lands This March 12, 1908. A.A. Sneed
        Come to hand and executed by leaving a copy with each, said George S.
Cooley and Ruben Swafford, this March 1908. J.L. Denton, Dept. S.

I surveyed said lands and placed corner stones where need and the boundary lines now are as follows: Beginning on a limestone rock on the South side of the Evensville and Washington road with 3 Blackjack Pointers and also a corner of G.S. Cooley and S.S. Franklin and running practically with the road N 40° W 44 poles; N 23°30' W 27 poles; N 48°30' W 42 poles to a point opposite Sneeds house; N 52° W 42 poles to a Stone corner to Sneed and Swafford, N 46°30' W 46 poles to a point on N side of old road; N 76° W with an old road bed 62.5 poles to a point in the Sam Crow line; then with the line of Ruf. Swafford then with this line N 32°18' E crossing the Public road 32 poles __?__ Sam Crows N.E. corner at 74 poles, in all 111 poles to a lime stone rock with Blackjack pointers N. of a hollow and corner to Cooley and Swafford, then S 47°18' E, passing Swaffords S.W. corner 101.8 poles 235.4 poles to a lime stone rock with 2 Red oak pointers, then S 32°18' W 95.4 poles to the Beginning.
Rufe Swafford and Sam Crow, Sworn Chainmen, Present and assisting J.T. Darwin, George S. Cooley and A.A. Sneed.   April 3, 1908.   J.L. Daniel, Surveyor

ALVIN SPENCE   (page 251)

Notice to Hon. Richard Knight
I, Alvin Spence, hereby serve Notice to all whom it may concern that on May 11, 1908 between the hours of 8 and 10 o'clock A.M. begin a Processioning Survey of lands by the County Surveyor J.L. Daniel, Beginning the Survey on my N.W. corner on the Ridge and continued the same from day to day until completed by Establishing corners and remarking lines, And you are notified and requested to be present and aid in the proper location of the same. Bring Your Title Papers.
April 16, 1908.   Alvin Spence
      I acknowledge servace on the above, Richard Knight
State of Tennessee, Rhea County
In pursuance to the above "Notice" I went on the day set out, May 11, 1908, for the purpose of carrying into effect the demands set out in the notice at 9:40 A.M. Present were Esq. James Gillespie, John Boyd and two sons Will and Charlie, Bob Hood, Rhea Purcer, Richard Knight and son, and Alvin Spence and son, J.G. Knight forbid me markin or running the line and demanded a Jury which was complied with and James Gillespie, John Boyd and son Will and Rhea Purcer were Summoned but each declined to serve. Adjurned at noon for dinner to meet back at this corner at 1:30 p.m. No one Came but Alvin Spence and sons. John Boyd sent two sons. A trial line was run from a Blackoak mk 4 and A1ft on bearing of S 28°30' E 117 poles, suspended till following day, Tuesday Set Stone at the corner on the Ridge and ran line on Bearing of S 29°30' E passing a 4 and Aft Black oak at 5 pole and one at 39.5 poles X [crossing] Boyds?) line at about 45 poles in all 216 poles to a Stake. Remarked the line till we crossed Boyds line
                           J.L. Daniel, Surveyor

J.W. KNOX   (page 252)

    PROCESSIONING SURVEY OF THE LANDS OF J.W. KNOX IN THE 4TH CIVIL DISTRICT

State of Tennessee, Rhea County
Office of County Surveyor, March 26, 1917
In pursuance of the following Notice to wit:
To Tom Nichols and Dave Holt, you are hereby Notified that I will in company with the County Surveyor on the 24th day of January 1917 proceed to Survey and reestablish certain lines and corners between your lands and my own and remark the same, said Survey will begin between the hours of nine and twelve oclock A.M. at the fallen pine corner. You are   (page 253)

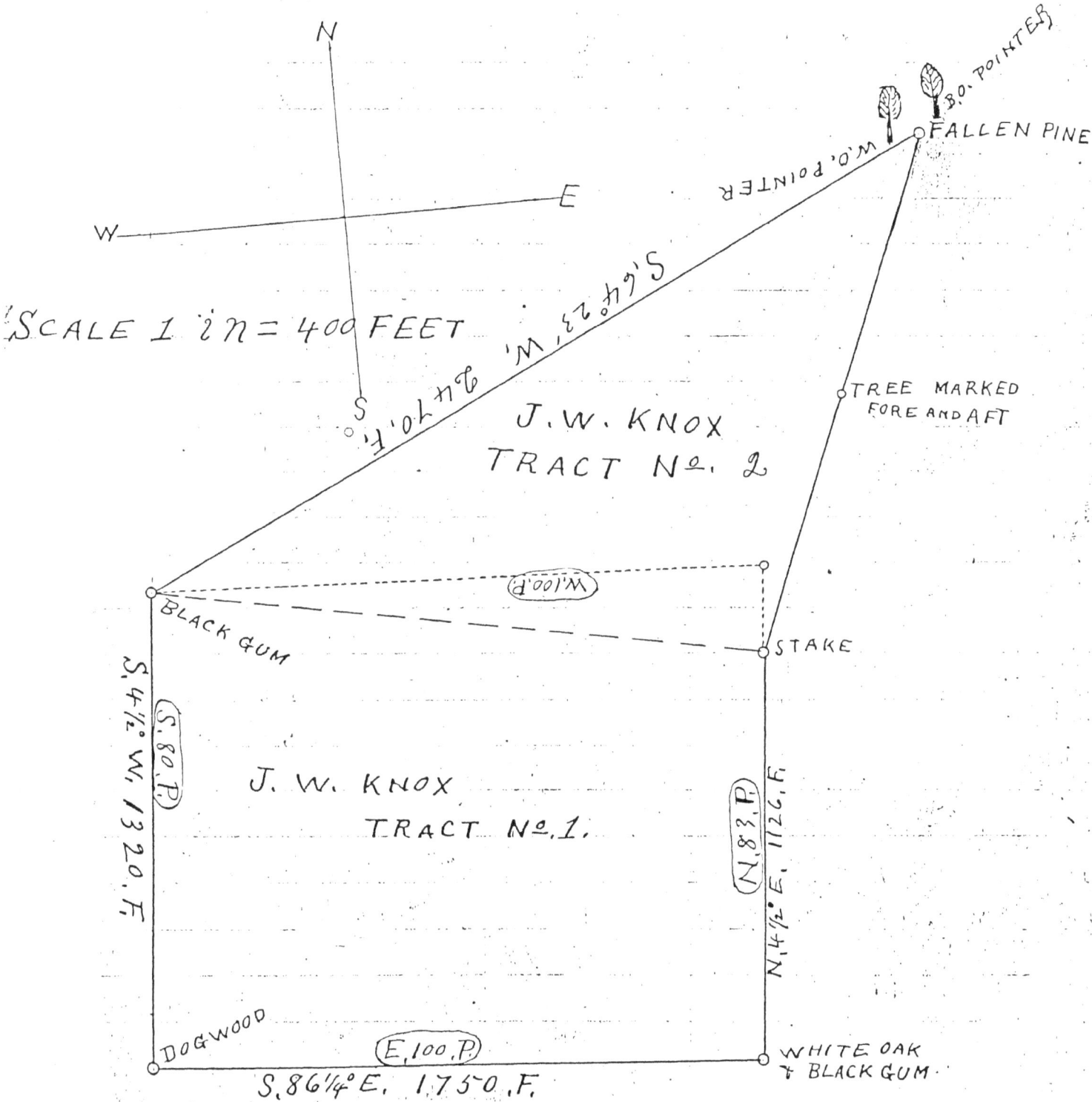

N

W —————— E

S

SCALE 1 in = 400 FEET

B.O. POINTER

FALLEN PINE

W.O. POINTER

S.64°23'W. 2440.F.

J. W. KNOX
TRACT No. 2

TREE MARKED
FORE AND AFT

W.100.P.

BLACK GUM

STAKE

S.4½°W. 1320.F.

S.80.P.

J. W. KNOX
TRACT No. 1

N.4½°E. 1126.F.

N.83.P.

DOGWOOD

E.100.P.

WHITE OAK
& BLACK GUM

S.86¼°E. 1750.F.

further Notified to bring with you all title papers or maps you may have pertaining to your land. Said Survey will continue from day to day untill completed unless otherwise continued this 28th day of Dec. 1916. James W. Knox

One copy of the above Notice was posted at the Court House door of Rhea Co. 20 days previous to said 24th day of Jan 1917, and one copy was posted at the voting place nearest to the lands in question it being in the 4th Civil district of Rhea Co., Tenn. and Tom Nichols and Dave Holt each had a Copy of the same Notice served on them as agents Representatives or owner of the adjoining lands and one copy of said Notice was handed to me with the Legal and proper return thereon by W.H. Smith, Constable for Said 4th District showing the same to have been served upon said parties more than 20 days pryor to the said 24 day of Jan. 1917.

I, J.W. Truex Surveyor for the County and in the State aforesaid did on the 24th day of Jan. 1917 and Succeeding day Survey and reestablish and remark certain lines and corners of the lands of James W. Knox as follows.

After all parties concerned in said survey or their representatives had arrived on the premises it was agreed that the best place to begin the survey was the South West corner of J.W. Knoxes first tract and what is known as the Dogwood corner of   (page 254)
said tract. I found at this point an old dogwood turned out by the roots but the old marks still on it. I then run the south line of said first tract by following an old marked line called for running due East. I run it on a variation of 3 3/4° 1750 ft. to a large stone marked F O X, and set at the root of an upturned White Oak tree and corner to said first tract. Thence with the East line of said tract it being an old marked line N 85½ E, 1126 feet to a stake set by me and corner to said Knoxes second tract and at the Junction of two old marked lines and the Eastern boundary line of the C.E. Shelton tract of land out of which the two tracts of J.W. Knox were purchased. Thence with the Eastern line of Knoxes second tract the same being one of the aforesaid old marked lines N 21½° E, Passing a center tree marked fore and aft at 747 feet in all 1508 feet to a stake set by me in the bed of an old fallen pine tree now nearly all rotten, a Blackoak and a White Oak marked as pointers, the marks on these trees appear to be very old, this last marked line seems to stop at this point as I could not find any marks beyond this point the afore said stake is a common corner between the lands of J.W. Knox and the land of Malinda A. Nichols Formerly owned by Theo Flora. Thence S 64°23' W 2470 feet to a stake set by me said stake being the North West and known as the Black Gum corner of J.W. Knoxes forst tract

(page 255)
also the West corner of said Knoxes Second tract, and corner to the Tenney E. Holt land. This last line running on S 64°23' W 2470 feet is the line in dispute, both Knox and Nichols deeds call for a fallen pine, and the above described fallen pine corner is the only place I could fine that would fill the conditions of both deeds, and the only point I could find with an old marked line or a marked line of any sort leading to it.

Therefore I decided that this point was the true and correct corner and I run and marked the line from there to the black gum corner of the said Knoxes first tract as per calls of said Knoxes deed. Thence with the West line of said first tract S 85½° W 1320 feet to the beginning.
Jesse Truex and Tom Burns, Sworn Cain Carriers
State of Tennessee, Rhea County
I hereby certify that the above report and description and map of the above named lands processioned by me, to the best of my knowledge and belief are true and correct and the Same is recorded in the Surveyors Book in my office on page 252 et seq. this Mar 26th 1917. J.W. Truex, Surveyor for Rhea Co. Tennessee

W.E. WYATT   (page 256)

PROCESSIONING SURVEY OF THE LAND OF W.E. WYATT IN THE 1ST CIVIL DISTRICT

State of Tennessee, Rhea County
Office of County Surveyor Dec 26, 1917
In persuance of the following Notice to wit:
To Alex and Matilda Reece. You are hereby Notified that I will in company with the County Surveyor of Rhea Co. Tenn. on the 20th day of Dec 1917 proceed to Survey and re-establish certain lines and corners between your land and mine and

re-mark the same. Said survey will begin between the hours of 9:00 A.M. and
12:00 oclock or noon   (page 257)
at the sweetgum tree on the West bank of the Creek at my Beginning point. You
are farther Notified to bring with you all of the papers or maps you may have
pertaining to your land. Said survey will continue from day to day untill completed unless otherwise continued.   (signed) W.E. Wyatt

A copy of the above Notice was posted at the Court House door in Dayton,
Rhea Co. Tenn. 20 days before the 20th day of Dec 1917 and one Copy of said Notice was posted at the nearest voting place to the land in question (it being
in the first Civil District Rhea Co. Tenn. and one Copy was handed to me with
the legal and proper return thereon showing that one copy of said Notice had
been legally served on Alex Reece and Matilda Reece by T.A. Hicks, constable 20

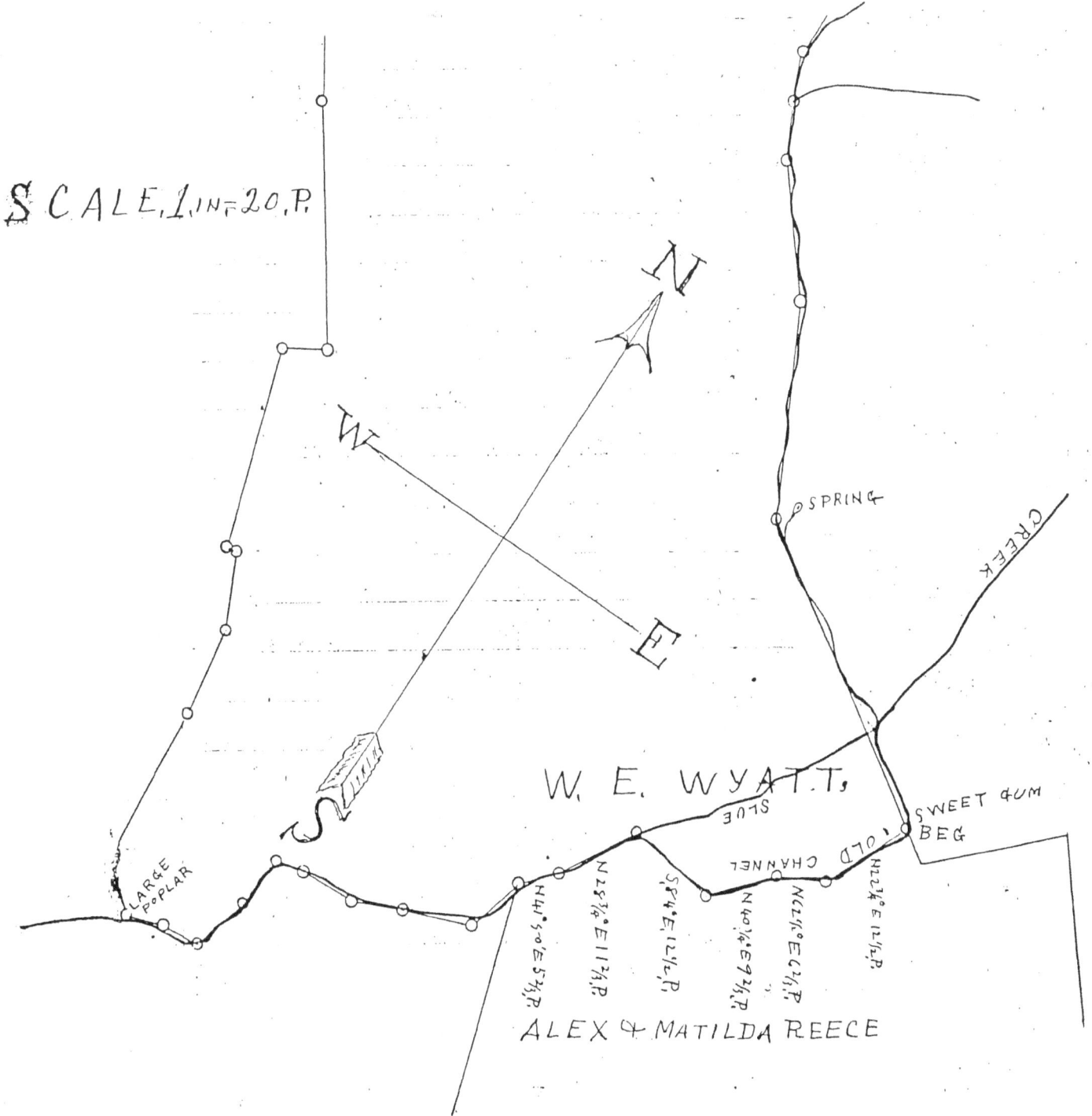

SCALE, 1 IN = 20 P.

N

W

E

S

SPRING

CREEK

W. E. WYATT,

SLUE

SWEET GUM
BEG

OLD CHANNEL

LARGE POPLAR

ALEX & MATILDA REECE

days pryor to the 20th day of Dec 1917.

I, J.W. Truex Surveyor for the County of Rhea State of Tenn. did on the 20th day of Dec 1917 and succeeding day proceede to survey and re-establish the following lines between the lands of W.E. Wyatt and Alex and Matilda Reece.

BEGINNING at a sweet gum tree and alder bush on the West bank of the Creek and in a line of the upper tract of the Stephen Breeding land and running Thence down the Creek as it meanders as follows. S 22 3/4° W   (page 258) 12½ p., S 62½° W 6 2/3 p., S 40 3/4° W 9 2/3 p., N 84° W 12½ p., S 28 3/4° W 11 2/3 p., S 41°50' W 5 2/3 p. to a point in the center of the Creek and corner to said Reece's land and in a line of said W.E. Wyatt.

The aforesaid Alex Reece and W.E. Wyatt both being present and acting as chain bearers, and both consented to this location of these lines between them and both parties bore their equal part of the expence of this survey.

J.W. Truex, Surveyor for Rhea County
State of Tennessee, Rhea County, Office of County Surveyor
This is to certify that the above plat and description of the lands herein before named and processioned by me to the best of my knowledge and belief is true and correct and the same is recorded in Surveyors book No. 1 in my office on page 256 et seq. this 26th of Dec 1917.   J.W. Truex, Surveyor for Rhea Co.

G.T. CUNNYNGHAM   (page 259)

PROCESSIONING SURVEY OF THE LAND OF G.T. CUNNINGHAM AT MORGAN'S SPRING ON WALDENS RIDGE IN 4TH CIVIL DISTRICT

State of Tennessee, Rhea County
Office of County Surveyor, November 20, 1919
In persuance of the following notice to wit: To Mrs. M.E. Soloman, George Morgan, Parrie Morgan Bridgman, H. Brown Morgan, and G.W. Spivey, you and each of you are hereby notified that I will in company with the County Surveyor on the 7th day of November 1919, proceed to survey and re-establish the line between your land and my own and re-mark the same. Said survey will begin between the hours of 9:00 and 12:00 at a point at the corner near Morgan Springs, being the original point were [sic] J.I. Riddle commenced to run with the division line in dividing said original 200 acre tract, and will survey each and every line of the tract of land conveyed to Calvin Morgan by W.P. McDonald et als by partition deed dated May 10, 1899, and registered in book 29, page 184 et seq. of the Register's Office of Rhea County, Tennessee.

You are further notified to bring with you all title papers or maps you may have pertaining to your land. Said survey will continue from day to day until completed unless othersise continued.
This Oct. 16, 1919.   (signed) G.T. Cunnyngham
One copy of the above notice was posted at the Courthouse door of Rhea County 20 days before the 7th day of November 1919, and one copy was posted at the nearest voting place to the land in question, it being in the 4th Civil District of Rhea County, Tennessee, and one copy was served on each of the following persons, Mrs. M.E. Solomon, George Morgan, Parrie Morgan Bridgman, H. Brown Morgan, and G.W. Spivey, and one copy of said notice was handed me with the legal and proper return thereon by Cain Burnett, Sheriff for Rhea County, Tenn., showing that said notice had been served on the above named parties more than 20 days prior to the said 7th day of November 1919.

I, J.W. Truex, Surveyor for the County and in the State aforesaid, did on the 7th day of November 1919, and succeeding days proceed to survey the aforesaid tract of land.

Beginning at a hickory tree near the Morgan Sulphur Spring, being the original point where J.I. Riddle commenced to run with the division line in dividing the original 200 acre tract; thence North 26°11' West 375 feet to a stone in said division line on North side of old road; thence with old road South 66 3/4° West 121 feet to an iron pin about

(page 262)

where the branch crosses said road; thence with the said old road again North 26°10' West 440 3/4 feet to an iron pin in the East side of the old road and corner to the Church lot; thence with a line of the Church lot North 63°55' East 121 feet to an iron pin in said original divisional line; thence with said line North 26°11' West passing a blackoak tree marked for a center tree at 423 feet in all 3344 feet to a stone at fork of road; thence North 12° East 173 feet to a stone with black oak pointer; thence South 77° East 726 feet to a stake, the north west corner of lot No. 5 in said division; thence with the West line of lot No. 5 South 12¼° East 3007 feet to a stake; thence South 63°55' West 100 feet to a stake directly opposite the north east corner of lot No. 1; thence South 23¼° East 23 feet to a stone marked E and north east corner to lot No. 1; thence with a line of lot No. 1 S 12½° E, 442 feet to the South east corner of lot No. 1; thence to the beginning.

J.W. Truex, Surveyor for Rhea County

State of Tennessee, Rhea County
Office of County Surveyor

This is to certify that the above plat and description of the lands herein named and processioned by me to the best of my knowledge

(page 263)

and belief is true and correct and the same is recorded in Surveyors book No. 1 in my office on page 259 et sequa, this the 20 day of November 1919.   J.W. Truex
Surveyor for Rhea County, Tenn.

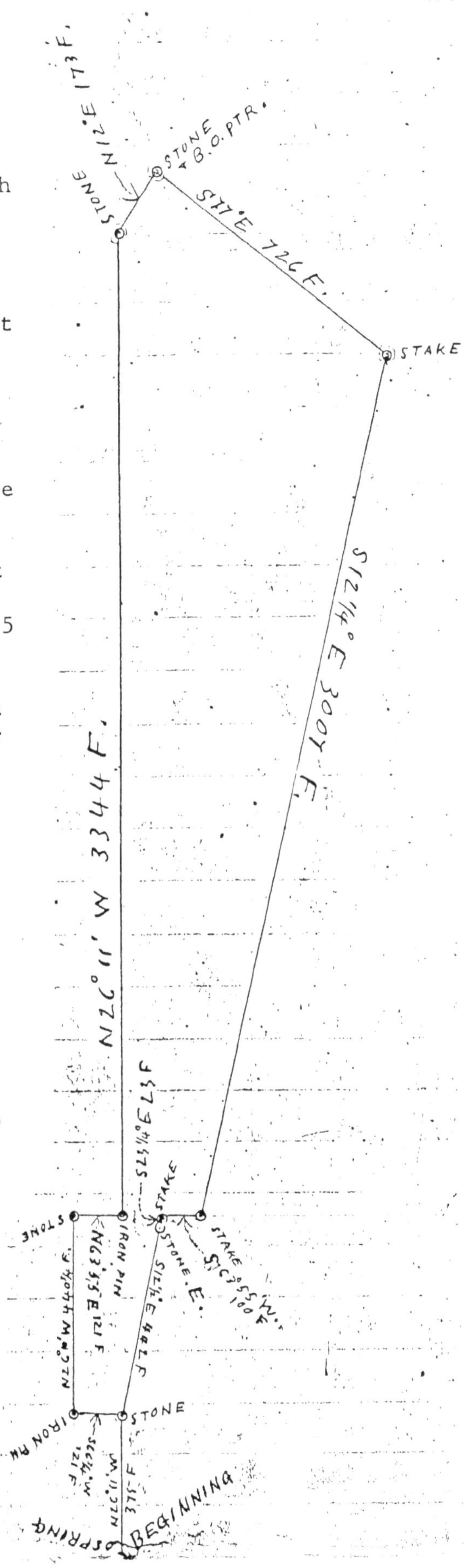

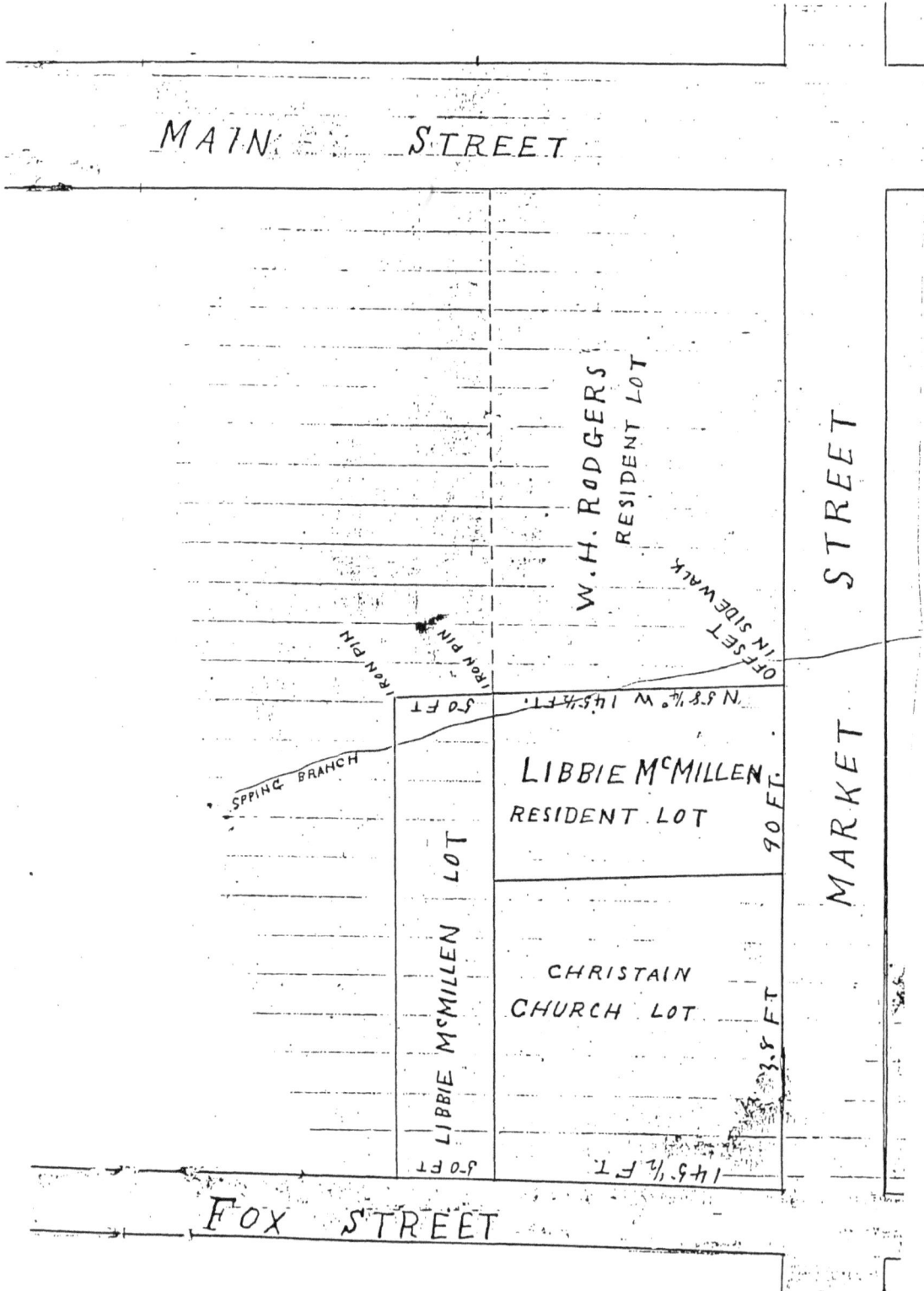

156

MAIN STREET

W.H. RODGERS RESIDENT LOT

OFFSET IN SIDE WALK

STREET

IRON PIN

IRON PIN

50 FT

N. 58 ¾° W. 145½ FT.

SPPING BRANCH

LIBBIE McMILLEN RESIDENT LOT

90 FT.

MARKET

LIBBIE McMILLEN LOT

CHRISTAIN CHURCH LOT

3.5 FT

50 FT

145½ FT.

FOX STREET

LIBBIE McMILLEN   (page 265)

State of Tennessee, Rhea County
Office of County Surveyor, May 25, 1921
In persuance of the following Notice to wit:
To W.H. Rodgers, you are hereby notified that I will in company with the County
Surveyor on the 24th day of May 1921 proceed to survey and re-establish the lines
and corners between your land and my own and remark the same. Said survey will
begin between the Hours of 8:00 & 9:00 A.M. at the North East corner of my resi-
dence lot and will survey my North West line which is the line between your lot
and mine.
        You are further Notified to bring with you all title papers or maps you
may have pertaining to your land. Said survey will continue from day to day untill completed unless otherwise continued.
This Apr 23rd 1921   Signed Mrs. Libbie McMillen & J.M. McMillen
        A copy of the above Notice was posted at the Court House door in Dayton
Rhea Co. Tenn. 20 days before the 24 day of May 1921, the same being the voting
place in the 3rd Civil District of Rhea Co. Tenn. wherein the land in question
is situated, and one copy of said Notice was handed to me with the proper and
legal return there on showing that one copy of said Notice had been legally
Served on   (page 266)
W.H. Rodgers by L.A. Smith, A deputy Sheriff of said County, 20 days pryor to
the 24th day of May 1921.
        I, J.W. Truex Surveyor for Rhea Co. Tenn. did on the 24th day of May
1921 proceed to Survey re-establish the following line between the lots of Libbie
McMillen and W.H. Rodgers. Beginning at a point on the West side of Market
street at an ofset in the concrete side walk near a large Sycamore tree standing
near the Spring branch this point appearing to be an undesputed corner between
the lots of said McMillen and Rodgers, and running thence at about Right Angle
to Market street the same being N 58¼° W 145½ feet to an iron rail driven in the
ground, Thence parallel with Market street 90 feet to the N.W. corner of the
Christan Church property. Thence with the N.E. line of said Church property and
paralell to the first line 145½ feet to the West line of Market street. Thence
with the West line of said street 90 feet to the beginning.
James Newell & J.W. Truex, Sworn C.C.
State of Tennessee, Rhea Co , Office of Co. Surveyor
        This is to certify that the above plat and description of the lot herein
before named and processioned by me to the Best of my knowledge & belief is true
and correct and the same is recorded in Surveyors book No. 1 in my office on
page 264 Et Seq. This the 25 day of May 1921. J.W. Truex, Surveyor

E.B. EWING   (page 267)

        PROCESSIONING SURVEY OF A LINE BETWEEN THE LAND OF E.B. EWING AND
                G.H. WEST IN THE 3RD CIVIL DISTRICT

State of Tennessee, Rhea County
Office of County Surveyor, March 11, 1922
In pursuance of the following Notice to wit:
To G.H. West, you are hereby Notified that I will in Company with the County Sur-
veyor of Rhea Co. Tenn. on the 9 day of March 1922 proceed to Survey and re-
establish the line and corners between your land and mine and re-mark the same.
Said Survey will begin between the hours of 9 oclock A.M. and 12 o'clock or noon
at the   (page 268)
North West corner of your lot on Washington Street being the lot conveyed to you
by S.M. Swaby and Wife on the 30th day of Oct 1903 recorded in book No 33 page

34 of the Registers office of Rhea Co. and being the North West corner of the Dr. A.C. Blevins Addition to Dayton. You are further Notified to bring with you all title papers or maps you may have pertaining to your land. Said Survey will continue from day to day untill completed unless otherwise continued.
This Feby 16, 1922   (signed)   E.B. Ewing

A copy of the above Notice was posted at the Court House door in Dayton Rhea Co Tenn. 20 days before the 9 day of March 1922 the same being the voting place in the third Civil district of Rhea Co. Tenn. wherein the lands in question are situated, and one copy of said Notice was handed to me with the proper and legal return thereon showing that Said Notice had been legaly served on G.H. West by Lud Parham, a Deputy Sheriff for said Co.

I did on the 9th day of March 1922 proceed to Survey and re-establish the line shown on map as line A.B. by beginning at a stone the North West corner of G.H. West's lot and corner to Mrs. Young and on the East side of Washington street, thence with the East side of said street S 57½° W 200 feet and drove an iron stake in the East line of said steeet and shown on map as point A. Then beginning at G.H. Wests East or N.E. corner the same being a corner to (blank) Powell and in W.L. Hodges line (I was informed by Powell that this corner was undesputed and satisfactory to all parties conserned), I then measured 200 feet along Hodges line (S 45 3/4° E) and located G.H. Wests South or S.E. corner as shown on map at point B. I drove an iron stake at this point and then run a strait line from the point A on Washington street to point B   S 33¼° E 505 feet

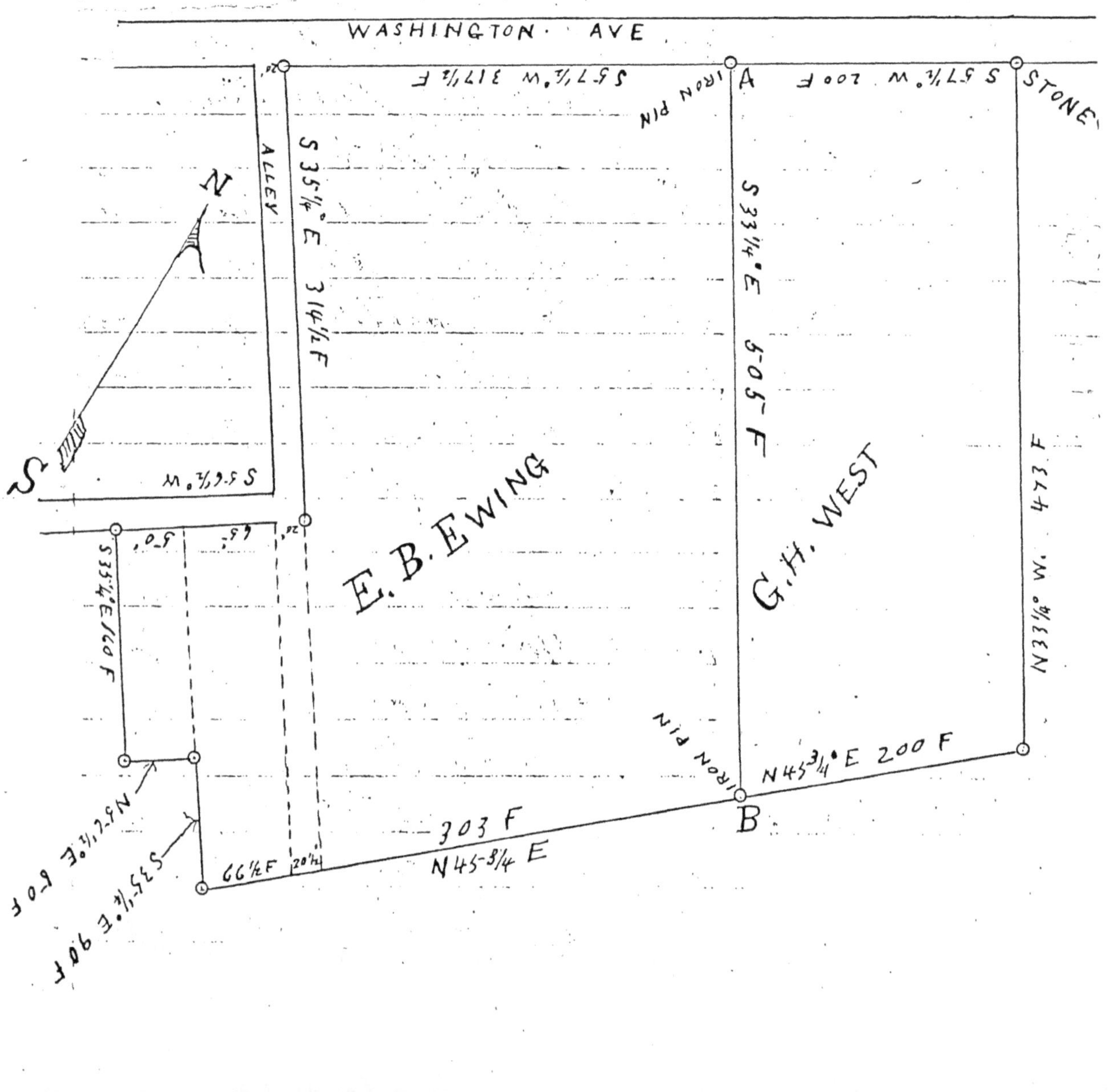

to Hodges line thence with Hodges line N 45 3/4 E 200 feet to Powells corner, thence with Powells line and Mrs. Youngs line N 33¼° W 473 feet to the Beginning. Francis Truex & Nick Purser, Sworn C.C.   J.W. Truex, Surveyor
State of Tennessee, Rhea County
Office of County Surveyor
This is to Certify that the above plat and description of the line herein before named and processioned by me to the best of my knowledge and belief is true and correct and the same is recorded in Surveyors book No. 1 in my office on page 267 Et Ewq. this the 11th day of March 1922.   J.W. Truex, Surveyor

W.F. WEIR   (page 271)

    PROCESSIONING SURVEY OF W.F. WEIRS LAND IN 3RD CIVIL DISTRICT

In persuance to the following Notice to wit:
To F.J. Paine, James Webb, Hoyl Ezell, C.W. Webb, Clint Norman, W.B. Allen, Cumberland Coal & Coak Co., Tom Evans, Fate Mathes, Sam Montgomery, and others, this is to Notify you and each of you that I will on the 10th day of June 1929 between the hours of 9 A.M. and 3 P.M. on said day proceed to procession my land lying on the side of Waldens ridge. Beginning at a stake at the foot of the mountain corner to lot No. 8 in the partetioning of the lands belonging to A. Paine Decased among his Heirs and in Sam Montgomerys line on the North side of the Paine old mountain Road and run and survey and mark the lines and establish corners to all my land in said locality and continue the survey from that day untill all the lines of said lands are surveyed and marked and you are further notified to bring with you all title papers you may have to any and all of your lands adjoining those of mine. This the 7th day of May 1929.
                              (signed)   W.F. Weir
A Copy of the above Notice was posted at the Court House door in Rhea County Tenn. 20 days previous to said 10th day of June 1929 and one Copy at the voting place nearest W.F. Weirs land also one copy reached me with the legal and proper return the same   (page 272)
showing that said Notice had been legaly served on each of the parties named therein by a Deputy Sheriff of Rhea Co Tenn. more than 20 days prior to the said 10th day of June 1929. I, J.W. Truex Surveyor for Rhea Co. Tennessee did on the 10th day of June 1929 (and continued for six days till completed) Survey all the lines marking the same and set up corner stones according to law for processioning land in Tennessee.
BEGINNING said survey at a stone in the Paine mountain old road and corner to lot No. 8 in the division of the land of A. Paine (Dec) and in Sam Montgomerys line. Thence with Montgomerys line and said old road as follows: N 2½° E 104 ft to a stone, N 32 3/4° W 224 ft to a stone, N 8° W 186 ft to a stone, N 3 3/4° W 190 ft to a stone, N 47° W 234 ft to a stone, N 78 3/4° W 88 ft to a stone, N 42° W 140 ft to a stone corner to said Montgomery. Thence with Montgomerys line N 33½° E 1591 feet to a stone corner to Mathes the same cource continued with Mathes line in all 2104 feet to a stone in the Evens line. Thence with Evens line N 51¼° W 1240 ft to the lower bluff of the mountain in all 1275 feet to a stone marked D.C.I. and corner to the Cumberland Coal and Coak Co. Thence with said Co.'s line along the lower bluff as follows: S 41° W 300 feet, S 40° W 235 feet, S 53° W 315 feet, due West 177 feet, S 41° W 689 feet, S 23° W 306 ft, S 48° W 322 ft, S 33° W 569 ft, S 45½° W 378 ft, S 60¼° W 439 ft
                                                              (page 273)
S 45½° W 368 ft crossing the Paine Road at this point then S 28½° W 516 ft, S 37½° W 243 ft, S 31 3/4° W 334 ft, S 43 3/4° W 315 ft to a stone marked D.C.I.

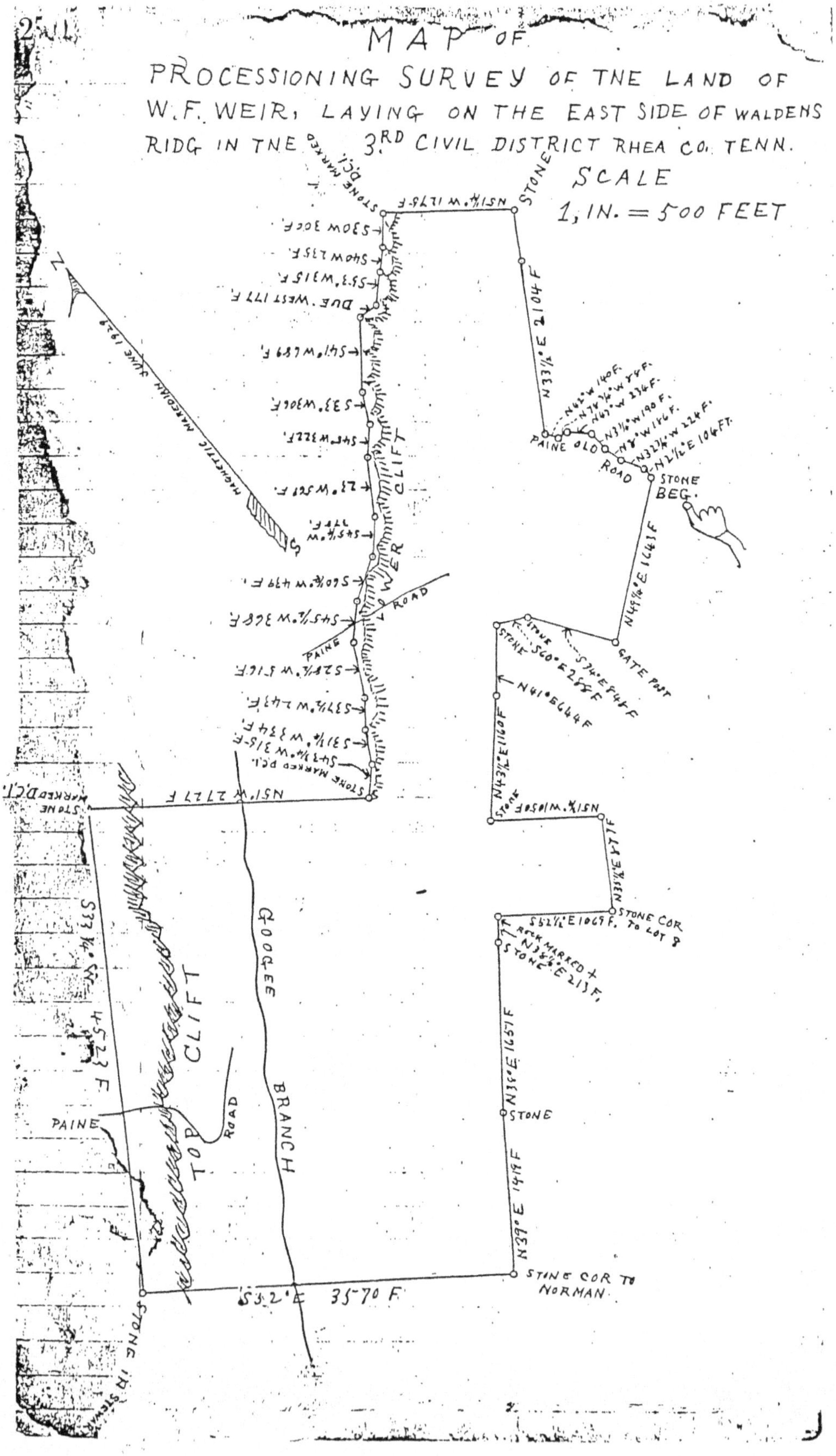

MAP of
PROCESSIONING SURVEY OF THE LAND OF
W.F. WEIR, LAYING ON THE EAST SIDE OF WALDENS
RIDG IN THE 3RD CIVIL DISTRICT RHEA CO. TENN.
SCALE
1 IN. = 500 FEET

N51½ W. 1175 F.

STONE MARKED D.C.

S30W 306F.
S8oW 135F.
S53°W 215F.
DUE WEST 177 F.
S41°W 689 F.
S33° W306F.
S44° W 322F.
27 W 521 F.
S45¾ W. 177F.
S60¾ W. 479 F.
S45 W. ¾ 366F
S28¾ W. 516F.
S37¼ W. 443F.
S31¾ W. 315F.
S4?¾ W. 334F.

LOWER CLIFT

MAGNETIC MARDIAN JUNE 1959

N51° W. 2727 F.

STONE MARKED D.C.

PAINE ROAD

STONE MARKED P.CL.

N37½ E 2104 F

STONE D.CL.

N4½°W 140F.
N4½ W 74F.
N2W½ W 276F.
N3¼ W 190F.
N4½ W 176F.
N33¼ W 224F.
N17½ E 106 FT.
PAINE OLD ROAD
STONE BEG.

N48½ E 1441 F

GATE POST

STONE
STONE S60° E 255 F
N41° E 644 F

N43°½ E 1100 F

N51½ W150F.
N14½ E 277 F

STONE COR. TO LOT 8

S52½° E 1069 F.
ROCK MARKED +
N3½° E 213 F.
STONE

N31° E 1651 F

STONE

S33 W. Co. 4527 F

TOP CLIFT

GOOGEE BRANCH

ROAD

PAINE

STONE IN STER?

N39° E 1418 F

STONE COR TO NORMAN

S32° E 3570 F

and corner to the afore said Co. Thence with an other line of said Co. N 51° W 2277 ft to the upper bluff of the mountain in all 2727 feet to a stone marked D.C.I. and corner to the afore said Co. Thence with another line of said Co. S 33 3/4° W crossing the Paine Road at 2828 feet in all 4523 feet to a stone marked D.C.I. and set in a line of the Stewart Coal Co.s land. Thence with said Stewart line S 52° E crossing top bluff at 363 feet crossing Googll branch at 1443 feet in all 3570 feet to a stone corner to Clint Norman. Thence with Normans line N 39° E 1419 feet to a stone corner to C.W. Webb, with 3 pines and chestnut oak marked as pointers. Thence with said Webbs line N 38° E 1651 ft to a stone corner to Hoyl Ezell. Thence with Ezells line N 38¼° E 213 feet to a Natural rock marked + on top and corner to said Ezell. Thence with another line of Ezell S 52½° E 1069 feet to a stone in said line and corner to lot No. 8 in the division of the A. Paine land. Thence with a line of said lot No. 8 N 35½° E 877 feet to a dogwood in J.A. Webbs line. Thence with said Webbs line N 51 3/4° W 1050 feet to a stone with 2 dogwoods & Blackoak marked for pointers and corner to J.A. Webb. Thence with another line of said Webb N 43½° E 1160 feet to a forked locus post corner to F.J. Paine. Thence with said Paines line N 41° E 644 feet to a stone in a drain and corner to said Paine.

(page 274)

Thence with another line of said Paine S 60° E 288 feet to stone corner to said Paine. Thence with another line of said Paine S 34° E 848 feet to a gate post corner to said Paine also corner to lot No. 8 in the division of the A. Paine land. Thence with a line of lot No. 8 N 49¼° E 1643 feet to the beginning.

J.W. Truex, Surveyor for Rhea County
J.A. Webb & Orville Paine, S.C.C.
State of Tennessee, Rhea County
Office of County Surveyor
I. J.W. Truex Surveyor for said County in said State do Certify that the above plat and descreption of the land herein before named and Processioned by me to the best of my knowledge and belief is true and correct, and is recorded in the Surveyors book No. 1 in my office on page 270 et seq. J.W. Truex, Surveyor

= = = = = = = = = = = = =

NOTE= The following information was written on a blank page at front of book:

Notes on Meridian Line
Temporary line set up by Roy V. Myres, Superintendent of D.C. & mines and Floyd Cunnyngham, Asst mine Sup., myself J.L. Daniel D.S., and Walter Daniel, assistant on Aug 11, 9:45 P.M. 1903, taking Easter Elongation the Asmuth angle 1°29' to East. On Aug Saturday 15, 4 P.M. 1903, Needle read N 1°30' E _____?
Franklin Transit read N 1°30' E & S 1°30' W.
Aug 25, 1903, 2:30 P.M., very hot after a shower.
      D.C.& I. Co Small transit   N 2°55' E
Aug 29, 1903, 7:30 A.M., Clear, my transit   N 2°50' E
Jan 28, 1904, 2:15 P.M., Cloudy & cool, my transit N 2°35' E

On page 402 was the following information:

Magnetic Variation of Needle as Register by Meredian Established by Roy V. Myres and J.L. Daniel in Court House Yard August 1903   2°35'

1906, July 2, 8:10 A.M. Clear and warm. Variation   2°30'

= = = = = = = = = = = = =

INDEX

DANE, David 61
DANIEL/DANILL, J.L. 137,139,145,146,
    149,150; Joseph 39,41,50; Thompson
    46,49,76
DARWIN, H.C. 149; J.T. 150; James 27,
    28; James A. 50,89; W.P. 131,137,139
DASSON, J.F. 145
DAVIS, R.D. 145; Rebecca 92; Sam 149
DAY, Jesse 27; John 4,11
DAYTON COAL AND IRON CO. LTD. 137
DAYTON COVE ROAD 137
DEAN, Thos 33,34
DENTON, J.L. 149; Jonathan 8
DERENS, John H. 13
DETHERAGE/DEATHERIDGE, Columbus 126;
    James 125
DEVIL'S FORK of Piney 3,15,41,121
DIXON, —— 24
DOLAN, —— 108
DONELSON, Stockly 48,65,68,75
DOTSON, Samuel 79
DOUGLAS/DOUGHLAS, John 57
DUDLEY, Calvin 108; Doctor 108; Samuel
    78,108
DUNAHOO, Thomas 36,37
DUNCAN, Massy 58; N.M. 134
DUNCAN CREEK 86
DUNLAP, Ephraim 75; J.L./Jacob L. 121,
    122; Jacob 111,115; John 50,107,111,
    114,115
DUNPETT, Elijah 90
DUSCAN CREEK 85,93
DUSKINS FORK of Piney 13,93,114,121
DUTCHMANS NOB 137
DYER, Joseph J. 109; Robert H. 108;
    Spills B. 12,58,60
DYER STILL HOUSE 58
EAST FORK of Piney 49,67
EASTLAND, A.J. 146; H.L. 146; Mark 146;
    Thomas B. 13
EBERLY, Peter W. 145
EDENS, L.T. 119
EDINGTON, Riley 131
EDMONDSON, Samuel 82
ELLIS, Adam L. 35; John 13,14
ENGLISH, George G. 16; Mathew 15,16,17,
    19; William 34; W.G./William G. 16,
    31,32,34,47,127
ERWIN, Benjamin 44,51,60
ESICS, Charles 145
EVANS, Hiram 48; Tom 159
EVERT, J.B. 124; W.D. 124
EVERETT'S COW FORD 120
EWING, E.B. 157,158

EZELL, Hoyl 159,161
FALKNER/FAULKNER, William 87,88
FALL CREEK 51,34,114
FANN, G.W. 129; James M. 129
FARMER, Aquilla 13
FERGUSON, Eli 58,106,107; James 3,44,
    94; James C. 123; John 43,76,121;
    Levi W. 44,48,90,123; Robert 3,6,12,
    13,44,88,90,94,123; S. 121; Samuel
    3; Samuel B. 44,90,123; Thomas 44,90
FERRIN BRANCH 133
FINE'S CAMP 36
FLACKNER, Henry 14
FLORA, Theo 152
FOSTER, Chester 131; Leander 131
FOUST, Phillip 121; W.M. 137,138
FOWLER, William 27
FRANKLIN, S.S. 150
FRAZIER, S.J.A. 129,130,134
FULLINGTON, —— 127
FULTON, Arthur 39,41,49,50; Flemming
    H. 50
FULTON'S GAP 50
FULTON'S TRACE 39,49,50
GAGES BRANCH 73,81
GANAWAY'S ROAD 139
GANSON, John 63
GARDENHIRE ADDITION 149
GARM---, Isaac 25
GARNER, William 15,16,77
GARRISON, John 6,44,46,50,63; Joseph
    4,6,44,50,106,107
GARRISON BRANCH 78
GARRISON'S FORK of Whites Creek 78
GASS, R.L. 131; W.T. 126,131,133,137,
    145
GATLETT(?), R.? 113
GEAR, A./Alexander 62,69,70,71,125;
    Jacob 69,71
GIBSON/GIPSON, A.C. 149; Benjamin C.
    19,20,21,60; Calvin D. 19,45; James
    51; Pleasant R. 19,21; William 51,83
GIBSONS SAW MILL 114
GILBREATH, —— 28,29
GILBREATH'S BRANCH 21,22,119,129
GILLAM, Nathaniel 75
GILLENWATERS, William T. 31,46,47,52,
    53,55,92
GILLENWATERS TRACE 53
GILLESPIE, —— 130; George 41,53,54,
    91; James 150
GIRTMAN'S TRACE 3
GLASCOCK, Asa 41
GOFF, Jean 32

GOOGLL BRANCH 161

GORDON, George 40; William B. 46,47,76

GORDON'S TURNPIKE ROAD 5,15,17,18,19,
20,27,40,51,53,60,83,114

GOTHARD, William 1,2; William B. 137

GRASHAM, John 115

GRASSY COVE 3,8,15

GREEN, — 78; John 83,84; Robert 38,
40,46

GREER, — 115; William 63,64,71,72,96

GREGORY, Thomas 129

GRIGSBY, James 34

GUTHRIE, George 113; Reese 113

HALEY, — 82,122,127; E.G. 83,84; Elijah 115; John 65,68,78,83

HAMMEL, John 1,139

HAMMET, John 17

HARRIS, Cornelius 37,95; Dawson 57; Wm?
William H. 113

HART'S TURNPIKE ROAD 128

HARVEY, John 40,47,49,76

HAYS/HAYES/HAYSE, Eli 137; Elijah 130;
James 37,48,49,51; James H. 49

HEDGECOTH, Pleasant 83,84

HEISKELL, John 146; L.M./Luke M. 131,
133

HEISKELL'S GAP 131

HELTON, Peter 39

HEMBREE, Benjamin 49

HENDERSON, J. 116; John 35; William 35

HENDERSON'S CREEK 120

HENRY, Cye 139; Henry 13,77; Mrs. R.F.
134; W.R. 134

HENRY'S FERRY 134

HICKMAN, E. 119

HICKS, T.A. 153

HILTON, James 60,61,62,64,65; John 61

HINSES CAMP BRANCH 17

HODGES, W.L. 158

HOLT, Dave 150,151; Tenney E. 152

HOLLAND, Huse 149

HOLLOWAY, Bermillion/Bramillian 32,45,
47; Burton 93; C.R. 149; John M. 131;
Major 30,32,38,46,47,93; R. 131; S.H.
131,132; Samuel 107; W.D. 131,133;
W.S. 131

HOOD, Bob 150

HOODENPYLE, G. 9

HOUP/HOUPT, Alexander 80,88; Jesse 88;
Val/Valentine 88

HOWERTON, — 28; Edmund/Edmond 27,89,
95; Jackson 28; Jeremiah 8; Micajah
27,28,89,95; Mandy E. 80; M. 81

HOWERTON'S MILL 80,95

HOWERTON'S TRACE 39

HOYT/HOIT, Hannah 89,108; Joseph L. 95?
95,99; Stephen 89,97,98,102,104

HUDGENS, Wilson 22

HUGHES, John W. 126

HUMPHREY, W.L. 121

HUNTSMAN, Adam 27

IGOU, Samuel 30

INGLE, Thomas 131; Vann(?) 131

INDIAN ROCK HOUSE 6,13

INLOW, John B. 85,110; Lewis 29,32;
Phillip 86,87,88

IRWIN, Ben 6

IVES, Thomas 81

IVY, Silas 40,60,77

JARRELL, John 21

JETT, John 13

JOHNSON, — 117; John 109

JOHNSON'S FORK of Piney 34,109,114,121,
133

JOLLY, A.J. 131; Isaac 126

JONES, J. 137; George S. 14

KEEDY ROAD 1

KENT, William 96,97; William O. 97,98,
99,100,101,102,104,105

KIMBROUGH, — 122,127; Joseph 65,68,79

KIMMEN, Thomas M. 7,8

KIUKA TRACE 31

KIUKA TURNPIKE 1,2,4,11,13,22,24,25,130

KNIGHT, Richard 150; Willard 145

KNOX, Daniel 8; David 2,5,8,10,11,49,55,
78; J.W./James W. 150,151,152

KNOX'S SPRING BRANCH 10,78

KNOX'S TRACE 8

LAUREL FORK of Richland Creek 22,57,72

LAUREL FORK of Whites Creek 34,45,66

LAWLESS, Benjamin 35,52

LEA, James 21,22,28

LEA PATH 121,125,129

LEAD MINE 14

LEVRETT, Joseph 25

LICK BRANCH 11,46,47

LIKENS, Isaac 109; Jonas 109

LINCOLN, Jesse 13

LITTLE LAUREL FORK of Whites Creek 31,
57,127

LITTLE RICHLAND CREEK 27,28,57

LOCKE, Adison 121,122,123; Franklin 15,
16,17,18,19,20,21,81,114,115,134;
Isabella T. 134,135; J.C. 146; John
16,17,19,20,27,72,74,75,81; Newton 81;
Ralph B. 16,20,21; Robert 76

LODEN, James 128

LONE MOUNTAIN 12,28,30,137

LONG, Joel 11,65; Joseph 82,89
LONG REACH TRACT 134,136
LOOPER/LUPER Allen 19,20,40,53,60,77,
   83,89; Gilbert 52,53,89; James 89
LOVING, Miles 27
LOWE'S GAP 13
LOWRY/LOURY, Adam 33; Henry 115; Jacob
   33,34; Joel 4,14; Samuel 13,14,34
LOY, Yancy 121,122
LOYD/LOID, —— 125; A. 111; James 23,
   111; John 111; L.P. 121; R. 111; R.P.
   120
McBRIDE, David 28,29; Polly 32; William
   27,30
McCLENDON, Dennis 114; John 63; Willis
   5,149
McCULLY, William 123
McDANIEL, Green Berry 35
McDONALD, R.F. 117,118,119,120,129,130,
   131,133,134; W.P. 154
McDONOUGH, James 118,120
McFALLS, Daniel 90,107,109
McFALLS BRANCH 66
McMILLEN, J.M. 157; Libbie 157
McPHERSON, J.L. 131,146; John 145
MADAN, John 4
MAJORS, Jesse 55; Peter 55,75; Thomas
   37,46
MAJORS BRANCH 66
MANESS, Wesley 22
MARSHALL, G.M. 149
MATHIS, —— 128; Fate 159
MATLOCK, John 115
MIDDLE FORK of Whites Creek 66
MILLER, Henry 63,64,71,105,126; Henry
   H. 80; John 12,60; Peter W. 79
MITCHELL, Robert 79
MOCCASON FORK of Piney 30
MONDAY/MUNDAY, —— 91; Arthur 37,38;
   William 37,91,92,128,130; Young B. 45
MONTEITH, Robert 62
MONTGOMERY, —— 136; Alex 131,132; Har-
   vey 77; James 62,77; R.C. 134; Sam 159
   159
MORGAN, —— 125,126; Calvin 154; Charles
   119,120,129; David 117; E.H. 117,119;
   G.W. 111; George 117,118,154; H. Brown
   154; Lewis 28,31,32,58,121; W. 118,
   120,130; Washington 4,11,21,23,58,117,
   119; William 120
MORGAN SPRINGS 154
MORGAN'S TURNPIKE 125
MUDDY CREEK RIDGE 146
MULLINS CABIN 44

MYNATT, B.K. 134; Mary 134
NAIL, Thomas 13
NEAL, Love 145; Sam 145
NEIL, John R. 131,137
NEILL, James 123
NELSON, —— 78; David 11; James C. 57,
   58; John S. 76
NEWELL, James 157
NICHOLS, Malinda A. 152; Tom 150,151
NICKOLDS, Henry O. 137
NORMAN, Clint 159,161
NORTH FORK of Piney 67
ORME, S.P. 114; Shiloh 114
ORTER CREEK 114
OTTER CREEK 35,77,114,127
OWENS, Alexander 34,50; Henry 34,49,50
OXIER, George 93
PAINE, A. 134,137,139,159,161; Bird
   72,74,75,81; Elvira 134; F.J. 159,
   161; Joe 139; Orville 26,69,71,73,
   74,81,161
PAINE'S ROAD/TURNPIKE/TRACE 35,74,100,
   103,159
PARHAM, Lud 158; Shamel 14
PARKE, Robert 4
PARKER, Joseph 114
PARSONS, James 30
PAUL, —— 90; Archibald D. 45,63; James
   15; John F. 39,63; Marten E. 35,36,
   45; Moses 39; Thomas G. 15
PEARCE, James 88,110; P.W. 145; Rhoda
   A. 134
PEARSON, J.H. 146
PEPPER, William 85,86,88
PHARRIS, Harrison 32; Peter L. 63;
   William W. 32,33
PICKET/PICKETT, —— 32; Charles 61,65;
   James 30; P.M. 117,118
PIKE, Oliver 3
PINE BRANCH 114,123
PINEY CREEK COAL & LAND CO. 137
PINEY RIVER/CREEK 1,3,4,5,6,8,9,10,12,
   13,17,26,37,39,41,43,44,46,48,49,50,
   51,55,58,60,62,68,71,76,83,90,93,94,
   106,107,110,112,114,121,123,132,133,
   137,139
PINEY TRACE 81
PLUMLEE/PLUMLYS, —— 118,119; Daniel
   117; Richard 115
POLEBRIDGE CREEK 97,102,117,120,129
POLECAT FORK of Piney 69,73
POSTAIN, William 30
POWDER MILL BRANCH 7,8
POWELL, —— 158,159

SOAK/SOKY CREEK 86,87,114
SOLOMON, Mrs. M.E. 154
SOUTH FORK of Piney 67
SPEARS, J.B. 145
SPEEWOOD SPRING 20
SPENCE, Alvin 150; J.G. 150
SPIVEY, G.W. 154
STANBOUGH, John 137,145
STEBINS, H.C. 131,133
STEVENS/STEPHENS, Bart/Bert L. 30,38,
   40,93; James 93; Wm M. 46,50
STEWART/STUART, —— 65; James 27,57,58,
   59,105,117; James H. 57; Laban 31,34
STEWART COAL & IRON CO. 161
STEWARTS TRACE 26
STINGING FORK of Piney 12,13,86,87,114
STOCK ROAD 112
STONER/STINER, Joseph 32; Michael 32
SWAN, Thomas B. 77
SWABY, S.M. 157
SWAFFORD, —— 129; Ruben 149; Rufe 150
SWAFFORD'S SALTING GROUND 129
SWAGGERTY COVE 3,49
SWEENY, —— 63
TAR KILN 17
TAYLOR, Joshua 39
TEAGUE CREEK 97,130
TENNESSEE RIVER 55,56,134
THEDYS TRACE 61
THOMAS, Joseph 13
THOMPSON, Absolem L. 45,50,75; Charles
   P. 117; Isaac 79; James W. 34,43,94;
   Jesse 27,30,31,32,33,34,35,36,37,38,
   39,40,41,43,44,45,46,47,48,49,50,52,
   53,54,55,57,58,60,61,62,63,64,65,69,
   71,75,76,77,78,79,81,91,112; J.P./
   Jesse P. 114,115,121,122,123,124,125,
   126,127,128,129,130,131,134; Joseph
   M. 94,115; Moses 78; Moses F. 131;
   Olivia(?) 131; Thomas 95; W.F. 127
THOMPSON'S BRANCH 66
THOMPSON'S TRACE 45,46,75
THURMAN, Charles 80; John 114
TORBETT, J.A. 149
TOWN CREEK 48
TRIPLETT, Abner 28
TROUP/TROOP, Benjamin H. 103
TRUEX, Francis 159; J.W. 152,154,155,
   157,159,161; Jesse 152
TUTTLE, —— 121,126
TYNERS CREEK 120
UPTON, William 121
VALLEY ROAD 56,133
VAN'S SPRING CREEK 65,66,67,133

VERNON, Absolom 33
VERNUM, Andrew 4; Nehemiah 4
WABLORD, Richard 112
WALKER, Anderson 108; B.F./Benjamin F.
   124,125; J.M. 125; John P. 128;
   Richard 5,79,80,88; Robert 53; Tho-
   mas 125
WALKER'S TURNPIKE 128
WALTON FERRY 15
WARD, Wm 131,133
WARMAN/WORMAN, William R. 36,37,39,
   41,46
WARREN, —— 112
WASSOM, John 146
WASSON, E.E. 114
WASSUM, Andrew 12,44,48,60; Jacob 12,
   48; J.L./Jacob L. 44,48,106,126,132
WASSUM'S SPRING 67
WATERHOUSE, —— 37,38,43,45,49,118,
   123,149; Alice 131; Blackstone 2,3,
   4,9,10; Callie 131; Cyrus 2,3,4,5,
   6,9,10,11,18,78,131; Darius 9,10,
   131,137; E.F. 131,134,136,145; Euclid
   9,10; Franklin 131,133; Myra 5,17;
   Richard 2,4,5,6,8,9,10,11,43,68,70,
   76,90,132; Richard G. 2,3,4,10,69,71;
   Ucled 131
WATERHOUSE MILL 67
WATERHOUSE PATH 43
WATERHOUSE'S IRON WORKS 106
WEAVER, David 137,139
WEBB, C.W. 159,161; J.A. 161; James
   159; William T. 85,86,88
WEIDENHOFFER, Henry 89,95,100,101,104
WEIR, W.F. 159
WEST, G.H. 149,157,158; W.T. 127
WEST FORK of Piney 69
WEST FORK of Whites Creek 7,8
WHEELER, —— 133; Mary 17; S.J. 131,
   133; Thomas H. 17,18,30
WHITE WALNUT BOTTOM 145
WHITEHEAD, Benjamin 43
WHITEOAK FLAT 37
WHITES CREEK 2,5,7,8,10,11,16,17,18,
   10,20,21,30,31,35,37,38,40,44,45,46,
   47,48,49,51,52,53,55,60,63,76,77,78,
   91,92,93,95,114,115,127,128
WIERICK, J.L. 146
WILLIAMS, E.P. 119
WILSON, Alex 68; G.W. 134; J./James 1,
   2,5,6,8,9,10,11,12,13,14,15,16,17,
   18,20,21; William M. 62
WINFIELD, Joseph 91,92
WITT, Jesse 4; John 11,22,38

168

WOLF CREEK 149
WRIGHT, Abraham G. 41,42,53; W.P. 125;
  Wiat 90
WYATT, W.E. 152,153,154

WYRICK, Alfred 126; Andrew 126; Solomon 126; William 126
YOUNG, Mrs. 159

APPENDIX

ORIGINAL INDEX FROM BOOK NO. 1

	Page	Entry No.	Acres
Bishop, Joseph	1	2 2	50
Bean, Edmund	21	1919	52
Barnett, James R.	45	1 101	200
Brinkley, Jesse	66	134	10
Bowling, Jeremiah	667	136	.10
Baker, Isaac	70	143	1
Breeding, Bryam	76	108	100
Benson, Robert	77	156	100
Bundren, James	85	155	300
Brown, James	103	150	200
Bundren, Claibourn	108	185,154	50,150
Brumble, Jesse	110	241	100
Bean, James C.	145	295	1000
Black, George W.	148	296	100
Brewer, Eli	162,163	254,208	100,200
Beaty, John M.	165	229	300
Birdett, George	184	320	300
Benson, Barclay S.	189	328	300
Bollinger, A.J.	191	—	1000
" J.H.	192	347	5000
" H.H.	193	344	5000
Bridgeman, B.F.	201	397	45
" & Rigsby	205	389	200
Burwick, John M.	206	421	50
" , William	219	400	300
Cooper, Robert	26,33	61,79	100,50
Chapman, W.H.	32	82	400
Clarke, Thomas	40	88	400
Creesy, Samuel	44	90	320
Carter, Levi	56	86	266
Chilton, Palatiah	59,62	118,141	120,100
Crews & Paul	85	167	500
Collins, Henry	141	258	100
Compton, William	146	294	100
Condley, John	159	300	100
Collins, Alfred	188	329	2000
Cawood & Wassum	212	431	——
Clift, William	217	378	5000
" J.W.	198	259	5000
Cunnyngham, G.T. Processioning	259		33 1/3
Day, John	9,21	21,34	50,600
Denton, Jonathan	15	38	100
Dyer, Spills Be	22,117	36,247	360,150
Day, Jesse	71	116	100
Daniel & Fulton	91	168	300
Dunlap, John	105,189,196	222,332,357	200,320,300
Dyer & Miller	119	36	360
Davis, Rebecca	165	256	50
Dudley, Samuel	185	326	37
Dyer, Robert H.	186	327	100
Deatheridge, James	212	426	250

	Page	Entry No.	Acres
Eastland, T.B., Jett & Co.	24	49	640
Ellis, John	25	44	100
English, William G.	28,78	65,169	200,600
" George G.	28	66	25
" Matthew	29	67	200
Ervin, Benjamin	53	68	200
Edens, L.T.	203	396	236
Ewing, E.B. Processioning	267		
Ferguson, Robert	7,13,168	13,31,277	80,300,1000
Farmer, Aquilla & Nail	25	48	300
Ferguson, John	54	95	300
Fowler, William	63	148	50
Fulton, Arthur	90,91,93,105	77,112,1	100,55,
	93,105	186,174	300,150
" & Daniel	91	168	100
Ferguson, Robert, S.B., Thos. & Levi W.W.	97	232	1000
Fulton, Fleming H.	106	194	200
Faulkner, William	157	269	5000
Foust & Riddle	206	421	50
Ferguson, Sarah	206	412	500
Foust, W.M. Processioning	233		59
Garrison, John	12	32	125
Gibson, Calvin D.	34	87	100
" Benj. C.	35,36	51,53	100,140
Goode, Edward	67	94	100
Gillenwaters, Wm T.	78,110	172.207	300,250
Grigsby, James	83	144	100
Green, Robert	92,93,100	139,56,191	50,200,300
Garrison, Joseph	97,107	33	640
Gipson, James	107	217	100
Gillenwaters & Roddy	109	243	150
Gear, Alexander	123,133	271,283	3000,5000
Greer, William	136	279	2000
Gordon, William B.	142	171	320
Garner & Swan	143	72,73	200,200
Grasham, John	197	—	1000
Gothard, William B.	232	436	10
Gillespie & Smith	111	193	200
Hammel, John	1	1	60
Howerton, Jeremiah	14	41	220
" Edmund	72	179	1832
Henderson, John	84	145	200
Hays, James	88	135	300
Holloway, Bermillion	99	166	300
Hilton, James	120	192	200
" John	121	157	300
Haley & Kimbrough	128,131	248,249	5000,5000
Haley, John	152	226,225	300,300
" Elijah	158	299	1100
Houpt, Valentine	153	297	300
Hoyt, Hannah	160	274	100
Holloway, Burton	166	165	200
" Major	166	159	400

	Page	Entry No.	Acres
Harris, Cornelius	170	162	200
Hoyt, Stephen	171,180	308,318	1000,2000
Harris, William H.	194	—	200
Hughes, John W.	213	428	100
Hembre, Benjamin	103	150	2000
Ivey, Silas	92	151	100
Ives, Thomas	150		3500
Inlow, John B.	154	266	5000
" Phillip	156	268	5000
" Lewis	75	120	140
Jett, John, Eastland & Co.	24	49	640
Kimmen, Thomas M.	14	22	50
Knox, David	104	211	1100
Kimbrough & Haley	128,131	248,249	5000,5000
Kent, William	170	307	1000
" William O.	172,171,173,	309,308,310,	1000,1000,1000,
" "	174,175,176,	311,312,313,	1000,1000,1000,
" "	177,178	314,315	1000,1000
Knox, J.W. Procession	252		
Lowry, Joel	8		50
Long, Joel	20	29	200
Looper, Allen	37,119	554,246	150,100
Lea, James	38	50	200
Luper, Gilbert	65	131	125
Lowry, Adam	81	181	100
Loyd, James	190	337	1000
Locke, Addison	207,208	415,414	5000,5000
Locke, Mrs. Isabella T. Procession	228		545 3/3
Morgan, Washington	41	75	100
" & Ragsdale	55	80	200
" , Lewis	57	85	100
Maloney, David	59	102	50
McClendon, Willis	71	34	5
McBride, William	72	121	1100
" David	75	120	140
" Polly	79	125	100
Monday, William	88	163	200
" Young B.	98	213	100
Miller, & Dyer	119	36	360
McClendon, John	125	204	70
Miller, Pharris & Qualls	126	282	
Montgomery, James	144	263	100
McFalls, Daniel	184,187	325,324	200,1280
McClendon, Dennis	196	357	300
Morgan & Pickett	200	399	1000
Morgan, E.H.	204	373	300
McClendon, Willes Part.	246		
McMillen, Libbie Processioning	264		
Nail, Thomas & Farmer	25	48	300
Neil, James	209	413	5000
Nichols & Ward	218	408	500
Orme, Shiloh & E.E. Wasson	194	350	2000
Paul, James & Thomas G.	27	60	100

	Page	Entry No.	Acres
Paine, Orville	47,48,49,	105,104,103,	480,640,1000,
" "	136,60,139,	119,236	100,2770,260
" "	149		640
Posten, William	63	92	100
Parsons & Wheeler	76	109	150
Pharris, Harrison	80	123	300
Paul & Crews	85	167	500
Paul, A.D.	99	209	150
Pharris, Qualls & Miller	126	282	5000
Preston, James	159	257	300
Plumlee & Thompson	197	380	—
Plimlee, Daniel	199	379	300
Pickett & Morgan	200	399	1000
Pickett, P.M.	201	386	605
Pyott, Thompson & Walker	216	433	4000
Paine, A. Processioning	234		400
Qualls, Gatewood	89,132,130	199,275,316	300,2000,1000
" Robert	134,124	239,202	1500,400
" & Miller	126	282	5000
Ragsdale, David	2,23,95,121	3,37,278,	50,100,800,
" "		47	100
Ransom, George	22	35	400
Richards, Richard	26	23	50
Runnion, William	41,42	70,83	50,50
Richards, Isaac	43,64	81,93	100,50
Romine, Samuel	43	82	100
Rose, Thomas	46	69	75
Rice, Theodorick B.	50,94	53,115	500,2000
Redwine, Wyley	54	59	200
Ragsdale,& Morgan	55	80	200
Ransom, Peggy	61	99	80
Rawlston, Elizabeth	81	149	100
" James	82	182	100
Reynolds & Thompson	82	173	100
Roddy, David	83	170	150
Riddle, Thomas	84	214	200
Ransom & Whitehead	96	100	200
Roddy & Gillenwaters	109	243	150
Roddy, David M.	112	245	100
Redwine, Wyley	113	238	100
Rhea, James	115	240	5000
Roddy, James	116,151	197,292	100,300
Romines, Job	127	127	400
Robinson, Robert	135	234	5000
Roddye, Jesse Junr	141	—	400
Reed, Zebulon	149,169	298,250	46,25
Roddy, Jesse Senior	151,160	291,301	200,300
Rice, Elijah C.	155	267	5000
Rigsby, J.M. & W.J.	202	393	405
Riddle, Joshua I.	204	388	600
Rigsby & Bridgeman	205	389	200
Riddle & Foust	206	421	50
Riddle, Mary & H.D.	211	429	—
Roddy,& Thompson	214	429	730

	Page	Entry No.	Acres
Shelton, David	39	76	100
Stewart, James	58,117,118	117,264,273	1000,200,1500
Stevens, William M.	668	137	500
" Burt L.	69,89	107,113,160	200,100,75
Sampley, Jesse	74	178	600
Smith, William B.	80,124	190,202	400,400
Seay, William H.	101	187	1000
Stewart, James H.	116	188	100
Silvey, William	137	——	3227
Swan & Garner	143	72,73	200,200
Smith, William	164	161	200
Shelton, Henry A.	181	319	3000
Short, George Washington	195	355	2000
Smith & West	215	444	402
Shuster, George	89	199	300
Shelow & Co. B.F. Processioning	222		
Smith, J.B.	221	425	200
Spence, Alvin Processioning	251		
Sneed, A.A. "	250		
Stoner, M.	80		
Shelow, B.F. & Co. "	222		
Shaver, John Q. Part.	238		
Spence, J.B. Processioning	240		
Thompson, Jesse	65,87	96,110	50,50
Triplett, Abner	73	146	100
Thompson & Reynolds	82	173	100
Thompson, Jesse	86,87,140	176,177,	100,150,
" "		110,206	50,400
" Moses	144	255	200
" James W.	167,168	195,196	200,75
Throup, William Benjamin H.	179	317	3200
Thompson & Plumlee	197	380	——
" & Roddy	214	429	730
" , Pyott & Walker	216	433	4000
Waterhouse, Richard G.	5,6,19,	8,11,43,	50,52,53,640,
" "	5,4,7	9,12	51,62½,65
" "	8,161	17,235	84,1000
" Blackstone	9,18	20,28	55,585
" Cyrus	10,20	24,42	80,170
" Myra	10	23	142½
" Euclid	16	27	520
" Darius	17	26	640
Wassum, Jacob	23,103	40,78	200,100
Wheeler, Mary	30,31	89,55	160,200
Witt, John	39	84	300
Wilson, James	45	30	200
Wheeler & Parsons	76	109	150
Whitehead & Ransom	96	100	200
Warman, William R.	100	111	50
Wassum, Andy	102	221	150
Wilson, William M.	122	261	200
Walker, Richard	147	281	500
Winfield, Joseph	164	205	400

174

www.ingramcontent.com/pod-product-compliance
Lightning Source LLC
Chambersburg PA
CBHW080240270326
41926CB00020B/4314